THE
FIFTH DISCIPLINE

T H E
FIFTH DISCIPLINE

THE ART AND
PRACTICE OF
THE LEARNING
ORGANIZATION

Peter M. Senge

CURRENCY   DOUBLEDAY

New York London Toronto Sydney Auckland

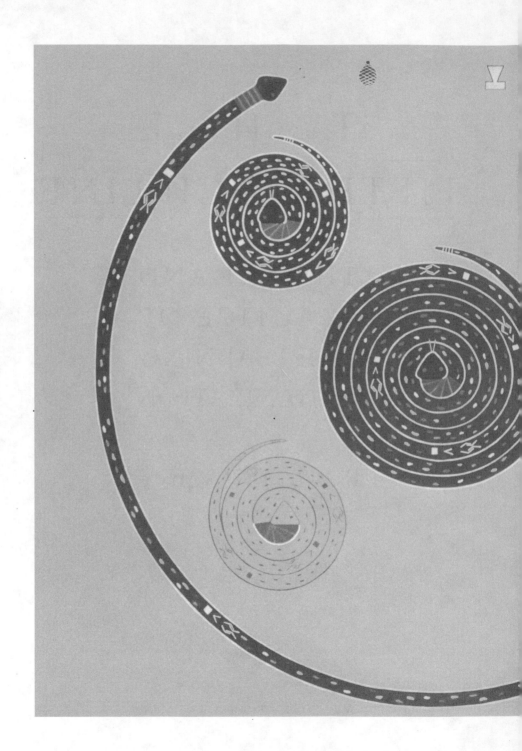

A Currency Book

PUBLISHED BY DOUBLEDAY
a division of Random House, Inc.

CURRENCY is a trademark of Random House, Inc., and DOUBLEDAY is a registered
trademark of Random House, Inc.

THE FIFTH DISCIPLINE was originally published in hardcover by Currency in 1990.
A hardcover of this edition has been published simultaneously.

Book design by Richard Oriolo

Permission to reprint Navajo sand painting given by the Wheelwright Museum of the
American Indian, Santa Fe, New Mexico. Photography by Kay V. Weist.

Cataloging-in-Publication Data for the hardcover edition
is on file with the Library of Congress.

ISBN 978-0-385-51725-6

PRINTED IN THE UNITED STATES OF AMERICA

All trademarks are the property of their respective companies.

SPECIAL SALES
Currency Books are available at special discounts for bulk purchases for sales promotions or
premiums. Special editions, including personalized covers, excerpts of existing books, and
corporate imprints, can be created in large quantities for special needs. For more information, write to Special Markets, Currency Books, specialmarkets@randomhouse.com

10 9 8 7 6

To Diane

CONTENTS

PART IV
REFLECTIONS FROM PRACTICE

PART V
CODA

INTRODUCTION TO THE REVISED EDITION

THE PREVAILING SYSTEM OF MANAGEMENT

In the spring of 1990, shortly after the writing and editing of the original edition of *The Fifth Discipline* was completed and publication was imminent, my editor at Doubleday asked me who I wanted to write a comment for the book jacket. As a first time author, I had never considered this. After thinking for a while I realized that there was no one I would rather have write something than Dr. W. Edwards Deming, revered around the world as a pioneer in the quality management revolution. I knew of no one who had had a greater impact on management practice. But I had never met Deming. I doubted that a letter with such a request from an unknown author, referring to work with which Deming was unfamiliar, would get a favorable response. Fortunately, through mutual friends at Ford, a copy of the manuscript did reach him. A few weeks later, to my surprise, a letter arrived at my home.

When I opened it I found a short paragraph written by Dr, Deming. Reading the first sentence, I stopped to catch my breath. Somehow he had said in a sentence what I had struggled to put into four hundred pages pages. It is amazing, I thought, how clear and direct you can be when you reach the end of your years (Deming was then almost 90). As I took in the totality of what he had written, I slowly started to realize he had unveiled a deeper layer of connections, and a bigger task, than I had previously understood:

Our prevailing system of management has destroyed our people. People are born with intrinsic motivation, self-respect, dignity, curiosity to learn, joy in learning. The forces of destruction begin with toddlers—a prize for the best Halloween costume, grades in school, gold stars—and on up through the university. On the job, people, teams, and divisions are ranked, reward for the top, punishment for the bottom. Management by Objectives, quotas, incentive pay, business plans, put together separately, division by division, cause further loss, unknown and unknowable.

As I subsequently learned, Deming had almost completely stopped using the terminology of "Total Quality Management," "TQM" or "TQ" because he believed it had become a superficial label for tools and techniques. The real work, which he simply called the "transformation of the prevailing system of management," lay beyond the aims of managers seeking only short-term performance improvements. This transformation, he believed, required "profound knowledge" largely untapped in contemporary institutions. Only one element of this profound knowledge, "theory of variation" (statistical theory and method), was associated with the common understanding of TQM. The other three elements, to my amazement, mapped almost directly onto the five disciplines: "understanding a system," " theory of knowledge" (the importance of mental models), and "psychology," especially "intrinsic motivation" (the importance of personal vision and genuine aspiration).

These elements of Deming's "profound knowledge" led eventually to the simplest and, today, most widely used way to present the five learning disciplines, a way that was not evident when the original book was completed. The five disciplines represent approaches (theories and methods) for developing three core learning capabilities: fostering aspiration, developing reflective conversation, and understanding complexity. Building on an idea from the original book, that the fundamental learning units in an organization are working teams (people who need one another to produce an outcome), we came to refer to these as the "core learning capabilities of teams" and symbolically represented them as a three-legged stool, to visually convey the importance of each—the stool would not stand if any of the three were missing.

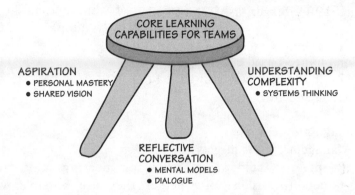

Even more important for me was Deming's idea that a common "system of management" governed modern institutions, and in particular formed a deep connection between work and school. He would often say, "We will never transform the prevailing system of management without transforming our prevailing system of education. They are the same system." So far as I know, his insight into this connection between work and school was original.

I believe that Deming came to this realization late in his life, in part as a way to make sense of why so few managers seemed able to actually implement real Quality Management as he conceived it. People failed, he realized, because they had been socialized in ways of thinking and acting that were embedded in their most formative institutional experiences. "The relationship between a boss and subordinate is the same as the relationship between a teacher and student," he said. The teacher sets the aims, the student responds to those aims. The teacher has the answer, the student works to get the answer. Students know when they have succeeded because the teacher tells them. By the time all children are 10 they know what it takes to get ahead in school and please the teacher —a lesson they carry forward through their careers of "pleasing bosses and failing to improve the system that serves customers." After Dr. Deming passed away in 1993, I spent many years thinking and talking with colleagues about what constituted this prevailing system of management as Deming understood it, eventually settling on eight basic elements:[1]

- Management by measurement:
  - Focusing on short-term metrics
  - Devaluing intangibles
    ("You can only measure 3 percent of what matters"
                                    – W.E. Deming)

- Compliance-based cultures
  - Getting ahead by pleasing the boss
  - Management by fear

- Managing outcomes
  - Management sets targets
  - People are held accountable for meeting management targets (regardless of whether they are possible within existing system and processes)

- "Right answers" vs. "wrong answers"
  - Technical problem solving is emphasized
  - Diverging (systemic) problems are discounted

- Uniformity
  - Diversity is a problem to be solved
  - Conflict is suppressed in favor of superficial agreement

- Predictability and controllability
  - To manage is to control
  - The "holy trinity of management" is planning, organizing, controlling

- Excessive competitiveness and distrust
  - Competition between people is essential to achieve desired performance
  - Without competition among people there is no innovation
    ("We've been sold down the river by competition"
                                    – W.E. Deming)

- Loss of the whole
  - Fragmentation
  - Local innovations do not spread

Today, most managers probably regard the "Quality Management revolution," like the organizational learning fad of the early 1990s, as history, far from the frontiers of today's challenges. But is that because we have achieved or abdicated the transformation Deming advocated? It is hard for me to contemplate a list like this one and not feel that these maladies still afflict most organizations today, and that it will take generations, not years, to change such deeply embedded beliefs and behaviors. Indeed, perhaps the most obvious question for many of us is: "Will this system of management ever change on a large scale?" Answering deep questions like this about the future requires looking carefully at the present.

A TIME OF CROSSCURRENTS

In the decade and a half since *The Fifth Discipline* was first published much has changed in the world. Our economies are more global than ever; consequently, so is business. Among businesses competing globally, cost and performance pressures are relentless. The time available for people to think and reflect is scarcer, if anything, and in many organizations, resources available for developing people are scarcer still. But there is more to think about than just accelerating change. The globalization of business and industrial development is raising the material standards of living for many, but also creating significant side effects in the form of a host of social and environmental sustainability challenges. All too often, the production of financial capital seems to occur at the expense of social and natural capital. Gaps between "haves" and "have-nots" are widening in many countries. Local environmental stresses, always a feature of industrial development, are now matched by problems on a larger scale, like global warming and weather instability. While the advocates for global industrial growth trumpet its benefits, people around the world are reacting, nonviolently and violently, to losses in traditional ways of living—and this shifting context is getting onto the strategic radar screen of many businesses.

At the same time, the interconnected world creates a greater awareness of others than has ever before existed. It is an unprecedented time of cultures colliding and in many instances learning from one another, and the promise of truly generative "dialogue among civilizations" holds great hope for the future. Young people around the world are creating a web of relationships that has never existed before. The frontiers of Western science, the underpinning of our modern worldview, are revealing a living world of flux and interdependency strangely familiar to aboriginal and native cultures, and one that might, in the words of cosmologist Brian Swimme, once again show us that we have "a meaningful place in the universe." And, as illustrated below, the organizational learning practices that were limited to a few pioneers fifteen years ago have taken deeper root and spread.

In short, it is a time of dramatically conflicting forces. Things are getting better and things are getting worse. The comments of former Czech president Vaclav Havel's to the U.S. Congress in the mid-1990s summarize these perilous times aptly:

> Today, many things indicate that we are going through a transitional period, when it seems that something is on the way out and something else is painfully being born. It is as if something were crumbling, decaying and exhausting itself, while something else, still indistinct, were arising from the rubble.

The shape of Havel's "something else" being born and the sorts of management and leadership skills it might require remain as fuzzy today as they were when he made these remarks a decade ago.

These conflicting forces play out within organizations as well, creating environments in which the need and possibility for learning capabilities are greater than ever, but so too are the challenges of building such capabilities. On one hand, building enterprises capable of continually adapting to changing realities clearly demands new ways of thinking and operating. So do the sustainability challenges, in many ways the archetypal organizational learning challenge of this era. In addition, organizations are becoming more networked, which is weakening traditional management hierarchies and potentially opening up new capacity for continual learning, innovation, and adaptation. On the other hand, the dysfunctions of the traditional management system keep many organizations in perpetual fire-fighting mode, with little time or energy for innovation. This frenzy and chaos also undermines the building of values-based management cultures and opens the door for opportunistic grabs at individual power and wealth.

VOICES FROM THE FRONT

When I was invited by Doubleday to create this new edition of *The Fifth Discipline*, I was initially ambivalent but then became excited. One of the great joys of the past fifteen years has been getting to know countless gifted practitioners of organizational learning— managers, school principals, community organizers, police chiefs, business and social entrepreneurs, military leaders, teachers—people who have somehow found an infinite array of imaginative ways to work with and utilize the five disciplines, even if they had never heard of or read the original book. A few of these figured prominently in the first book, like Arie de Geus and the recently deceased Bill O'Brien. Since then, the worldwide growth of the Society for Organizational Learning (SoL) has brought me in touch with hundreds more such practitioners. In their own ways, each has created an alternative system of management based on love rather than fear, curiosity rather than an insistence on "right" answers, and learning rather than controlling. Now I could use the excuse of this revised edition to talk with many of them.

Those interviews and conversations led to my making many changes in the text of this book and to a new section, Part IV, "Reflections from Practice." The interviews provided fresh insights into how master practitioners initiate change and deal creatively with the challenges of sustaining momentum. In addition to many business successes, people revealed a host of new possibilities in applying organizational learning tools and principles in areas few of us could have imagined fifteen years ago: from growing more environmentally sound businesses and industries to addressing societal problems like gang violence, transforming school systems, promoting economic development, undertaking the improvement of global food production, and reducing poverty. In all these settings, openness, reflection, deeper conversations, personal mastery, and shared visions uniquely energize change; and understanding the systemic causes of problems is crucial.

The interviews also clarified core ideas that implicitly bound together the original work.

- *There are ways of working together that are vastly more satisfying and more productive than the prevailing system of management.* As one senior executive said, reflecting on her first learning experiment—"just getting people to talk to one another" as a way to rethink how their organization was structured—". . . was the most fun I had ever had in business, and the ideas that emerged are still creating a competitive advantage for the company fifteen years later."

- *Organizations work the way they do because of how we work, how we think and interact; the changes required ahead are not only in our organizations but in ourselves as well.* "The critical moment comes when people realize that this learning organization work is about each one of us," commented a twenty-year veteran of corporate organizational learning projects. "Personal mastery is core. If you get the personal mastery element of these changes right, everything else falls into place."

- *In building learning organizations there is no ultimate destination or end state, only a lifelong journey.* "This work requires great reservoirs of patience," commented the president of a global NGO (nongovernmental organization), "but I believe the results we achieve are more sustainable because the people involved have really grown. It also prepares people for the ongoing journey. As we learn, grow, and tackle more systemic challenges, things do not get easier."

I believe that, the prevailing system of management is, at its core, dedicated to mediocrity. It forces people to work harder and harder to compensate for failing to tap the spirit and collective intelligence that characterizes working together at their best. Deming saw this clearly, and I believe that now, so do a growing number of leaders committed to growing organizations capable of thriving in and contributing to the extraordinary challenges and possibilities of the world we are living into.

PART I

How Our Actions
Create Our Reality . . .
and How We Can
Change It

1

"GIVE ME A LEVER LONG ENOUGH...AND SINGLE-HANDED I CAN MOVE THE WORLD"

From a very early age, we are taught to break apart problems, to fragment the world. This apparently makes complex tasks and subjects more manageable, but we pay a hidden, enormous price. We can no longer see the consequences of our actions; we lose our intrinsic sense of connection to a larger whole. When we then try to "see the big picture," we try to reassemble the fragments in our minds, to list and organize all the pieces. But, as physicist David Bohm says, the task is futile—similar to trying to reassemble the fragments of a broken mirror to see a true reflection. Thus, after a while we give up trying to see the whole altogether.

The tools and ideas presented in this book are for destroying the illusion that the world is created of separate, unrelated forces. When we give up this illusion—we can then build "learning organizations," organizations where people continually expand their capacity to create the results they truly desire, where new and expansive patterns of thinking are nurtured, where collective aspiration is set free, and where people are continually learning how to learn together.

As the world becomes more interconnected and business becomes more complex and dynamic, work must become more "learningful." It is no longer sufficient to have one person learning for the organization, a Ford or a Sloan or a Watson or a Gates. It's just not possible any longer to figure it out from the top, and have everyone else following the orders of the "grand strategist." The organizations that will truly excel in the future will be the organizations that discover how to tap people's commitment and capacity to learn at all levels in an organization.

Learning organizations are possible because, deep down, we are all learners. No one has to teach an infant to learn. In fact, no one has to teach infants anything. They are intrinsically inquisitive, masterful learners who learn to walk, speak, and pretty much run their households all on their own. Learning organizations are possible because not only is it our nature to learn but we love to learn. Most of us at one time or another have been part of a great team, a group of people who functioned together in an extraordinary way—who trusted one another, who complemented one anothers's strengths and compensated for one another's limitations, who had common goals that were larger than individual goals, and who produced extraordinary results. I have met many people who have experienced this sort of profound teamwork—in sports, or in the performing arts, or in business. Many say that they have spent much of their life looking for that experience again. What they experienced was a learning organization. The team that became great didn't start off great—it *learned* how to produce extraordinary results.

One could argue that the entire global business community is learning to learn together, becoming a learning community. Whereas once many industries were dominated by a single, undisputed leader—one IBM, one Kodak, one Xerox—today industries, especially in manufacturing, have dozens of excellent companies. American, European, or Japanese corporations are pulled forward by innovators in China, Malaysia, or Brazil, and they in turn, are pulled by the Koreans and Indians. Dramatic improvements take place in corporations in Italy, Australia, Singapore—and quickly become influential around the world.

There is also another, in some ways deeper, movement toward learning organizations, part of the evolution of industrial society. Material affluence for the majority has gradually shifted people's orientation toward work—from what Daniel Yankelovich called an "instrumental" view of work, where work was a means to an end, to a more "sacred" view, where people seek the "intrinsic" benefits of work.[1] "Our grandfathers worked six days a week to earn what most of us now earn by Tuesday afternoon," says Bill O'Brien, former CEO of Hanover Insurance. "The ferment in management will continue until we build organizations that are more consistent with man's higher aspirations beyond food, shelter and belonging."

Moreover, many who share these values are now in leadership positions. I find a growing number of organizational leaders who, while still a minority, feel they are part of a profound evolution in the nature of work as a social institution. "Why can't we do good works at work?" asked Edward Simon, former president of Herman Miller, a sentiment I often hear repeated today. In founding the "Global Compact," UN Secretary General Kofi Annan invited businesses around the world to build learning communities that elevate global standards for labor rights, and social and environmental responsibility.

Perhaps the most salient reason for building learning organizations is that we are only now starting to understand the capabilities such organizations must possess. For a long time, efforts to build learning organizations were like groping in the dark until the skills, areas of knowledge, and paths for development of such organizations became known. What fundamentally will distinguish learning organizations from traditional authoritarian "controlling organizations" will be the mastery of certain basic disciplines. That is why the "disciplines of the learning organization" are vital.

DISCIPLINES OF THE LEARNING ORGANIZATION

On a cold, clear morning in December 1903, at Kitty Hawk, North Carolina, the fragile aircraft of Wilbur and Orville Wright proved that powered flight was possible. Thus was the airplane invented; but it would take more than thirty years before commercial aviation could serve the general public.

Engineers say that a new idea has been "invented" when it is proven to work in the laboratory. The idea becomes an "innovation" only when it can be replicated reliably on a meaningful scale at practical costs. If the idea is sufficiently important, such as the telephone, the digital computer, or commercial aircraft, it is called a "basic innovation," and it creates a new industry or transforms an existing industry. In these terms, learning organizations have been invented, but they have not yet been innovated.

In engineering, when an idea moves from an invention to an innovation, diverse "component technologies" come together. Emerging from isolated developments in separate fields of research, these components gradually form an ensemble of technologies that are critical to one another's success. Until this ensemble forms, the idea, though possible in the laboratory, does not achieve its potential in practice.[2]

The Wright brothers proved that powered flight was possible, but the McDonnel Douglas DC-3, introduced in 1935, ushered in the era of commercial air travel. The DC-3 was the first plane that supported itself economically as well as aerodynamically. During those intervening thirty years (a typical time period for incubating basic innovations), myriad experiments with commercial flight had failed. Like early experiments with learning organizations, the early planes were not reliable and cost-effective on an appropriate scale.

The DC-3, for the first time, brought together five critical component technologies that formed a successful ensemble. They were: the variable-pitch propeller, retractable landing gear, a type of lightweight molded body construction called "monocque," a radial air-cooled engine, and wing flaps. To succeed, the DC-3 needed all five; four were not enough. One year earlier, the Boeing 247 was introduced with all of them except wing flaps. Boeing's engineers found that the plane, lacking wing flaps, was unstable on takeoff and landing, and they had to downsize the engine.

Today, I believe, five new component technologies are gradually converging to innovate learning organizations. Though developed separately, each will, I believe, prove critical to the others' success, just as occurs with any ensemble. Each provides a vital dimension in building organizations that can truly "learn," that can continually enhance their capacity to realize their highest aspirations:

Systems Thinking. A cloud masses, the sky darkens, leaves twist upward, and we know that it will rain. We also know the storm runoff will feed into groundwater miles away, and the sky will clear by tomorrow. All these events are distant in time and space, and yet they are all connected within the same pattern. Each has an influence on the rest, an influence that is usually hidden from view. You can only understand the system of a rainstorm by contemplating the whole, not any individual part of the pattern.

Business and other human endeavors are also systems. They,

too, are bound by invisible fabrics of interrelated actions, which often take years to fully play out their effects on each other. Since we are part of that lacework ourselves, it's doubly hard to see the whole pattern of change. Instead, we tend to focus on snapshots of isolated parts of the system, and wonder why our deepest problems never seem to get solved. Systems thinking is a conceptual framework, a body of knowledge and tools that has been developed over the past fifty years, to make the full patterns clearer, and to help us see how to change them effectively.

Though the tools are new, the underlying worldview is extremely intuitive; experiments with young children show that they learn systems thinking very quickly.

Personal Mastery. "Mastery" might suggest gaining dominance over people or things. But mastery can also mean a special level of proficiency. A master craftsman doesn't dominate pottery or weaving. People with a high level of personal mastery are able to consistently realize the results that matter most deeply to them— in effect, they approach their life as an artist would approach a work of art. They do that by becoming committed to their own lifelong learning.

Personal mastery is the discipline of continually clarifying and deepening our personal vision, of focusing our energies, of developing patience, and of seeing reality objectively. As such, it is an essential cornerstone of the learning organization—the learning organization's spiritual foundation. An organization's commitment to and capacity for learning can be no greater than that of its members. The roots of this discipline lie in both Eastern and Western spiritual traditions, and in secular traditions as well.

But few organizations encourage the growth of their people in this manner. This results in vast untapped resources: "People enter business as bright, well-educated, high-energy people, full of energy and desire to make a difference," says Hanover's O'Brien. "By the time they are 30, a few are on the fast track and the rest 'put in their time' to do what matters to them on the weekend. They lose the commitment, the sense of mission, and the excitement with which they started their careers. We get damn little of their energy and almost none of their spirit."

And surprisingly few adults work to rigorously develop their own personal mastery. When you ask most adults what they want from their lives, they often talk first about what they'd like to get rid of: "I'd like my mother-in-law to move out," they say, or "I'd like my back problems to clear up." The discipline of personal mastery starts with clarifying the things that really matter to us, of living our lives in the service of our highest aspirations.

Here, I am most interested in the connections between personal learning and organizational learning, in the reciprocal commitments between individual and organization, and in the special spirit of an enterprise made up of learners.

Mental Models. Mental models are deeply ingrained assumptions, generalizations, or even pictures or images that influence how we understand the world and how we take action. Very often, we are not consciously aware of our mental models or the effects they have on our behavior. For example, we may notice that a co-worker dresses elegantly, and say to ourselves, "She's a country club person." About someone who dresses shabbily, we may feel, "He doesn't care about what others think." Mental models of what can or cannot be done in different management settings are no less deeply entrenched. Many insights into new markets or outmoded organizational practices fail to get put into practice because they conflict with powerful, tacit mental models.

For example, in the early 1970s, Royal Dutch/Shell, became one of the first large organizations to understand how pervasive was the influence of hidden mental models. Shell's success in the 1970s and 1980s (rising from one of the weakest of the big seven oil companies to one of the strongest along with Exxon) during a period of unprecedented changes in the world oil business—the formation of OPEC, extreme fluctuations in oil prices and availability, and the eventual collapse of the Soviet Union—came in large measure from learning how to surface and challenge managers' mental models as a discipline for preparing change. Arie de Geus, Shell's Coordinator of Group Planning during the 80s, said that continuous adaptation and growth in a changing business environment depends on "institutional learning, which is the process whereby management teams change their shared mental models of the company, their markets, and their competitors. For this reason, we think of planning as learning and of corporate planning as institutional learning."[3]

The discipline of working with mental models starts with turning the mirror inward; learning to unearth our internal pictures of the world, to bring them to the surface and hold them rigorously to scrutiny. It also includes the ability to carry on "learningful" conversations that balance inquiry and advocacy, where people expose their own thinking effectively and make that thinking open to the influence of others.

Building Shared Vision. If any one idea about leadership has inspired organizations for thousands of years, it's the capacity to hold a shared picture of the future we seek to create. One is hard-pressed to think of any organization that has sustained some measure of greatness in the absence of goals, values, and missions that become deeply shared throughout the organization. IBM had "service"; Polaroid had instant photography; Ford had public transportation for the masses and Apple had "computers for the rest of us."[4] Though radically different in content and kind, all these organizations managed to bind people together around a common identity and sense of destiny.

When there is a genuine vision (as opposed to the all-too-familiar "vision statement"), people excel and learn, not because they are told to, but because they want to. But many leaders have personal visions that never get translated into shared visions that galvanize an organization. All too often, a company's shared vision has revolved around the charisma of a leader, or around a crisis that galvanizes everyone temporarily. But, given a choice, most people opt for pursuing a lofty goal, not only in times of crisis but at all times. What has been lacking is a discipline for translating individual vision into shared vision—not a "cookbook" but a set of principles and guiding practices.

The practice of shared vision involves the skills of unearthing shared "pictures of the future" that foster genuine commitment and enrollment rather than compliance. In mastering this discipline, leaders learn the counterproductiveness of trying to dictate a vision, no matter how heartfelt.

Team Learning. How can a team of committed managers with individual IQs above 120 have a collective IQ of 63? The discipline of team learning confronts this paradox. We know that teams can learn; in sports, in the performing arts, in science, and even, occasionally, in business, there are striking examples where the intelligence of the team exceeds the intelligence of the individuals in the team, and where teams develop extraordinary capacities for coordinated action. When teams are truly learning, not only are they producing extraordinary results, but the individual members are growing more rapidly than could have occurred otherwise.

The discipline of team learning starts with "dialogue," the capacity of members of a team to suspend assumptions and enter into a genuine "thinking together." To the Greeks dia-logos meant a free-flowing of meaning through a group, allowing the group to discover insights not attainable individually. Interestingly, the practice of dialogue has been preserved in many "primitive" cultures, such as that of the American Indian, but it has been almost completely lost to modern society. Today, the principles and practices of dialogue are being rediscovered and put into a contemporary context. (Dialogue differs from the more common "discussion," which has its roots with "percussion" and "concussion," literally a heaving of ideas back and forth in a winner-takes-all competition.)

The discipline of dialogue also involves learning how to recognize the patterns of interaction in teams that undermine learning. The patterns of defensiveness are often deeply ingrained in how a team operates. If unrecognized, they undermine learning. If recognized and surfaced creatively, they can accelerate learning.

Team learning is vital because teams, not individuals, are the fundamental learning unit in modern organizations. This is where the rubber meets the road; unless teams can learn, the organization cannot learn.

If a learning organization were an engineering innovation, such as the airplane or the personal computer, the components would be called "technologies." For an innovation in human behavior, the components need to be seen as *disciplines*. By "discipline," I do not mean an "enforced order" or "means of punishment," but a body of theory and technique that must be studied and mastered to be put into practice. A discipline (from the Latin *disciplina*, to learn) is a developmental path for acquiring certain skills or competencies. As with any discipline, from playing the piano to electrical engineering, some people have an innate gift, but anyone can develop proficiency through practice.

To practice a discipline is to be a lifelong learner. You never arrive; you spend your life mastering disciplines. You can never say, "We are a learning organization," any more than you can say, "I am an enlightened person." The more you learn, the more acutely aware you become of your ignorance. Thus, a corporation cannot be "excellent" in the sense of having arrived at a permanent excellence; it is always in the state of practicing the disciplines of learning, of getting better or worse.

That organizations can benefit from disciplines is not a totally new idea. After all, management disciplines such as accounting have been around for a long time. But the five learning disciplines differ from more familiar management disciplines in that they are personal disciplines. Each has to do with how we think and how we interact and learn with one another. In this sense, they are more like artistic disciplines than traditional management disciplines. Moreover, while accounting is good for "keeping score," we have never approached the subtler tasks of building organizations, of enhancing their capabilities for innovation and creativity, of crafting strategy and designing policy and structure through assimilating new disciplines. Perhaps this is why, all too often, great organizations are fleeting, enjoying their moment in the sun, then passing quietly back to the ranks of the mediocre.

Practicing a discipline is different from emulating a model. All too often, new management innovations are described in terms of the "best practices" of so-called leading firms. I believe benchmarking best practices can open people's eyes as to what is possible, but it can also do more harm than good, leading to piecemeal copying and playing catch-up. As one seasoned Toyota manager commented after hosting over a hundred tours for visiting executives, "They always say 'Oh yes, you have a Kan-Ban system, we do also. You have quality circles, we do also. Your people fill out standard work descriptions, ours do also.' They all see the parts and have copied the parts. What they do not see is the way all the parts work together." I do not believe great organizations have ever been built by trying to emulate another, any more than individual greatness is achieved by trying to copy another "great person."

When the five component technologies converged to create the DC-3 the commercial airline industry began. But the DC-3 was not the end of the process. Rather, it was the precursor of a new industry. Similarly, as the five component learning disciplines converge they will not create *the* learning organization but rather a new wave of experimentation and advancement.

THE FIFTH DISCIPLINE

It is vital that the five disciplines develop as an ensemble. This is challenging because it is much harder to integrate new tools than simply apply them separately. But the payoffs are immense.

This is why systems thinking is the fifth discipline. It is the discipline that integrates the disciplines, fusing them into a coherent body of theory and practice. It keeps them from being separate gimmicks or the latest organization change fads. Without a systemic orientation, there is no motivation to look at how the disciplines interrelate. By enhancing each of the other disciplines, it continually reminds us that the whole can exceed the sum of its parts.

For example, vision without systems thinking ends up painting lovely pictures of the future with no deep understanding of the forces that must be mastered to move from here to there. This is one of the reasons why many firms that have jumped on the "vision bandwagon" in recent years have found that lofty vision alone fails to turn around a firm's fortunes. Without systems thinking, the seed of vision falls on harsh soil. If nonsystemic thinking predominates, the first condition for nurturing vision is not met: a genuine belief that we can make our vision real in the future. We may say "We can achieve our vision" (most American managers are conditioned to this belief), but our tacit view of current reality as a set of conditions created by somebody else betrays us.

But systems thinking also needs the disciplines of building shared vision, mental models, team learning, and personal mastery to realize its potential. Building shared vision fosters a commitment to the long term. Mental models focus on the openness needed to unearth shortcomings in our present ways of seeing the world. Team learning develops the skills of groups of people to look for the larger picture beyond individual perspectives. And personal mastery fosters the personal motivation to continually learn how our actions affect our world. Without personal mastery, people are so steeped in the reactive mindset ("someone/something else is creating my problems") that they are deeply threatened by the systems perspective.

Lastly, systems thinking makes understandable the subtlest aspect of the learning organization—the new way individuals perceive themselves and their world. At the heart of a learning organization is a shift of mind—from seeing ourselves as separate from the world to connected to the world, from seeing problems as caused by someone or something "out there" to seeing how our own actions create the problems we experience. A learning organization is a place where people are continually discovering how they create their reality. And how they can change it. As Archimedes said, "Give me a lever long enough . . . and single-handed I can move the world."

METANOIA—A SHIFT OF MIND

When you ask people about what it is like being part of a great team, what is most striking is the meaningfulness of the experience. People talk about being part of something larger than themselves, of being connected, of being generative. It becomes quite clear that, for many, their experiences as part of truly great teams stand out as singular periods of life lived to the fullest. Some spend the rest of their lives looking for ways to recapture that spirit.

The most accurate word in Western culture to describe what happens in a learning organization is one that hasn't had much currency for the past several hundred years. It is a word we have used in our work with organizations for some ten years, but we always caution them, and ourselves, to use it sparingly in public. The word is "metanoia" and it means a shift of mind. The word has a rich history. For the Greeks, it meant a fundamental shift or change, or more literally transcendence (*"meta"*—above or beyond, as in "metaphysics") of mind (*"noia,"* from the root *"nous,"* of mind). In the early (Gnostic) Christian tradition, it took on a special meaning of awakening shared intuition and direct knowing of the highest, of God. "Metanoia" was probably the key term of such early Christians as John the Baptist. In the Catholic corpus the word "metanoia" was eventually translated as "repent."

To grasp the meaning of "metanoia" is to grasp the deeper meaning of "learning," for learning also involves a fundamental shift or movement of mind. The problem with talking about "learning organizations" is that the "learning" has lost its central meaning in contemporary usage. Most people's eyes glaze over if you talk to them about "learning" or "learning organizations." The words tend to immediately evoke images of sitting passively in schoolrooms, listening, following directions, and pleasing the teacher by avoiding making mistakes. In effect, in everyday use, learning has come to be synonymous with "taking in information." "Yes, I learned all about that at the training yesterday." Yet, taking in information is only distantly related to real learning. It would be nonsensical to say, "I just read a great book about bicycle riding—I've now learned that."

Real learning gets to the heart of what it means to be human. Through learning we re-create ourselves. Through learning we become able to do something we never were able to do. Through learning we reperceive the world and our relationship to it. Through learning we extend our capacity to create, to be part of the generative process of life. There is within each of us a deep hunger for this type of learning. As anthropologist Edward Hall says, "Humans are the learning organism par excellence. The drive to learn is as strong as the sexual drive—it begins earlier and lasts longer."[5]

This, then, is the basic meaning of a "learning organization"—an organization that is continually expanding its capacity to create its future. For such an organization, it is not enough merely to survive. "Survival learning" or what is more often termed "adaptive learning" is important—indeed it is necessary. But for a learning organization, "adaptive learning" must be joined by "generative learning," learning that enhances our capacity to create.

A few brave organizational pioneers are pointing the way, but the territory of building learning organizations is still largely unexplored. It is my fondest hope that this book can accelerate that exploration.

PUTTING THE IDEAS INTO PRACTICE

I take no credit for inventing the five major disciplines of this book. The five disciplines described below represent the experimentation, research, writing, and invention of hundreds of people. But I have worked with all of the disciplines for years, refining ideas about them, collaborating on research, and introducing them to organizations throughout the world.

When I first entered graduate school at MIT I was already convinced that most of the problems faced by humankind concerned our inability to grasp and manage the increasingly complex systems of our world. Little has happened since to change my view. Today, the environmental crisis, the continuing gap between "haves and have-nots" and consequent social and political instability, the persisting global arms race, the international drug trade, and the explosive U.S. budget, trade deficits, and consequent financial fragility all attest to a world where problems are becoming increasingly complex and interconnected. From the start at MIT I was drawn to the work of Jay Forrester, a computer pioneer who had shifted fields to develop what he called "system dynamics." Jay maintained that the causes of many pressing public issues, from urban decay to global ecological threat, lay in the very well-intentioned policies designed to alleviate them. These problems were "actually systems" that lured policymakers into interventions that focused on obvious

symptoms not underlying causes, which produced short-term benefit but long-term malaise, and fostered the need for still more symptomatic interventions.

As I began my doctoral work, I began to meet business leaders
who came to visit our MIT group to learn about systems thinking.
These were thoughtful people, deeply aware of the inadequacies of
prevailing ways of managing. Unlike most academics, they were
engaged, not detached intellectuals, and many were working to
build new types of organizations—decentralized, nonhierarchical
organizations dedicated to the well-being and growth of employees
as well as to success. Some had crafted radical corporate philoso-
phies based on core values of freedom and responsibility. Others
had developed innovative organization designs. All shared a commitment and a capacity to innovate that I found lacking in other
sectors. Gradually, I came to realize why business is the locus of
innovation in an open society. Despite whatever hold past thinking
may have on the business mind, business has a freedom to experiment missing in the public and education sectors and, often, in non-
profit organizations. It also has a clear bottom line, so that experiments can be evaluated, at least in principle, by objective criteria.

But why were they interested in systems thinking? Too often, the
most daring organizational experiments were foundering. Local
autonomy produced business decisions that were disastrous for the
organization as a whole. "Team building" exercises focused on better relationships among people who often still held radically different mental models of the business system. Companies pulled
together during crises, and then lost all their inspiration when business improved. Organizations which started out as booming successes, with the best possible intentions toward customers and
employees, found themselves trapped in downward spirals that got
worse the harder they tried to fix them.

When I was a student and young professor, we all believed that
the tools of systems thinking could make a difference in these companies. As I worked with different companies, I came to see why
systems thinking was not enough by itself. It needed a new type of
management practitioner to really make the most of it. At that time,
in the mid-1970s, there was a nascent sense of what such a management practitioner could be. But it had not yet crystallized. It began
to do so with the formation of a "CEO group" that met regularly at
MIT starting around 1980 that included William O'Brien of
Hanover Insurance, Arie de Geus of Shell, Edward Simon from
Herman Miller, and Ray Stata, CEO of Analog Devices. The group

continued for over a decade eventually drawing participants from Apple, Ford, Harley-Davidson, Philips, Polaroid, and Trammell Crow.

For over twenty-five years I have also been involved in developing and conducting leadership workshops, which have introduced people from all walks of life to the fifth discipline ideas that grew out of our work at MIT. These ideas combined initially with Innovation Associate's path-breaking work on building shared vision and personal mastery and the workshops continue today as part of the global Society for Organizational Learning (SoL). When *The Fifth Discipline* was originally published, over four thousand managers had attended these workshops and they were in fact the "target audience" to whom the book was aimed. (When it became apparent that many more people were using the book as an introduction to organizational learning, we created *The Fifth Discipline Fieldbook* in 1994, thinking that a book of practical tools, stories, and tips might in fact be a better introduction.) Over the course of these experiences the initial focus on corporate senior executives broadened, as it became evident that the basic disciplines of systems thinking, personal mastery, mental models, team learning and shared vision were relevant for teachers, public administrators and elected officials, students, and parents. All were in leadership positions of importance. All were in "organizations" that had still untapped potential for creating their future. All felt that to tap that potential required developing their own capacities, that is, learning.

So, this book is for the learners, especially those of us interested in the art and practice of collective learning.

For managers, this book should help in identifying the specific practices, skills, and disciplines that can make building learning organizations less of an occult art (though an art nonetheless).

For parents, this book should help in letting our children be our teachers, as well as we are theirs—for they have much to teach us about learning as a way of life.

For citizens, the dialogue about why contemporary organizations are not especially good learners and about what is required to build learning organizations reveals some of the tools needed by communities and societies if they are to become more adept learners.

2

DOES YOUR
ORGANIZATION
HAVE A LEARNING
DISABILITY?

Few large corporations live even half as long as a person. In 1983, a Royal Dutch/Shell study found that one-third of the firms that had been in the Fortune "500" in 1970 had vanished.[1] Shell estimated that the average lifetime of the largest industrial enterprises is less than forty years, roughly half the lifetime of a human being! Since then this study has been repeated by EDS and several other corporations, and served as a point of reference in James Collins' *Good to Great,* published in 2001. The chances are fifty-fifty that readers of this book will see their present firm disappear during their working career.

In most companies that fail, there is abundant evidence in advance that the firm is in trouble. This evidence goes unheeded, however, even when individual managers are aware of it. The organization as a whole cannot recognize impending threats, understand the implications of those threats, or come up with alternatives.

Perhaps under the laws of "survival of the fittest," this continual death of firms is fine for society. Painful though it may be for the employees and owners, it is simply a turnover of the economic soil, redistributing the resources of production to new companies and new cultures. But what if the high corporate mortality rate is only a symptom of deeper problems that afflict all companies, not just the ones that die? What if even the most successful companies are poor learners—they survive but never live up to their potential? What if, in light of what organizations *could* be, "excellence" is actually "mediocrity"?

It is no accident that most organizations learn poorly. The way they are designed and managed, the way people's jobs are defined, and, most importantly, the way we have all been taught to think and interact (not only in organizations but more broadly) create fundamental learning disabilities. These disabilities operate despite the best efforts of bright, committed people. Often the harder they try to solve problems, the worse the results. What learning does occur takes place despite these learning disabilities—for they pervade all organizations to some degree.

Learning disabilities are tragic in children, especially when they go undetected. They are no less tragic in organizations, where they also go largely undetected. The first step in curing them is to begin to identify the seven learning disabilities:

1. "I AM MY POSITION"

We are trained to be loyal to our jobs—so much so that we confuse them with our own identities. When a large American steel company began closing plants in the early 1980s, it offered to train the displaced steelworkers for new jobs. But the training never "took"; the workers drifted into unemployment and odd jobs instead. Psychologists came in to find out why, and found the steelworkers suffering from acute identity crises. "How could I do anything else?" asked the workers. "I *am* a lathe operator."

When asked what they do for a living, most people describe the tasks they perform every day, not the *purpose* of the greater enterprise in which they take part. Most see themselves within a system over which they have little or no influence. They do their job, put in their time, and try to cope with the forces outside of their control. Consequently, they tend to see their responsibilities as limited to the boundaries of their position.

Many years ago, managers from a Detroit auto maker told me of stripping down a Japanese import to understand why the Japanese were able to achieve extraordinary precision and reliability at lower cost on a particular assembly process. They found the same standard type of bolt used three times on the engine block. Each time it mounted a different type of component. On the American car, the same assembly required three different bolts, which required three different wrenches and three different inventories of bolts—making the car much slower and more costly to assemble. Why did the Americans use three separate bolts? Because the design organization in Detroit had three groups of engineers, each responsible for "their" component only. The Japanese had one designer responsible for the entire engine mounting, and probably much more. The irony is that each of the three groups of American engineers considered their work successful because their bolt and assembly worked just fine.

When people in organizations focus only on their position, they have little sense of responsibility for the results produced when all positions interact. Moreover, when results are disappointing, it can be very difficult to know why. All you can do is assume that "someone screwed up."

2. "THE ENEMY IS OUT THERE"

A friend once told the story of a boy he coached in Little League, who after dropping three fly balls in right field, threw down his glove and marched into the dugout. "No one can catch a ball in that darn field," he said.

There is in each of us a propensity to find someone or something outside ourselves to blame when things go wrong. Some organizations elevate this propensity to a commandment: "Thou shalt always find an external agent to blame." Marketing blames manufacturing: "The reason we keep missing sales targets is that our quality is not competitive." Manufacturing blames engineering. Engineering blames marketing: "If they'd only quit screwing up our designs and let us design the products we are capable of, we'd be an industry leader."

The "enemy is out there" syndrome is actually a by-product of "I am my position," and the nonsystemic ways of looking at the world that it fosters. When we focus only on our position, we do not see how our own actions extend beyond the boundary of that position.

When those actions have consequences that come back to hurt us, we misperceive these new problems as externally caused. Like the person being chased by his own shadow, we cannot seem to shake them.

The "Enemy Is Out There" syndrome is not limited to assigning blame within the organization. During its last years of operation, the once highly successful People Express Airlines slashed prices, boosted marketing, and bought Frontier Airlines—all in a frantic attempt to fight back against the perceived cause of its demise: increasingly aggressive competitors. Yet, none of these moves arrested the company's mounting losses or corrected its core problem, service quality that had declined so far that low fares were its only remaining pull on customers.

For years American companies who had lost market share to foreign competitors blamed cheap foreign wages, labor unions, government regulators, or customers who "betrayed us" by buying products from someone else. "The enemy is out there," however, is almost always an incomplete story. "Out there" and "in here" are usually part of a single system. This learning disability makes it almost impossible to detect the leverage we can use "in here" on problems that straddle the boundary between us and "out there."

3. THE ILLUSION OF TAKING CHARGE

Being "proactive" is in vogue. Managers frequently proclaim the need for taking charge in facing difficult problems. What is typically meant by this is that we should face up to difficult issues, stop waiting for someone else to do something, and solve problems before they grow into crises. In particular, being proactive is frequently seen as an antidote to being "reactive"—waiting until a situation gets out of hand before taking a step. But is taking aggressive action against an external enemy really synonymous with being proactive?

Once, a management team in a leading property and liability insurance company with whom we were working got bitten by the proactiveness bug. The head of the team, a talented vice president for claims, was about to give a speech proclaiming that the company wasn't going to get pushed around anymore by lawyers litigating more and more claims settlements. The firm would beef up its own legal staff so that it could take more cases through to trial by verdict, instead of settling them out of court.

Then we and some members of the team began to look more systemically at the probable effects of the idea: the likely fraction of cases that might be won in court, the likely size of cases lost, the monthly direct and overhead costs regardless of who won or lost, and how long cases would probably stay in litigation. Interestingly, the team's scenarios pointed to increasing total costs because, given the quality of investigation done initially on most claims, the firm simply could not win enough of its cases to offset the costs of increased litigation. The vice president tore up his speech.

All too often, proactiveness is reactiveness in disguise. Whether in business or politics, if we simply become more aggressive fighting the "enemy out there," we are reacting—regardless of what we call it. *True proactiveness comes from seeing how we contribute to our own problems.* It is a product of our way of thinking, not our emotional state.

4. THE FIXATION ON EVENTS

Two children get into a scrap on the playground and you come over to untangle them. Lucy says, "I hit him because he took my ball." Tommy says, "I took her ball because she won't let me play with her airplane." Lucy says, "He can't play with my airplane because he broke the propeller." Wise adults that we are, we say, "Now, now, children—just get along with each other." But are we really any different in the way we explain the entanglements we find ourselves caught in? We are conditioned to see life as a series of events, and for every event, we think there is one obvious cause.

Conversations in organizations are dominated by concern with events: last month's sales, the new budget cuts, last quarter's earnings, who just got promoted or fired, the new product our competitors just announced, the delay that just was announced in our new product, and so on. The media reinforces an emphasis on short-term events—after all, if it's more than two days old it's no longer "news." Focusing on events leads to "event" explanations: "The Dow Jones average dropped sixteen points today," announces the newspaper, "because low fourth-quarter profits were announced yesterday." Such explanations may be true, but they distract us from seeing the longer-term patterns of change that lie behind the events and from understanding the causes of those patterns.

Our fixation on events is actually part of our evolutionary programming. If you wanted to design a cave person for survival, ability to contemplate the cosmos would not be a high-ranking design criterion. What is important is the ability to see the saber-toothed tiger over your left shoulder and react quickly. The irony is that, today, the primary threats to our survival, both of our organizations and of our societies, come not from sudden events but from slow, gradual processes: the arms race, environmental decay, the erosion of a society's public education system, and decline in a firm's design or product quality (relative to competitors' quality) are all slow, gradual processes.

Generative learning cannot be sustained in an organization if people's thinking is dominated by short-term events. If we focus on events, the best we can ever do is predict an event before it happens so that we can react optimally. But we cannot learn to create.

5. THE PARABLE OF THE BOILED FROG

Maladaptation to gradually building threats to survival is so pervasive in systems studies of corporate failure that it has given rise to the parable of the "boiled frog." If you place a frog in a pot of boiling water, it will immediately try to scramble out. But if you place the frog in room temperature water, and don't scare him, he'll stay put. Now, if the pot sits on a heat source, and if you gradually turn up the temperature, something very interesting happens. As the temperature rises from 70 to 80 degrees F., the frog will do nothing. In fact, he will show every sign of enjoying himself. As the temperature gradually increases, the frog will become groggier and groggier, until he is unable to climb out of the pot. Though there is nothing restraining him, the frog will sit there and boil. Why? Because the frog's internal apparatus for sensing threats to survival is geared to sudden changes in his environment, not to slow, gradual changes.

The American automobile industry has had a long-standing case of boiled frog. In the 1960s, it dominated North American sales. That began to change very gradually. Certainly, Detroit's Big Three did not see Japan as a threat to their survival in 1962, when the Japanese share of the U.S. market was below 4 percent. Nor in 1967, when it was less than 10 percent. Nor in 1974, when it was under 15 percent. By the time the Big Three began to look critically at their own practices and core assumptions, it was the early 1980s, and the Japanese share of the American market had risen to 21.3 percent. By 1990, the Japanese share was approaching 25 percent, and by 2005 it was closer to 40 percent.[2] Given the financial health of the U.S. car companies it is unclear whether this particular frog will ever regain the strength to pull itself out of the hot water.

Learning to see slow, gradual processes requires slowing down our frenetic pace and paying attention to the subtle as well as the dramatic. If you sit and look into a tidepool, initially you won't see much of anything going on. However, if you watch long enough, after about ten minutes the tidepool will suddenly come to life. The world of beautiful creatures is always there, but moving a bit too slowly to be seen at first. The problem is our minds are so locked in one frequency, it's as if we can only see at 78 rpm; we can't see anything at 33-1/3. We will not avoid the fate of the frog until we learn to slow down and see the gradual processes that often pose the greatest threats.

6. THE DELUSION OF LEARNING FROM EXPERIENCE

The most powerful learning comes from direct experience. Indeed, we learn eating, crawling, walking, and communicating through direct trial and error—through taking an action and seeing the consequences of that action; then taking a new and different action. But what happens when we can no longer observe the consequences of our actions? What happens if the primary consequences of our actions are in the distant future or in a distant part of the larger system within which we operate? We each have a "learning horizon," a breadth of vision in time and space within which we assess our effectiveness. When our actions have consequences beyond our learning horizon, it becomes impossible to learn from direct experience.

Herein lies the core learning dilemma that confronts organizations: *we learn best from experience but we never directly experience the consequences of many of our most important decisions.* The most critical decisions made in organizations have systemwide consequences that stretch over years or decades. Decisions in R&D have first-order consequences in marketing and manufacturing. Investing in new manufacturing facilities and processes influences quality and delivery reliability for a decade or more. Promoting the right people into leadership positions shapes strategy and organizational climate for years. These are exactly the types of decisions where there is the least opportunity for trial and error learning.

Cycles are particularly hard to see, and thus learn from, if they last longer than a year or two. As systems-thinking writer Draper Kauffman, Jr., points out, most people have short memories. "When a temporary oversupply of workers develops in a particular field," he writes, "everyone talks about the big surplus and young people are steered away from the field. Within a few years, this creates a shortage, jobs go begging, and young people are frantically urged into the field—which creates a surplus. Obviously, the best time to start training for a job is when people have been talking about a surplus for several years and few others are entering it. That way, you finish your training just as the shortage develops."[3]

Traditionally, organizations attempt to surmount the difficulty of coping with the breadth of impact from decisions by breaking themselves up into components. They institute functional hierarchies that are easier for people to "get their hands around." But, functional divisions grow into fiefdoms, and what was once a convenient division of labor mutates into the "stovepipes" that all but cut off contact between functions. The result: analysis of the most important problems in a company, the complex issues that cross functional lines, becomes a perilous or nonexistent exercise.

7. THE MYTH OF THE MANAGEMENT TEAM

Striding forward to do battle with these dilemmas and disabilities is "the management team," the collection of savvy, experienced managers who represent the organization's different functions and areas of expertise. Together, they are supposed to sort out the complex cross-functional issues that are critical to the organization. What confidence do we have, really, that typical management teams can surmount these learning disabilities?

All too often, teams in business tend to spend their time fighting for turf, avoiding anything that will make them look bad personally, and pretending that everyone is behind the team's collective strategy—maintaining the appearance of a cohesive team. To keep up the image, they seek to squelch disagreement; people with serious reservations avoid stating them publicly, and joint decisions are watered-down compromises reflecting what everyone can live with, or else reflecting one person's view foisted on the group. If there is disagreement, it's usually expressed in a manner that lays blame, polarizes opinion, and fails to reveal the underlying differences in assumptions and experience in a way that the team as a whole could learn from.

"Most management teams break down under pressure," writes Harvard's Chris Argyris—a longtime student of learning in management teams. "The team may function quite well with routine issues. But when they confront complex issues that may be embarrassing or threatening, the 'teamness' seems to go to pot."[4]

Argyris argues that most managers find collective inquiry inherently threatening. School trains us never to admit that we do not know the answer, and most corporations reinforce that lesson by rewarding the people who excel in advocating their views, not inquiring into complex issues. (When was the last time someone was rewarded in your organization for raising difficult questions about the company's current policies rather than solving urgent problems?) Even if we feel uncertain or ignorant, we learn to protect ourselves from the pain of appearing uncertain or ignorant. That very process blocks out any new understandings which might threaten us. The consequence is what Argyris calls "skilled incompetence"—teams full of people who are incredibly proficient at keeping themselves from learning.

DISABILITIES AND DISCIPLINES

These learning disabilities have been with us for a long time. In *The March of Folly*, Barbara Tuchman traces the history of devastating large-scale policies "pursued contrary to ultimate self-interest,"[5] from the fall of the Trojans through the U.S. involvement in Vietnam. In story after story, leaders could not see the consequences of their own policies, even when they were warned in advance that their own survival was at stake. Reading between the lines of Tuchman's writing, you can see that the fourteenth-century Valois monarchs of France suffered from "I am my position" disabilities—when they devalued currency, they literally didn't realize they were driving the new French middle class toward insurrection.

In the mid-1700s Britain had a bad case of boiled frog. The British went through "a full decade," wrote Tuchman, "of mounting conflict with the [American] colonies without any [British official]

sending a representative, much less a minister, across the Atlantic
. . . to find out what was endangering the relationship . . ."[6] By 1776,
the start of the American Revolution, the relationship was irrevoca-
bly endangered. Elsewhere, Tuchman describes the Roman Catholic
cardinals of the fifteenth and sixteenth centuries, a tragic management "team" in which piety demanded that they present an appearance of agreement. However, behind-the-scenes backstabbing (in
some cases, literal backstabbing) brought in opportunistic popes
whose abuses of office provoked the Protestant Reformation.

More recently, historian Jared Diamond tells similar stories of
arrogance and blindness leading to demise, only this time the victims are entire civilizations. From the Mayas to the Easter Islanders,
Diamond shows how powerful dominant empires collapse, often in
remarkably short periods of time. Like failing organizations, most
of those inside the empire sense that all is not quite right, but their
instincts are to more strongly defend their traditional ways of doing
things rather than to question them—let alone develop the capacity
to change those ways.[7]

We live in no less perilous times today, and the same learning disabilities persist, along with their consequences. The five disciplines
of the learning organization can, I believe, act as antidotes to these
learning disabilities. But first, we must see the disabilities more
clearly—for they are often lost amid the bluster of day-to-day
events.

3

PRISONERS OF
THE SYSTEM, OR
PRISONERS OF OUR
OWN THINKING?

In order to see the learning disabilities in action, it helps to start with a laboratory experiment—a microcosm of how real organizations function, where you can see the consequences of your decisions play out more clearly than is possible in real organizations. For this reason, we often invite people to take part in a simulation called the "beer game," first developed in the 1960s at MIT's Sloan School of Management. Because it is a laboratory replica of a real setting, rather than reality itself, we can isolate the disabilities and their causes more sharply than is possible in real organizations. This reveals that the problems originate in basic ways of thinking and interacting, more than in peculiarities of organization structure and policy.

The beer game does this by immersing us in a type of organization which is rarely noticed but widely prevalent: a production/distribution system, the kind responsible for producing and shipping consumer and commercial goods in all industrial countries. In this case, it's a system for producing and distributing a single brand of beer. The players at each position are completely free to make any decision that seems prudent. Their only goal is to manage their position as best they can to maximize their profits.[1]

As with many games, the playing of a single session of the beer game can be told as a story. There are three main characters in the story—a retailer, a wholesaler, and the marketing director of a brewery.[2] This story is told, in turn, through each players' eyes.

THE RETAILER

Imagine that you're a retail merchant. Perhaps you're the franchise manager of a brightly lit twenty-four-hour chain store at a suburban intersection. Or maybe you own a mom-and-pop grocery on a street of Victorian-era brownstones. Or a discount beverage outlet on a remote highway.

No matter what your store looks like, or whatever else you sell, beer is a cornerstone of your business. Not only do you make a profit on it, but it draws customers in to buy, perhaps, popcorn and potato chips. You stock at least a dozen different brands of beer, and keep a rough tally of how many cases of each are in your back room, which is where you keep your inventory.

Once each week, a trucker arrives at the rear entrance of your store. You hand him a form on which you've filled in that week's order. How many cases of each brand do you want delivered? The trucker, after he makes his other rounds, returns your order to your beer wholesaler, who then processes it, arranges outgoing orders in a proper sequence, and ships the resulting order to your store. Because of all that processing, you're used to a four-week delay on average on your orders; in other words, a delivery of beer generally arrives in your store about four weeks after you order it.

You and your beer wholesaler never speak to each other directly. You communicate only through those check marks on a piece of paper. You probably have never even met him; you know only the truck driver. And that's for good reason: you have hundreds of products in your store. Dozens of wholesalers dole them out to you. Meanwhile, your beer wholesaler handles deliveries to several hundred stores, in a dozen different cities. Between your steady deluge of customers and his order-shuffling, who has time for chitchat? That single number is the only thing you need to say to each other.

One of your steadiest beer brands is called Lover's Beer. You are dimly aware that it's made by a small but efficient brewery located about three hundred miles away from you. It's not a super-popular brand; in fact, the brewery doesn't advertise at all. But every week, as regularly as your morning newspaper deliveries, four cases of Lover's Beer sell from the shelves. Sure, the customers are young— most are in their 20s—and fickle; but somehow, for every one who graduates to Miller or Bud, there's a younger sister or brother to replace him.

To make sure you always have enough Lover's Beer, you try to keep twelve cases in the store at any time. That means ordering four cases each Monday, when the beer truck comes. Week after week after week. By now, you take that four-case turnover for granted; it's inextricably wedded to the image in your mind of the beer's per-formance. You don't even articulate it to yourself when placing the order: "Oh, yeah," runs the automatic litany. "Lover's Beer. Four cases."

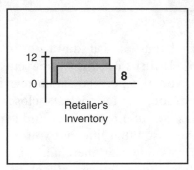

Week 2

Week 2: Without warning, one week in October (let's call it Week 2), sales of the beer double. They jump from four cases to eight. That's all right, you figure; you have an eight-case surplus in your store. You don't know why they've sold so much more suddenly. Maybe someone is having a party. But to replace those extra cases, you raise your order to eight. That will bring your inventory back to normal.

Week 3: Strangely enough, you also sell eight cases of Lover's Beer the *next* week. And it's not even spring break. Every once in a while, in those rare moments between sales, you briefly ponder the reason why. There's no advertising campaign for the beer; you would have received a mailing about it. Unless the mailing got lost, or you accidentally threw it out. Or maybe there's another reason . . . but a customer comes in, and you lose your train of thought.

At the moment the deliveryman comes, you're still not thinking much about Lover's Beer, but you look down at your sheet and see that he's brought only four cases this time. (It's from the order you placed four weeks ago.) You only have four cases left in stock, which means—unless there's a drop-back in sales—you're going to sell out all your Lover's Beer this week. Prudence dictates an order of at least eight cases to keep up with sales. Just to be on the safe side, you order twelve so you can rebuild your inventory.

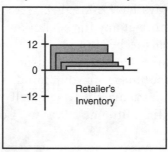

Week 4

Week 4: You find time on Tuesday to quiz one or two of your younger customers. It turns out that a new music video appeared a month or so back on the popular cable television channels. The video's recording group, the Iconoclasts, closes their song with the line, "I take one last sip of Lover's Beer and run into the sun." You don't know why they used that line, but your wholesaler would have told you if there was any new merchandising deal. You think of calling the wholesaler, but a delivery of potato chips arrives and the subject of Lover's Beer slips your mind.

When your next delivery of beer comes in, only five cases of beer arrive. You're chagrined now because you have only one case in stock. You're almost sold out. And thanks to this video, demand might go up even *further*. Still, you know that you have some extra cases on order, but you're not sure exactly how many. Better order at least sixteen more.

Week 5: Your one case sells out Monday morning. Fortunately, you receive a shipment for seven more cases of Lover's (apparently your wholesaler is starting to respond to your higher orders). But all are sold by the end of the week, leaving you with absolutely zero inventory. Glumly, you stare at the empty shelf. Better order another sixteen. You don't want to get a reputation for being out of stock of popular beers.

Week 6: Sure enough, customers start coming in at the beginning of the week, looking for Lover's. Two are loyal enough to wait for your backlog. "Let us know as soon as it comes in," they say, "and we'll be back to buy it." You note their names and phone numbers: they've promised to buy one case each.

Only six cases arrive in the next shipment. You call your two "backlogged" customers. They stop in and buy their shares; the rest of the beer sells out before the end of the week. Again, two customers give you their names to call as soon as your next shipment arrives. You wonder how many more you could have sold had your shelves not been empty at the end of the week. Seems there's been a run on the beer: none of the stores in the area have it. This beer is hot, and it's apparently getting more popular all the time.

After two days of staring at the parched, empty shelf, it doesn't feel right to order any less than another sixteen cases. You're tempted to order more, but you restrain yourself because you know the big orders you've been placing will start to arrive soon. But when . . . ?

Week 7: The delivery truck brings only five cases this week, which means that you're facing another week of empty shelves. As soon as you fill your back orders, Lover's Beer is sold out again, this time within two days. This week, amazingly, five customers give you their names. You order another sixteen and silently pray that your big orders will start arriving. You think of all the lost potato chip sales.

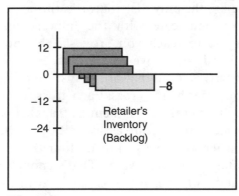

Week 8

Week 8: By now, you're watching Lover's Beer more closely than any other product you sell. The suspense is palpable: every time a customer buys a six-pack of that quiet beer, you notice it. People seem to be talking about the beer. Eagerly, you wait for the trucker to roll in the sixteen cases you expect. . .

But he brings only five. "What do you mean, five?" you say. "Gee, I don't know anything about it," the deliveryman tells you. "I guess they're backlogged. You'll get them in a couple of weeks." A couple of *weeks!?!* By the time you call your backlogged customers, you'll be sold out before you can sell a single new case. You'll be without a bottle of Lover's on your shelf all week. What will this do to your reputation?

You place an order for twenty-four more cases—twice as much as you had planned to order. What is that wholesaler *doing* to me, you wonder? Doesn't he know what a ravenous market we have down here? What's going through his mind, anyway?

THE WHOLESALER

As the manager of a wholesale distributing firm, beer is your life. You spend your days at a steel desk in a small warehouse stacked high with beer of every conceivable brand: Miller, Bud, Coors, Rolling Rock, a passel of imported beers—and, of course, regional beers such as Lover's Beer. The region you serve includes one large city, several smaller satellite cities, a web of suburbs, and some outlying rural areas. You're not the only beer wholesaler here, but you're very well established. For several small brands, including Lover's Beer, you are the only distributor in this area.

Mostly, you communicate with the brewery using the same method retailers use to reach you. You scribble numbers onto a form which you hand your driver each week. Four weeks later, on average, the beer arrives to fill that order. Instead of ordering by the case, however, you order by the gross. Each gross is about enough to fill a small truck, so you think of them as truckloads. Just as your typical retailer orders about four cases of Lover's Beer from you, week after week after week, so you order four truckloads from the brewery, week after week after week. That's enough to give you a typical accumulation of twelve truckloads' worth in inventory at any given time.

By Week 8, you had become almost as frustrated and angry as your retailers. Lover's Beer had always been a reliably steady brand. But a few weeks ago—in Week 4, actually—those orders had abruptly started rising sharply. The next week, orders from retailers had risen still further. By Week 8, most stores were ordering three or four times their regular amount of beer.

At first, you had easily filled the extra orders from your inventory in the warehouse. And you had been prescient; noting that there was a trend, you had immediately raised the amount of Lover's Beer you ordered from the brewery. In Week 6, after seeing an article in *Beer Distribution News* about the rock video, you had raised your brewery order still further, to a dramatic twenty truckloads per week. That was five times as much beer as your regular order. But you had needed that much; the beer's popularity was doubling, tripling, and even quadrupling, to judge from the stores' demand.

By Week 6, you had shipped out all the beer you had in inventory and entered the hellishness of backlog. Each week you sent out what you could, and sent the stores paperwork equivalents of IOUs to cover the rest. A few of the larger chain stores called you and got what preferential treatment you could offer, but the Lover's Beer in your inventory was gone. At least you knew it would be only a couple of weeks more before the extra beer you ordered would begin to arrive.

In Week 8, when you called the brewery to ask if there was any way to speed up their deliveries (and to let them know that you were upping your order to thirty truckloads), you were dismayed to find out that they had only just stepped up production two weeks before. They were just learning of the increase in demand. How could they be so slow?

Now it's **Week 9.** You're getting orders for twenty truckloads'

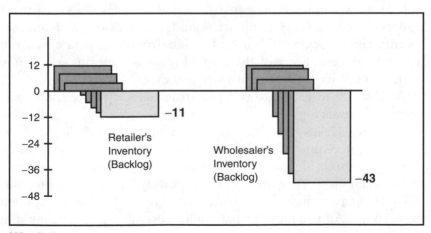

Week 9

worth of Lover's Beer per week, and you still don't have it. By the end of last week, you had backlogged orders of another twenty-nine truckloads. Your staff is so used to fielding calls that they've asked you to install an answering machine devoted to an explanation about Lover's Beer. But you're confident that, this week, the twenty truckloads you ordered a month ago will finally arrive.

However, only six truckloads arrive. Apparently the brewery is still backlogged, and the larger production runs are only now starting to get shipped out. You call some of your larger chains and assure them that the beer they ordered will be coming shortly.

Week 10 is infuriating. The extra beer you were expecting—at least twenty truckloads' worth—doesn't show. The brewery simply couldn't ramp up production that fast. Or so you guess. They only send you eight truckloads. It's impossible to reach anybody on the phone down there—they're apparently all on the factory floor, manning the brewery apparatus.

The stores, meanwhile, are apparently selling the beer wildly. You're getting unprecedented orders—for twenty-six truckloads this week. Or maybe they're ordering so much because *they* can't get any of the beer from you. Either way, you have to keep up. What if you can't get any of the beer and they go to one of your competitors?

You order forty truckloads from the brewery.

In **Week 11,** you find yourself tempted to take extra-long lunches at the bar around the corner from your warehouse. Only *twelve* truckloads of Lover's Beer arrive. You still can't reach anybody at the brewery. And you have over *a hundred* truckloads' worth of orders to fill: seventy-seven truckloads in backlog, and another twenty-eight truckloads' worth of orders from the stores which you receive this week. Some of those backlog costs come due, and you're afraid to tell your accountant what you expect.

You've got to get that beer: you order *another* forty truckloads from the brewery.

By **Week 12,** it's clear. This new demand for Lover's Beer is a far more major change than you expected. You sigh with resignation when you think of how much money you could make if you only had enough in stock. How could the brewery have *done* this to you? Why did demand have to rise so *quickly?* How are you ever expected to keep up? All you know is that you're never going to get caught in this situation again. You order sixty more truckloads.

For the next four weeks, the demand continues to outstrip your supply. In fact, you can't reduce your backlog at all in **Week 13.**

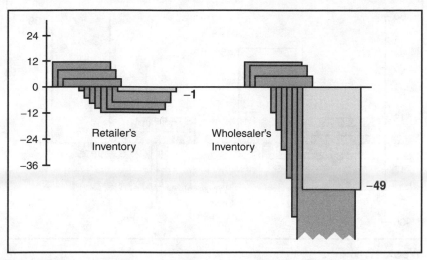

Week 14

You finally start receiving larger shipments from the brewery in **Weeks 14 and 15.** At the same time, orders from your stores drop off a bit. Maybe in the previous weeks, you figure, they overordered a bit. At this point, anything that helps work off your backlog is a welcome reprieve.

And now, in **Week 16,** you finally get almost *all* the beer you asked for weeks ago: fifty-five truckloads. It arrives early in the week, and you stroll back to that section of the warehouse to take a look at it, stacked on pallets. It's as much beer as you keep for any major brand. And it will be moving out soon.

Throughout the week, you wait expectantly for the stores' orders to roll in. You even stop by the intake desk to see the individual forms. But on form after form, you see the same number written: zero. Zero. Zero. Zero. Zero. What's wrong with these people? Four weeks ago, they were screaming at you for the beer, now, they don't even want any.

Suddenly, you feel a chill. Just as your trucker leaves for the run that includes the brewery, you catch up with him. You initial the form, and cross out the twenty-four truckloads you had ordered, replacing it with a zero of your own.

Week 17: The next week, sixty more truckloads of Lover's Beer arrive. The stores still ask for—zero. You still ask for—zero. One hundred and nine truckloads of the stuff sit in your warehouse. You could bathe in the stuff every day, and it wouldn't make a dent.

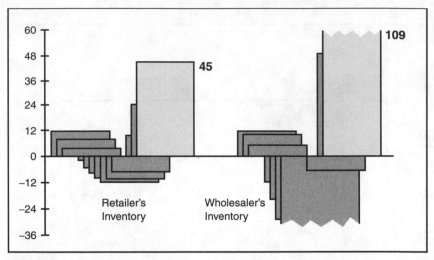

Week 17

Surely the stores will want more *this* week. After all, that video is still running. In your brooding thoughts, you consign every retailer to the deepest corner of hell; the corner reserved for people who don't keep their promises.

And, in fact, the retailers once again order zero cases of Lover's Beer from you. You, in turn, order zero truckloads from the brewery. And yet, the brewery continues to deliver beer. Sixty more truckloads appear on your dock this week. Why does that brewery have it in for you? When will it ever end?

THE BREWERY

Imagine that you were hired four months ago to manage distribution and marketing at the brewery, where Lover's Beer is only one of several primary products. Yours is a small brewery, known for its quality, not its marketing savvy. That's why you were hired.

Now, clearly, you have been doing something right. Because in only your second month (Week 6 of this game), new orders began to rise dramatically. By the end of your third month on the job, you felt the satisfaction of getting orders for forty gross of beer per *week,* up dramatically from the four when you started. And you shipped out . . . well, you shipped out thirty.

Because breweries get backlogs too. It takes (in your brewery, at least) two weeks from the time you decide to brew a bottle of beer until the moment when that beer is ready for shipment. Admittedly, you kept a few weeks' worth of beer in your warehouse, but those stocks were exhausted by Week 7, only two weeks after the rising orders came in. The next week, while you had back orders for nine gross and another twenty-four gross in new orders, you could send out only twenty-two gross. By that time you were a hero within your company. The plant manager had given everyone incentives to work double-time, and was feverishly interviewing for new factory help.

You had lucked out with that Iconoclasts video mentioning the beer. You had learned about the video in Week 3—from letters written by teenagers to the brewery. But it had taken until Week 6 to see that video translate into higher orders.

Even by Week 14, the factory had *still* not caught up with its backlogged orders. You had regularly requested brew batches of seventy gross or more. You had wondered how large your bonus would be that year. Maybe you could ask for a percentage of the profits, at least once you caught up with back orders. You had even idly pictured yourself on the cover of *Marketing Week.*

Finally, you *had* caught up with the backlog in Week 16. But the next week, your distributors had asked for only nineteen gross. And last week, **Week 18,** they had not asked for any more beer at all. Some of the order slips actually had orders crossed out on them.

Now, it's **Week 19.** You have a hundred gross of beer in inventory. And the orders, once again, ask for virtually no new deliveries. Zero beer. Meanwhile the beer you've been brewing keeps rolling in. You place the phone call you've dreaded making to your boss. "Better hold off on production for a week or two," you say. "We've got"—

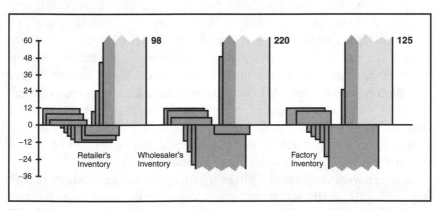

Week 21

and you use a word you've picked up in business school—"a discontinuity." There is silence on the other end of the phone. "But I'm sure it's only temporary," you say.

The same pattern continues for four more weeks: **Weeks 20, 21, 22, and 23.** Gradually your hopes of a resurgence slide, and your excuses come to sound flimsier and flimsier. Those distributors screwed us, you say. The retailers didn't buy enough beer. The press and that rock video hyped up the beer and got everybody sick of it. At root, it's the fickle kids—they have no loyalty whatsoever. How could they buy hundreds of cases one month, and nothing at all the next?

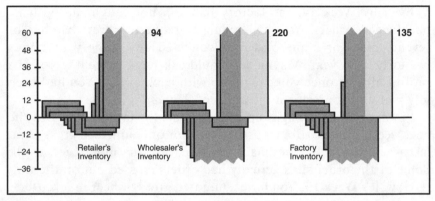

Week 24

Nobody misses you when you borrow the company car at the beginning of **Week 24.** Your first stop is the wholesaler's office. Not only is it the first time you have ever met face to face, it's only the second time you have ever spoken. There has never been anything to say until this crisis. You greet each other glumly, and then the wholesaler takes you out to the back warehouse. "We haven't gotten an order for your brand in two months," says the wholesaler. "I feel completely jerked around. Look! We still have 220 truckloads here."

What must have happened, you decide together, is that demand rose rapidly, and then fell dramatically. Another example of the fickleness of the public. If the retailers had stayed on top of it and warned you, this would never have happened.

You are working over the phrasing of a marketing strategy report in your mind on the way home when, on a whim, you decide to stop at the store of a retailer you pass along the way. Fortuitously, the owner of the store is in. You introduce yourself and the retailer's face breaks into a sardonic grin. Leaving an assistant in charge of the shop, the two of you walk next door to a luncheonette for a cup of coffee.

The retailer has brought along the shop's inventory tally notebooks, and spreads them open across the table. "You don't know how much I wanted to strangle you a few months ago."

"Why?" you ask

"Look—we're stuck with ninety-three cases in our back room. At this rate, it's going to be another six weeks before we order any more."

Six weeks, you think to yourself. And then you pull out a pocket calculator. If *every* retailer in this area waits six weeks before ordering any more beer, and then only orders a few cases a week, it's going to be a year or more before they put a dent in those 220 truckloads sitting at the wholesaler's. "This is a tragedy," you say. "Who let it happen—I mean, how can we keep it from happening again?"

"Well, it's not *our* fault," says the retailer, after sipping some coffee. "We were selling four cases of beer when that music video came out. Then, in Week 2, we sold eight cases."

"And then it mushroomed," you say. "But then why did it die down?"

"No, you don't understand," says the retailer. "The demand never mushroomed. And it never died out. We *still* sell eight cases of beer—week after week after week. But *you* didn't send us the beer we wanted. So we had to keep ordering, just to make sure we had enough to keep up with our customers."

"But we got the beer out as soon as it was necessary."

"Then maybe the wholesaler screwed up somehow," says the retailer. "I've been wondering if I should switch suppliers. Anyway, I wish you'd do a coupon promotion or something, so I could make back some of my costs. I'd like to unload some of those ninety-three cases."

You pick up the tab for coffee. On your trip back, you plan the wording of your resignation notice. Obviously, you'll be blamed for any layoffs or plant closings that come out of this crisis—just as the wholesaler blamed the retailer, and the retailer blamed the wholesaler, and both of them wanted to blame you. At least it's early enough that you can quit with some dignity. If only you could come up with some explanation to show that it wasn't your fault—to show that you were the victim, instead of the culprit . . .

LESSONS OF THE
BEER GAME

1. *Structure Influences Behavior*
Different people in the same structure tend to produce quali-
tatively similar results. When there are problems, or performance fails to live up to what is intended, it is easy to find someone or something to blame. But, more often than we realize,
systems cause their own crises, not external forces or individuals' mistakes.

2. *Structure in Human Systems Is Subtle*
We tend to think of "structure" as external constraints on the
individual. But, *structure* in complex living systems, such as
the "structure" of the multiple "systems" in a human body (for
example, the cardiovascular and neuromuscular) *means the
basic interrelationships that control behavior.* In human systems, structure includes how people make decisions—the
"operating policies" whereby we translate perceptions, goals,
rules, and norms into actions.

3. *Leverage Often Comes from New Ways of Thinking*
In human systems, people often have potential leverage that
they do not exercise because they focus only on their own decisions and ignore how their decisions affect others. In the beer
game, players have it in their power to eliminate the extreme
instabilities that invariably occur, but they fail to do so because
they do not understand how they are creating the instability in
the first place.

People in the business world love heroes. We lavish praise and
promotion on those who achieve visible results. But if something
goes wrong, we feel intuitively that somebody must have screwed up.

In the beer game, there are no such culprits. There is no one to
blame. Each of the three players in our story had the best possible
intentions: to serve his customers well, to keep the product moving
smoothly through the system, and to avoid penalties. Each partici-

pant made well-motivated, clearly defensible judgments based on reasonable guesses about what might happen. There were no villains, but there was a crisis nonetheless—built into the structure of the system.

In the last twenty years, the beer game has been played thousands of times in classes and management training seminars. It has been played on five continents, among people of all ages, nationalities, cultural origins, and vastly varied business backgrounds. Some players had never heard of a production/distribution system before; others had spent a good portion of their lives working in such businesses. Yet every time the game is played the same crises ensue. First, there is growing demand that can't be met. Orders build throughout the system. Inventories are depleted. Backlogs grow. Then the beer arrives en masse while incoming orders suddenly decline. By the end of the experiment, almost all players are sitting with large inventories they cannot unload—for example, it is not unusual to find brewery inventory levels in the hundreds overhanging orders from wholesalers for eight, ten, or twelve cases per week.[3]

If literally thousands of players, from enormously diverse backgrounds, all generate the same qualitative behavior patterns, the causes of the behavior must lie beyond the individuals. The causes of the behavior must lie in the structure of the game itself.

Moreover beer game-type structures create similar crises in real-life production-distribution systems. For instance, in 1985, personal computer memory chips were cheap and readily available; sales went down by 18 percent and American producers suffered 25 to 60 percent losses.[4] But in late 1986 a sudden shortage developed and was then exacerbated by panic and overordering. The result was a 100 to 300 percent increase in prices for the same chips.[5] A similar surge and collapse in demand occurred in the semiconductor industry in 1973 to 1975. After a huge order buildup and increases in delivery delays throughout the industry, demand collapsed and you could have virtually any product you wanted off any supplier's shelf overnight. Within a few years, Siemens, Signetics, Northern Telecom, Honeywell, and Schlumberger all entered the business by buying weakened semiconductor manufacturers.[6]

In mid-1989, General Motors, Ford, and Chrysler, as the May 30 *Wall Street Journal* put it, "were simply producing far more cars than they were selling, and dealer inventories were piling up . . . The companies already are idling plants and laying off workers at rates not seen for years."[7] Entire national economies undergo the same sorts of surges in demand and inventory overadjustments, due to what economists call the "inventory accelerator" theory of business cycles.

Similar boom and bust cycles continue to recur in diverse service businesses. For example, real estate is notoriously cyclic, often fueled by speculators who drive up prices to attract investors to new projects. "The phone would ring," Massachusetts condominium developer Paul Quinn told the *MacNeil-Lehrer Newshour* in 1989, "in our offices, and we said 'How are we going to handle this? We'll tell everybody to send in a $5,000 check with their name and we'll put them on the list.' The next thing we knew, we had over 150 checks sitting on the desk." The glut followed quickly on the boom: "It was a slow, sinking feeling," Quinn said, interviewed in a seaside town full of unsold developments. "Now's the time to start building for the next boom. Unfortunately, the people in the real estate industry are too busy trying to address the problems they have left over from the last one."[8]

In fact, reality in production-distribution systems is often worse than the beer game. A real retailer can order from three or four wholesalers at once, wait for the first group of deliveries to arrive, and cancel the other orders. Real producers often run up against production capacity limits not present in the game, thereby exacerbating panic throughout the distribution system. In turn, producers invest in additional capacity because they believe that current demand levels will continue into the future, then find themselves strapped with excess capacity once demand collapses.

The dynamics of production-distribution systems such as the beer game illustrate the first principle of systems thinking:

STRUCTURE INFLUENCES BEHAVIOR

When placed in the same system, people, however different, tend to produce similar results.

The systems perspective tells us that we must look beyond individual mistakes or bad luck to understand important problems. We must look beyond personalities and events. We must look into the underlying structures which shape individual actions and create the conditions where types of events become likely. As Donella Meadows expresses it:

A truly profound and different insight is the way you begin to see that the system causes its own behavior.[9]

This same sentiment was expressed over a hundred years ago by a systems thinker of an earlier vintage. Two thirds of the way through *War and Peace,* Leo Tolstoy breaks off from his narrative about the history of Napoleon and czarist Russia to contemplate why historians, in general, are unable to explain very much:

The first fifteen years of the nineteenth century present the spectacle of an extraordinary movement of millions of men. Men leave their habitual pursuits; rush from one side of Europe to the other; plunder, slaughter one another, triumph and despair; and the whole current of life is transformed and presents a quickened activity, first moving at a growing speed, and then slowly slackening again. What was the cause of that activity, or from what laws did it arise? asked the human intellect.

The historians, in reply to that inquiry, lay before us the sayings and doings of some dozens of men in one of the buildings in the city of Paris, summing up those doings and sayings by one word—revolution. Then they give us a detailed biography of Napoleon, and of certain persons favorably or hostilely disposed to him; talk of the influence of some of these persons upon others; and then say that this it is to which the activity is due; and these are its laws.

But, the human intellect not only refuses to believe in that explanation, but flatly declares that the method of explanation is not a correct one . . . The sum of men's individual wills produced both the revolution and Napoleon; and only the sum of those wills endured them and then destroyed them.

"But whenever there have been wars, there have been great military leaders; whenever there have been revolutions in states, there have been great men," says history. "Whenever there have been great military leaders there have, indeed, been wars," replies the human reason; "but that does not prove that the generals were the cause of the wars, and that the factors leading to warfare can be found in the personal activity of one man. . . ."[10]

Tolstoy argues that only in trying to understand underlying "laws of history," his own synonym for what we now call systemic structures, lies any hope for deeper understanding:

For the investigation of the laws of history, we must completely
change the subject of observations, must let kings and ministers
and generals alone, and study the homogeneous, infinitesimal
elements by which the masses are led. No one can say how far it
has been given to man to advance in that direction in understanding the laws of history. But it is obvious that only in that direction lies any possibility of discovering historical laws; and that
the human intellect has hitherto not devoted to that method of
research one millionth part of the energy that historians have put
into the description of the doings of various kings, ministers, and
generals . . .[11]

The term "structure," as used here, doesn't mean the "logical
structure" of a carefully developed argument or the reporting
"structure" as shown by an organization chart. Rather, systemic
structure is concerned with the key interrelationships that influence
behavior over time. These are not interrelationships between people,
but among key variables, such as population, natural resources, and
food production in a developing country; or engineers' product ideas
and technical and managerial know-how in a high-tech company.

In the beer game, the structure that caused wild swings in orders
and inventories involved the multiple-stage supply chain and the
delays intervening between different stages, the limited information
available at each stage in the system, and the goals, costs, perceptions, and fears that influenced individuals' orders for beer. But it is
very important to understand that when we use the term "systemic
structure" we do not just mean structure outside the individual. The
nature of structure in human systems is subtle because we are part
of the structure. This means that we often have the power to alter
structures within which we are operating.

However, more often than not, we do not perceive that power. In
fact, we usually don't see the structures at play much at all. Rather,
we just find ourselves feeling compelled to act in certain ways.

In 1973, psychologist Philip Zimbardo performed an experiment
in which college students were placed in the roles of prisoners and
guards in a mock prison set up in the basement of the psychology
building at Stanford. What started as mild resistance by the "prisoners" and assertiveness by the "guards," steadily escalated into
increasing rebelliousness and abusiveness, until the "guards" began
to physically abuse the "prisoners" and the experimenters felt the
situation was dangerously out of control. The experiment was

ended prematurely, after six days, when students began to suffer from depression, uncontrollable crying, and psychosomatic illnesses.[12]

I'll never forget one particularly chilling illustration of the power of structure in international politics. It occurred in a private meeting with a high-ranking member of the Soviet embassy, a few months after the Soviets had sent troops into Afghanistan. The official talked, eloquently and sincerely, about how the U.S.S.R. had been the first to recognize the country after its founding. The U.S.S.R. had been the first to come to its aid, repeatedly, when there was internal strife or instability. Beginning in the late 1970s, as threats from guerrilla factions increased, the ruling government asked for increasing Soviet aid. Modest assistance led to greater needs for broader help. It came to a point, the official explained, where "We really had no choice but to intervene militarily."

As I listened to this tale, I couldn't help but think of how retailers or wholesalers in the beer game will explain, when the game is over, that they really had no choice but to keep increasing their orders. It also brought to mind similar stories of American officials, ten or fifteen years earlier, trying to explain how the United States became entangled in Vietnam.

What, exactly, does it mean to say that structures generate particular patterns of behavior? How can such controlling structures be recognized? How would such knowledge help us to be more successful in a complex system?

The beer game provides a laboratory for exploring how structure influences behavior. Each player—retailer, wholesaler, and brewery—made only one decision per week: how much beer to order. The retailer is the first to boost orders significantly, with orders peaking around Week 12. At that point, the expected beer fails to arrive on time—because of backlogs at the wholesale and brewery levels. But the retailer, not thinking of those backlogs, dramatically increases orders to get beer at any cost. That sudden jump in orders is then amplified through the whole system—first by the wholesaler, and then by the brewery. Wholesaler orders peak at about 40, and brewery production peaks at about 80.

The result is a characteristic pattern of buildup and decline in orders at each position, amplified in intensity as you move "upstream," from retailers to breweries. In other words, the further from the ultimate consumer, the higher the orders, and the more dramatic the collapse. In fact, virtually all brewery players go through major crises, ending with near-zero production rates only weeks after having produced 40, 60, 100 or more gross per week.[13]

The other characteristic pattern of behavior in the game can be seen in the inventories and backlogs. The retailer's inventory begins to drop below zero at around Week 5. The retailer's backlog continues to increase for several weeks and the retailer doesn't get back to a positive inventory until around Weeks 12 to 15. Similarly, the wholesaler is in backlog from around Week 7 through around Weeks 15 to 18, and the brewery from Week 9 through Weeks 18 to 20. Once inventories begin to accumulate, they reach large values (about 40 for the retailer, 80 to 120 for the wholesaler, and 60 to 80 for the brewery by Week 30)—much larger than intended. So each position goes through an inventory-backlog cycle: first there is insufficient inventory, then there is too much inventory.

These characteristic patterns of overshoot and collapse in ordering and inventory-backlog cycles occur *despite stable consumer demand.* The actual consumer orders experienced only one change. In Week 2, consumer orders doubled—going from four cases of beer per week to eight. They remained at eight cases per week for the rest of the game.

In other words, after a one-time increase, consumer demand, for the rest of the simulation, was perfectly flat! Of course, none of the players other than the retailer knew consumer demand, and even the retailers saw demand only week by week, with no clue about what would come next.

After the beer game, we ask the people who played wholesalers and brewers to draw what they think the consumer orders were. Most draw a curve which rises and falls, just as their orders rose and fell.[14] In other words, the players assume that if orders in the game rose and collapsed, this must have been due to a surge and collapse in consumer orders. Such assumptions of an "external cause" are characteristic of nonsystemic thinking.

Players' guesses regarding consumer demand shed light on our deeply felt need to find someone or something to blame when there are problems. Initially, after the game is over, many believe that the culprits are the players in the other positions. This belief is shattered by seeing that the same problems arise in all plays of the game, regardless of who is manning the different positions. Many then direct their search for a scapegoat toward the consumer. "There must have been a wild buildup and collapse in consumer demand," they reason. But when their guesses are compared with the flat customer orders, this theory too is shot down.

This has a devastating impact on some players. I'll never forget the president of a large trucking firm sitting back, wide-eyed, staring at the beer game charts. At the next break, he ran to the telephones. "What happened?" I asked when he returned.

"Just before we came here," he said, "my top management team had concluded a three-day review of operations. One of our divisions had tremendously unstable fluctuations in fleet usage. It seemed pretty obvious that the division president didn't have what it took to get the job done. We automatically blamed the man, just as each of us in the experiment automatically blamed the brewery. It just hit me that the problems were probably structural, not personal. I just dashed out to call our corporate headquarters and cancel his termination process."

Once they see that they can no longer blame one another, or the customer, the players have one last recourse—*blame the system.* "It's an unmanageable system," some say. "The problem is that we couldn't communicate with each other." Yet this too turns out to be an untenable position. In fact, given the "physical system" of inventories, shipping delays, and limited information, there is substantial room for improving most teams' scores.

REDEFINING YOUR SCOPE OF INFLUENCE: HOW TO IMPROVE PERFORMANCE IN THE BEER GAME

To begin to see the possibilities for improvement, consider the outcomes if each player did nothing to correct his or her inventory or backlog. Following the "no strategy" strategy, each player would simply place new orders equal to orders he or she received. This is about the simplest ordering policy possible. If you receive new incoming orders for four cases of beer, you place orders for four. If you receive incoming orders for eight, you place orders for eight. Given the pattern of consumer demand in this game, that means ordering four cases or truckloads every week—until you receive your first order of eight. Thereafter you order eight.

When this strategy is followed unswervingly by all three players, all three positions settle into a form of stability by Week 11. The retailer and wholesaler never quite catch up with their backlogs. Backlogs develop, as in the basic game, due to the delays in getting orders filled. Backlogs persist because the players make no effort to correct them—because the "no strategy" strategy precludes placing the orders in excess of orders received needed to correct backlogs.

Is the "no strategy" strategy successful? Probably, most players would say no. After all, the strategy generates persistent backlogs. Everyone throughout the system is kept waiting longer than necessary for his orders to be filled. In real life, such a situation would, undoubtedly, invite competitors to enter a market and provide better delivery service. Only producers/distributors with monopolies on markets would be likely to stick to such a strategy.[15]

But the strategy eliminates the buildup and collapse in ordering, and the associated wild swings in inventories. Moreover, total cost generated by all positions in the "no strategy" strategy is lower than what is achieved by 75 percent of the teams that play the game![16] In other words, the majority of players in the game, many of them experienced managers, do much worse than if they simply placed orders equal to the orders they receive. In trying to correct the imbalances that result from "doing nothing," most players make matters worse—in many cases dramatically worse.

On the other hand, about 25 percent of the players score better than the "no strategy" strategy, and about 10 percent score very much better. In other words, success is possible. But it requires a shift of view for most players. It means getting to the heart of fundamental mismatches between common ways of thinking about the game—what we will later call our "mental model" of it—and the actual reality of how the game works. Most players see their job as "managing their position" in isolation from the rest of the system. What is required is to see how their position interacts with the larger system.

Consider how you feel if you are a typical player at any position. You pay close attention to your own inventory, costs, backlog, orders, and shipments. Incoming orders come from "outside"—most wholesalers and brewers, for instance, are shocked by the implacable mystery of those latter-half orders, which *should* be high numbers, but instead appear week after week as "zero, zero, zero, zero." You respond to new orders by shipping out beer, but you have little sense of how those shipments will influence the next round of orders. Likewise, you have only a fuzzy concept of what happens to the orders you place; you simply expect them to show up as new shipments after a reasonable delay. Your perspective of the system looks something like the figure on the next page.

Given this picture of the situation, if you need beer it makes sense to place more orders. If your beer doesn't arrive when expected, you place still more orders. Given this picture of the situ-

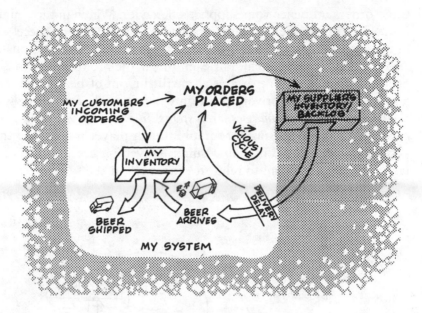

MY SYSTEM

ation, your job is to manage your position, reacting to changes in the external inputs of incoming orders, beer arrivals, and your supplier's delivery delay.

What the typical "manage your position" view misses is the ways that your orders interact with others' orders to influence the variables you perceive as "external." The players are part of a larger system that most perceive only dimly. For example, if they place a large number of orders, they can wipe out their supplier's inventory, thereby causing their supplier's delivery delay to increase. If they, then, respond (as many do) by placing still more orders, they create a "vicious cycle" that increases problems throughout the system.

This vicious cycle can be set off by any player who panics, anywhere within the system—whether retailer, or wholesaler. Even factories can create the same effect, simply by failing to produce enough beer. Eventually, as one vicious cycle influences other vicious cycles, the resulting panic spreads up and down the entire production-distribution system. Once the panic builds momentum, I have seen players generate orders that are twenty to fifty times what is actually needed to correct real inventory imbalances.

To improve performance in the beer game players must redefine their scope of influence. As a player in any position, your influence is broader than the limits of your own position. You don't simply place orders which go off into the ether and return as beer supplies;

those orders influence your supplier's behavior. Which in turn might influence yet another supplier's behavior. In turn, your success is not just influenced by your orders; it is influenced by the actions of everyone else in the system. For example, if the brewery runs out of beer, then pretty soon, everyone else will run out of beer. Either the larger system works, or your position will not work. *Interestingly, in the beer game and in many other systems, in order for you to succeed others must succeed as well.* Moreover, each player must share this systems viewpoint—for, if any single player panics and places a large order, panics tend to reinforce throughout the system.

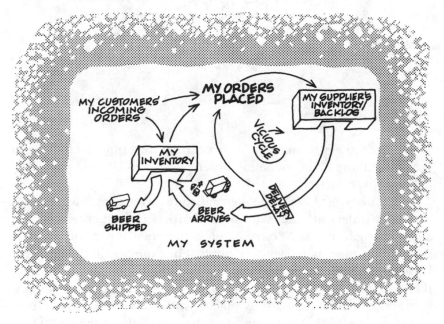

There are two key guidelines for players in the game.

First, keep in mind the beer you ordered but that, because of the delay, has not yet arrived. I call this the "take two aspirin and wait" rule. If you have a headache and need to take aspirin, you don't keep taking aspirin every five minutes until your headache goes away. You wait patiently for the aspirin to take effect because you know that aspirin operates with a delay. Many players keep ordering beer every week until their inventory discrepancy goes away.

Second, don't panic. When your supplier can't get you the beer you want as quickly as normal, the worst thing you can do is order more beer. Yet, that is exactly what many players do. It takes discipline to contain the overwhelming urge to order more when backlogs are building and your customers are screaming. But, without that discipline, you and everyone else will suffer.

These guidelines are consistently missed by most players because they are evident only if you understand the interactions that cross the boundaries between different positions. The "take two aspirin and wait" guideline comes from understanding the delay embedded in the response of your supplier's shipments to changes in your orders placed. The "don't panic" guideline comes from understanding the vicious cycle created when the orders you place exacerbate your supplier's delivery delay.

How well can players do if they follow these guidelines?

It is not possible to totally eliminate all overshoots in orders and all inventory/backlog cycles. It is possible to hold these instabilities to a very modest level, a small fraction of what occurred in Lover's Beer. It is possible to achieve total costs that are one-fifth of the "do nothing" strategy, or about one-tenth the typical costs achieved by teams. In other words, substantial improvements are possible.

THE LEARNING DISABILITIES AND
OUR WAYS OF THINKING

All of the learning disabilities described in Chapter 2 operate in the beer game:

- Because they "become their position," people do not see how their actions affect the other positions.
- Consequently, when problems arise, they quickly blame each other—"the enemy" becomes the players at the other positions, or even the customers.
- When they get "proactive" and place more orders, they make matters worse.
- Because their overordering builds up gradually, they don't realize the direness of their situation until it's too late.
- By and large, they don't learn from their experience because the most important consequences of their actions occur elsewhere in the system, eventually coming back to create the very problems they blame on others.[17]
- The "teams" running the different positions (usually there are two or three individuals at each position) become consumed

with blaming the other players for their problems, precluding any opportunity to learn from one another's experience.[18]

The deepest insights in the beer game come from seeing how these learning disabilities are related to alternative ways of thinking in complex situations. For most participants, the overall experience of playing the game is deeply dissatisfying because it is purely reactive. Yet, most eventually realize that the source of the reactiveness lies in their own focus on week-by-week events. Most of the players in the game get overwhelmed by the shortages of inventory, surges in incoming orders, disappointing arrivals of new beer. When asked to explain their decisions, they give classic "event explanations." I ordered forty at Week 11 because my retailers ordered thirty-six and wiped out my inventory." So long as they persist in focusing on events, they are doomed to reactiveness.

The systems perspective shows that there are multiple levels of explanation in any complex situation, as suggested by the diagram below. In some sense, all are equally "true." But their usefulness is quite different. Event explanations—"who did what to whom"—doom their holders to a reactive stance. As discussed earlier, event explanations are the most common in contemporary culture, and that is exactly why reactive management prevails.

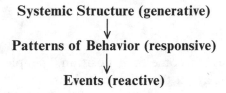

Systemic Structure (generative)

↓

Patterns of Behavior (responsive)

↓

Events (reactive)

"Pattern of behavior" explanations focus on seeing longer-term trends and assessing their implications. For example, in the beer game, a pattern of behavior explanation would be: "Production/distribution systems are inherently prone to cycles and instability, which become more severe the further you move from the retailer. Therefore, sooner or later, severe crises are likely at the brewery." Pattern of behavior explanations begin to break the grip of short-term reactiveness. At least they suggest how, over a longer term, we can *respond* to shifting trends.[19]

The third level of explanation, the "structural" explanation, is the least common and most powerful. It focuses on answering the question, "What causes the patterns of behavior?" In the beer game, a structural explanation must show how orders placed, shipments, and inventory interact to generate the observed patterns of instability and amplification, taking into account the effects of built-in delays in filling new orders, and the vicious cycle that arises when rising delivery delays lead to more orders placed. Though rare, structural explanations, when they are clear and widely understood, have considerable impact.

An exceptional example of a leader providing such insight was Franklin Roosevelt, when he went on the radio on March 12, 1933, to explain the four-day "banking holiday." In a time of panic, Roosevelt calmly explained how the banking system worked, structurally. "Let me state the simple fact that when you deposit money in a bank the bank does not put the money into a safe-deposit vault," he said. "It invests your money in many different forms of credit—bonds, mortgages. In other words, the bank puts your money to work to keep the wheels turning around . . ." He explained how banks were required to maintain reserves, but how those reserves were inadequate if there were widespread withdrawals; and why closing the banks for four days was necessary to restore order. In so doing, he generated public support for a radical but necessary action, and his reputation as a master of public communication.[20]

The reason that structural explanations are so important is that only they address the underlying causes of behavior at a level at which patterns of behavior *can be changed.* Structure produces behavior, and changing underlying structures can produce different patterns of behavior. In this sense, structural explanations are inherently *generative.* Moreover, since structure in human systems includes the "operating policies" of the decision makers in the system, redesigning our own decision making redesigns the system structure.[21]

For most players of the game, the deepest insight usually comes when they realize that their problems, *and* their hopes for improvement, are inextricably tied to how they think. Generative learning cannot be sustained in an organization where event thinking predominates. It requires a conceptual framework of "structural" or systemic thinking, the ability to discover structural causes of behavior. Enthusiasm for "creating our future" is not enough.

As the players in the beer game come to understand the structures that cause its behavior, they see more clearly their power to change that behavior, to adopt ordering policies that work in the larger system. They also discover a bit of timeless wisdom delivered years ago by Walt Kelly in his famous line from "Pogo": "We have met the enemy and he is us."

PART II

The Fifth
Discipline:
The Cornerstone
of the Learning
Organization

4

THE LAWS OF
THE FIFTH
DISCIPLINE[1]

1. *Today's problems come from yesterday's "solutions."*

Once there was a rug merchant who saw that his most beautiful carpet had a large bump in its center.[2] He stepped on the bump to flat-
ten it out—and succeeded. But the bump reappeared in a new spot
not far away. He jumped on the bump again, and it disappeared—
for a moment, until it emerged once more in a new place. Again and
again he jumped, scuffing and mangling the rug in his frustration;
until finally he lifted one corner of the carpet and an angry snake
slithered out.

Often we are puzzled by the causes of our problems; when we
merely need to look at our own solutions to other problems in the
past. A well-established firm may find that this quarter's sales are
off sharply. Why? Because the highly successful rebate program last
quarter led many customers to buy then rather than now. Or a new
manager attacks chronically high inventory costs and "solves" the
problem—except that the sales force is now spending 20 percent
more time responding to angry complaints from customers who are

still waiting for late shipments, and the rest of its time trying to convince prospective customers that they can have "any color they want so long as it's black."

Police enforcement officials will recognize their own version of this law: arresting narcotics dealers on 30th Street, they find that they have simply transferred the crime center to 40th Street. Or, even more insidiously, they learn that a new citywide outbreak of drug-related crime is the result of federal officials intercepting a large shipment of narcotics—which reduced the drug supply, drove up the price, and caused more crime by addicts desperate to maintain their habit.

Solutions that merely shift problems from one part of a system to another often go undetected because, unlike the rug merchant, those who "solved" the first problem are different from those who inherit the new problem.

2. *The harder you push, the harder the system pushes back.*

In George Orwell's *Animal Farm,* the horse Boxer always had the same answer to any difficulty: "I will work harder," he said. At first, his well-intentioned diligence inspired everyone, but gradually, his hard work began to backfire in subtle ways. The harder he worked, the more work there was to do. What he didn't know was that the pigs who managed the farm were actually manipulating them all for their own profit. Boxer's diligence actually helped to keep the other animals from seeing what the pigs were doing.[3] Systems thinking has a name for this phenomenon: "compensating feedback": when well-intentioned interventions call forth responses from the system that offset the benefits of the intervention. We all know what it feels like to be facing compensating feedback—the harder you push, the harder the system pushes back; the more effort you expend trying to improve matters, the more effort seems to be required.

Examples of compensating feedback are legion. Many of the best-intentioned government interventions fall prey to compensating feedback. In the 1960s there were massive programs to build low-income housing and improve job skills in decrepit inner cities in the United States. Many of these cities were even worse off in the 1970s despite the largesse of government aid. Why? One reason was that low-income people migrated from other cities and from rural areas to those cities with the best aid programs. Eventually, the new housing units became overcrowded and the job training programs were swamped with applicants. All the while, the city's tax base continued to erode, leaving more people trapped in economically depressed areas.

Similar compensating feedback processes have operated to thwart food and agricultural assistance to developing countries. More food available has been "compensated for" by reduced deaths due to malnutrition, higher net population growth, and eventually more malnutrition.

Similarly, periodic efforts to correct the U.S. trade imbalance by letting the value of the dollar fall are often compensated for by foreign competitors who let prices of their goods fall in parallel (for countries whose currency is "pegged to the dollar," prices adjust automatically). Efforts by foreign powers to suppress indigenous guerrilla fighters often lead to further legitimacy for the guerrillas' cause, thereby strengthening their resolve and support, and leading to still more resistance.

Many companies experience compensating feedback when one of their products suddenly starts to lose its attractiveness in the market. They push for more aggressive marketing; that's what always worked in the past, isn't it? They spend more on advertising, and drop the price; these methods may bring customers back temporarily, but they also draw money away from the company, so it cuts corners to compensate. The quality of its service (say, its delivery speed or care in inspection) starts to decline. In the long run, the more fervently the company markets, the more customers it loses.

Nor is compensating feedback limited to large systems—there are plenty of personal examples. Take the person who quits smoking only to find himself gaining weight and suffering such a loss in self-image that he takes up smoking again to relieve the stress. Or the protective mother who wants so much for her young son to get along with his schoolmates that she repeatedly steps in to resolve problems and ends up with a child who never learns to settle differences by himself. Or the enthusiastic newcomer so eager to be liked that she never responds to subtle criticisms of her work and ends up embittered and labeled "a difficult person to work with."

Pushing harder, whether through an increasingly aggressive intervention or through increasingly stressful withholding of natural instincts, is exhausting. Yet, as individuals and organizations, we not only get drawn into compensating feedback, we often glorify the suffering that ensues. When our initial efforts fail to produce lasting improvements, we push harder—faithful, as was Boxer, to the creed that hard work will overcome all obstacles, all the while blinding ourselves to how we are contributing to the obstacles ourselves.

3. *Behavior grows better before it grows worse.*

Low-leverage interventions would be much less alluring if it were not for the fact that many actually work, in the short term. New houses get built. The unemployed are trained. Starving children are spared. Lagging orders turn upward. We stop smoking, relieve our child's stress, and avoid a confrontation with a new coworker. Compensating feedback usually involves a "delay," a time lag between the short-term benefit and the long-term disbenefit. *The New Yorker* once published a cartoon in which a man sitting in an armchair pushes over a giant domino encroaching upon him from the left. "At last, I can relax," he's obviously telling himself in the cartoon. Of course, he doesn't see that the domino is toppling another domino, which in turn is about to topple another, and another, and that the chain of dominoes behind him will eventually circle around his chair and strike him from the right.

The "better before worse" response to many management interventions is what makes political decision making so counterproductive. By "political decision making," I mean situations where factors other than the intrinsic merits of alternative courses of action weigh in making decisions—factors such as building one's own power base, or "looking good," or "pleasing the boss." In complex human systems there are always many ways to make things look better in the short run. Only eventually does the compensating feedback come back to haunt you.

The key word is "eventually." The delay in, for example, the circle of dominoes, explains why systemic problems are so hard to recognize. A typical solution feels wonderful, when it first cures the symptoms. Now there's improvement; or maybe even the problem has gone away. It may be two, three, or four years before the problem returns, or some new, worse problem arrives. By that time, given how rapidly most people move from job to job, someone new is sitting in the chair.

4. *The easy way out usually leads back in.*

In a modern version of an ancient Sufi story, a passerby encounters a drunk on his hands and knees under a street lamp. He offers to help and finds out that the drunk is looking for his house keys. After several minutes, he asks, "Where did you drop them?" The drunk replies that he dropped them outside his front door. "Then why look for them here?" asks the passerby. "Because," says the drunk, "there is no light by my doorway."

We all find comfort applying familiar solutions to problems, sticking to what we know best. Sometimes the keys are indeed under the street lamp; but very often they are off in the darkness. After all, if the solution *were* easy to see or obvious to everyone, it probably would already have been found. Pushing harder and harder on familiar solutions, while fundamental problems persist or worsen, is a reliable indicator of nonsystemic thinking—what we often call the "what we need here is a bigger hammer" syndrome.

5. *The cure can be worse than the disease.*

Sometimes the easy or familiar solution is not only ineffective; sometimes it is addictive and dangerous. Alcoholism, for instance, may start as simple social drinking—a solution to the problem of low self-esteem or work-related stress. Gradually, the cure becomes worse than the disease; among its other problems it makes self-esteem and stress even worse than they were to begin with.

The long-term, most insidious consequence of applying nonsystemic solutions is increased need for more and more of the solution. This is why ill-conceived government interventions are not just ineffective, they are "addictive" in the sense of fostering increased dependency and lessened abilities of local people to solve their own problems. The phenomenon of short-term improvements leading to long-term dependency is so common, it has its own name among systems thinkers—it's called "shifting the burden to the intervenor." The intervenor may be federal assistance to cities, food relief agencies, or welfare programs. All "help" a host system, only to leave the system fundamentally weaker than before and more in need of further help.

Finding examples of shifting the burden to the intervenor, as natural resource expert and writer Donella Meadows says, "is easy and fun and sometimes horrifying"[4] and hardly limited to government intervenors. We shift the burden of doing simple math from our knowledge of arithmetic to a dependency on pocket calculators. We take away extended families, and shift the burden for care of the aged to nursing homes. In cities, we shift the burden from diverse local communities to housing projects. The Cold War shifted responsibility for peace from negotiation to armaments, thereby strengthening the military and related industries. In business, we can shift the burden to consultants or other "helpers" who make the company dependent on them, instead of training the client managers to solve problems themselves. Over time, the intervenor's power grows—whether it be a drug's power over a person, or the military budget's hold over an economy, the size and scope of foreign assistance agencies, or the budget of organizational "relief agencies."

"Shifting the burden" structures show that any long-term solution must, as Meadows says, "strengthen the ability of the system to shoulder its own burdens." Sometimes that is difficult; other times it is surprisingly easy. A manager who has shifted the burden of his personnel problems onto a human relations specialist may find that the hard part is deciding to take the burden back; once that happens, learning how to handle people is mainly a matter of time and commitment.

6. *Faster is slower.*

This, too, is an old story: the tortoise may be slower, but he wins the race. For most American business people the best rate of growth is fast, faster, fastest. Yet, virtually all natural systems, from ecosystems to animals to organizations, have intrinsically optimal rates of growth. The optimal rate is far less than the fastest possible growth. When growth becomes excessive—as it does in cancer—the system itself will seek to compensate by slowing down; perhaps putting the organization's survival at risk in the process. The story of People Express airlines offers a good example of how faster can lead to slower—or even full stop—in the long run.

Observing these characteristics of complex systems, noted biologist and essayist Lewis Thomas said, "When you are dealing with a complex social system, such as an urban center or a hamster, with things about it that you are dissatisfied with and eager to fix, you cannot just step in and set about fixing with much hope of helping. This realization is one of the sore discouragements of our century."[5]

When managers first start to appreciate how these systems principles have operated to thwart many of their own favorite interventions, they can be discouraged and disheartened. The systems principles can even become excuses for inaction—for doing nothing rather than possibly taking actions that might backfire, or even make matters worse. This is a classic case of a little knowledge being a dangerous thing. For the real implications of the systems perspective are not inaction but a new type of action rooted in a new way of thinking—systems thinking is both more challenging *and* more promising than our normal ways of dealing with problems.

7. *Cause and effect are not closely related in time and space.*

Underlying all of the above problems is a fundamental characteristic of complex human systems: cause and effect are not close in time and space. By "effects," I mean the obvious symptoms that indicate that there are problems—drug abuse, unemployment, starving children, falling orders, and sagging profits. By "cause" I mean the interaction of the underlying system that is most responsible for generating the symptoms, and which, if recognized, could lead to changes producing lasting improvement. Why is this a problem? Because most of us assume they *are*—most of us assume, most of the time, that cause and effect *are* close in time and space.

When we play as children, problems are never far away from their solutions—as long, at least, as we confine our play to one group of toys. Years later, as managers, we tend to believe that the world works the same way. If there is a problem on the manufacturing line, we look for a cause in manufacturing. If salespeople can't meet targets, we think we need new sales incentives or promotions. If there is inadequate housing, we build more houses. If there is inadequate food, the solution must be more food.

As the players in the beer game described in Chapter 3 eventually discover, the root of our difficulties is neither recalcitrant problems nor evil adversaries—but ourselves. There is a fundamental mismatch between the nature of reality in complex systems and our predominant ways of thinking about that reality. The first step in correcting that mismatch is to let go of the notion that cause and effect are close in time and space.

8. *Small changes can produce big results—but the areas of highest leverage are often the least obvious.*

Some have called systems thinking the "new dismal science" because it teaches that most obvious solutions don't work—at best, they improve matters in the short run, only to make things worse in the long run. But there is another side to the story. For systems thinking also shows that small, well-focused actions can sometimes produce significant, enduring improvements, if they're in the right place. Systems thinkers refer to this principle as "leverage."

Tackling a difficult problem is often a matter of seeing where the high leverage lies, a change which—with a minimum of effort— would lead to lasting, significant improvement.

The only problem is that high-leverage changes are usually highly *nonobvious* to most participants in the system. They are not "close in time and space" to obvious problem symptoms. This is what makes life interesting.

Buckminster Fuller had a wonderful illustration of leverage that also served as his metaphor for the principle of leverage—the "trim tab." A trim tab is a small "rudder on the rudder" of a ship. It is only a fraction the size of the rudder. Its function is to make it easier to turn the rudder, which, then, makes it easier to turn the ship. The larger the ship, the more important is the trim tab because a large volume of water flowing around the rudder can make it difficult to turn.

But what makes the trim tab such a marvelous metaphor for leverage is not just its effectiveness, but its nonobviousness. If you knew absolutely nothing about hydrodynamics and you saw a large oil tanker plowing through the high seas, where would you push if you wanted the tanker to turn left? You would probably go to the bow and try to push it to the left. Do you have any idea how much force it requires to turn an oil tanker going fifteen knots by pushing on its bow? The leverage lies in going to the stern and pushing the tail end of the tanker to the right, in order to turn the front to the left. This, of course, is the job of the rudder. But in what direction does the rudder turn in order to get the ship's stern to turn to the right? Why, to the left, of course.

You see, ships turn because their rear end is "sucked around." The rudder, by being turned into the oncoming water, compresses the water flow and creates a pressure differential. The pressure differential pulls the stern in the opposite direction as the rudder is turned. This is exactly the same way that an airplane flies: the airplane's wing creates a pressure differential and the airplane is "sucked" upward.

The trim tab—this very small device that has an enormous effect on the huge ship—does the same for the rudder. When it is turned to one side or the other, it compresses the water flowing around the rudder and creates a small pressure differential that "sucks the rudder" in the desired direction. But, if you want the rudder to turn to the left, what direction do you turn the trim tab?—to the right, naturally.

The entire system—the ship, the rudder, and the trim tab—is marvelously engineered through the principle of leverage. Yet, its functioning is totally nonobvious if you do not understand the force of hydrodynamics.

So, too, are the high-leverage changes in human systems nonobvious *until* we understand the forces at play in those systems.

There are no simple rules for finding high-leverage changes, but there are ways of thinking that make it more likely. Learning to see underlying structures rather than events is a starting point; each of the systems archetypes developed below suggests areas of high- and low-leverage change.

Thinking in terms of processes of change rather than snapshots is another.

9. *You* can *have your cake and eat it too—but not at once.*

Sometimes, the knottiest dilemmas, when seen from the systems point of view, aren't dilemmas at all. They are artifacts of "snapshot" rather than "process" thinking, and appear in a whole new light once you think consciously of change over time.

For years, for example, American manufacturers thought they had to choose between low cost and high quality. "Higher quality products cost more to manufacture," they thought. "They take longer to assemble, require more expensive materials and components, and entail more extensive quality controls." What they didn't consider was all the ways that increasing quality and lowering costs could go hand in hand, over time. What they didn't consider was how basic improvements in work processes could eliminate rework, eliminate quality inspectors, reduce customer complaints, lower warranty costs, increase customer loyalty, and reduce advertising and sales promotion costs. They didn't realize that they could have both goals, if they were willing to wait for one while they focused on the other. Investing time and money to develop new skills and methods of assembly, including new methods for involving everyone responsible for improving quality, is an up-front "cost." Quality and costs may both go up in the ensuing months; although some cost savings (like reduced rework) may be achieved fairly quickly, the full range of cost savings may take several years to harvest.

Many apparent dilemmas, such as central versus local control, and happy committed employees versus competitive labor costs, and rewarding individual achievement versus having everyone feel valued, are by-products of static thinking. They only appear as rigid "either-or" choices, because we think of what is possible at a fixed point in time. Next month, it may be true that we must choose one or the other, but the real leverage lies in seeing how both can improve over time.[6]

10. *Dividing an elephant in half does not produce two small elephants.*

Living systems have integrity. Their character depends on the whole. The same is true for organizations; to understand the most challenging managerial issues requires seeing the whole system that generates the issues.

Another Sufi tale illustrates the point of this law. As three blind men encountered an elephant, each exclaimed aloud. "It is a large rough thing, wide and broad, like a rug," said the first, grasping an ear. The second, holding the trunk, said, "I have the real facts. It is a straight and hollow pipe." And the third, holding a front leg, said, "It is mighty and firm, like a pillar." Are the three blind men any different from the heads of manufacturing, marketing, and research in many companies? Each sees the firm's problems clearly, but none see how the policies of their department interact with the others. Interestingly, the Sufi story concludes by observing that "Given these men's way of knowing, they will never know an elephant."

Seeing "whole elephants" does not mean that every organizational issue can be understood only by looking at the entire organization. Some issues *can* be understood only by looking at how major functions such as manufacturing, marketing, and research interact; but there are other issues where critical systemic forces arise within a given functional area; and others where the dynamics of an entire industry must be considered. The key principle, called the "principle of the system boundary," is that the interactions that must be examined are those most important to the issue at hand, *regardless* of parochial organizational boundaries.

What makes this principle difficult to practice is the way organizations are designed to keep people from seeing important interactions. One obvious way is by enforcing rigid internal divisions that inhibit inquiry across divisional boundaries, such as those that grow up between marketing, manufacturing, and research. Another is by leaving problems behind us, for someone else to clean up. Many European cities have avoided the problems of crime, entrenched poverty, and helplessness that afflict so many American inner cities because they have forced themselves to face the balances that a healthy urban area must maintain. One way they have done this is by maintaining large "green belts" around the city that discourage the growth of suburbs and commuters who work in the city but live outside it. By contrast, many American cities have encouraged steady expansion of surrounding suburbs, continually enabling wealthier residents to move further from the city center and its problems. (Impoverished areas today, such as Harlem in New York and Roxbury in Boston were originally upper-class suburbs.) Corporations do the same thing by continually acquiring new businesses and "harvesting" what they choose to regard as mature businesses rather than reinvesting in them.

Incidentally, sometimes people go ahead and divide an elephant in half anyway. You don't have two small elephants then; you have a mess. By a "mess," I mean a complicated problem where there is no leverage to be found because the leverage lies in interactions that cannot be seen from looking only at the piece you are holding.

11. *There is no blame.*

We all tend to blame someone else—the competitors, the press, the changing mood of the marketplace, the government—for our problems. Systems thinking shows us that there is no separate "other"; that you and the someone else are part of a single system. The cure lies in your relationship with your "enemy."

5

A SHIFT OF MIND

SEEING THE WORLD ANEW

There is something in all of us that loves to put together a puzzle, that loves to see the image of the whole emerge. The beauty of a person, or a flower, or a poem lies in seeing all of it. It is interesting that the words "whole" and "health" come from the same root (the Old English *hal,* as in "hale and hearty"). So it should come as no surprise that the unhealthiness of our world today is in direct proportion to our inability to see it as a whole.

Systems thinking is a discipline for seeing wholes. It is a framework for seeing interrelationships rather than things, for seeing patterns of change rather than static "snapshots." It is a set of general principles—distilled over the course of the twentieth century, spanning fields as diverse as the physical and social sciences, engineering, and management. It is also a set of specific tools and techniques, originating in two threads: in "feedback" concepts of cybernetics and in "servo-mechanism" engineering theory dating back to the nineteenth century. During the last thirty years, these tools have been applied to help us understand a wide range of corporate, urban, regional, economic, political, ecological, and even physiological systems.[1] And systems thinking is a sensibility—for the subtle interconnectedness that gives living systems their unique character.

Today, systems thinking is needed more than ever because we are becoming overwhelmed by complexity. Perhaps for the first time in history, humankind has the capacity to create far more information than anyone can absorb, to foster far greater interdependency than anyone can manage, and to accelerate change far faster than anyone's ability to keep pace. Certainly the scale of complexity is without precedent. All around us are examples of "systemic breakdowns"—problems such as global warming, climate change, the international drug trade, and the U.S. trade and budget deficits—problems that have no simple local cause. Similarly, organizations break down, despite individual brilliance and innovative products, because they are unable to pull their diverse functions and talents into a productive whole.

Complexity can easily undermine confidence and responsibility—as in the frequent refrain, "It's all too complex for me," or "There's nothing I can do. It's the system." Systems thinking is the antidote to this sense of helplessness that many feel as we enter the "age of interdependence." Systems thinking is a discipline for seeing the "structures" that underlie complex situations, and for discerning high from low leverage change. That is, by seeing wholes we learn how to foster health. To do so, systems thinking offers a language that begins by restructuring how we think.

I call systems thinking the fifth discipline because it is the conceptual cornerstone that underlies all of the five learning disciplines of this book. All are concerned with a shift of mind from seeing parts to seeing wholes, from seeing people as helpless reactors to seeing them as active participants in shaping their reality, from reacting to the present to creating the future. Without systems thinking, there is neither the incentive nor the means to integrate the learning disciplines once they have come into practice. As the fifth discipline, systems thinking is the cornerstone of how learning organizations think about their world.

Originally *The Fifth Discipline* included an analysis of the most "poignant example" of the need for systems thinking of its time, the U.S.-U.S.S.R. arms race, "a race to see who could get fastest to where no one wants to go." I noted that this tragic "race" had "drained the U.S. economy and devastated the Soviet economy," and commented at the end that it would only change when one of the antagonists concluded that they were no longer "willing to play." Ironically within a year of writing that, the collapse of the Soviet Union brought the tragic U.S.-U.S.S.R. arms race to an abrupt end. But today, the U.S. and much of the world finds itself caught in another race that appears to be heading toward where no one wants to go, the so-called "war on terrorism."

The roots of the war on terrorism, like the US-Soviet arms race, lie not in rival political ideologies, nor in particular arms, but in a way of thinking both sides shared. The United States establishment, for example, has been governed by a viewpoint that essentially resembled the following:

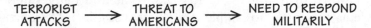

$$\text{TERRORIST ATTACKS} \longrightarrow \text{THREAT TO AMERICANS} \longrightarrow \text{NEED TO RESPOND MILITARILY}$$

The terrorists' view of their situation resembles this:

$$\text{US MILITARY ACTIVITY} \longrightarrow \text{PERCEIVED AGGRESSIVENESS OF U.S.} \longrightarrow \text{TERRORIST RECRUITS}$$

From the American viewpoint, terrorists networks like Al Qaeda have been the aggressor, and U.S. military expansion has been a defensive response to the threat. From the terrorist viewpoint, the United States, both economically and militarily, has been the aggressor, and the expansion of recruits bears evidence that many share this view.

But the two straight lines form a circle. The two antagonists' individual, "linear," or nonsystemic viewpoints interact to create a "system," a set of variables that influence one another:

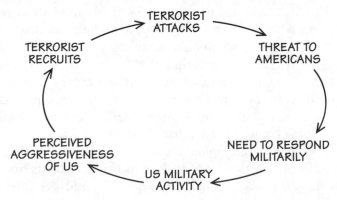

The systems view of the war on terrorism shows a perpetual cycle of aggression. The United States responds to a perceived Threat to Americans by increasing U.S. military activities, which increases the Perceived Aggressiveness of the U.S., which leads to more Terrorist Recruits, which eventually leads to more Terrorist Activities and increases the Threat to the United States, which leads to more U.S. military activities, which increases the Terrorist Recruits, which . . . and so on, and so on. From their individual viewpoints, each side focuses on its short-term goals. Both sides respond to perceived threats. But their actions end up creating escalating danger for everyone. Here, as in many systems, doing the obvious thing does not produce the obvious, desired outcome. The longer-term result of each side's efforts is heightened insecurity for all.

Interestingly, the U.S. in particular has failed to adopt a true systems view, despite an abundance of "systems analysts" studying the terrorists' weapons and resources and state-of-the art information technology, including complex computer simulations.[3] Why then have these supposed tools for dealing with complexity not empowered us to escape the illogic of the war on terrorism?

The answer lies in the same reason that sophisticated tools of forecasting and business analysis, as well as elegant strategic plans, usually fail to produce dramatic breakthroughs in managing a business. They are all designed to handle the sort of complexity in which there are many variables: *detail complexity. But there is a second type of complexity.* The second type is *dynamic complexity,* situations where cause and effect are subtle, and where the effects over time of interventions are not obvious. Conventional forecasting, planning, and analysis methods are not equipped to deal with dynamic complexity. Following a complex set of instructions to assemble a machine involves detail complexity, as does taking inventory in a discount retail store. But none of these situations is especially complex dynamically.

When the same action has dramatically different effects in the short run and the long, there is dynamic complexity. When an action has one set of consequences locally and a very different set of consequences in another part of the system, there is dynamic complexity. When obvious interventions produce nonobvious consequences, there is dynamic complexity. A gyroscope is a dynamically complex machine: If you push downward on one edge, it moves to the left; if you push another edge to the left, it moves upward. Yet, how trivially simple is a gyroscope when compared with the complex dynamics of an enterprise, where it takes days to produce something, weeks to develop a new marketing promotion, months to hire and train new people, and years to develop new products, nurture management talent, and build a reputation for quality—and all these processes interact continually.

The real leverage in most management situations lies in understanding dynamic complexity, not detail complexity. Balancing market growth and capacity expansion is a dynamic problem. Developing a profitable mix of price, product (or service) quality, design, and availability that make a strong market position is a dynamic problem. Improving quality, lowering total costs, and satisfying customers in a sustainable manner is a dynamic problem.

Unfortunately, most systems analyses focus on detail complexity not dynamic complexity. Simulations with thousands of variables and complex arrays of details can actually distract us from seeing patterns and major interrelationships. In fact, sadly, for most people "systems thinking" means "fighting complexity with complexity," devising increasingly "complex" (we should really say "detailed") solutions to increasingly "complex" problems. In fact, this is the antithesis of real systems thinking.

The war on terrorism is, most fundamentally, a problem of dynamic complexity. Insight into the causes and possible cures requires seeing the interrelationships, such as between U.S. actions to become more secure and the perceived image of aggression. It requires seeing the delays between action and consequence, such as the delay between a U.S. decision to intervene militarily and the growth in terrorist recruits. And it requires seeing patterns of change, not just snapshots, such as the continuing escalation.

Seeing the major interrelationships underlying a problem leads to new insight into what might be done. In the case of the war on terrorism, as in any escalation dynamic, the obvious question is, "Can the vicious cycle be run in reverse?" "Can the war on terrorism be run backward to create a slowly building cycle of security?" Obviously, there are a great many other factors in the global and Middle East geopolitical system that influence the simple escalation dynamic shown above. But any real progress will surely hinge on much deeper insight into how people of the region themselves (including those who are potential recruits to or supporters of terrorism) perceive security and their own genuine aspirations for progress and development. Simply imposing an external view of progress, especially one promulgated by a party seen to be an aggressor in the conflict, cannot reduce perceived threats.

The essence of the discipline of systems thinking lies in a shift of mind:

- seeing interrelationships rather than linear cause-effect chains, and
- seeing processes of change rather than snapshots

The practice of systems thinking starts with understanding a simple concept called "feedback" that shows how actions can reinforce or counteract (balance) each other. *It builds to learning to recognize types of "structures" that recur again and again:* an arms race is a generic or archetypal pattern of escalation, at its heart no different from turf warfare between two street gangs, the demise of a marriage, or the advertising battles of two companies fighting a price war for market share. Eventually, systems thinking forms a rich language for describing a vast array of interrelationships and patterns of change. Ultimately, *it simplifies life* by helping us see the deeper patterns lying behind the events and the details.

Learning any new language is difficult at first. But as you start to master the basics, it gets easier. Research with young children has shown that many learn systems thinking remarkably quickly.[4] It appears that we have latent skills as systems thinkers that are undeveloped, even repressed by formal education in linear thinking. Hopefully, what follows will help rediscover some of those latent skills and bring to the surface the systems thinker that is within each of us.

SEEING CIRCLES OF CAUSALITY[5]

Reality is made up of circles but we see straight lines. Herein lie the beginnings of our limitation as systems thinkers. One of the reasons for this fragmentation in our thinking stems from our language. Language shapes perception. What we see depends on what we are prepared to see. Western languages, with their subject-verb-object structure, are biased toward a linear view.[6] If we want to see systemwide interrelationships, we need a language of interrelationships, a language made up of circles. Without such a language, our habitual ways of seeing the world produce fragmented views and counterproductive actions—as it has done for decision makers in the war on terrorism. Such a language is important in facing dynamically complex issues and strategic choices, especially when individuals, teams, and organizations need to see beyond events and into the forces that shape change.

To illustrate the rudiments of the new language, consider a very simple system—filling a glass of water. You might think, "That's not a system—it's too simple." But think again.

From the linear viewpoint, we say, "I am filling a glass of water." What most of us have in mind looks pretty much like the following picture:

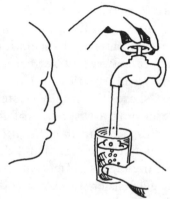

But, in fact, as we fill the glass, we are watching the water level rise. We monitor the "gap" between the level and our goal, the desired water level. As the water approaches the desired level, we adjust the faucet position to slow the flow of water, until it is turned off when the glass is full. In fact, when we fill a glass of water we operate in a water-regulation system involving five variables: our desired water level, the glass's current water level, the gap between the two, the faucet position, and the water flow. These variables are organized in a circle or loop of cause-effect relationships which is called a "feedback process." The process operates continuously to bring the water level to its desired level.

People get confused about feedback because we often use the word in a somewhat different way—to gather opinions about an act we have undertaken. "Give me some feedback on the brewery decision," you might say. "What did you think of the way I handled it?" In that context, "positive feedback" means encouraging remarks and "negative feedback" means bad news. But in systems thinking, feedback is a broader concept. It means any reciprocal flow of

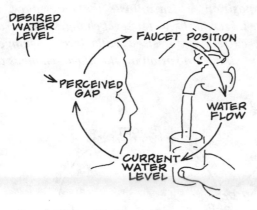

influence. In systems thinking it is an axiom that every influence is both *cause* and *effect*. Nothing is ever influenced in just one direction.

HOW TO READ A SYSTEMS DIAGRAM

The key to seeing reality systemically is seeing circles of influence rather than straight lines. This is the first step to breaking out of the reactive mindset that comes inevitably from "linear" thinking. Every circle tells a story. By tracing the flows of influence, you can see patterns that repeat themselves, time after time, making situations better or worse.

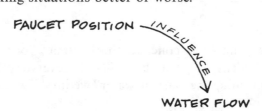

From any element in a situation, you can trace arrows that represent influence on another element:

Above, the faucet position arrow points to water flow. Any change made to the faucet position will alter the flow of water. But arrows never exist in isolation:

To follow the story, start at any element and watch the action ensue, circling as the train in a toy railroad does through its recurring journey. A good place to start is with the action being taken by the decision maker:

I set the faucet position, which adjusts the water flow, which changes the water level. As the water level changes, the perceived gap (between the current and desired water levels) changes. As the gap changes, my hand's position on the faucet changes again. And so on . . .

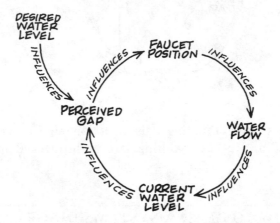

When reading a feedback circle diagram, the main skill is to see the story that the diagram tells: how the structure creates a particular pattern of behavior (or, in a complex structure, several patterns of behavior) and how that pattern might be influenced. Here the story is filling the water glass and gradually closing down the faucet as the glass fills.

Though simple in concept, the feedback loop overturns deeply ingrained ideas—such as causality. In everyday English when we say, "I am filling the glass of water" we imply, without thinking very

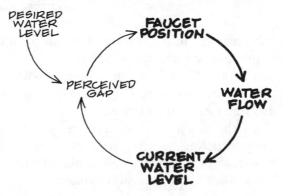

much about it, a one-way causality—"I am causing the water level to rise." More precisely, "My hand on the faucet is controlling the rate of flow of water into the glass." Clearly, this statement describes only half of the feedback process: the linkages from faucet position to flow of water to water level.

But it would be just as true to describe only the other half of the process: "The level of water in the glass is controlling my hand."

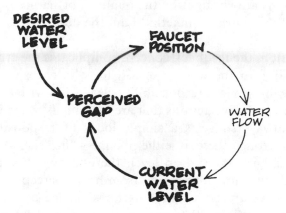

Both statements are equally incomplete. The more complete statement of causality is that my intent to fill a glass of water creates a system that causes water to flow in when the level is low, then shuts the flow off when the glass is full. In other words, the structure causes the behavior and the structure is brought into play by my intention and action. This distinction is important because seeing only individual actions and missing the structure underlying the actions, as we saw in the beer game in Chapter 3, lies at the root of our powerlessness in complex situations.

In fact, all causal attributions made in everyday English are highly suspect! Most are embedded in linear ways of seeing. They are at best partially accurate, inherently biased toward describing portions of reciprocal processes, not the entire process.

Another idea overturned by the feedback perspective is anthropocentrism—or seeing ourselves as the center of activities. The simple description, "I am filling the glass of water," suggests a world of human actors standing at the center of activity, operating on an inanimate reality. *From the systems perspective, the human actor is part of the feedback process, not standing apart from it. This represents a profound shift in awareness.* It allows us to see how we are continually both influenced by and influencing our reality. It is the shift in awareness so ardently advocated by ecologists in their cries that we see ourselves as part of nature, not separate from nature. It is the shift in awareness recognized by many of the world's great philosophical systems—for example, the *Bhagavad Gita*'s chastisement:

> All actions are wrought by the qualities of nature only. The self, deluded by egoism, thinketh: "I am the doer."[7]

In addition, the feedback concept complicates the ethical issue of responsibility. In the war on terrorism, who is responsible? From each side's linear view, responsibility clearly lies with the other side: "It is their aggressive actions that are causing us to respond." A linear view always suggests a simple locus of responsibility. When things go wrong, there is either blame—"he, she, it did it"—or guilt—"I did it." At a deep level, there is no difference between blame and guilt, for both spring from linear perceptions. From the linear view, we are always looking for someone or something that must be responsible—they can even be directed toward hidden agents within ourselves. When my son was 4 years old, he used to say, "My stomach won't let me eat it," when turning down his vegetables. We may chuckle, but is his assignment of responsibility really different from the adult who says, "My neuroses keep me from trusting people."

In mastering systems thinking, we give up the assumption that there is an individual, or individual agent, responsible. The feedback perspective suggests that *everyone shares responsibility for problems generated by a system*. That doesn't necessarily imply that everyone involved can exert equal leverage in changing the system.

But it does imply that the search for scapegoats—a particularly alluring pastime in individualistic cultures such as ours in the United States—is a blind alley.

Finally, the feedback concept illuminates the limitations of our language. When we try to describe in words even a very simple system, such as filling the water glass, it gets very awkward: "When I fill a glass of water, there is a feedback process that causes me to adjust the faucet position, which adjusts the water flow and feeds back to alter the water position. The goal of the process is to make the water level rise to my desired level." This is precisely why a new language for describing systems is needed. If it is this awkward to describe a system as simple as filling a water glass, *imagine our difficulties using everyday English to describe the multiple feedback processes in an organization.*

All this takes some getting used to. We are steeped in a linear language for describing our experience. We find simple statements about causality and responsibility familiar and comfortable. It is not that they must be given up, any more than you give up English to learn French. There are many situations where simple linear descriptions suffice and looking for feedback processes would be a waste of time. But not when dealing with problems of dynamic complexity.

REINFORCING AND BALANCING FEEDBACK AND DELAYS: THE BUILDING BLOCKS OF SYSTEMS THINKING

There are two distinct types of feedback processes: reinforcing and balancing. *Reinforcing* (or amplifying) feedback processes are the engines of growth. Whenever you are in a situation where things are growing, you can be sure that reinforcing feedback is at work. Reinforcing feedback can also generate accelerating decline—a pattern of decline where small drops amplify themselves into larger and larger drops, such as the decline in bank assets when there is a financial panic.

Balancing (or stabilizing) feedback operates whenever there is a goal-oriented behavior. If the goal is to be not moving, then balancing feedback will act the way the brakes in a car do. If the goal is to be moving at sixty miles per hour, then balancing feedback will cause you to accelerate to sixty but no faster. The goal can be an explicit target, as when a firm seeks a desired market share, or it can be implicit, such as a bad habit, which despite disavowing, we stick to nevertheless.

In addition, many feedback processes contain *"delays,"* interruptions in the flow of influence which make the consequences of actions occur gradually.

All ideas in the language of systems thinking are built up from these elements, just as English sentences are built up from nouns and verbs. Once we have learned the building blocks, we can begin constructing stories: the systems archetypes of the next chapter.

REINFORCING FEEDBACK: DISCOVERING HOW
SMALL CHANGES CAN GROW

If you are in a reinforcing feedback system, you may be blind to how small actions can grow into large consequences—for better or for worse. Seeing the system often allows you to influence how it works.

For example, managers frequently fail to appreciate the extent to which their own expectations influence subordinates' performance. If I see a person as having high potential, I give him special attention to develop that potential. When he flowers, I feel that my original assessment was correct and I help him still further. Conversely, those I regard as having lower potential languish in disregard and inattention, perform in a disinterested manner, and further justify, in my mind, the lack of attention I give them.

Psychologist Robert Merton first identified this phenomenon as the "self-fulfilling prophecy."[8] It is also known as the "Pygmalion effect," after the famous George Bernard Shaw play (later to become *My Fair Lady*). Shaw in turn had taken his title from Pygmalion, a character in Greek and Roman mythology, who believed so strongly in the beauty of the statue he had carved that it came to life.

Pygmalion effects have been shown to operate in countless situations.[9] An example occurs in schools, where a teacher's opinion of a student influences the behavior of that student. Jane is shy and does particularly poorly in her first semester at a new school (because her parents are fighting constantly). This leads her teacher to form an opinion that she is unmotivated. Next semester, the teacher pays less attention to Jane and she does poorly again, withdrawing further. Over time, Jane gets caught in an ever-worsening spiral of withdrawal, poor performance, labeling by her teachers, inattention, and further withdrawing. Thus, students are unintentionally "tracked" into a high self-image of their abilities, where they get personal attention, or a low self-image, where their poor classwork is reinforced in an ever-worsening spiral.

In *reinforcing processes* such as the Pygmalion effect, a small change builds on itself. Whatever movement occurs is amplifed, producing more movement in the same direction. A small action snowballs, with more and more and still more of the same, resembling compounding interest. Some reinforcing (amplifying) processes are "vicious cycles," in which things start off badly and grow worse. A "gas crisis" is a classic example. Once word that gasoline is becoming scarce gets out it sets off a spate of trips to local service stations, to fill up. Once people start seeing lines of cars, they are convinced that the crisis is here. Panic and hoarding then set in. Before long, everyone is "topping off" their tanks when they are only one-quarter empty, lest they be caught when the pumps go dry. The same thing happens when there is a run on food or water before a major storm and people expect power to be out and normal supplies to disappear. A run on a bank is another example, as is a panic to sell of a type of stock when the word gets out that values are falling. All are escalation structures where small moves in an undesirable direction set off reinforcing spiral.

But there's nothing inherently bad about reinforcing loops. There are also virtuous cycles—processes that reinforce in desired directions. For instance, physical exercise can lead to a reinforcing spiral; you feel better, thus you exercise more, thus you're rewarded by feeling better and exercise still more. The war on terrorism run in reverse, if it can be sustained, would make another virtuous cycle. The growth of any new product involves reinforcing spirals. For example, many products grow from "word of mouth." Word of mouth about a product can reinforce a snowballing demand (as occurred with the Volkswagen Beetle and the ipod) as satisfied customers tell others who then become satisfied customers, who tell still others. With today's network devices the physical act of sharing information (or songs) adds another reinforcing dynamic: once one person has such a device, the information can only be shared with others with similar devices.

Here is how you might diagram the positive word-of-mouth process that drives growth in sales and satisfaction:

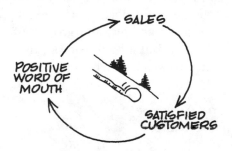

SALES

POSITIVE WORD OF MOUTH

SATISFIED CUSTOMERS

HOW TO READ A REINFORCING
CIRCLE DIAGRAM

Reinforcing Sales Process Caused by Customers Talking to Each Other About Your Product

This diagram shows a reinforcing feedback process wherein actions *snowball*. Again, you can follow the process by walking yourself around the circle:

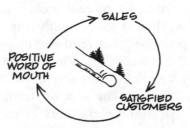

If the product is a good product, more sales means more satisfied customers, which means more positive word of mouth. That will lead to still more sales, which means even more widespread word of mouth . . . and so on. On the other hand, if the product is defective, the virtuous cycle becomes a vicious cycle: sales lead to fewer satisfied customers, less positive word of mouth, and fewer sales; which leads to still less positive word of mouth and fewer sales.

The behavior that results from a reinforcing loop is either accelerating growth or accelerating decline. For example, the nuclear-arms race has produced an accelerating growth of arms stockpiles over the past half century. But a bank run produces an accelerating decline in a bank's deposits.

Folk wisdom speaks of reinforcing loops in terms such as "snowball effect," "bandwagon effect," or "vicious circle," and in phrases describing particular systems: "the rich get richer and the poor get poorer." In business, we know that "momentum is everything," in building confidence in a new product or within a fledgling organization. We also know about reinforcing spirals running the wrong way. "The rats are jumping ship" suggests a situation where, as soon as a few people lose confidence, their defection will cause others to defect in a vicious spiral of eroding confidence. Word of mouth can easily work in reverse, and (as occurred with contaminated over-the-counter drugs) produce marketplace disaster.

Both good news and bad news reinforcing loops accelerate so quickly that they often take people by surprise. A French schoolchildren's jingle illustrates the process. First there is just one lily pad in a corner of a pond. But every day the number of lily pads doubles. It takes thirty days to fill the pond, but for the first twenty-eight days, no one even notices. Suddenly, on the twenty-ninth day, the pond is half full of lily pads and the villagers become concerned. But by this time there is little that can be done. The next day their worst fears come true. That's why environmental dangers are so worrisome, especially those that follow reinforcing patterns. By the time the problem is noticed, it may be too late. Extinctions of species often follow patterns of slow, gradually accelerating decline over long time periods, then rapid collapse. So do extinctions of corporations.

But pure accelerating growth or decline rarely continues unchecked in nature, because reinforcing processes rarely occur in isolation. Eventually, limits are encountered—which can slow growth, stop it, divert it, or even reverse it. Even the lily pads stop growing when the limit of the pond's perimeter is encountered. These limits are one form of *balancing feedback,* which, after reinforcing processes, is the second basic element of systems thinking.

BALANCING PROCESSES: DISCOVERING THE SOURCES OF STABILITY AND RESISTANCE

If you are in a balancing system, you are in a system that is seeking stability. If the system's goal is one you like, you will be happy. If it is not, you will find all your efforts to change matters frustrated—until you can either change the goal or weaken its influence.

Nature loves a balance—but many times, human decision makers act contrary to these balances, and pay the price. For example, managers under budget pressure often cut back staff to lower costs, but eventually discover that their remaining staff is now overworked, and their costs have not gone down at all—because the remaining work has been farmed out to consultants, or because overtime has made up the difference. The reason that costs don't stay down is that *the system has its own agenda.* There is an implicit goal, unspoken but very real—the amount of work that is expected to get done.

In a balancing (stabilizing) system, there is a self-correction that attempts to maintain some goal or target. Filling the glass of water is a balancing process with the goal of a full glass. Hiring new employees is a balancing process with the goal of having a target work force size or rate of growth. Steering a car and staying upright on a bicycle are also examples of balancing processes, where the goal is heading in a desired direction.

Balancing feedback processes are everywhere. They underlie all goal-oriented behavior. Complex organisms such as the human body contain thousands of balancing feedback processes that maintain temperature and balance, heal our wounds, adjust our eyesight to the amount of light, and alert us to threat. A biologist would say that all of these processes are the mechanisms by which our body achieves *homeostasis*—its ability to maintain conditions for survival in a changing environment. Balancing feedback prompts us to eat when we need food, and to sleep when we need rest, or to put on a sweater when we are cold.

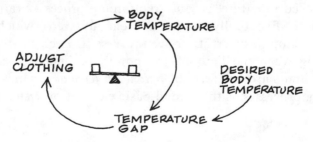

As in all balancing processes, the crucial element—our body temperature—gradually adjusts itself toward its desired level:

Organizations and societies resemble complex organisms because they too have myriad balancing feedback processes. In corporations, the production and materials ordering process is constantly adjusting in response to changes in incoming orders; short-term (discounts) and long-term (list) prices adjust in response to changes in demand or competitors' prices; and borrowing adjusts with changes in cash balances or financing needs.

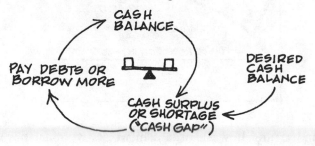

Planning creates longer-term balancing processes. A human resource plan might establish long-term growth targets in head count and in skill profile of the work force to match anticipated needs. Market research and R&D plans shape new product development and investments in people, technologies, and capital plant to build competitive advantage.

What makes balancing processes so difficult in management is that the goals are often implicit, and no one recognizes that the balancing process exists at all. I recall a good friend who tried, fruitlessly, to reduce burnout among professionals in his rapidly growing training business. He wrote memos, shortened working hours, even closed and locked offices earlier—all attempts to get people to stop overworking. But all these actions were offset—people ignored the memos, disobeyed the shortened hours, and took their work home with them when the offices were locked. Why? Because an unwritten norm in the organization stated that the *real* heroes, the people who really cared and who got ahead in the organization, worked seventy hours a week—a norm that my friend had established himself by his own prodigious energy and long hours.

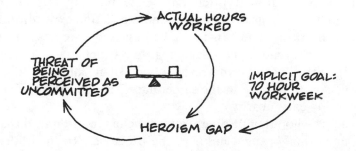

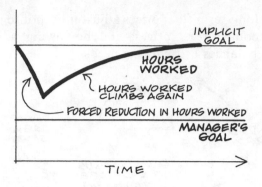

To understand how an organism works we must understand its balancing processes—those that are explicit *and* implicit. We could master long lists of body parts, organs, bones, veins, and blood vessels and yet we would not understand how the body functions—until we understood how the neuromuscular system maintains balance, or how the cardiovascular system maintains blood pressure and oxygen levels. This is why many attempts to redesign social systems fail. The state-controlled economy fails because it severs the multiple self-correcting processes that operate in a free market system.[10] This is why corporate mergers often fail. When two hospitals in Boston, both with outstanding traditions of patient care, were merged several years ago, the new larger hospital had state-of-the-art facilities but lost the spirit of personal care and employee loyalty that had characterized the original institutions. In the merged hospital, subtle balancing processes in the older hospitals that monitored quality, paid attention to employee needs, and maintained friendly relationships with patients were disrupted by new administrative structures and procedures.

Though simple in concept, balancing processes can generate surprising and problematic behavior if they go undetected.

In general, balancing loops are more difficult to see than reinforcing loops because it often *looks* like nothing is happening. There's no dramatic growth of sales and marketing expenditures, or nuclear arms, or lily pads. Instead, the balancing process maintains the status quo, even when all participants want change. The feeling, as Lewis Carroll's Queen of Hearts put it, of needing "all the running you can do to keep in the same place," is a clue that a balancing loop may exist nearby.

Leaders who attempt organizational change often find themselves unwittingly caught in balancing processes. To the leaders, it looks as though their efforts are clashing with sudden resistance

HOW TO READ A BALANCING
CIRCLE DIAGRAM
Balancing Process for Adjusting Cash Balance to Cash Surplus or Shortage

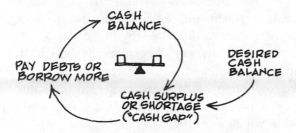

This diagram shows a balancing feedback process.

To walk yourself through the process, it's generally easiest to start at the gap—the discrepancy between what is desired and what exists:

Here, there is a shortfall in cash on hand for our cashflow needs. (In other words, there's a gap between our desired and actual cash balances.)

Then look at the actions being taken to correct the gap:

We borrow money, which makes our cash balance larger, and the gap decreases.

The chart shows that a balancing process is always operating to reduce a gap between what is desired and what exists. Moreover, such goals as desired cash balances change over time with growth or decline in the business. Regardless, the balancing process will continue to work to adjust actual cash balances to what is needed, even if the target is moving.

that seems to come from nowhere. In fact, as my friend found when he tried to reduce burnout, the resistance is a response by the system, trying to maintain an implicit system goal. Until this goal is recognized, the change effort is doomed to failure. So long as the leader continues to be the model, his work habits will set the norm. Either he must change his habits, or establish new and different models.

Whenever there is resistance to change, you can count on there being one or more "hidden" balancing processes. Resistance to change is neither capricious nor mysterious. It almost always arises from threats to traditional norms and ways of doing things. Often these norms are woven into the fabric of established power relationships. The norm is entrenched because the distribution of authority and control is entrenched. Rather than pushing harder to overcome resistance to change, artful leaders discern the source of the resistance. They focus directly on the implicit norms and power relationships within which the norms are embedded.

DELAYS: WHEN THINGS HAPPEN . . . EVENTUALLY

As we've seen, systems seem to have minds of their own. Nowhere is this more evident than in delays—interruptions between your actions and their consequences. Delays can make you badly overshoot your mark, or they can have a positive effect if you recognize them and work with them.

In a classic article in the *Sloan Management Review*, Ray Stata, former CEO of Analog Devices and founder of the Massachusetts High Technology Council, wrote that "One of the highest leverage points for improving system performance, is the minimization of system delays." Stata was referring to an increasing awareness in the late 1980s among American manufacturers that their traditional focus on tight control of inventories in warehouses was inherently lower leverage than their Japanese counterparts approach to reducing delays, so that over- and understocking don't occur in the first place. This gradually gave rise to the idea of "time based competition": "The way leading companies manage time," says George Stalk, vice president of the Boston Consulting Group, "—in production, in new product development, in sales and distribution—represents the most powerful new source of competitive disadvantage." In turn, appreciating how important it was to reduce delays evolved into a cornerstone of "flexible manufacturing" and today's "lean manufacturing."[11]

Delays between actions and consequences are everywhere in human systems. We invest now to reap a benefit in the distant future; we hire a person today but it may be months before he or she is fully productive; we commit resources to a new project knowing that it will be years before it will pay off. But delays are often unappreciated and lead to instability. For example, the decision makers in the beer game consistently misjudged the delays that kept them from getting orders filled when they thought they would.

Delays, when the effect of one variable on another takes time, constitute the third basic building block for a systems language. Virtually all feedback processes have some form of delay. But often the delays are either unrecognized or not well understood. This can result in "overshoot," going further than needed to achieve a desired result. The delay between eating and feeling full has been the neme-sis of many a happy diner; we don't yet feel full when we should stop eating, so we keep going until we are over stuffed. The delay between starting a new construction project and its completion results in overbuilding real estate markets and an eventual shakeout. In the beer game, the delay between placing and receiving orders for beer regularly results in overordering.

Unrecognized delays can also lead to instability and breakdown, especially when they are long. Adjusting the shower temperature, for instance, is far more difficult when there is a ten-second delay before the water temperature adjusts, then when the delay takes only a second or two.

HOW TO READ A DELAY

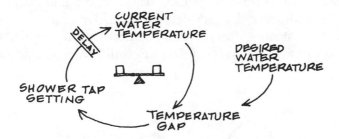

Balancing Process with a Delay: A Sluggish Shower

Here's our earlier "water faucet" feedback diagram again—but this time, with antiquated plumbing. Now there's a significant delay between the time you turn the faucet, and the time you see change in the water flow. Those two cross-hatch lines represent the delay.

Arrows with cross-hatch lines don't tell you how many seconds (or years) the delay will last. You only know it's long enough to make a difference.

When you follow an arrow with a delay, add the word "eventually" to the story you tell in your mind. "I moved the faucet handle, which eventually changed the water flow." Or, "I began a new construction project and, eventually, the houses were ready." You may even want to skip a beat—"one, two"—as you talk through the process.

During that ten seconds after you turn up the heat, the water remains cold. You receive no response to your action; so you *perceive* that your act has had no effect. You respond by continuing to

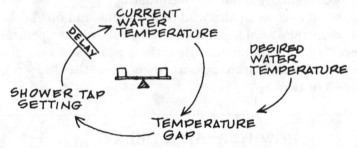

turn up the heat. When the hot water finally arrives, a 190-degree water gusher erupts from the faucet. You jump out and turn it back; and, after another delay, it's frigid again. On and on you go, through the balancing loop process. Each cycle of adjustments compensates somewhat for the cycle before. A diagram would look like this:

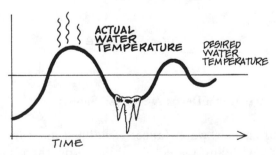

The more aggressive you are in your behavior—the more drastically you turn the knobs—the longer it will take to reach the right temperature. That's one of the lessons of balancing loops with delays: that aggressive action often produces exactly the opposite of what is intended. It produces instability and oscillation, instead of moving you more quickly toward your goal.

Delays are no less problematic in reinforcing loops. In the war on terrorism example, each side perceives itself as gaining advantage from expanding its activities because of the delay in the other side's response. This delay may span from days to months and even years because of the time required to gather resources for the next cycle of attacks. In part it is this temporary perceived advantage that keeps the escalation process going. If each side were able to respond instantly to buildups of its adversary, incentives to keep building would be nil.

The systems viewpoint is generally oriented toward the long-term view. That's why delays and feedback loops are so important. In the short term, you can often ignore them; they're inconsequential. They only come back to haunt you in the long term.

Reinforcing feedback, balancing feedback, and delays are all fairly simple. They come into their own as building blocks for the "systems archetypes"—more elaborate structures that recur in our personal and work lives again and again.

6

NATURE'S TEMPLATES: IDENTIFYING THE PATTERNS THAT CONTROL EVENTS

Some years ago, I witnessed a tragic accident while on an early spring canoe trip in Maine. We had come to a small dam, and put in to shore to portage around the obstacle. A second group arrived, and a young man who had been drinking decided to take his rubber raft over the dam. When the raft overturned after going over the dam, he was dumped into the freezing water. Unable to reach him, we watched in horror as he struggled desperately to swim downstream against the backwash at the base of the dam. His struggle lasted only a few minutes; then he died of hypothermia. Immediately, his limp body was sucked down into the swirling water. Seconds later, it popped up, ten yards downstream, free of the maelstrom at the base of the dam. What he had tried in vain to achieve in the last moments of his life, the currents accomplished for him within seconds after his death. Ironically, it was his very struggle against the forces at the base of the dam that killed him. He didn't know that the only way out was "counterintuitive. If he hadn't tried to keep his head above water, but instead dived down to where the current flowed downstream, he would have survived.

This tragic story illustrates the essence of the systems perspective, first shown in the beer game in Chapter 3, and again in the war on terrorism at the beginning of Chapter 5. *Structures of which we are unaware hold us prisoner.* Conversely, learning to see the structures within which we operate begins a process of freeing ourselves from previously unseen forces and ultimately mastering the ability to work with them and change them.

One of the most important, and potentially most empowering, insights to come from the young field of systems thinking is that certain patterns of structure recur again and again. These "systems archetypes" or "generic structures" embody the key to learning to see structures in our personal and organizational lives. The systems archetypes—of which there are only a relatively small number[1]— suggest that not all management problems are unique, something that experienced managers know intuitively.

If reinforcing and balancing feedback and delays are like the nouns and verbs of systems thinking, then the systems archetypes are analogous to basic sentences or simple stories that get retold again and again. Just as in literature there are common themes and recurring plot lines that get recast with different characters and settings, a relatively small number of these archetypes are common to a very large variety of management situations.

The systems archetypes reveal an incredibly elegant simplicity underlying the complexity of management issues. As we learn how to recognize more and more of these kinds of archetypes, it becomes possible for us to see more and more places where there is leverage in facing difficult challenges, and to explain these opportunities to others.

As we learn more about the systems archetypes, they will no doubt contribute toward one of our most vexing problems, a problem against which managers and leaders struggle incessantly—specialization and the fractionation of knowledge. In many ways, the greatest promise of the systems perspective is the unification of knowledge across all fields—for these same archetypes recur in biology, psychology, and family therapy; in economics, political science, and ecology; as well as in management.[2]

Because they are subtle, when the archetypes arise in a family, an ecosystem, a news story, or a corporation, you often don't see them so much as feel them. Sometimes they produce a sense of *deja vu,* a hunch that you've seen this pattern of forces before. "There it is again," you say to yourself. Though experienced managers already know many of these recurring plot lines intuitively, they often don't know how to explain them. The systems archetypes provide that language. They can make explicit much of what otherwise is simply "management judgment."

Mastering the systems archetypes starts an organization on the path of putting the systems perspective into practice. It is not enough to espouse systems thinking, to say, "We must look at the big picture and take the long-term view." It is not enough to appreciate basic systems principles, as expressed in the laws of the fifth discipline (Chapter 4) or as revealed in simulations such as the beer game (Chapter 3). It is not even enough to see a particular structure underlying a particular problem (perhaps with the help of a consultant). *This can lead to solving a problem, but it will not change the thinking that produced the problem in the first place.* For learning organizations, only when managers start thinking in terms of the systems archetypes, does systems thinking become an active daily agent, continually revealing how we create our reality.

The purpose of the systems archetypes is to recondition our perceptions, so as to be more able to see structures at play, and to see the leverage in those structures. Once a systems archetype is identified, it will always suggest areas of high- and low-leverage change. Presently, researchers have identified about a dozen systems archetypes, nine of which are presented and used in this book (Appendix 2 contains a summary of the archetypes used here). All of the archetypes are made up of the systems building blocks: reinforcing processes, balancing processes, and delays. Below are two that recur frequently, that are steppingstones to understanding other archetypes and more complex situations.

ARCHETYPE 1: LIMITS TO GROWTH

DEFINITION

A reinforcing (amplifying) process is set in motion to produce a desired result. It creates a spiral of success but also creates inadvertent secondary effects (manifested in a balancing process) which eventually slow down the success.

MANAGEMENT PRINCIPLE

Don't push growth; remove the factors limiting growth.

WHERE IT IS FOUND

The limits to growth structure is useful for understanding all situations where growth bumps up against limits. For example, organizations grow for a while, but then stop growing. Working groups get better for a while, but stop getting better. Individuals improve themselves for a period of time, then plateau.

Many sudden but well-intentioned efforts for improvement bump up against limits to growth. A farmer increases his yield by adding fertilizer, until the crop grows larger than the rainfall of the region can sustain. A crash diet works at first to shave off a few pounds of fat, but then the dieter loses his or her resolve. We might "solve" sudden deadline pressures by working longer hours; eventually, however, the added stress and fatigue slow down our work speed and quality, compensating for the longer hours.

People who try to break a bad habit such as criticizing others frequently come up against limits to growth. At first, their efforts pay off. They criticize less. The people around them feel more supported. The others reciprocate with positive feelings, which makes the person feel better and criticize less. This is a reinforcing spiral of improved behavior, positive feelings, and further improvement. But, then, their resolve weakens. Perhaps they start to find themselves facing the aspects of others' behavior that really give them the most trouble: it was easy to overlook a few little things, but *this* is another matter. Perhaps, they just become complacent and stop paying as close attention to their knee-jerk criticisms. For whatever reason, before long, they are back to their old habits.

Once, in one of our seminars, a participant said, "Why, that's just like falling in love." Cautiously, I asked, "How so?" She responded, "Well, first, you meet. You spend a little time together and it's wonderful. So you spend more time together. And it's more wonderful. Before long, you're spending all your free time together. Then you get to know each other better. He doesn't always open the door for you, or isn't willing to give up bowling with his buddies—every other night. He discovers that you have a jealous streak, or a bad temper, or aren't very neat. Whatever it is, you start to see each other's shortcomings." As you learn each other's flaws, she reminded the rest of us, the dramatic growth in feelings comes to a sudden halt—and may even reverse itself, so that you feel worse about each other than you did when you first met.

STRUCTURE

In each case of limits to growth, there is a reinforcing (amplifying) process of growth or improvement that operates on its own for a period of time. Then it runs up against a balancing (or stabilizing) process, which operates to limit the growth. When that happens, the rate of improvement slows down, or even comes to a standstill.

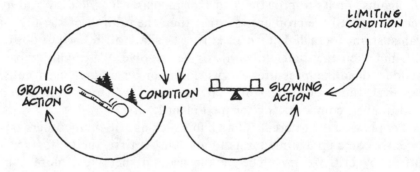

UNDERSTANDING AND USING THE STRUCTURE

Limits to growth structures operate in organizations at many levels. For example, a high-tech organization grows rapidly because of its ability to introduce new products. As new products grow, revenues grow, the R&D budget grows, and the engineering and research staff grows. Eventually, this burgeoning technical staff becomes increasingly complex and difficult to manage. The management burden often falls on senior engineers, who in turn have less time to spend on engineering. Diverting the most experienced engineers from engineering to management results in longer product development times, which slow down the introduction of new products.[3]

To read any limits to growth structure diagram, for example, start with the reinforcing circle of growth. That circle provides the structure with its initial momentum. Walk yourself around the circle: remind yourself how new product growth might generate revenues,

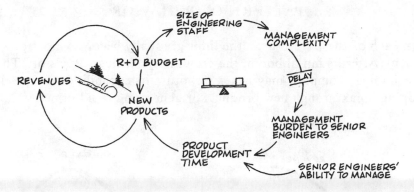

which in turn can be reinvested to generate more new products. At some point, however, the forces will shift—here, for example, the growth in R&D budget eventually leads to complexity beyond the senior engineers' ability to manage without diverting precious time from product development. After a delay (whose length depends on the rate of growth, complexity of products, and engineers' management skills), new product introductions slow, slowing overall growth.

　　Another example of limits to growth occurs when a professional organization, such as a law firm or consultancy, grows very rapidly when it is small, providing outstanding promotion opportunities. Morale grows and talented junior members are highly motivated, expecting to become partners within ten years. But as the firm gets larger, its growth slows. Perhaps it starts to saturate its market niche. Or it might reach a size where the founding partners are no longer interested in sustaining rapid growth. However the growth rate slows, this means fewer promotion opportunities, more infighting among junior members, and an overall decline in morale. The limits to growth structure can be diagrammed as follows:[4]

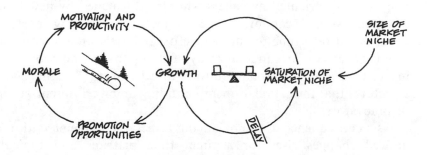

PATTERN OF BEHAVIOR

In each of these structures, the limit gradually becomes more powerful. After its initial boom, the growth mysteriously levels off. The technology company may never recapture its capabilities for developing breakthrough new products or generating rapid growth.

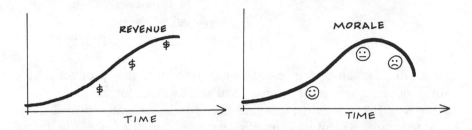

Eventually, growth may slow so much that the reinforcing spiral may turn around and run in reverse. The law firm or consulting firm loses its dominance in its market niche. Before long, morale in the firm has actually started on a downward spiral, caused by the reinforcing circle running in reverse.

Limits to growth structures often frustrate organizational changes that seem to be gaining ground at first, then run out of steam. For example, many change efforts fail, despite making some initial progress. As intended changes start to be implemented, problem solving and results start to improve, which strengthens commitment to the intended changes. But the more successful the changes become, the more threatening they can also become, and those threatened begin to undermine the change implementation. In *The Dance of Change* fieldbook,[5] we identified several specific ways such balancing processes can thwart otherwise promising change initiatives: control-oriented managers who are threatened by new levels of openness and candor; delays in metrics that show costs of changes but take time to show benefits; polarization and competition between converts to a new way of doing things and people trying to conserve mainstream culture; and fragmented management structures that thwart relationship building among different groups of innovators.

As a consequence of the balancing forces, the implementation of desired changes rises for a time—then plateaus and typically declines. Often, the response of the advocates of the disappointing results makes things worse. The more aggressively the advocates try to drive their desired changes, the more people feel threatened and the more resistance arises.

You see similar dynamics with implementing "Just in Time" inventory and other "lean" or "flexible" manufacturing systems, all of which depend on relationships of trust between suppliers and manufacturers. Initial improvements in production flexibility and cost are not sustained. Often, the supplier in these systems eventually demands to be a sole source to offset the risk in supplying the manufacturer overnight. This threatens the manufacturer, who is used to placing multiple orders with different suppliers or playing suppliers' off against one another in bidding wars. The manufacturer's commitment to the new supply system then wavers as will the supplier's. Thus, the more likely they are to hedge those risks by sticking to traditional practices of multiple suppliers and multiple customers, thereby undermining the trust a JIT system requires.[6]

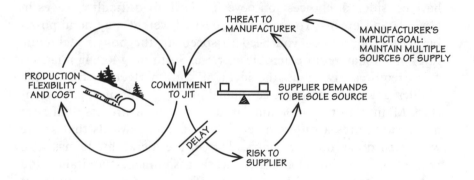

HOW TO ACHIEVE LEVERAGE

Typically, most people react to limits to growth situations by trying to push hard: if you can't break your bad habit, become more diligent in monitoring your own behavior; if your relationship is having problems, spend more time together or work harder to make the relationship work; if staff are unhappy, keep promoting junior staff to make them happy; if the flow of new products is slowing down, start more new product initiatives to offset the problems with the ones that are bogged down; or advocate change initiatives more strongly.

It's an understandable response. In the early stages when you can see improvement, you want to do more of the same—after all, it's working so well. When the rate of improvement slows down, you want to compensate by striving even harder. Unfortunately, the more vigorously you push the familiar levers, the more strongly the balancing process resists, and the more futile your efforts become. Sometimes, people just give up their original goal—lowering their goal to stop criticizing others, or giving up on change aims or lean manufacturing improvements (or more likely keeping the official program but never achieving anywhere near the potential impact of successful change).

But there is another way to deal with limits to growth situations. *In each of them, leverage lies in the balancing loop—not the reinforcing loop. To change the behavior of the system, you must identify and change the limiting factor.* This may require actions you may not yet have considered, choices you never noticed, or difficult changes in rewards and norms. To reach your desired weight may be impossible by dieting alone—you need to speed up the body's metabolic rate, which may require aerobic exercise. Sustaining loving relationships requires giving up the ideal of the "perfect partner"—the implicit goal that limits the continued improvement of any relationship. Maintaining morale and productivity as a professional firm matures requires a different set of norms and rewards that salute work well done, not a person's place in the hierarchy. It may also require distributing challenging work assignments equitably and not to "partners only." Maintaining effective product development processes as a firm grows requires dealing with the management burden brought on by an increasingly complex research and engineering organization. Some firms do this by decentralizing, some by bringing in professionals skilled in managing creative engineers (which is not easy), and some by management development for engineers who want to manage.

Not surprisingly, where change initiatives like lean manufacturing succeed they are part of a broader change in management practice and relationships both among employees and with key business partners like employee and suppliers. In particular, successes usually involve genuine efforts to redistribute control, and deal with the threats of giving up unilateral control. Usually this is part of long-term processes of building a different quality of relationship with key suppliers, and then in turn helping those suppliers grow their capabilities. These changes are necessary in order to overcome the distrust that lies behind traditional goals of maintaining unilateral control—because if these goals do not change all the clever managerial interventions in the world will not overcome the strength of the balancing forces to maintain the status quo. This is why veterans of successfully leading lean manufacturing efforts always emphasize that this is a "cultural change," not just a technical change.

But there is another lesson from the limits to growth structure as well. There will always be more limiting processes. When one source of limitation is removed or made weaker, growth returns until a new source of limitation is encountered. The skillful leader is always focused on the next set of limitations and working to understand their nature and how they can be addressed. In some settings, like the growth of a biological population, the fundamental lesson is that growth eventually will stop. Efforts to extend the growth by removing limits can actually be counterproductive, forestalling the eventual day of reckoning, which given the pace of change that reinforcing processes can create (remember the French lily pads) may be sooner than we think.

HOW TO CREATE YOUR OWN "LIMITS TO GROWTH" STORY

The best way to understand an archetype is to diagram your own version of it. The more actively you work with the archetypes, the better you will become at recognizing them and finding leverage.

Most people have many limits to growth structures in their lives. The easiest way to recognize them is through the pattern of behavior. Is there a situation in which things get better and better at first, and then mysteriously stop improving? Once you have such a situation in mind, see if you can identify the appropriate elements of the reinforcing and balancing loops.[7]

First, identify the reinforcing process—what is getting better and what is the action of activity leading to improvement? (There may be other elements of the reinforcing process, but there are always at least a condition which is improving, and an action leading to the improvement.) It might, for instance,

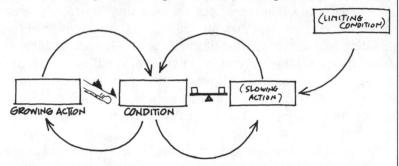

be the story of an organizational improvement: an equal opportunity hiring program, for example. The growing action is the equal opportunity program itself; and the condition is the percentage of women and minorities on staff. For example, as the percentage of women in management increases, confidence in or commitment to the program increases, leading to still further increases in women in management.

There is, however, bound to be a limiting factor, typically an implicit goal, or norm, or a limiting resource. The second step is to identify the limiting factor and the balancing process it creates. What "slowing action" or resisting force starts to come into play to keep the condition from continually improving? In this case, some managers might have an idea in their minds of how many women or minority executives are "too much." That unspoken number is the limiting factor; as soon as that threshold is approached, the slowing action—manager's resistance— will kick in. Not only will they resist more equal opportunity hires, but they may make life exceptionally difficult for the new people already in place.

Once you've mapped out your situation, look for the leverage. It won't involve pushing harder; that will just make the resistance stronger. More likely, it will require weakening or removing the limiting condition.

For the best results, test your limits to growth story in real life. Talk to others about your perception. Test your ideas about leverage in small real-life experiments first. For example, you might seek out one person whom you perceive as holding an implicit quota for "enough women," but who is also approachable, and ask him. (See the reflection and inquiry skills section in Chapter 9, "Mental Models," for how to do this effectively.)

ARCHETYPE 2:
SHIFTING THE BURDEN

DEFINITION

An underlying problem generates symptoms that demand attention. But the underlying problem is difficult for people to address, either because it is obscure or costly to confront. So people "shift the burden" of their problem to other solutions—well-intentioned, easy fixes which seem extremely efficient. Unfortunately, the easier "solutions" only ameliorate the symptoms; they leave the underlying problem unaltered. The underlying problem grows worse, unnoticed because the symptoms apparently clear up, and the system loses whatever abilities it had to solve the underlying problem.

MANAGEMENT PRINCIPLE

Beware the symptomatic solution. Solutions that address only the symptoms of a problem, not fundamental causes, tend to have short-term benefits at best. In the long term, the problem resurfaces and there is increased pressure for symptomatic response. Meanwhile, the capability for fundamental solutions can atrophy.

WHERE IT IS FOUND

Shifting the burden structures are common in our personal as well as organizational lives. They come into play when there are obvious symptoms of problems that cry out for attention, and quick and ready "fixes" that can make these symptoms go away, at least for a while.

Consider the problem of stress that comes when our personal workload increases beyond our capabilities to deal with it effectively. We juggle work, family, and community in a never-ending blur of activity. If the workload increases beyond our capacity (which tends to happen for us all) the only fundamental solution is to limit the workload. This can be tough—it may mean passing up a promotion that will entail more travel. Or it may mean declining a position on the local school board. It means prioritizing and making choices. Instead, people are often tempted to juggle faster, relieving the stress with alcohol, drugs, or a more benign form of "stress reduction" (such as exercise or meditation). But, of course, drinking doesn't really solve the problem of overwork—it only masks the problem by temporarily relieving the stress. The problem comes back, and so does the need for drinking. Insidiously, the shifting the burden structure, if not interrupted, generates forces that are all-too-familiar in contemporary society. These are the dynamics of avoidance, the result of which is increasing dependency, and ultimately addiction.

A shifting the burden structure lurks behind many "solutions" which seem to work effectively, but nonetheless leave you with an uneasy feeling that they haven't quite taken care of the problem. Managers may believe in delegating work to subordinates but still rely too much on their own ability to step in and handle things at the first sign of difficulty, so that the subordinate never gets the necessary experience to do the job. Businesses losing market share to foreign competitors may seek tariff protection and find themselves unable to operate without it. A Third World nation, unable to face difficult choices in limiting government expenditures in line with its tax revenues, finds itself generating deficits that are financed through printing money and inflation. Over time, inflation becomes a way of life, more and more government assistance is needed, and chronic deficits become accepted as inevitable. Shifting the burden structures also include food relief programs that "save" farmers from having to grow crops, and pesticides that temporarily remove vermin, but also eliminate natural controls, making it easier for the pest to surge back in the future.

STRUCTURE

The shifting the burden structure is composed of two balancing (stabilizing) processes. Both are trying to adjust or correct the same

problem symptom. The top circle represents the symptomatic intervention; the quick fix. It solves the problem symptom quickly, but
only temporarily. The bottom circle has a delay. It represents a more
fundamental response to the problem, one whose effects take longer
to become evident. However, the fundamental solution works far
more effectively—it may be the only enduring way to deal with the
problem.

Often (but not always), in shifting the burden structures there is
also an additional reinforcing (amplifying) process created by "side
effects" of the symptomatic solution. When this happens, the side
effects often make it even more difficult to invoke the fundamental
solution—for example, the side effects of drugs administered to correct a health problem. If the problem was caused originally by an
unhealthy lifestyle (smoking, drinking, poor eating habits, lack of
exercise), then the only fundamental solution lies in a change in
lifestyle. The drugs (the symptomatic solution) make the symptom
better, and remove pressure to make difficult personal changes. But
they also have side effects that lead to still more health problems,
making it even more difficult to develop a healthy lifestyle.

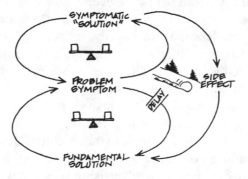

UNDERSTANDING AND USING THE STRUCTURE

The shifting the burden structure explains a wide range of behaviors where well-intended "solutions" actually make matters worse
over the long term. Opting for "symptomatic solutions" is enticing.
Apparent improvement is achieved. Pressures, either external or
internal, to do something about a vexing problem are relieved. But
easing a problem symptom also reduces any perceived need to find
more fundamental solutions. Meanwhile, the underlying problem
remains unaddressed and may worsen, and the side effects of the
symptomatic solution make it still harder to apply the fundamental

solution. Over time, people rely more and more on the symptomatic solution, which seemingly becomes the only solution. Without anyone making a conscious decision, people have "shifted the burden" to increasing reliance on symptomatic solutions.

Interactions between corporate staff and line managers are fraught with shifting the burden structures. For example, busy managers are often tempted to bring in human resource specialists to sort out personnel problems. The HR expert may solve the problem, but the manager's ability to solve other related problems has not improved. Eventually, other personnel issues will arise and the manager will be just as dependent on the HR expert as before. The very fact that the outside expert was used successfully before makes it even easier to turn to the expert again. "We had a new batch of difficulties, so we brought in the personnel specialists again. They are getting to know our people and our situation well, so they are very efficient." Over time, HR experts become increasingly in demand, staff costs soar, and managers' development (and respect) declines.

Shifting the burden structures often underlie unintended drifts in strategic direction and erosion in competitive position. A group of executives in a high-tech firm were deeply concerned that their company was "losing its edge" by not bringing dramatic new products to market. It was less risky to improve existing products. However, they feared that a culture of incrementalism rather than breakthrough was being fostered. The safer, more predictable, easier-to-plan-for-and-organize processes of improvement innovation were becoming so entrenched that the managers wondered if the company was still capable of basic innovation.

As I listened, I recalled a similar strategic drift described by managers of a leading consumer goods producer, which had become more and more dependent on advertising versus new product devel-

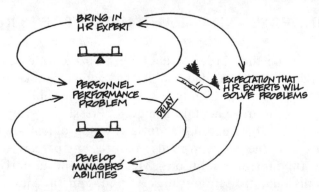

opment. Whenever business sagged for one of its many products, the tendency was to run a new advertising promotion. The advertising culture had become so entrenched, that the last three CEOs had all been ex-advertising executives, who frequently wrote ad copy personally. Meanwhile, the flow of major new products had dwindled to a trickle under their leadership.

A special case of shifting the burden, which recurs with alarming frequency, is eroding goals. Whenever there is a gap between our goals and our current situation there are two sets of pressures: to improve the situation and to lower our goals. How these pressures are dealt with is central to the discipline of personal mastery, as will be shown in Chapter 8.

Societies collude in eroding goals all the time. For example the federal "full employment" target in the United States (the level of unemployment considered acceptable) slid from 4 percent in the 1960s to 6 to 7 percent by the early 1980s when unemployment was hovering near 10 percent. (In other words, we were willing to tolerate 50 to 75 percent more unemployment as "natural.") Likewise, 3 to 4 percent inflation was considered severe in the early 1960s, but a victory for anti-inflation policies by the early 1980s. In 1992 President Clinton inherited the largest budget deficit in U.S. history, which, with the help of the Budget Omnibus Act in 1993, was converted into a record budget surplus of $200 billion by the end of the 1990s. In 2005, the Bush Administration called for a "war on the deficit" which now stands at about $318 billion. This eroding goal structure can be diagrammed as follows:

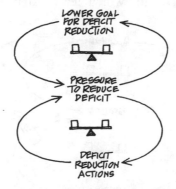

As we will see in the next two chapters, similar eroding goal dynamics play out in organizations around goals for quality, goals for innovation, goals for personal growth of employees, and goals for organizational improvement. In effect, we all can become "addicted" to lowering our goals. Or, as a bumper sticker I saw recently said, "If all else fails, lower your goals."

PATTERN OF BEHAVIOR

Regardless of the choice of symptomatic solution, it works—in a way. Drinking, for example, lifts some tension, at least for a while. It relieves the problem symptom. If it didn't, people wouldn't drink. But it also gives the person the feeling of having solved the problem, thereby diverting attention from the fundamental problem—controlling the workload. Failing to take a stand may well cause the workload to gradually increase further, since most of us are continually besieged by more demands on our time than we can possibly respond to. Over time, the workload continues to build, the stress returns, and the pressure to drink increases.

What makes the shifting the burden structure insidious is the subtle reinforcing cycle it fosters, increasing dependence on the symptomatic solution. Alcoholics eventually find themselves physically addicted. Their health deteriorates. As their self-confidence and judgment atrophy, they are less and less able to solve their original workload problem. To trace out the causes of the reinforcing cycle, just imagine you are moving around the "figure eight" created by the two interacting feedback processes: stress builds, which leads to more alcohol, which relieves stress, which leads to less perceived need to adjust workload, which leads to more workload, which leads to more stress.

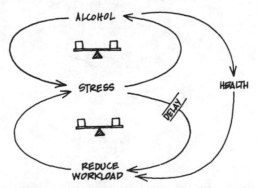

These are the generic dynamics of addiction. In fact, almost all forms of addiction have shifting the burden structures underlying them. All involve opting for symptomatic solutions, the gradual atrophy of the ability to focus on fundamental solutions, and the increasing reliance on symptomatic solutions. By this definition, organizations and entire societies are subject to addiction as much as are individuals.

Shifting the burden structures tend to produce periodic crises, when the symptoms of stress surface. The crises are usually resolved with more of the symptomatic solution, causing the symptoms to temporarily improve. What is often less evident is a slow, long-term drift to lower levels of health: financial health for the corporation or physical health for the individual. The problem symptom grows worse and worse. The longer the deterioration goes unnoticed, or the longer people wait to confront the fundamental causes, the more difficult it can be to reverse the situation. While the fundamental response loses power, the symptomatic response grows stronger and stronger.

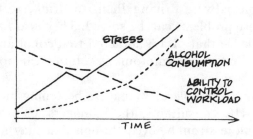

HOW TO ACHIEVE LEVERAGE

Dealing effectively with shifting-the-burden structures requires a combination of strengthening the fundamental response and weakening the symptomatic response. The character of organizations is often revealed in their ability (or inability) to face shifting-the-burden structures. Strengthening fundamental responses requires a long-term orientation and a sense of shared vision. Without a vision of succeeding through new product innovation, pressures to divert investment into short-term problem-solving will be overwhelming. Without a vision of skilled "people-oriented" managers, the time and energy to develop those skills will not be forthcoming. Without a shared vision of the role government can and should play, and for which people will provide tax revenues to support, there can be no long-term solution to balance government spending and income.

Weakening the symptomatic response requires willingness to tell the truth about palliatives and "looking good" solutions. Managers might acknowledge, for example, that heavy advertising steals market share from competitors, but doesn't expand the market in any significant way. And politicians must admit that the resistance they face to raising taxes comes from the perception that the government is corrupt. Until they deal credibly with perceived corruption, they will neither be able to raise taxes nor reduce spending.

A splendid illustration of the principles of leverage in shifting the burden structures can be found in the approach of some of the most effective alcoholism and drug treatment programs. They insist that people face their addiction on one hand, while offering support groups and training to help them rehabilitate on the other. For example, the highly successful Alcoholics Anonymous creates powerful peer support to help people revitalize their ability to face whatever problems were driving them to drink, with a sense of vision that those problems can be solved. They also force individuals to acknowledge that "I am addicted to alcohol and will be for my entire life," so that the symptomatic solution can no longer function in secret.[8]

In the business example of managers becoming more and more dependent on HR consultants, the managers' own abilities must be developed more strongly, even though that may mean a larger initial investment. The HR experts must become coaches and mentors, not problem solvers, helping managers develop their own personal skills.

Sometimes symptomatic solutions *are* needed—for example, in treating a person suffering from a disease created by smoking or drinking. But symptomatic solutions must always be acknowledged as such, *and* combined with strategies for rehabilitating the capacity for fundamental solution, if the shifting the burden dynamic is to be interrupted. If symptomatic solutions are employed *as if* they are fundamental solutions, the search for fundamental solutions stops and shifting the burden sets in.

HOW TO CREATE YOUR OWN "SHIFTING THE BURDEN" STORY

There are three clues to the presence of a shifting the burden structure. First, there's a problem that gets gradually worse over the long term—although every so often it seems to get better for a while. Second, the overall health of the system gradually worsens. Third, there's a growing feeling of helplessness. People start out feeling euphoric—they've solved their problem!—but instead end up feeling as if they are victims.

In particular, look for situations of dependency, in which you have a sense that the real issues, the deeper issues, are never quite dealt with effectively. Again, once you have such a situation in mind, see if you can identify the appropriate elements of the reinforcing and balancing loops.

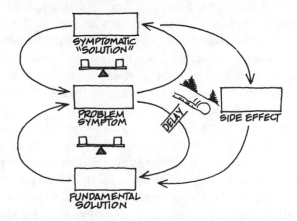

Start by identifying the "problem symptom." This will be the "squeaky wheel" that demands attention—such as stress, subordinates' inabilities to solve pressing problems, falling market share. Then identify a "fundamental solution" (there may be more than one)—a course of action that would, you believe, lead to enduring improvement. Then, identify one or several "symptomatic solutions" that might ameliorate symptoms for a time.

In fact, "fundamental solutions" and "symptomatic solutions" are relative terms, and what is most valuable is recognizing the multiple ways in which a problem can be addressed, from the most fundamental to the most superficial.

Then identify the possible negative "side effects" of the symptomatic solution.

The primary insights in shifting the burden will come from (1) distinguishing different types of solutions; (2) seeing how reliance on symptomatic solutions can reinforce further reliance. The leverage will always involve strengthening the bottom circle, and/or weakening the top circle. Just as with limits to growth, it's best to test your conclusions here with small actions—and to give the tests time to come to fruition. In particular, strengthening an atrophied ability will most likely take a long period of time.

Limits to growth and shifting the burden are but two of the basic systems archetypes. Several others are introduced in the following chapters. (Appendix 2 summarizes all the archetypes used in this book.) As the archetypes are mastered, they become combined into more elaborate systemic descriptions. The basic "sentences" become parts of paragraphs. The simple stories become integrated into more involved stories, with multiple themes, many characters, and more complex plots.

But the archetypes start the process of mastering systems thinking. By using the archetypes, we start to see more and more of the circles of causality that surround our daily activity. Over time, this leads naturally to thinking and acting more systemically.

To see how the archetypes get put into practice, the next chapter examines one way in which limits to growth and shifting the burden have proven useful—in understanding the ways a company with great growth potential can fail to realize that potential.

7

SELF-LIMITING OR
SELF-SUSTAINING
GROWTH

It's hard to disagree with the *principle* of leverage. But the leverage in most real-life systems is not obvious to most of the actors in those systems. Our non-systemic ways of thinking consistently lead us to focus on low-leverage changes. Because we don't see the structures underlying our actions, we focus on symptoms where the stress is greatest. We repair or ameliorate the symptoms. But such efforts only make matters better in the short run, at best, and often worse in the long run. The purpose of the systems archetypes, such as limits to growth and shifting the burden, is to help people see those structures and thus find the leverage, especially amid the pressures and crosscurrents of real-life business situations.

For example, let's look at a real story that we have seen again and again. In fact, the following case is a mosaic pieced together from several specific instances where the same story unfolded.[1]

WHEN WE CREATE OUR OWN
"MARKET LIMITATIONS"

In the mid-1980s a new electronics company was founded with a unique high-tech product—a new type of high-end computer. Thanks to its engineering know-how and distinctive technology, WonderTech had a virtual lock on its market niche. There was enormous demand for its products, and there were enough investors to guarantee no financial constraints.

Yet the company, which began with meteoric growth, never sustained its rapid growth after its first three years. Eventually it declined into bankruptcy.

That fate would have seemed unthinkable during WonderTech's first three years, when sales doubled annually. In fact, sales were so good that backlogs of orders began to pile up midway through its second year. Even with steadily increasing manufacturing capacity (more factories, more shifts, more advanced technology), the demand grew so fast that delivery times slipped a bit. Originally the company had promised to deliver machines within eight weeks, and it intended to return to that standard; but with some pride, the top management told investors, "Our computers are so good that some customers are willing to wait fourteen weeks for them. We know it's a problem, and we're working to fix it, but nonetheless they're *still* glad to get the machines, and they love 'em when they get 'em."

The top management knew that they had to add production capacity. After six months of study, while manufacturing changed from a one-shift to a two-shift operation, they decided to borrow the money to build a new factory. To make sure the growth kept up, they pumped much of the incoming revenue directly back into sales and marketing. Since the company sold its products only through a direct sales force, that meant hiring and training more salespeople. During the company's third year, the sales force doubled.

But despite this, sales started to slump at the end of the third year. By the middle of the fourth year, sales had dropped off to crisis levels. The curve of sales, so far, looked like the figure on the next page.

At this point, the new factory came on-line. "We've hired all these people," said the vice president of manufacturing. "What are we going to do with them?" The top management began to panic about what to tell their investors, after they had spent all this money

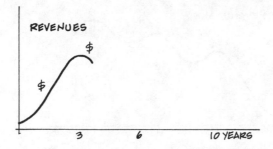

on a new manufacturing facility. It was as if everyone in the company simultaneously turned and looked at one person: the marketing and sales vice president.

Not surprisingly, the marketing and sales VP had become a rising star in the company. His force had done so well during the initial boom that he had anticipated a promotion. Now there was a slump, and he was under pressure to turn sales around. So he took the most likely course of action. He held high-powered sales meetings with a single message: "Sell! Sell! Sell!" He fired the low performers. He increased sales incentives, added special discounts, and ran new advertising promotions describing the machine in an exciting new way.

And indeed, sales rose again. The sales and marketing VP found himself once more hailed as a hero, a born-again motivator who could take charge of a tough situation. Once again, WonderTech was in the happy position of having rapidly rising orders. Eventually, backlogs began to grow again. And after a year, delivery times began to rise again—first to ten weeks, then to twelve, and eventually to sixteen. The debate over adding capacity started anew. But this time, having been stung on the last occasion, the top management was still more cautious. Eventually, approval of a new facility was granted, but no sooner had the papers been signed than a new sales crisis started. The slump was so bad that the sales and marketing vice president lost his job.

Over the next several years, and through a succession of marketing managers, the same situation recurred. High sales growth occurred in spurts, always followed by periods of low or no growth. The pattern looked like the figure on the next page.

The company prospered modestly, but never came close to fulfilling its original potential. Gradually, the top managers began to fear that other firms would learn how to produce competing products. They frantically introduced ill-conceived improvements in the prod-

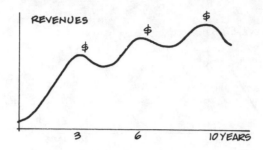

uct. They continued to push hard on marketing. But sales never returned to the original rate of growth. The "wonder" went out of WonderTech. Eventually, the company collapsed.

In his final statement to the lingering members of his executive team, the CEO said, "We did great under the circumstances, but the demand just isn't there. Clearly it was a limited market—a niche which we have effectively filled."

The tale of WonderTech is hardly a novel one. Of every ten startup companies, one-half will disappear within their first five years, only four survive into their tenth year, and only three into their fifteenth year.[2] Whenever a company fails, people always point to specific events to explain the "causes" of the failure: product problems, inept managers, loss of key people, unexpectedly aggressive competition, or business downturns. Yet, the deeper systemic causes for unsustained growth go unrecognized. With the aid of the systems archetypes, these causes often can be understood and, in many cases, successful policies can be formulated. The irony of WonderTech is that, given its product and its market potential, it could have grown vigorously for many years, not just two or three.

WonderTech's managers could not see the reasons for their own decline. This was not for lack of information. They had all the significant facts—the same facts that you have after reading this story. But they could not see the structures implicit in those facts.

As a systems thinker trying to diagnose WonderTech's problem, you would look for clues—anything that might suggest an archetype. You'd begin with the most obvious pattern of behavior: growth leaped up at first, amplifying itself to grow stronger and stronger. But the growth gradually slowed, and eventually sales stopped growing altogether. This pattern is the classic symptom of limits to growth.

There are many possible reinforcing (amplifying) processes that could have produced WonderTech's original rapid sales growth.

Investment in products, investment in advertising, good word of mouth—all could have reinforced past success into future success. But one especially evident in the WonderTech story was the reinforcing process created by investing revenues in increasing the sales force: more sales meant more revenues, which meant hiring salespeople, which meant more sales.

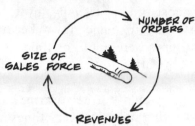

The other part of any limits to growth structure, of course, are balancing (stabilizing) processes. Something made sales growth slow. But sales only slow down when a market is saturated, when competition grows, or when customers grow disenchanted. In this case, the need for the WonderTech computer was still strong, and there was no significant competition. There was one factor which turned customers off: long delivery times. As backlogs rise relative to production capacity, delivery times increase. A reputation for poor delivery service builds, eventually making it harder for WonderTech's salespeople to make more sales. The limits to growth structure, then, looks like this:

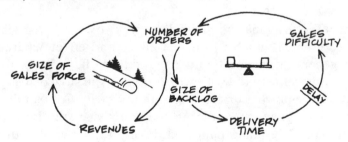

In a limits to growth structure, the worst thing you can do is push hard on the reinforcing process. But that's exactly what Wonder-Tech's managers did. They tried to reignite the "engine of growth" through sales incentives, marketing promotions, and minor product improvements—none of which had any leverage. In a limits-to-growth structure, the leverage lies with the balancing process.

Why wasn't that balancing process noticed? First, WonderTech's financially oriented top management did not pay much attention to their delivery service. They mainly tracked sales, profits, return on investment, and market share. So long as these were healthy, delivery times were the least of their concerns. Plus, delivery times were rising when sales growth and profits were rising rapidly, so there was little overall concern. When financial performance weakened, pressures shifted to boost orders. Usually, by this time, delivery times were already starting to come down because orders were falling. Thus, whether times were good, or times were bad, the top management paid little attention to the time customers had to wait to get their computers.

Even if they had, they would not necessarily have seen delivery time as a key factor affecting sales. Delivery times had been getting longer and longer, for more than a year and a half, before the first sales crisis hit. This reinforced an attitude among top management: "Customers don't care about late shipments." But that complacency was misplaced; customers *were* concerned, but their concern was obscured, to WonderTech's management, by a built-in delay in the system. A customer would say, "I want the machine delivered in eight weeks." The salesperson would say fine. But after nine, ten, or twelve weeks, there would still be no machine. After several more months, gossip would filter out. However, the number of potential customers was vast. And the gossip had little effect until it eventually mushroomed into a widespread reputation This delay between "Delivery Time" and "Sales Difficulty" could be six months or longer.

WonderTech's managers had fallen prey to the classic learning disability of being unable to detect cause and effect separated in time. In general, if you wait until demand falls off, and *then* get concerned about delivery time, it's way too late. The slow delivery time has already begun to correct itself—temporarily. At WonderTech, delivery times grew worse during the third year, the last year of rapid growth. They then improved during the downturn that followed; but grew worse again when sales rose.

Over the entire ten-year history of the firm, there was an overall trend of rising delivery times, interrupted by periodic improvements. Alongside that was a gradual decline in the overall health of the system—as seen in slowing growth and declining profits. The company made money in spurts, but lost money like mad in every downturn. The euphoria of the early growth period gave way to discouragement and, eventually, despair. People felt, at the end, as if they were victims. Privately, the CEO said the company had been misled by initial marketing projections that forecast a huge potential market that was never realized.

What no one realized was that the situation at WonderTech also characterized a classic shifting the burden structure. There was a problem symptom (delivery time) that worsened steadily, albeit with periodic improvements. The overall health of the enterprise was also steadily worsening, and there was a growing feeling of victimization. As a systems thinker, you would first identify that key problem symptom, and then the symptomatic and fundamental responses to it. In this case, the fundamental response (the lower circle in the diagram below) is to expand production capacity to control delivery time. Delivery times above WonderTech's standard indicate the need for more capacity, which, once it comes on-line, will correct long delivery times. But if this fundamental response is slow in coming, the burden shifts to the symptomatic response (the upper circle) of customer dissatisfaction in declining orders. Since WonderTech's managers didn't solve the problem of long delivery times by adding manufacturing capacity rapidly enough, disgruntled would-be customers "solved" the problem by walking away.

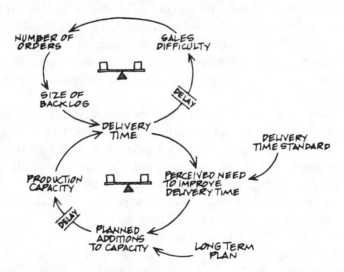

Moreover, because WonderTech management largely disregarded the disgruntled customer process to operate, the symptomatic response tended to get stronger and stronger—just as you'd expect from a shifting the burden structure. This occurred as WonderTech's reputation for poor delivery service spread through its market;

whenever WonderTech entered a new period of rising delivery times, word spread more and more rapidly. Meanwhile, the fundamental response grew weaker. Having been stung when they added capacity that was left idle by falling orders in year four, WonderTech's top management grew increasingly cautious in committing to new capacity additions. That meant that new capacity took longer and longer to come on-line—or never came on-line at all. By the time WonderTech's managers were finally ready to add capacity, the symptomatic response had already relieved the pressure, delivery times had started to fall, and the capacity expansion was no longer justified. "Let's wait a little longer before building," they said, "to make sure the demand is there."

In effect, there was a horse race going on between the two responses. Over time, the symptomatic response became more rapid, while the fundamental response became more sluggish. The net effect was that gradually the "disgruntled customer" response assumed more and more of the burden for controlling delivery times.

WonderTech's fate could have been reversed. There was a point of leverage in the underlying structure that was largely overlooked: the firms' original goal of an eight-week delivery time. In the shifting the burden structure, the first thing a systems thinker looks for is what might be weakening the fundamental response. In this case, the firm had a delivery time standard—eight weeks—but it obviously never meant a great deal to the financially preoccupied top managers.

After three years, the actual operating standard to which manufacturing had become accustomed was about ten weeks, and they had great trouble meeting that when business was booming. Over time, as delivery problems returned, the standard continued to drift. No one thought much about it, least of all top management.

As it happened, the *second* marketing and sales vice president periodically relayed his customers' dissatisfaction with poor deliveries to the management team. His counterpart in manufacturing acknowledged that they occasionally got behind their backlogs, but only when their capacity was inadequate. But the top managers said, "Yes, we know it's a problem, but we can't rush into major investments unless we're certain demand will be sustained." They didn't realize that demand would never be sustained until they made the investment.

We will never know for certain what might have happened if the company had held tight to its original goal of eight-week delivery times and invested aggressively in manufacturing capacity to meet this goal. But simulations based on this structure (combining limits to growth and shifting the burden) and on actual sales figures have been conducted in which the delivery time standard is not allowed to erode, forcing more aggressive capacity expansion. In these simulations, sales continue to grow rapidly throughout the ten years, although there are still periodic plateaus. Delivery time fluctuates, but does not drift upward and the delivery time standard is constant at eight weeks. WonderTech now realizes its growth potential. At the end of the ten years, sales are many times higher than in the original case.[3]

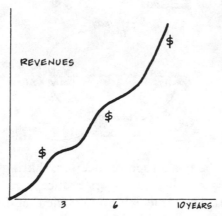

The original sales and marketing vice president had grasped these problems intuitively. He argued from the outset that WonderTech was assessing its factory capacity all wrong. "We only compare capacity to the number of orders we have," he said, "instead of the potential volume of orders that we would have if we were operating at our target delivery times." Unfortunately, the VP's arguments were interpreted as excuses for poor sales performance, and his insights went unheeded. It didn't help that he had no way, conceptually, to explain his thinking. Had he been able to describe the systems archetypes, perhaps more people would have grasped what seemed intuitive to him.

In fact, the subtle dynamics of WonderTech confirm an intuition of many experienced managers: that it is vital to hold to critical performance standards "through thick and thin," and to do whatever it takes to meet those standards. The standards that are most important are those that matter the most to the customer. They usually include product quality (design and manufacture), delivery times, service reliability and quality, and friendliness and concern of service personnel. The systemic structure at WonderTech converts this management intuition into an explicit theory, which shows how eroding standards and sluggish capacity expansion can undermine the growth of an entire enterprise. The complete structure comes from integrating limits to growth and shifting the burden:

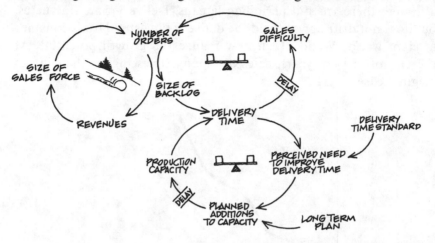

As shown here, the two structures overlap, sharing one balancing process—where disgruntled customers reduce their orders due to long delivery times. The same balancing circle that diverts attention from adding capacity (in shifting the burden) also keeps sales from expanding (in limits to growth). Whether the disgruntled customer circle becomes dominant depends on how the firm capacity expansion response when delivery times are long. If standards are allowed to drift, the firm's response is weakened and the burden shifts to the disgruntled customers. In other words, the company unwittingly becomes addicted to the limiting of its own growth.

SEEING THE FOREST
AND THE TREES

The systemic structure underlying WonderTech explains many complex situations where companies that were once growing rapidly and were highly successful fail mysteriously—companies like People Express Airlines, once the fastest growing airline in U.S. history. In fact, this structure is another systems archetype called "growth and underinvestment," a bit more complicated than the two previous archetypes. This archetype operates whenever a company limits its own growth through underinvestment. Underinvestment means building less capacity than is needed to serve rising customer demand. You can recognize growth and underinvestment by the failure of a firm to achieve its potential growth despite everyone's working tremendously hard (a sign of the underinvestment). Usually, there is continuing financial stress—which, ironically, is both cause and consequence of underinvestment. Financial stress makes aggressive investment difficult or impossible, but today's financial stress originates in the underinvestment of the past. If you look closely, you will also see eroding or declining quality standards. (By quality we mean all the things that matter to a customer, such as product quality, service quality, and delivery reliability). Standards erode, or fail to continually advance with competition, which results in a failure to invest in building capacity to serve customer needs. ("Investing" may mean adding or improving physical capacity, work processes, organizational structures, or training personnel.) Disgruntled customers then go elsewhere. Reduced customer demand eliminates the symptoms of unmet demand and the perceived need to invest in more capacity, as well as reducing financial resources needed to invest.

When these forces afflict entire industries—as started to happen in U.S. manufacturing industries, such as steel, autos, machine tools, and consumer electronics in the 1960s and the 1970s—the result is vulnerability to foreign competitors with higher standards and stronger investment policies. In each of these industries, loss of market share to foreign competitors was blamed on external factors yet had its origins, at least in part, in weak standards for customer satisfaction, underinvestment, and unhappy customers. Again, the decline happens so slowly that it's difficult to detect, and it is often masked by "shifting the burden" palliatives such as increased advertising, discounting, "restructuring," or tariff protection.

Two things make this pattern hard to see. First it is gradual. If all this happened in a month, the whole organization or industry would be mobilized to prevent it. But gradually eroding goals and declining growth are insidious. This is the structure that underlies the "boiled frog" syndrome discussed in the learning disabilities of Chapter 2. The frog's standards for safe water temperature steadily erode as its condition slowly deteriorates, until its capacity to respond to the threat of boiling disappears entirely.

Second, managers in the middle of the syndrome see so many urgent problems requiring attention—and they are unequipped to see the larger patterns. The art of systems thinking lies in being able to recognize increasingly (dynamically) complex and subtle structures, such as that at WonderTech amid the wealth of details, pressures, and cross currents that attend all real management settings. In fact, the essence of mastering systems thinking as a management discipline lies in seeing patterns where others see only events and forces to react to. Yet few are trained to see detail and dynamic complexity. How many CEOs today can stand and give a fifteen-minute speech that lays out a compelling explanation of the systemic causes of an important issue, and the high- and low-leverage strategies for dealing with that issue?

We all know the metaphor of being unable to "see the forest for the trees." Unfortunately, when most of us "step back" we just see lots of trees. We pick our favorite one or two and focus all our attention and change efforts on those.

In effect, the art of systems thinking lies in seeing through the detail complexity to the underlying structures generating change. Systems thinking does not mean ignoring detail complexity. Rather, it means organizing detail complexity into a coherent story that illuminates the causes of problems and how they can be remedied in enduring ways. For example, at a technology firm like WonderTech, grasping the reality of the situation begins with assimilating details like:

PRODUCTION CAPACITY	HUMAN RESOURCES	COMPETITIVE FACTORS
Machine capacity	Service personnel	Market size
Shifts	Manufacturing	Market segments
Manufacturing	personnel	Technology trends
Scheduling	Maintenance	Reputation
"Tac time"	Hiring	Service quality
Process technology	Training	Competitor service
Supply channels and	Turnover	quality
delivery schedules	Morale	Prices
Energy costs	Productivity	Attractiveness for talent,
Competitor plans	Experience	capital, and labor
Service hours	Team management	productivity
	Job rotation	
	Stock ownership	

The increasing complexity of today's world leads many managers to assume that they lack information they need to act effectively. I would suggest that the fundamental "information problem" faced by managers is not too little information but too much information. What we most need are ways to know what is important and what is not important, what variables to focus on and which to pay less attention to—and we need ways to do this that can help groups or teams develop shared understanding.

Mastering such basic archetypes as growth and underinvestment is the first step in developing the capability of seeing the forest *and* the trees—of seeing information in terms of broad *and* detailed patterns. Only by seeing both can you respond powerfully to the challenge of complexity and change.

Ultimately, mastering the language of systems thinking also requires the other complementary learning disciplines. Each contributes important principles and tools that make individuals, teams, and organizations more able to make the shift from seeing the world primarily from a linear perspective to seeing and acting systemically.

PART III

The Core Disciplines: Building the Learning Organization

8

PERSONAL MASTERY

THE SPIRIT OF THE
LEARNING ORGANIZATION

Organizations learn only through individuals who learn. Individual learning does not guarantee organizational learning. But without it no organizational learning occurs.

A small number of organizational leaders are recognizing the radical rethinking of corporate philosophy which a commitment to individual learning requires. Kazuo Inamori, founder and president of Kyocera until his retirement in 1995 (a world leader in fine ceramics technology and electronics), says this:

Whether it is research and development, company management, or any other aspect of business, the active force is "people." And people have their own will, their own mind, and their own way of thinking. If the employees themselves are not sufficiently motivated to challenge the goals of growth and technological devel-

opment . . . there will simply be no growth, no gain in productivity, and no technological development.[1]

Tapping the potential of people, Inamori believes, will require
new understanding of the "subconscious mind," "willpower," and
"action of the heart . . . sincere desire to serve the world." He taught
that Kyocera employees should look inward as they continually
strive for "perfection," guided by the corporate motto, "Respect
Heaven and Love People." In turn, he believes that his duty as a
manager starts with "providing for both the material good and spiritual welfare of my employees."

Half a world away in a totally different industry, another builder
of a company that achieved some measure of long-term success, Bill
O'Brien, former president of Hanover Insurance, aspired to

> . . . organizational models that are more congruent with human
> nature. Our traditional hierarchical organizations are not
> designed to provide for people's higher order needs, self-respect
> and self-actualization. The ferment in management will continue
> until organizations begin to address these needs, for all employees.

Like Inamori, O'Brien argued that managers must redefine their
job. They must give up "the old dogma of planning, organizing and
controlling," and realize "the almost sacredness of their responsibility for the lives of so many people." Managers' fundamental task,
according to O'Brien, is "providing the enabling conditions for people to lead the most enriching lives they can."

Lest these sentiments seem overly romantic for building a business, I should point out that Kyocera has gone from startup to
$9 billion in sales in forty-five years, borrowing almost no money,
often achieving profit levels that have been the envy of even
Japanese firms. Hanover was at the rock bottom of the property
and liability industry in 1969 when O'Brien's predecessor, Jack
Adam, began its reconstruction around a core set of values and
beliefs about people. When O'Brien retired in 1990, the company
operated consistently in the upper quarter of its industry in profits
and grew 50 percent faster than the industry in the preceding
decade.[2]

No less a source of business acumen than Henry Ford observed,

> The smallest indivisible reality is, to my mind, intelligent and is

waiting there to be used by human spirits if we reach out and call them in. We rush too much with nervous hands and worried minds. We are impatient for results. What we need . . . is reinforcement of the soul by the invisible power waiting to be used . . . I know there are reservoirs of spiritual strength from which we human beings thoughtlessly cut ourselves off . . . I believe we shall someday be able to know enough about the source of power, and the realm of the spirit to create something ourselves . . .

I firmly believe that mankind was once wiser about spiritual things than we are today. What we now only believe, they knew.[3]

"Personal mastery" is the phrase we use for the discipline of personal growth and learning. People with high levels of personal mastery are continually expanding their ability to create the results in life they truly seek. From their quest for continual learning comes the spirit of the learning organization.

MASTERY AND PROFICIENCY

Personal mastery goes beyond competence and skills, though it is grounded in competence and skills. It goes beyond spiritual unfolding or opening, although it requires spiritual growth. It means approaching one's life as a creative work, living life from a creative as opposed to reactive viewpoint. As my long-time colleague Robert Fritz puts it:

Throughout history, almost every culture has had art, music, dance, architecture, poetry, storytelling, pottery, and sculpture. The desire to create is not limited by beliefs, nationality, creed, educational background, or era. The urge resides in all of us . . . [it] is not limited to the arts, but can encompass all of life, from the mundane to the profound.[4]

When personal mastery becomes a discipline—an activity we integrate into our lives—it embodies two underlying movements. The first is continually clarifying what is important to us. We often spend so much time coping with problems along our path that we forget why we are on that path in the first place. The result is that we only have a dim, or even inaccurate, view of what's really important to us.

The second is continually learning how to see current reality more clearly. We've all known people entangled in counterproductive relationships, who remain stuck because they keep pretending everything is all right. Or we have been in business meetings where everyone says, "We're on course relative to our plan," yet an honest look at current reality would show otherwise. In moving toward a desired destination, it is vital to know where you are now.

The juxtaposition of vision (what we want) and a clear picture of current reality (where we are relative to what we want) generates what we call "creative tension": a force to bring them together, caused by the natural tendency of tension to seek resolution. The essence of personal mastery is learning how to generate and sustain creative tension in our lives.

"Learning" in this context does not mean acquiring more information, but expanding the ability to produce the results we truly want in life. It is lifelong generative learning. And learning organizations are not possible unless they have people at every level who practice it.

Sadly, the term "mastery" suggests gaining dominance over people or things. But mastery can also mean a special level of proficiency. A master craftsperson, for instance, doesn't *dominate* pottery or weaving. But the craftsperson's skill allows the best pots or fabrics to emerge from the workshop. Similarly, personal mastery suggests a special level of proficiency in every aspect of life—personal and professional.

People with a high level of personal mastery share several basic characteristics. They have a special sense of purpose that lies behind their visions and goals. *For such a person, a vision is a calling rather than simply a good idea.* They see current reality" as an ally, not an enemy. They have learned how to perceive and work with forces of change rather than resist those forces. They are deeply inquisitive, committed to continually seeing reality more and more accurately. They feel connected to others and to life itself. Yet they sacrifice none of their uniqueness. They feel as if they are part of a larger creative process, which they can influence but cannot unilaterally control.

People with a high level of personal mastery live in a continual learning mode. They never "arrive." Sometimes, language, such as the term "personal mastery," creates a misleading sense of definiteness, of black and white. But personal mastery is not something you possess. It is a process. It is a lifelong discipline. People with a high level of personal mastery are acutely aware of their ignorance, their incompetence, their growth areas. And they are deeply self-confident. Paradoxical? Only for those who do not see that "the journey is the reward."

At Hanover, O'Brien wrote about "advanced maturity" as entailing building and holding deep values, making commitments to goals larger than oneself, being open, exercising free will, and continually striving for an accurate picture of reality. Such people, he asserted, also have a capacity for delayed gratification, which makes it possible for them to aspire to objectives which others would disregard, even considering "the impact of their choices on succeeding generations." In an interesting foreshadowing of interest in "emotional intelligence" a decade later, he pointed to a deficiency in modern society's commitment to human development:

> Whatever the reasons, we do not pursue emotional development with the same intensity with which we pursue physical and intellectual development. This is all the more unfortunate because full emotional development offers the greatest degree of leverage in attaining our full potential.[5]

"WHY WE WANT IT"

"The total development of our people," O'Brien adds, "is essential to achieving our goal of corporate excellence." Whereas once the morals of the marketplace seemed to require a level of morality in business that was lower than in other activities, "We believe there is no fundamental tradeoff between the higher virtues in life and economic success. We believe we can have both. In fact, we believe that, over the long term, the more we practice the higher virtues of life, the more economic success we will have."

In essence, O'Brien is articulating his own version of the most common rationale whereby organizations come to support personal mastery—or whatever words they use to express their commitment to the growth of their people. People with high levels of personal mastery are more committed. They take more initiative. They have a broader and deeper sense of responsibility in their work. They learn faster. For all these reasons, many organizations espouse a commitment to fostering personal growth among their employees because they believe it will make the organization stronger.

But O'Brien articulated another reason for pursuing personal mastery, one that we've come to see as a necessary complement:

Another and equally important reason why we encourage our people in this quest is the impact which full personal development can have on individual happiness. To seek personal fulfillment only outside of work and to ignore the significant portion of our lives which we spend working, would be to limit our opportunities to be happy and complete human beings.[6]

In other words, why do we want personal mastery? We want it because we want it. It is a pivotal moment in the evolution of an organization when enough people take this stand, a stand of being intrinsically committtted to the well-being of people. Traditionally, organizations have supported people's development instrumentally—if people grew and developed, then the organization would be more effective. Leaders like O'Brien go one step further: "In the type of organization we seek to build, the fullest development of people is on an equal plane with financial success."

To see people's development as a means toward the organization's ends subtly devalues the relationship that can exist between individual and organization. Max de Pree, retired CEO of Herman Miller, speaks of a "covenant" between organization and individual, in contrast to the traditional "contract" ("an honest day's pay in exchange for an honest day's work"). "Contracts," says De Pree, "are a small part of a relationship. A complete relationship needs a covenant . . . a covenantal relationship rests on a shared commitment to ideas, to issues, to values, to goals, and to management processes . . . Covenantal relationships reflect unity and grace and poise. They are expressions of the sacred nature of relationships."[7]

In Japan, a *Christian Science Monitor* reporter visiting the Matsushita Corporation observed that "There is an almost religious atmosphere about the place, as if work itself were considered something sacred." Inamori of Kyocera says that his commitment to personal mastery simply evolved from the traditional Japanese commitment to lifetime employment. "Our employees agreed to live in a community in which they would not exploit each other, but rather help each other so that we may each live our life fully."

"You know the system is working," O'Brien added, "when you see a person who came to work for the company ten years ago who was unsure of him or herself and had a narrow view of the world and their opportunities. Now that person is in charge of a department of a dozen people. He or she feels comfortable with responsibility, digests complex ideas, weighs different positions, and develops solid reasoning behind choices. Other people listen with care to what this person says. The person has larger aspirations for family, company, industry, and society."

There is an unconditional commitment, an unequivocating courage, in the stand that an organization truly committed to personal mastery takes. We want it because we want it.

RESISTANCE

Who could resist the benefits of personal mastery? Many people and organizations do. Taking a stand for the full development of your people is a radical departure from the traditional contract between employee and institution. In some ways, it is the most radical departure from traditional business practices in the learning organization.

There are obvious reasons why companies resist encouraging personal mastery. It is "soft," based in part on unquantifiable concepts such as intuition and personal vision. No one will ever be able to measure to three decimal places how much personal mastery contributes to productivity and the bottom line. In a materialistic culture such as ours, it is difficult even to discuss some of the premises of personal mastery. "Why do people need to talk about this stuff?" someone may ask. "Isn't it obvious? Don't we already know it?"

A more daunting form of resistance is cynicism. In combating cynicism, it helps to know its source. Scratch the surface of most cynics and you find a frustrated idealist—someone who made the mistake of converting ideals into expectations. For example, many of those cynical about personal mastery once held high ideals about people. Then they found themselves disappointed, hurt, and eventually embittered because people fell short of their ideals. O'Brien used to point out that burnout does not just come from working too hard. "There are teachers, social workers, and clergy," says O'Brien, "who work incredibly hard until they are 80 years old and never suffer "burnout"—because they have an accurate view of human nature, of our potential and limitations. They don't over-romanticize people, so they don't feel the great psychological stress when people let them down."

Finally, some fear that personal mastery will threaten the established order of a well-managed company. This is a valid fear. *To empower people in an unaligned organization can be counterproductive.* If people do not share a common vision, and do not share common mental models about the business reality within which they operate, empowering people will only increase organizational stress and the burden of management to maintain coherence and direction. This is why the discipline of personal mastery must always be seen as one among the set of disciplines of a learning organization. An organizational commitment to personal mastery would be naive and foolish if leaders in the organization lacked the capabilities of building shared vision and shared mental models to guide local decision makers.

THE DISCIPLINE OF PERSONAL MASTERY

The way to begin developing a sense of personal mastery is to approach it as a discipline, as a series of practices and principles that must be applied to be useful. Just as one becomes a master artist by continual practice, so the following principles and practices lay the groundwork for continually expanding the discipline of personal mastery.

PERSONAL VISION

Personal vision comes from within. Several years ago I was talking with a young woman about her vision for the planet. She said many lovely things about peace and harmony, about living in balance with nature. As beautiful as these ideas were, she spoke about them unemotionally, as if these were things that she should want. I asked her if there was anything else. After a pause, she said, "I want to live on a green planet," and started to cry. As far as I know, she had never said this before. The words just leaped from her, almost with a will of their own. Yet, the image they conveyed clearly had deep meaning to her—perhaps even levels of meaning that she didn't understand.

Most adults have little sense of real vision. We have goals and objectives, but these are not visions. When asked what they want, many adults will say what they want to get rid of. They'd like a better job—that is, they'd like to get rid of the boring job they have. They'd like to live in a better neighborhood, or not have to worry about crime, or about putting their kids through school. They'd like it if their mother-in-law returned to her own house, or if their back stopped hurting. Such litanies of "negative visions" are sadly commonplace, even among very successful people. They are the byproduct of a lifetime of fitting in, of coping, of problem solving. As a teenager in one of our programs once said, "We shouldn't call them 'grown ups' we should call them 'given ups.'"

A subtler form of diminished vision is "focusing on the means not the result." Many senior executives, for example, choose "high market share" as part of their vision. But why? "Because I want our company to be profitable." Now, you might think that high profits is an intrinsic result in and of itself, and indeed it is for some. But for surprisingly many other leaders, profits too are a means toward a still more important result. Why choose high annual profits? "Because I want us to remain an independent company, to keep from being taken over." Why do you want that? "Because I want to keep our integrity and our capacity to be true to our purpose in starting the organization." While all the goals mentioned are legitimate, the last—being true to our purpose—has the greatest intrinsic significance to these executives. All the rest are means to the end, means which might change in particular circumstances. *The ability to focus on ultimate intrinsic desires, not only on secondary goals, is a cornerstone of personal mastery.*

Real vision cannot be understood in isolation from the idea of purpose. By purpose, I mean an individual's sense of why he or she is alive. No one could prove or disprove the statement that human beings have purpose. It would be fruitless even to engage in the debate. But as a working premise, the idea has great power. One implication is that happiness may be most directly a result of living consistently with your purpose. George Bernard Shaw expressed the idea pointedly when he said:

> This is the true joy in life, the being used for a purpose recognized by yourself as a mighty one . . . the being a force of nature instead of a feverish, selfish little clod of ailments and grievances complaining that the world will not devote itself to making you happy.[8]

This same principle has been expressed in some organizations as "genuine caring." In places where people felt uncomfortable talking about personal purpose, they felt perfectly at ease talking about genuine caring. When people genuinely care, they are naturally committed. They are doing what they truly want to do. They are full of energy and enthusiasm. They persevere, even in the face of frustration and setbacks, because what they are doing is what they must do. It is *their work.*

Everyone has had experiences when work flows fluidly; when one feels in tune with a task and works with a true economy of means. Someone whose vision calls him to a foreign country, for example, may find himself learning a new language far more rapidly than he ever could before. You can often recognize your personal vision because it creates such moments; it is the goal pulling you forward that makes all the work worthwhile.

But vision is different from purpose. Purpose is similar to a direction, a general heading. Vision is a specific destination, a picture of a desired future. Purpose is abstract. Vision is concrete. Purpose is "advancing man's capability to explore the heavens." Vision is "a man on the moon by the end of the 1960s." Purpose is "being the best I can be," "excellence." Vision is breaking the four minute mile.

It can truly be said that nothing happens until there is vision. But it is equally true that a vision with no underlying sense of purpose, no calling, is just a good idea—all "sound and fury, signifying nothing."

Conversely, purpose without vision has no sense of appropriate scale. "You and I may be tennis fans and enjoy talking about ground strokes, our backhands, the thrill of chasing down a corner shot, of hitting a winner. We may have a great conversation, but then we find out that I am gearing up to play at my local country club and you are preparing for Wimbledon. We share the same enthusiasm and love of the game, but at totally different scales of proficiency. Until we establish the scales we have in mind, we might think we are communicating when we're not."

Ultimately, vision is intrinsic not relative. It's something you desire for its intrinsic value, not because of where it stands you relative to another. Relative visions may be appropriate in the interim, but they will rarely lead to greatness. Nor is there anything wrong with competition. Competition, which literally means "striving together" (from the Latin *competrere*) is one of the best structures yet invented by humankind to allow each of us to bring out the best in each other. But after the competition is over, after the vision has (or has not) been achieved, it is your sense of purpose that draws you further, that compels you to set a new vision. *This, again, is why personal mastery must be a discipline. It is a process of continually focusing and refocusing on what one truly wants, on one's visions.*

Vision is multifaceted. There are material facets of our visions, such as where we want to live and how much money we want to have in the bank. There are personal facets, such as health, freedom, and being true to ourselves. There are service facets, such as helping others or contributing to the state of knowledge in a field. All are part of what we truly want. Modern society tends to direct our attention to the material aspects, and simultaneously foster guilt for our material desires. Society places some emphasis on our personal desires—for example, it is almost a fetish in some circles to look trim and fit—and relatively little on our desires to serve. In fact, it is easy to feel naive or foolish by expressing a desire to make a contribution. Be that as it may, it is clear from working with thousands of people that personal visions span all these dimensions and more. It is also clear that it takes courage to hold visions that are not in the social mainstream.

But it is exactly that courage to take a stand for one's vision that distinguishes people with high levels of personal mastery. Or, as the Japanese say of the master's stand, "When there is no break, not even the thickness of a hair comes between a man's vision and his action."[9]

In some ways, clarifying vision is one of the easier aspects of personal mastery. A more difficult challenge, for many, conies in facing current reality.

HOLDING CREATIVE TENSION

People often have great difficulty talking about their visions, even when the visions are clear. Why? Because we are acutely aware of the gaps between our vision and reality. "I would like to start my own company," but "I don't have the capital." Or, "I would like to pursue the profession that I really love," but "I've got to make a living." These gaps can make a vision seem unrealistic or fanciful. They can discourage us or make us feel hopeless. But the gap between vision and current reality is also a source of energy. If there was no gap, there would be no need for any action to move toward the vision. Indeed, the gap is *the* source of creative energy. We call this gap *creative tension*.[10]

Imagine a rubber band, stretched between your vision and current reality. When stretched, the rubber band creates tension, representing the tension between vision and current reality. What does tension seek? Resolution or release. There are only two possible ways for the tension to resolve itself: pull reality toward the vision or pull the vision toward reality. Which occurs will depend on whether we hold steady to the vision.

VISION

CURRENT
REALITY

The principle of creative tension is the central principle of personal mastery, integrating all elements of the discipline. Yet, it is easily misunderstood. For example, the very term "tension" suggests anxiety or stress. But creative tension doesn't feel any particular way. It is the force that comes into play at the moment when we acknowledge a vision that is at odds with current reality.

Still, creative tension often leads to feelings or emotions associated with anxiety, such as sadness, discouragement, hopelessness, or worry. This happens so often that people easily confuse these emotions with creative tension. People come to think that the creative process *is all about being in a state of anxiety.* But it is important to realize that these "negative" emotions that may arise when there is creative tension are not creative tension itself. These emotions are what we call *emotional tension.*

If we fail to distinguish emotional tension from creative tension, we predispose ourselves to lowering our vision. If we feel deeply discouraged about a vision that is not happening, we may have a strong urge to lighten the load of that discouragement. There is one immediate remedy: lower the vision! "Well, it wasn't really that important to shoot seventy-five. I'm having a great time shooting in the eighties."

Or, "I don't really care about being able to play in recital. I'll have to make money as a music teacher in any case; I'll just concentrate there." The dynamics of relieving emotional tension are insidious because they can operate unnoticed. Emotional tension can always be relieved by adjusting the one pole of the creative tension that is completely under our control at all times—the vision. The feelings that we dislike go away because the creative tension that was their source is reduced. Our goals are now much closer to our current reality. Escaping emotional tension is easy—the only price we pay is abandoning what we truly want, our vision.

The dynamics of emotional tension deeply resemble the dynamics of eroding goals that so troubled WonderTech in Chapter 7. The interaction of creative tension and emotional tension is a shifting the burden dynamic, similar to that of eroding goals, that can be represented as follows:

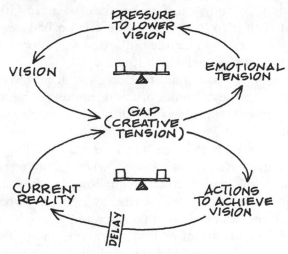

When we hold a vision that differs from current reality, a gap exists (the creative tension) which can be resolved in two ways. The lower balancing process represents the "fundamental solution": taking actions to bring reality into line with the vision. But changing reality takes time. This is what leads to the frustration and emotional tension in the upper balancing process, the "symptomatic solution" of lowering the vision to bring it into line with current reality.

But a onetime reduction in the vision usually isn't the end of the story. Sooner or later new pressures pulling reality away from the (new, lowered) vision arise, leading to still more pressures to lower the vision. The classic "shifting the burden" dynamic ensues, a subtle reinforcing spiral of failure to meet goals, frustration, lowered vision, temporary relief, and pressure anew to lower the vision still further. Gradually, the "burden" is shifting increasingly to lowering the vision.

At WonderTech, relieving emotional tension took the form of decline in key operating standards for delivery performance that seemed impossible to meet. The decline was especially difficult to see because it was gradual. During each crisis at Wonder Tech delivery standards eroded just a bit relative to where they had settled after the last crisis. So, too, do eroding personal goals go unrecognized, as we gradually surrender our dreams for the relationships we want to have, the work we want to do, and the type of world we want to live in.

In organizations, goals erode because of low tolerance for emotional tension. Nobody wants to be the messenger with bad news. The easiest path is to just pretend there is no bad news, or better yet, declare victory—to redefine the bad news as not so bad by lowering the standard against which it is judged.

The dynamics of emotional tension exist at all levels of human activity. They are the dynamics of compromise, the path of mediocrity. As Somerset Maugham said, "Only mediocre people are always at their best."

We allow our goals to erode when we are unwilling to live with emotional tension. On the other hand, when we understand creative tension and allow it to operate by not lowering our vision, vision becomes an active force. Robert Fritz says, "It's not what the vision is, it's what the vision does." Truly creative people use the gap between vision and current reality to generate energy for change.

For example, Alan Kay, who directed the research at Xerox Palo Alto Research Center (PARC) which in many ways gave birth to the personal computer, actually had a vision for a different machine, which he called the "dynabook." This would be a book that was interactive. A child could test out his or her understanding, play games, and creatively rearrange the static presentation of ideas offered by the traditional book. Kay failed, in a sense, because the "dynabook" never became a reality. But the vision reshaped the computer industry. The prototype machines developed at PARC achieved the functionality—windows, pull-down menus, mouse control, iconic displays (images rather than words)—that was introduced commercially almost ten years later in the Macintosh.

Bill Russell, the legendary center for the Boston Celtics basketball team during its historic run of eleven professional championships in thirteen years, used to keep his own personal scorecard. He graded himself after every game on scale from one to one hundred. In his career he never achieved more than sixty-five. Now, given the way most of us are taught to think about goals, we would regard Russell as an abject failure. The poor soul played in over twelve hundred basketball games and never achieved his standard! Yet, it was the striving for that standard that made him arguably the best basketball player ever.[11]

It's not what the vision is, it's what the vision does.

Mastery of creative tension transforms the way one views "failure." Failure is, simply, a shortfall, evidence of the gap between vision and current reality. Failure is an opportunity for learning—about inaccurate pictures of current reality, about strategies that didn't work as expected, about the clarity of the vision. Failures are not about our unworthiness or powerlessness. Ed Land, founder and president of Polaroid for decades and inventor of instant photography, had one plaque on his wall. It read:

A mistake is an event, the full benefit of which has not yet been turned to your advantage.

Mastery of creative tension brings out a capacity for perseverance and patience. A Japanese executive in one of our seminars once told me how, in his view, Japanese and Americans have quite different attitudes toward time. He said that, "U.S. businessmen in Japan to negotiate business deals often find the Japanese evasive and reticent to 'get down to business.' The American arrives in Japan on a tight, carefully planned five-day schedule and immediately wants to get to work. Instead, the Japanese greet them with a polite, formal tea ceremony instead, never getting down to nuts and bolts. As the days go by, the Japanese keep their slow pace, while the Americans become antsier and antsier. For the American," the executive said, "time is the enemy. For the Japanese, time is an ally."

More broadly, current reality itself is, for many of us, the enemy. We fight against what is. We are not so much drawn to what we want to create as we are repelled by what we have, from our current reality. By this logic, the deeper the fear, the more we abhor what is, the more "motivated" we are to change. "Things must get bad enough, or people will not change in any fundamental way."

This leads to the mistaken belief that fundamental change *requires* a threat to survival, a "burning platform" in the words of some. This crisis theory of change is remarkably widespread. Yet, it is also a dangerous oversimplification. Often in workshops or presentations, I will ask, "How many of you believe people and organizations only change, fundamentally, when there is a crisis?" Reliably, 75 to 90 percent of the hands go up. Then I ask people to consider a life where everything is exactly the way they would like— there are absolutely no problems of any sort in work, personally, professionally, in their relationships, or their community. Then I ask, "What is the first thing you would seek if you had a life of absolutely no problems?" The answer, overwhelmingly, is "change —to create something new." So human beings are more complex than we often assume. We both fear and seek change. Or, as one seasoned organization change consultant once put it, "People don't resist change. They resist being changed."

Mastery of creative tension leads to a fundamental shift in our whole posture toward reality. Current reality becomes the ally not the enemy. *An accurate, insightful view of current reality is as important as a clear vision.* Unfortunately, most of us are in the habit of imposing biases on our perceptions of current reality. "We learn to rely on our concepts of reality more than on our observations," writes Robert Fritz. "It is more convenient to assume that reality is similar to our preconceived ideas than to freshly observe what we have before our eyes."[12] If the first choice in pursuing personal mastery is to be true to your own vision, the second fundamental choice in support of personal mastery is commitment to the truth.

The two are equally vital to generating creative tension. Or, as Fritz puts it, "The truly creative person knows that all creating is achieved through working with constraints. Without constraints there is no creating."

"STRUCTURAL CONFLICT": THE POWER OF YOUR POWERLESSNESS

Many people, even highly successful people, harbor deep beliefs contrary to their personal mastery. Very often, these beliefs are below the level of conscious awareness. To see what I mean, try the following experiment. Say out loud the following sentence: "I can create my life exactly the way I want it, in all dimensions—work, family, relationships, community, and larger world." Notice your internal reaction to this assertion, the "little voice" in the back of your head. "Who's he kidding?" "He doesn't really believe that." "Personally and in work, sure—but, not 'community' and 'the larger world.'" "What do I care about the 'larger world' anyhow?" All of these reactions are evidence of deep-seated beliefs.

Fritz, who has worked with literally tens of thousands of people to develop their creative capacities, has concluded that practically all of us have a "dominant belief that we are not able to fulfill our desires." Where does this belief come from? Fritz argues that it is an almost inevitable by-product of growing up:

> As children we learn what our limitations are. Children are right-fully taught limitations essential to their survival. But too often this learning is generalized. We are constantly told we can't have or can't do certain things, and we may come to assume that we have an inability to have what we want."[13]

Most of us hold one of two contradictory beliefs that limit our ability to create what we really want. The more common is belief in our powerlessness—our inability to bring into being all the things we really care about. The other belief centers on unworthiness— that we do not deserve to have what we truly desire. Fritz claims that he has met only a handful of individuals who do not seem to have one or the other of these underlying beliefs. Such an assertion is difficult to prove rigorously because it is difficult to measure deep beliefs. But if we accept it as a working premise, it illuminates systemic forces that can work powerfully against creating what we really want.

Fritz uses a metaphor to describe how contradictory underlying beliefs work as a system, counter to achieving our goals. Imagine, as you move toward your goal, there is a rubber band, symbolizing creative tension, pulling you in the desired direction. But imagine also a second rubber band, anchored to the belief of powerlessness or unworthiness. Just as the first rubber band tries to pull you toward your goal, the second pulls you back toward the underlying belief that you can't (or don't deserve to) have your goal. Fritz calls the system involving both the tension pulling us toward our goal and the tension anchoring us to our underlying belief "structural conflict," because it is a structure of conflicting forces: pulling us simultaneously toward and away from what we want.

Thus, the closer we come to achieving our vision, the more the second rubber band pulls us away from our vision. This force can manifest itself in many ways. We might lose our energy. We might question whether we really wanted the vision. "Finishing the job" might become increasingly difficult. Unexpected obstacles develop in our path. People let us down. All this happens even though we are unaware of the structural conflict system, because it originates in deep beliefs of which we are largely unaware—in fact, our unaware-ness contributes to the power of structural conflict.

Given beliefs in our powerlessness or unworthiness, structural conflict implies that systemic forces come into play to keep us from

BELIEF IN
POWERLESSNESS
OR UNWORTHINESS   YOUR   YOUR
                              CURRENT   VISION
                              REALITY

succeeding *whenever* we seek a vision. Yet, we *do* succeed sometimes, and in fact many of us have become adept at identifying and achieving goals, at least in some areas of our lives. How do we overcome the forces of structural conflict.

Fritz has identified three generic strategies for coping with the forces of structural conflict, each of which has its limitations."[14] Letting our vision erode is one such coping strategy. The second is "conflict manipulation," in which we try to manipulate ourselves into greater effort toward what we want by creating artificial conflict, such as through focusing on avoiding what we don't want. Conflict manipulation is the favored strategy of people who incessantly worry about failure, of managers who excel at motivational chats that point out the highly unpleasant consequences if the company's goals are *not* achieved, and of social movements that attempt to mobilize people through fear. In fact, sadly, most social movements operate through conflict manipulation or "negative vision," focusing on getting away from what we don't want, rather than on creating what we do want: antidrugs, antinuclear arms, antinuclear power, antismoking, anti-abortion, or antigovernment corruption.

But many ask, "What's wrong with a little worry or fear if it helps us achieve our goals?" The response of those who seek personal mastery is the simple question: "Do you really want to live your life in a state of fear of failure?" The tragedy is that many people who get hooked on conflict manipulation come to believe that *only* through being in a state of continual anxiety and fear can they be successful. These are the people who, rather than shunning emotional tension, actually come to glorify it. For them, there is little joy in life. Even when they achieve their goals, they immediately begin worrying about losing what they have gained.

Fritz's third generic strategy is the strategy of willpower where we simply psych ourselves up to overpower all forms of resistance to achieving our goals. Lying behind willpower strategies, he suggests, is the simple assumption that we motivate ourselves through heightened volition. Willpower is so common among highly successful people that many see its characteristics as synonymous with success: a maniacal focus on goals, willingness to pay the price, ability to defeat any opposition and surmount any obstacle.

The problems with willpower are many, but they may hardly be noticed by the person focused narrowly on success. First, there is little economy of means; in systems thinking terms, we act without leverage. We attain our goals, but the effort is enormous and we may find ourselves exhausted and wondering if it was worth it when we have succeeded. Ironically, people hooked on willpower may actually look for obstacles to overcome, dragons to slay, and enemies to vanquish—to remind themselves and others of their own prowess. Second, there are often considerable unintended consequences. Despite great success at work, the master of willpower will often find that he or she has gone through two marriages and has terrible relationships with his or her children. Somehow, the same dogged determination and goal orientation that works at work doesn't quite turn the trick at home.

Worse still, just as with all of the coping strategies, willpower leaves the underlying system of structural conflict unaltered. In particular, the underlying belief in powerlessness has not really changed. Despite significant accomplishments, many highly successful people still feel a deep, usually unspoken, sense of powerlessness in critical areas of their lives—such as in their personal and family relationships, or in their ability to achieve a sense of peace and spiritual fulfillment.

These coping strategies are, to a certain extent, unavoidable.

They are deeply habitual and cannot be changed overnight. We all-tend to have a favorite strategy—mine has long been willpower," as those close to me can attest.

Where then is the leverage in dealing with structural conflict? If structural conflict arises from deep underlying beliefs, then it can be changed only by changing the beliefs. But psychologists are virtually unanimous that fundamental beliefs such as powerlessness or unworthiness cannot be changed readily. They are developed early in life (remember all those "can'ts" and "don'ts" that started when you were 2?). For most of us, beliefs change gradually as we accumulate new experiences—as we develop our personal mastery. But if mastery will not develop so long as we hold unempowering beliefs, and the beliefs will change only as we experience our mastery, how may we begin to alter the deeper structures of our lives?

COMMITMENT TO THE TRUTH

We may begin with a disarmingly simple yet profound strategy for dealing with structural conflict: telling the truth.

Commitment to the truth often seems to people an inadequate strategy. "What do I need to do to change my behavior?" "How do I change my underlying belief?" People often want a formula, a technique, something tangible that they can apply to solve the problem of structural conflict. But, in fact, being committed to the truth is far more powerful than any technique.

Commitment to the truth does not mean seeking the Truth, the absolute final word or ultimate cause. Rather, it means a relentless willingness to root out the ways we limit or deceive ourselves from seeing what is, and to continually challenge our theories of why things are the way they are. It means continually broadening our awareness, just as the great athlete with extraordinary peripheral vision keeps trying to see more of the playing field. It also means continually deepening our understanding of the structures underlying current events. Specifically, people with high levels of personal mastery see more of the structural conflicts underlying their own behavior.

Thus, the first critical task in dealing with structural conflicts is to recognize them, *and* the resulting behavior, when they are operating. It can be very difficult to recognize these coping strategies while we are playing them out, especially because of tensions and pressures that often accompany them. It helps to develop internal warning signals, such as when we find ourselves blaming something or somebody for our problems: "The reason I'm giving up is nobody appreciates me," or "The reason I'm so worried is that they'll fire me if I don't get the job done."

In my life, for example, for many years my experience was that people let me down at critical junctures in major projects. When this happened, I would bulldoze through, overcoming the obstacle of their disloyalty or incompetence. It took many years before I recognized this as a recurring pattern, my own special form of the willpower strategy, rooted in a deep feeling of being powerless to change the way others let me down. Invariably, I ended up feeling "I've got to do it all myself."

Once I recognized this pattern, I began to act differently when this happened. I became angry less often. Rather, there was a twinge of recognition—"Oh, there goes my pattern." I looked more deeply at how my own actions were part of the outcome, either by creating tasks that were impossible to accomplish, or by undermining or not supporting the other person. Further, I worked to develop skills to discuss such situations with the people involved without producing defensiveness. Chapter 9, "Mental Models," illustrates these skills.

I would never have developed those skills or known how to put them into practice without a shift of mind. So long as I saw the problem in terms of events, I was convinced that my problems were externally caused—"*they* let me down." Once I saw the problem as structurally caused, I began to look at what I could do, rather than at what "they had done."

Structures of which we are unaware hold us prisoner. Once we can see them and name them, they no longer have the same hold on us. This is as much true for individuals as it is for organizations. In fact, an entire field is evolving, structural family therapy, based on the assumption that individual psychological difficulties can be understood and changed only by understanding the structures of interdependencies within families and close personal relationships. Once these structures are recognized, in the words of David Kantor, a pioneer in the field, "It becomes possible to begin to alter structures to free people from previously mysterious forces that dictated their behavior."[15]

Discovering structures at play is the stock-in-trade of people with high levels of personal mastery. Sometimes these structures can be readily changed. Sometimes, as with structural conflict, they change only gradually. Then the need is to work more creatively within them while acknowledging their origin, rather than fighting the structures. Either way, once an operating structure is recognized, the structure itself becomes part of "current reality." The greater my commitment to the truth, the more creative tension comes into play because current reality is seen more for what it really is. In the context of creative tension, commitment to the truth becomes a generative force, just as vision becomes a generative force.

One of the classic illustrations of this process is Charles Dickens's *A Christmas Carol*. Through the visitations of the three ghosts on Christmas Eve, Scrooge sees more and more of the reality from which he has turned away. He sees the reality of his past, how the choices he made steadily whittled away his compassion and increased his self-centeredness. He sees the reality of his present, especially those aspects of reality that he has avoided, such as Tiny Tim's illness. And he sees the reality of his likely future, the future that will occur if he continues in his present ways. But then he wakes up. He realizes that he is not the captive of these realities. He realizes that he has a choice. He chooses to change.

Significantly, Scrooge can't make the choice to change before he becomes more aware of his current reality. In effect, Dickens says that life always avails the option of seeing the truth, no matter how blind and prejudiced we may be. And if we have the courage to respond to that option, we have the power to change ourselves profoundly. Or, to put it in more classic religious terms, only through the truth do we come to grace.

The power of the truth, seeing reality more and more as it is, cleansing the lens of perception, awakening from self-imposed distortions of reality—are different expressions of a common principle in almost all the world's great philosophic and religious systems. Buddhists strive to achieve the state of "pure observation," of seeing reality directly. Hindus speak of "witnessing," observing themselves and their lives with an attitude of spiritual detachment. The power of the truth was no less central to early Christian thinking, although it has lost its place in Christian practice over the last two thousand years. In fact, the Hebrew symbols used to form the word *Yeheshua,* "Jesus," include the symbols for Jehovah, with the additional letter *shin* inserted in the middle. The symbols for Jehovah carry the meaning, "That which was, is, and will be." The inserted *shin* modifies the meaning to "that which was, is, and will be, *delivers*." This is the probable origin of the statement "The truth shall set you free."

USING THE SUBCONSCIOUS, OR, YOU DON'T REALLY NEED TO FIGURE IT ALL OUT

One of the most fascinating aspects of people with high levels of personal mastery is their ability to accomplish extraordinarily complex tasks with grace and ease. We have all marveled at the breathtakingly beautiful artistry of the championship ice skater or the prima ballerina. We know that their skills have been developed through years of diligent training, yet the ability to execute their artistry with such ease and seeming effortlessness is still wondrous.

Implicit in the practice of personal mastery is another dimension of the mind, the subconscious., through which *all of us* deal with complexity. What distinguishes people with high levels of personal mastery is they have developed a higher level of rapport between their normal awareness and this other dimension we have come to call the subconscious.[16] What most of us take for granted and exploit haphazardly, they approach as a discipline.

Is the subconscious relevant in management and organizations? Inamori of Kyocera says:

> When I am concentrating . . . I enter the subconscious mind. It is said that human beings possess both a conscious and subconscious mind, and that our subconscious mind has a capacity that is larger by a factor of ten . . . "
>
> When I talk about our "mind," I risk being called crazy. Nonetheless, I think therein may lie the hint to the secret that may determine our future.

O'Brien of Hanover likewise sees tapping mental capabilities formerly ignored as central to building the new organization:

> The greatest unexplored territory in the world is the space between our ears. Seriously, I am certain that learning organizations will find ways to nurture and focus the capabilities within us all that today we call "extraordinary."

But what is extraordinary is actually closely related to aspects of our lives that are so ordinary that we hardly notice them. Our lives are full of myriad complex tasks which we handle quite competently with almost no conscious thought. Try an experiment: touch the top of your head. Now, *how* did you do that? For most of us, the answer resembles, "Well, I just thought about my hand on my head—or, I formed a mental image of my hand on top of my head—and *voila,* it just was there." But at a neurophysiological level, raising your hand to the top of your head is an extraordinarily complex task, involving hundreds of thousands of neural firings as signals move from the brain to your arm and back again. This entire complex activity is coordinated without our conscious awareness. Likewise, if you had to think about every detail of walking, you'd be in big trouble. Walking, talking, eating, putting on your shoes, and riding a bicycle are all accomplished with almost no conscious attention— yet all are, in fact, enormously complex tasks.

These tasks are accomplished reliably because there is an aspect of our mind that is exceedingly capable of dealing with complexity. In some sense it does not matter what we call this other aspect. The term "subconscious" is suggestive because it implies operating below or behind our conscious awareness. Others call it "uncon- scious" or "automatic mind." Whatever it is called, without this dimension of mind it would be quite impossible to explain how human beings ever succeed in mastering any complex task. For one thing we can say confidently is that these tasks are not accom- plished through our normal awareness and thinking alone.

Equally important, the subconscious is critical to how we learn. At one point in your life you were unable to carry out "mundane" tasks such as walking, talking and eating. Each had to be *learned*. The infant does not get the spoon in her mouth the first time out— it goes over the left shoulder, then the right shoulder, then the cheek. Only gradually does she learn to reliably reach her mouth. Initially, any new task requires a great deal of conscious attention and effort. As we "learn" the skills required of the task, the whole activity gradually shifts from conscious attention to subconscious control.

As another example, when you first learned to drive a car, it took considerable conscious attention, especially if your were learning to drive on a standard transmission. In fact, you might have found it difficult to carry on a conversation with the person next to you. If that person had asked you to "slow down, downshift, and turn right" at the next corner, you might have given up then and there. Yet, within a few months or less, you executed the same task with little or no conscious attention. It had all become "automatic." Amazingly, before long you drove in heavy traffic while carrying on a conversation with the person sitting next to you—apparently giving almost no conscious attention to the literally hundreds of variables you had to monitor and respond to.

When we first learn to play the piano or any musical instrument, we start by playing scales. Gradually, we move up to simple and then more complex compositions, leaving scales behind as a task that can be handled with little conscious attention. Even concert pianists, when sitting down to an unfamiliar piece will play that piece at half speed in order to allow concentration on the mechanics of hand and pedal positions, rhythm and tempo. But when the concert comes, the same pianist places no conscious attention on the mechanics of playing the piece. This leaves his conscious attention to focus exclusively on the aesthetics of the performance.

We have all mastered a vast repertoire of skills through training the subconscious. Once learned, they become so taken for granted, so subconscious, we don't even notice when we are executing them. But, for most of us, we have never given careful thought to *how* we mastered these skills and how we might continue to develop deeper and deeper *rapport* between our normal awareness and subconscious. Yet, these are matters of the greatest importance to the discipline of personal mastery.[17]

This is why, for instance, many people committed to continually developing personal mastery practice some form of meditation. Whether it is through contemplative prayer or other methods of simply quieting the conscious mind, regular meditative practice can be extremely helpful in working more productively with the subconscious mind. The subconscious appears to have no particular volition. It neither generates its own objectives nor determines its own focus. It is highly subject to direction and conditioning—what we pay attention to takes on special significance to the subconscious. In our normal highly active state of mind, the subconscious is deluged with contradictory thoughts and feelings. In a quieter state of mind, when we then focus on something of particular importance, some aspect of our vision, the subconscious is undistracted.

Moreover, there are particular ways that people with high levels of personal mastery direct their focus. As discussed earlier, they *focus on the desired result itself,* not the "process" or the means they assume necessary to achieve that result.

Focusing on the desired intrinsic result is a skill. For most of us it is not easy at first, and takes time and patience to develop. For most of us, as soon as we think of some important personal goal, almost immediately we think of all the reasons why it will be hard to achieve—the challenges we will face and the obstacles we will have to overcome. While this is very helpful for thinking through alternative strategies for achieving our goals, it is also a sign of lack of discipline when thoughts about the process of achieving our vision continually crowd out our focus on the outcomes we seek. We must work at learning how to separate what we truly want, from what we think we need to do in order to achieve it.

A useful starting exercise for learning how to focus more clearly on desired results is to take any particular goal or aspect of your vision. First imagine that that goal is fully realized. Then ask yourself the question, "If I actually had this, what would it get me?" What people often discover is that the answer to that question reveals deeper desires lying behind the goal. In fact, the goal is actually an interim step they assume is necessary to reach a more important result. For example, a person has a goal of reaching a certain level in the organizational hierarchy. When she asks herself, "What would it get me to be a senior VP?" she discovers that the answer is "respect of my peers" or "being where the action is." Though she may still aspire to the position, she now sees that there is also a deeper result she desires—a result she can start to hold as part of her vision now, independent of where she is in the organizational hierarchy. (Moreover, if she doesn't clarify "the result" she truly seeks, she may reach her stated goal and find that the more senior position is somehow still dissatisfying.)

The reason this skill is so important is precisely because of the responsiveness of the subconscious to a clear focus. When we are unclear between interim goals and more intrinsic goals, the subconscious has no way of prioritizing and focusing.

Making clear choices is also important. Only after choice are the capabilities of the subconscious brought fully into play. In fact, making choices and focusing on the results that are important to us may be one of the highest leverage uses of our normal awareness.

Commitment to the truth is also important for developing subconscious rapport—for the same basic reasons that lie detectors work. Lie detectors work because when most human beings do not tell the truth they create some level of internal stress, which in turn generates measurable physiological effects—blood pressure, pulse rate, and respiration. So, not only does deceiving ourselves about current reality prevent the subconscious from having accurate information about where we are relative to our vision, but it also creates distracting input to the subconscious, just as our "chatter" about why we can't achieve our vision is distracting. The principle of creative tension recognizes that the subconscious operates most effectively when it is focused clearly on our vision and current reality.

The art of working effectively with the subconscious incorporates many techniques. An effective way to focus the subconscious is through imagery and visualization. For example, world-class swimmers have found that by imagining their hands to be twice their actual size and their feet to be webbed, they actually swim faster. "Mental rehearsal" of complex feats has become routine psychological training for diverse professional performers.

But the real effectiveness of all of this still hinges on knowing what it is that is most important to you. In the absence of knowing what truly matters to you, the specific practices and methods of working with the subconscious run the risk of becoming mechanical techniques—simply a new way of manipulating yourself into being more productive. This is not an idle concern. Almost all spiritual traditions warn against adopting the techniques of increased mental powers without diligently continuing to refine one's sense of genuine aspiration.

Ultimately, what matters most in developing the subconscious rapport characteristic of masters is the genuine caring for a desired outcome, the deep feeling of it being the "right" goal toward which to aspire. The subconscious seems especially receptive to goals in line with our deeper aspirations and values. According to some spiritual disciplines, this is because these deeper aspirations input directly to, or are part of, the subconscious mind.

A wonderful example of what can be accomplished in the pursuit of something truly important to a person is the story of Gilbert Kaplan, a highly successful publisher and editor of a leading investment periodical. Kaplan first heard Mahler's Second Symphony in a rehearsal in 1965. He "found himself unable to sleep. I went back for the performance and walked out of the hall a different person. It was the beginning of a long love affair." Despite his having had no formal musical training, he committed time and energy and a

considerable sum of his personal finances (he had to hire an orchestra) to the pursuit of learning how to conduct the piece. Today, his
performances of the symphony have received the highest praise of
critics throughout the world. *The New York Times* praised his 1988
recording of the symphony with the London Symphony Orchestra
as one of the five finest classical recordings of the year and the
president of the New York Mahler Society called it "the outstanding recorded performance." A strict reliance on only conscious
learning could never have achieved this level of artistry, even with
all the willpower in the world. It had to depend on a high level of
subconscious rapport which Kaplan could bring to bear on his new
"love affair."

In many ways, the key to developing high levels of mastery in
subconscious rapport comes back to the discipline of developing
personal vision. This is why the concept of vision has always figured
so strongly in the creative arts. Picasso once said:

> It would be very interesting to record photographically, not the
> stages of a painting, but its metamorphoses. One would see per-
> haps by what course a mind finds its way toward the crystalliza-
> tion of its dream. But what is really very serious is to see that the
> picture does not change basically, that the initial vision remains
> almost intact in spite of appearance.[18]

PERSONAL MASTERY AND THE FIFTH DISCIPLINE

As individuals practice the discipline of personal mastery, several
changes gradually take place within them. Many of these are quite
subtle and often go unnoticed. In addition to clarifying the structures that characterize personal mastery as a discipline (such as creative tension, emotional tension, and structural conflict), the systems perspective also illuminates subtler aspects of personal
mastery—especially: integrating reason and intuition; continually
seeing more of our connectedness to the world; compassion; and
commitment to the whole.

INTEGRATING REASON AND INTUITION

According to an ancient Sufi story, a blind man wandering lost in a forest tripped and fell. As the blind man rummaged about the forest floor he discovered that he had fallen over a cripple. The blind man and the cripple struck up a conversation, commiserating on their fate. The blind man said, "I have been wandering in this forest for as long as I can remember, and I cannot see to find my way out." The cripple said, "I have been lying on the forest floor for as long as I can remember, and I cannot get up to walk out." As they sat there talking, suddenly the cripple cried out. "I've got it," he said. "You hoist me up onto your shoulders and I will tell you where to walk. Together we can find our way out of the forest." According to the ancient storyteller, the blind man symbolized rationality. The cripple symbolized intuition. We will not find our way out of the forest until we learn how to integrate the two.

Intuition in management has recently received increasing attention and acceptance, after many decades of being officially ignored. Now numerous studies show that experienced managers and leaders rely heavily on intuition—that they do not figure out complex problems entirely rationally. They rely on hunches, recognize patterns, and draw intuitive analogies and parallels to other seemingly disparate situations.[19] There are even courses in management schools on intuition and creative problem solving. But we have a very long way to go, in our organizations and in society, toward reintegrating intuition and rationality.

People with high levels of personal mastery do not set out to integrate reason and intuition. Rather, they achieve it naturally—as a by-product of their commitment to use all resources at their disposal. They cannot afford to choose between reason and intuition, or head and heart, any more than they would choose to walk on one leg or see with one eye.

Bilateralism is a design principle underlying the evolution of advanced organisms. Nature seems to have learned to design in pairs; it not only builds in redundancy but achieves capabilities not possible otherwise. Two legs are critical for rapid, flexible locomotion. Two arms and hands are vital for climbing, lifting, and manipulating objects. Two eyes give us stereoscopic vision, and along with two ears, depth perception. Is it not possible that, following the same design principle, reason and intuition are designed to work in harmony for us to achieve our potential intelligence?

Systems thinking may hold a key to integrating reason and intuition. Intuition eludes the grasp of linear thinking, with its exclusive emphasis on cause and effect that are close in time and space. The result is that most of our intuitions don't make sense—that is, they can't be explained in terms of linear logic.

Very often, experienced managers have rich intuitions about complex systems, which they cannot explain. Their intuitions tell them that cause and effect are not close in time and space, that obvious solutions will produce more harm than good, and that short-term fixes produce long-term problems. But they cannot explain their ideas in simple linear cause-effect language. They end up saying, "Just do it this way. It will work."

For example, many managers sense the dangers of eroding goals or standards but cannot fully explain how they create a reinforcing tendency to underinvest and a self-fulfilling prophecy of underrealized market growth. Or, managers may feel that they are focusing on tangible, easily measured indicators of performance and masking deeper problems, and even exacerbating these problems. But they cannot explain convincingly why these are the wrong performance indicators or how alternatives might produce improved results. Both of these intuitions can be explained when the underlying systemic structures are understood.

The conflict between intuition and linear, nonsystemic thinking has planted the seed that *rationality* itself is opposed to intuition. This view is demonstrably false if we consider the synergy of reason and intuition that characterizes virtually all great thinkers. Einstein said, "I never discovered anything with my rational mind." He once described how he discovered the principle of relativity by imagining himself traveling on a light beam. Yet, he could also take brilliant intuitions and convert them into succinct, rationally testable propositions.

As managers gain facility with systems thinking as an alternative language, they find that many of their intuitions become explicable. Eventually, reintegrating reason and intuition may prove to be one of the primary contributions of systems thinking.

SEEING OUR CONNECTEDNESS TO THE WORLD

When he was just six weeks old, our son Ian did not yet seem to know his hands and feet. I suspect that he was aware of them, but he was clearly not aware that they were *his* hands and feet, or that he could control their actions. One day, he got caught in a terrible reinforcing feedback loop. He had taken hold of his ear with his left hand. It was clearly agitating him, as you could tell from his pained expression and increasing flagellations. But, as a result of being agitated, he pulled harder. This increased his discomfort, which led him to get more agitated and pull still harder. The poor little guy might have kept going like this for some time if I hadn't detached his hand and quieted him down.

Not knowing that his hand was actually within his control, he perceived the source of his discomfort as an external force. Sound familiar? Ian's plight was really no different from the beer game players of Chapter 3, who reacted to suppliers' delivery times as if they were external forces, or the arms race participants in Chapter 5 ("A Shift of Mind") who reacted to each other's arms buildups as if they had no power to change them.

As I thought about Ian, I began to think that a neglected dimension of personal growth lies in "closing the loops"—in continually discovering how apparent external forces are actually interrelated with our own actions. Fairly soon, Ian will recognize his feet and hands and learn he can control their motions. Then he will discover that he can control his body position—if it is unpleasant on his back, he can roll over. Then will come internal states such as temperature, and the realization that they can be influenced by moving closer or further from a heat source such as Mommy or Daddy. Eventually comes Mommy and Daddy themselves, and the realization that their actions and emotions are subject to his influence. At each stage in this progression, there will be corresponding adjustments in his internal pictures of reality, which will steadily change to incorporate more of the feedback from his actions to the conditions in his life.

But for most of us, sometime early in life this process of closing the loops is arrested. As we get older, our rate of discovery slows down; we see fewer and fewer new links between our actions and external forces. We become locked into ways of looking at the world that are, fundamentally, no different from little Ian's.

The learning process of the young child provides a beautiful metaphor for the learning challenge faced by us all: to continually expand our awareness and understanding, to see more and more of the interdependencies between actions and our reality, to see more and more of our connectedness to the world around us. We will probably never perceive fully the multiple ways in which we influence our reality. But simply being open to the possibility is enough to free our thinking.

Einstein expressed the learning challenge when he said:

[the human being] experiences himself, his thoughts and feelings as something separated from the rest—a kind of optical delusion of our consciousness. This delusion is a kind of prison for us, restricting us to our personal desires and to affection for a few persons nearest to us. Our task must be to free ourselves from this prison by widening our circle of compassion to embrace all living creatures and the whole of nature in its beauty.

The experience of increasing connectedness which Einstein describes is one of the subtlest aspects of personal mastery, one that derives most directly from the systems perspective. His "widening . . . circle of compassion" is another.

COMPASSION

The discipline of seeing interrelationships gradually undermines older attitudes of blame and guilt. We begin to see that *all of us* are trapped in structures, structures embedded both in our ways of thinking and in the interpersonal and social milieus in which we live. Our knee-jerk tendencies to find fault with one another gradually fade, leaving a much deeper appreciation of the forces within which we all operate.

This does not imply that people are simply victims of systems that dictate their behavior. Often, the structures are of our own creation. But this has little meaning until those structures are seen. For most of us, the structures within which we operate are invisible. We are neither victims nor culprits but human beings controlled by forces we have not yet learned how to perceive.

We are used to thinking of compassion as an emotional state, based on our concern for one another. But it is also grounded in a level of awareness. In my experience, as people see more of the systems within which they operate, and as they understand more clearly the pressures influencing one another, they naturally develop more compassion and empathy.

COMMITMENT TO THE WHOLE

"Genuine commitment," according to Bill O'Brien, "is always to something larger than ourselves." Inamori talks about "action of our heart," when we are guided by "sincere desire to serve the world." Such action, he says, "is a very important issue since it has great power."

The sense of connectedness and compassion characteristic of individuals with high levels of personal mastery naturally leads to a broader vision. Without it, all the subconscious visualizing in the world is deeply self-centered—simply a way to get what I want.

Individuals committed to a vision beyond their self-interest find they have energy not available when pursuing narrower goals, as will organizations that tap this level of commitment. "I do not believe there has been a single person who has made a worthwhile discovery or invention," Inamori states, "who has not experienced a spiritual power." He describes the will of a person committed to a larger purpose as "a cry from the soul which has been shaken and awakened."

FOSTERING PERSONAL MASTERY IN AN ORGANIZATION

It must always be remembered that embarking on any path of personal growth is a matter of choice. No one can be forced to develop his or her personal mastery. It is guaranteed to backfire. Organizations can get into considerable difficulty if they become too aggressive in promoting personal mastery for their members.

Still many have attempted to do just that by creating compulsory internal personal growth training programs. However well intentioned, such programs are probably the most sure-fire way to impede the genuine spread of commitment to personal mastery in an organization. Compulsory training, or "elective" programs that people feel expected to attend if they want to advance their careers, conflict directly with freedom of choice.

For example, there have been numerous instances of overzealous managers requiring employees to participate in personal development training, which the employees regarded as contradictory to their own religious beliefs. Several of these have resulted in legal action against the organization.[20]

What then can leaders intent on fostering personal mastery do?

They can work relentlessly to foster a climate in which the principles of personal mastery are practiced in daily life. That means building an organization where it is safe for people to create visions, where inquiry and commitment to the truth are the norm, and where challenging the status quo is expected—especially when the status quo includes obscuring aspects of current reality that people seek to avoid.

Such an organizational climate will strengthen personal mastery in two ways. First, it will continually reinforce the idea that personal growth is truly valued in the organization. Second, to the extent that individuals respond to what is offered, it will provide an "on the job training" that is vital to developing personal mastery. As with any discipline, developing personal mastery must become a continual, ongoing process. There is nothing more important to an individual committed to his or her own growth than a supportive environment. An organization committed to personal mastery can provide that environment by continually encouraging personal vision, commitment to the truth, and a willingness to face honestly the gaps between the two.

Many of the practices most conducive to developing one's own personal mastery—developing a more systemic worldview, learning how to reflect on tacit assumptions, expressing one's vision and listening to others' visions, and joint inquiry into different people's views of current reality—are embedded in the disciplines for building learning organizations. So, in many ways, the most positive actions that an organization can take to foster personal mastery involve working to develop all five learning disciplines in concert.

The core leadership strategy is simple: be a model. Commit yourself to your own personal mastery. Talking about personal mastery may open people's minds somewhat, but actions always speak louder than words. There's nothing more powerful you can do to encourage others in their quest for personal mastery than to be serious in your own quest. And keep reminding yourself, in the words of MIT Sloan School professor Edgard Schein, that organizations are by their nature "coercive systems."

9

MENTAL MODELS

WHY THE BEST IDEAS FAIL

One thing all managers know is that many of the best ideas never get put into practice. Brilliant strategies fail to get translated into action. Systemic insights never find their way into operating policies. A pilot experiment may prove to everyone's satisfaction that a new approach leads to better results, but widespread adoption of the approach never occurs.

We are coming increasingly to believe that this "slip 'twixt cup and lip" stems, not from weak intentions, wavering will, or even nonsystemic understanding, but from *mental models*. More specifically, new insights fail to get put into practice because they conflict with deeply held internal images of how the world works, images that limit us to familiar ways of thinking and acting. That is why the discipline of managing mental models—surfacing, testing, and improving our internal pictures of how the world works—promises to be a major breakthrough for building learning organizations.

None of us can carry an organization in our minds—or a family, or a community. What we carry in our heads are images, assumptions, and stories. Philosophers have discussed mental models for centuries, going back at least to Plato's parable of the cave. "The Emperor's New Clothes" is a classic story, not about fatuous people, but about people bound by mental models. Their image of the monarch's dignity kept them from seeing his naked figure as it was.

In surveying the accomplishments of cognitive science in his book *The Mind's New Science,* Howard Gardner writes, "To my mind, the major accomplishment of cognitive science has been the clear demonstration of . . . a level of mental representation" active in diverse aspects of human behavior.[1] Our "mental models" determine not only how we make sense of the world, but how we take action. Harvard's Chris Argyris, who has worked with mental models and organizational learning for forty years, puts it this way: "Although people do not [always] behave congruently with their espoused theories [what they say], they do behave congruently with their theories-in-use [their mental models]."[2]

Mental models can be simple generalizations such as "people are untrustworthy," or they can be complex theories, such as my assumptions about why members of my family interact as they do. But what is most important to grasp is that mental models are active—they shape how we act. If we believe people are untrustworthy, we act differently from the way we would if we believed they were trustworthy. If I believe that my son lacks self-confidence and my daughter is highly aggressive, I will continually intervene in their exchanges to prevent her from damaging his ego.

Why are mental models so powerful in affecting what we do? In part, because they affect what we see. Two people with different mental models can observe the same event and describe it differently, because they've looked at different details and made different interpretations. When you and I walk into a crowded party, we both take in the same basic sensory data, but we pick out different faces. As psychologists say, we observe selectively. This is no less true for supposedly "objective" observers such as scientists than for people in general. As Albert Einstein once wrote, "Our theories determine what we measure." For years, physicists ran experiments that contradicted classical physics, yet no one "saw" the data that these experiments eventually provided, leading to the revolutionary theories—quantum mechanics and relativity—of twentieth-century physics.[3]

The way mental models shape our perceptions is no less important in management. I will never forget visiting with a group of Detroit auto executives after their first factory visits to Japan over twenty years ago. This was right around the time that US automakers were finally waking up to the fact that Japan was steadily gaining market and profit share in their industry—and it might be attributed to how they managed, not just because they had "cheap" labor or protected home markets. A little way into the conversation, it was clear that the Detroit executives were unimpressed. I asked why and one said, "They didn't show us real plants." When I inquired as to what he meant by this, he responded "There were no inventories in any of the plants. I've been in manufacturing operations for almost thirty years and I can tell you those were not real plants. They had clearly been staged for our tour." Today we all know that they were indeed real plants, examples of the "Just-in-time" inventory systems that the Japanese had been working on for many years that dramatically reduced the need for in-process inventories throughout the manufacturing system. Within a few years these same US firms would be racing desperately to catch up to these manufacturing innovations . . . but that evening the Detroit execs had not seen anything to alarm them.

Or consider the customer belief that dominated the Big Three of Detroit for decades (and many feel still does)—that American consumers mostly cared about styling. According to management consultant Ian Mitroff, these beliefs about styling were part of a pervasive set of long-standing and unquestioned assumptions for success at General Motors:[4]

GM is in the business of making money, not cars.

Cars are primarily status symbols. Styling is therefore more important than quality.

The American car market is isolated from the rest of the world.

Workers do not have an important impact on productivity or product quality.

Everyone connected with the system has no need for more than a fragmented, compartmentalized understanding of the business.

The point here is not that GM or the Detroit industry in general were wrong. As Mitroff points out, these principles had served the industry well for many years. But the industry treated these principles as "a magic formula for success for all time, when all it had found was a particular set of conditions . . . that were good for a limited time."

The problems with mental models lie not in whether they are right or wrong—by definition, all models are simplifications. The problems with mental models arise when they become implicit— when they exist below the level of our awareness. The Detroit automakers didn't say, "We have a *mental model* that all people care about is styling." They said, "All people care about is styling." Because we remain unaware of our mental models, the models remain unexamined. Because they are unexamined, the models remain unchanged. As the world changes, the gap widens between our mental models and reality, leading to increasingly counterproductive actions.[5]

As the Detroit automakers demonstrated, entire industries can develop chronic misfits between mental models and reality. In some ways, close-knit industries are especially vulnerable because all the member companies look to each other for standards of best practice.

Failure to appreciate mental models has undermined many efforts to foster systems thinking. In a classic study many years ago, a leading American industrial goods manufacturer—the largest in its industry—found itself steadily losing market share. Hoping to analyze their situation, top executives sought help from an MIT team of system dynamics specialists. Based on computer models, the team concluded that the firm's problems stemmed from the way its executives managed inventories and production. Because it cost so much to store its bulky, expensive products, production managers held inventories as low as possible and aggressively cut back production whenever orders turned down. The result was unreliable and slow delivery, even when production capacity was adequate. In fact, the team's computer simulations predicted that deliveries would lag further during business downturns than during booms— a prediction which ran counter to conventional wisdom, but which turned out to be true.

Impressed, the firm's top executives put into effect a new policy based on the analysts' recommendations. From now on, when orders fell, they would maintain production rates and try to improve delivery performance. During a modest business downturn the following year, the experiment worked beyond anyone's expectations; thanks to prompter deliveries and more repeat buying from satisfied customers, the firm's market share increased during the downturn. The managers were so pleased that they set up their own internal systems group. But the new policies were never taken to heart, and the improvement proved temporary. During the ensuing business recovery, the managers stopped worrying about delivery service. Four years later, when a more severe recession hit, the company went back to their original policy of dramatic production cutbacks.

Why discard such a successful experiment? The reason was the mental models deeply embedded in the firm's management traditions. Every production manager knew that there was no more sure-fire way to destroy one's career than to be held responsible for stockpiling unsold goods in the warehouse. Generations of top management had preached the gospel of commitment to inventory control. Despite the new experiment, the old mental model was still alive and well.

The inertia of deeply entrenched mental models can overwhelm even the best systemic insights. This has been a bitter lesson for many a purveyor of new management tools, not only for systems thinking advocates.

But if mental models can *impede* learning—freezing companies and industries in outmoded practices—why can't they also help *accelerate* learning? This simple question became, over time, the impetus for the discipline of bringing mental models to the surface and challenging them so they can be improved.

INCUBATING A NEW BUSINESS WORLDVIEW

Perhaps the first large corporation to discover the power of mental models in learning was Royal Dutch/Shell. Although the origins of this story go back a quarter century, Shell's journey to develop ways of building consensus in a global, multi-cultural business are still instructive today. The story starts just prior to the historic turbulence of the world oil business that began with the formation of OPEC.

From its beginnings, Shell was multi-cultural: the firm was formed originally in 1907 from a "gentleman's agreement" between Royal Dutch Petroleum and the London-based Shell Transport and

Trading Company. Consequently, Shell managers had developed a self-described "consensus-style" of management respectful of differing cultural perspectives. But as the company grew to more than a hundred operating companies around the world, led by managers from almost as many different cultures, people found themselves trying to build consensus across vast gulfs of style and understanding.

In 1972, one year before OPEC, but Shell's scenario planning group had already concluded that the stable, predictable world familiar to Shell's managers was about to change—in ways that influence corporate strategies and global geo-politics still today. After analyzing long-term trends of oil production and consumption, senior planner Pierre Wack and his team could see that Europe, Japan, and the U.S. were becoming increasingly dependent on oil imports, and that these came from a small number of oil-exporting countries. Although diverse culturally and politically, they had some important things in common. Iran, Iraq, Libya, and Venezuela were becoming increasingly concerned with falling reserves. Saudi Arabia,on the other hand, was reaching the limits of its ability to productively invest oil revenues. In other words, all were gaining economic power as large producers and all had a motivation to limit production. To the Shell planners, these trends meant that the historical, smooth growth in oil demand and supply would eventually give way to chronic supply shortfalls, excess demand, and a "seller's market" controlled by the oil-exporting nations. While Shell's planners did not predict the OPEC cartel per se, they foresaw the types of changes that OPEC would eventually bring about. Yet, attempts to impress upon Shell's managers the radical shifts ahead largely failed.

In principle, Shell's "Group Planning" staff were in an ideal position to disseminate insights about the changes ahead. Group Planning was the central planning department, responsible for coordinating planning activities in operating companies worldwide. At the time, Group Planning was developing scenario planning as a practical method for summarizing alternative future trends. The planners at Shell began to build the coming discontinuities into their scenarios. But their audience of Shell managers found these new scenarios so contradictory to their years of experience with predictable growth that they paid little attention to them.

At this point, Wack and his colleagues realized that they had fundamentally misperceived their task. In a famous *Harvard Business Review* article he wrote over a decade later, Wack said that, from that moment, "We no longer saw our task as producing a documented view of the future . . . Our real target was the 'microcosms' our decision makers . . . Unless we influenced the mental image, the picture of reality held by critical decision-makers, our scenarios would be like water on a stone."[6] If the planners had once thought their job was delivering information to the decision makers, it was now clear that their task was to help managers rethink their worldview. In particular, the Group Planners developed a new set of scenarios in January and February, 1973 which forced the managers to identify all of the assumptions that had to be true in order for the managers' "trouble-free" future to occur. This revealed a set of assumptions only slightly more likely to come true than a fairy tale.

Group Planning now built a new set of scenarios, carefully designed to take off from the current mental models of Shell managers. Then they helped managers begin the process of constructing a new mental model—by helping them think through how they would have to manage in this new world. For example, exploration for oil would have to expand to new countries, while refinery building would have to slow down because of higher prices and consequently slower demand growth. Also, with greater instability, nations would respond differently. Some, with free-market traditions, would let the price rise freely; others with controlled-market policies, would try to keep it low. Thus, control to Shell's locally based operating companies would have to increase to enable them to adapt to local conditions.

Although many Shell managers remained skeptical, they took the new scenarios seriously because they began to see that their present understandings were untenable. The exercise had begun to unfreeze managers' mental models and incubate a new worldview.

When the OPEC oil embargo suddenly became a reality in the winter of 1973–74, Shell responded differently from the other major oil companies. They slowed down their investments in refineries, and designed refineries that could adapt to whatever type of crude oil was available. They forecast energy demand at a consistently lower level than their competitors did, and consistently more accurately. They quickly accelerated development of oil fields outside OPEC.

While competitors reined in their divisions and increased centralized control—a common response to crisis—Shell did the opposite. This gave their operating companies more room to maneuver.

Shell's managers responded differently because they interpreted their reality differently. They saw themselves entering a new era of supply shortages, lower growth, and price instability. Because they had come to expect the 1970s to be a decade of turbulence (Wack's scenarios called it the decade of "the rapids"), they responded as if the turbulence would continue. Shell had discovered the power of managing mental models.

The net result of Shell's efforts was a significant shift in business fortunes. In 1970, Shell had been considered the weakest of the seven largest oil companies. Forbes called it the "Ugly Sister" of the "Seven Sisters." By 1979 it was perhaps the strongest; certainly it and Exxon were in a class by themselves.[7] By the early 1980s, bringing managers' mental models to the surface was an important part of the planning process at Shell. About a half-year prior to the collapse of oil prices in 1986, Group Planning, under the direction of coordinator Arie de Geus, produced a fictitious *Harvard Business School*-style case study of an oil company coping with a sudden world oil glut. Managers had to critique the oil company's decisions and in doing prepare themselves mentally for another dramatic shift in their reality. Two years later, a similar exercise was conducted around the fall of the Soviet Union, two years before this too became a reality.

Learning how to work with mental models was a key element in BP's rapid rise during the last fifteen years to the number two ranked global oil company in sales and volume (after Exxon), although their approach was very different from Shell's. At BP the vehicle was not a centralized planning staff, as had been the case at Shell, but a fervent commitment to distribute decision-making power and authority.

By the late 1990s, BP had one hundred and fifty local profit centers, and business unit mangers had much greater authority. "We were all familiar with Shell's use of scenarios to foster challenging mental models," says CIO and Group VP John Leggate. "But the way they did it through the central planning function did not seem to be the way we wanted to go. John Browne (BP's CEO since 1995) was passionate about building a performance culture and this meant that more people had to have bottom-line business accountability and think issues through for themselves. Pushing down profit-and-loss responsibility can be hard to do in a large highly integrated business like ours, but we gradually succeeded. The danger of distributing power well is that you become fragmented, which makes ensuring that learning occurs across the business difficult.

"What has helped prevent that from happening here are the variety of networks we've developed to keep connecting people, and a climate of openly talking about our problems and challenging each other's thinking. Continually questioning ourselves has become the basis for our discipline of mental models—though we have never used that terminology extensively."

WORKING WITH MENTAL MODELS IN PRACTICE

The Shell and BP stories suggest three facets to developing an organization's capacity to surface and test mental models: tools that promote personal awareness and reflective skills, "infrastructures" that try to institutionalize regular practice with mental models, and a culture that promotes inquiry and challenging our thinking. It is hard to say which is most important. Indeed, it is the connections among them that matter most. For example, it is one thing to espouse cultural norms like "openness" but practicing them requires real commitment and skills that many managers lack, and developing those skills requires regular opportunities to practice, the whole point of infrastructures that embed reflection in the work environment.

OVERCOMING "THE BASIC DISEASES OF THE HIERARCHY"

Not surprisingly, CEOs tend to emphasize developing the organizational culture. "In the traditional authoritarian organization, the dogma was managing, organizing, and controlling," says Hanover's CEO Bill O'Brien. "In the learning organization, the new 'dogma' will be vision, values, and mental models. The healthy corporations will be ones which can systematize ways to bring people together to develop the best possible mental models for facing any situation at hand." O'Brien thought about cultural change in terms of basic "diseases of traditional hierarchies" and the required antidotes. "We set out," he said, "to find what would give the necessary organization and discipline to have work be more congruent with human nature. We gradually identified a set of core values that are actually principles that overcome the basic diseases of the hierarchy."

Two of these values in particular, "openness" and "merit," led Hanover to develop its approach to "managing mental models." Openness was seen as an antidote to "the disease of gamesplaying that dominated people's behavior in face-to-face meetings. Nobody described an issue at 10:00 in the morning at a business meeting the way they described the issue at 7:00 that evening, at home or over drinks with friends." Merit—making decisions based on the best interests of the organization—was Hanover's antidote to "decision-making based on bureaucratic politics, where the name of the game is getting ahead by making an impression, or, if you're already at the top, staying there."[8] Together openness and merit embodied a deep belief that decision-making processes could be transformed if people become more able to surface and discuss productively their different ways of looking at the world.

But articulating these values was but a first step. While some confuse value statements with cultural change, O'Brien and his colleagues could see that impressive words were not enough. "If openness and merit were so useful," they asked, "why did they seem so difficult?"

This question eventually led O'Brien to Chris Argyris, whose writings resonated with Hanover's managers' experience. Argyris's "action science," offered theory and method for examining "the reasoning that underlies our actions."[9] Teams and organizations trap themselves, he says, in "defensive routines" that insulate our mental models from examination. Consequently we develop "skilled incompetence,"a marvelous oxymoron to describe being "highly skillful at protecting ourselves from pain and threat posed by learning situations," but because we fail to learn we remain incompetent at producing the results we really want. Most importantly, Argyris had developed tools designed to be effective in organizations and was a masterful facilitator in their use.

About this same time, I found this out for myself when when we invited Argyris to do a workshop with a half-dozen members of our research team at MIT. Ostensibly an academic presentation of Argyris's methods, it quickly evolved into a powerful demonstration of what action science practitioners call "reflection in action." He asked each of us to recount a conflict with a client, colleague, or family member. We had to recall not only what was said, but what we were thinking and did not say. As he began to work with these "cases" it became almost immediately apparent how each of us contributed to the conflict through our own thinking. For example, we all made sweeping generalizations about the others that determined what we said and how we behaved. Yet, we never communicated the generalizations. I might think, "Joe believes I'm incompetent," but I would never ask Joe directly about it. I would simply go out of my way to try continually to make myself look respectable to Joe. Or, "Bill [my boss] is impatient and believes in quick and dirty solutions," so I go out of my way to give him simple solutions even though I don't think they will really get to the heart of difficult issues.

Within a matter of minutes, literally, I watched the level of alertness and "presentness" of the entire group rise ten notches—thanks not so much to Argyris's personal charisma, but to his skillful way of getting each of us to see for ourselves how we got in trouble and then blamed it on others. As the afternoon moved on, all of us were led to see (sometimes for the first time in our lives) subtle patterns of reasoning which underlay our behavior; and how those patterns continually got us stuck. I had never had such a dramatic demonstration of my own mental models in action. But even more interesting, it became clear that, with proper training, I could become much more aware of my mental models and how they operated. This was exciting.

From their work with Argyris and his colleague Lee Bolman, O'Brien realized that, "Despite our philosophy, we had a very long way to go to being able to have the types of open, productive discussion about critical issues that we all desired. In some cases, Argyris' work revealed painfully obvious gamesplaying that we had come to accept. Chris held an incredibly high standard of real openness, of seeing our own thinking and cutting the crap. Yet, he was also not simply advocating "tell everyone everything"—he was illustrating the skills of engaging difficult issues so that everyone learned. Clearly, this was important new territory if we were really going to live our core values of openness and merit."

In the ensuing years, Hanover integrated training in Argyris' tools with a workshop on the "limitations of mechanistic thinking" developed by philosopher, John Beckett. "Beckett showed," says O'Brien, "that if you look closely at how Eastern cultures approach basic moral, ethical, and managerial issues, they do make sense. Then he shows that Western ways of approaching these issues also make sense. But the two can lead to opposite conclusions. This leads to discovering that there is more than one way to look at complex issues. It helped enormously in breaking down the walls between the disciplines in our company, and between different ways of thinking." The two combined to have a profound impact on many managers' understanding of mental models. "Many saw for the first time in their life that all we ever have are assumptions, never "truths," that we always see the world through our mental models and that the mental models are always incomplete, and, especially in Western culture, chronically nonsystemic."

BP has followed a somewhat similar path of broad training, reaching over 5000 "First Level Leaders" in three years with a four-day program that includes the basics of personal mastery and working with mental models. "We have tried to make the tools and ideas of organizational learning part of our basic ways of managing," says Leggate. The "pacesetter program," aimed at developing networks of refinery managers who could share best practices, help one another, and learn collectively "was our first major cross-border network capacity-building effort, and it showed us that people appreciated and could use these tools. Since then, similar introductions have occurred throughout the organization."

INSTITUTIONALIZING PRACTICE

Obviously, introductory training, no matter how broadly available, needs to be followed by the opportunity to practice regularly and build skills. I have seen many ways to institutionalize reflection and surfacing mental models through "infrastructures" that make these part of regular management practice. (Chapter 14, "Strategies," gives an extended description of learning infrastructures.)

Shell's approach was to institutionalize working with mental models through its planning process. De Geus, as coordinator of Group Planning, and his colleagues sought to rethink the role of planning in large institutions. It is less important, they concluded, to produce perfect plans than to use planning to force managers to think about their assumptions and thereby accelerate learning as a whole. Long-term success, according to De Geus, depends on, "the process whereby management teams change their shared mental models of their company, their markets, and their competitors. For this reason we think of planning as learning and of corporate planning as institutional learning."

Hanover instituted "internal boards of directors" to bring senior management and local management together regularly to challenge and expand the thinking behind business unit decision making. The aim was to create a management structure that would foster open examination of key assumptions about important business issues at the business unit level, and also foster more interaction among senior managers who compromised the boards around these issues.

Harley-Davidson likewise made changes in management structures, but they implemented a radically different top management structure—in part to make working with mental models part of managerial work. Around the same time that many Harley managers were learning the basics of organizational learning through introductory SoL (Society for Organizational Learning) workshops, they created their "circle organization," re-conceiving traditional top management roles in terms of three overlapping circles of activity: "create demand," "produce product," and "provide support." These circles intentionally blurred the traditional top management hierarchy, and led to many "bosses" becoming "circle coaches."

"One of the most exciting innovations of our new structure was 'the circle coach'," says Rich Teerlink, former CEO. The circle coach was typically someone who would otherwise have been a VP of a fragmented function, like product development or manufacturing. In their concept of the job, the Harley managers envisioned the circle coach as someone who would "possess acute communication, listening, and influencing skills, and would be highly regarded by all the circle members and by the motor company president." "We didn't put it in writing at the time because we didn't want it to sound jargonny," says Teerlink, "but we had in mind that the circle coach would facilitate getting people's different mental models into the open, and indeed it has been very effective in doing so."

TOOLS AND SKILLS

Though Shell, BP, Hanover, and Harley-Davidson took very different approaches to developing capacity to work with mental models, their work involved developing skills in two broad categories: skills of reflection and skills of inquiry. Skills of reflection concern slowing down our own thinking processes so that we can become more aware of how we form our mental models and the ways they influence our actions. Inquiry skills concern how we operate in face-to-face interactions with others, especially in dealing with complex and conflictual issues. Together with the tools and methods used to develop these skills these constitute the core of the discipline of mental models:

- Facing up to distinctions between espoused theories (what we say) and theories-in-use (the implied theory in what we do)
- Recognizing "leaps of abstraction" (noticing our jumps from observation to generalization)
- Exposing the "left-hand column" (articulating what we normally do not say)
- Balancing inquiry and advocacy (skills for effective collaborative learning)

THE DISCIPLINE OF MENTAL MODELS

REFLECTIVE PRACTICE

Though highly personal at one level, effective work with mental models is also pragmatic, that is, it is tied to bringing key assumptions about important business issues to the surface. This is vital because the most crucial mental models in any organization are those shared by key decision makers. Those models, if unexamined, limit an organization's range of actions to what is familiar and comfortable. Second, managers themselves, not just consultants or advisors, have to develop reflective and the face-to-face learning skills, or else there will be little impact on actual decisions and actions.

Argyris's longtime colleague Donald Schon of MIT studied the importance of reflection in professions including medicine, architecture, and management. While many professionals seem to stop learning as soon as they leave graduate school, those who become lifelong learners become what he calls "reflective practitioners." The ability to reflect on one's thinking while acting, for Schon, distinguishes the truly outstanding professionals:

Phrases like "thinking on your feet," "keeping your wits about you," and "learning by doing" suggest not only that we can think about doing but that we can think about doing something while doing it . . . When good jazz musicians improvise together . . . they feel the direction of the music that is developing out of their interwoven contributions, and they make new sense of it and adjust their performance to the new sense they have made.[10]

Reflective practice is the essence of the discipline of mental models. For managers this requires both business skills and reflective and interpersonal skills. Because managers are inherently pragmatic, training them in "mental modeling" or "balancing inquiry and advocacy," with no connection to pressing business issues, will usually be rejected. Or, it will lead to people having "academic" skills they do not use. On the other hand, without reflective and interpersonal learning skills, learning is inevitably reactive, not generative. Generative learning, in my experience, requires people at all levels who can surface and challenge their mental models before external circumstances compel them to do so.

ESPOUSED THEORY VERSUS THEORY-IN-USE

Learning is eventually always about action, and one basic reflective skill involves using gaps between what we say and what we do as a vehicle for becoming more aware. For example, I may profess a view (an espoused theory) that people are basically trustworthy. But I never lend friends money and jealously guard all my possessions. Obviously, my theory-in-use, my deeper mental model, differs from my espoused theory.

While gaps between espoused theories and theories-in-use might be cause for discouragement, or even cynicism, they needn't be. Often they arise as a consequence of vision, not hypocrisy. For example, it may be truly part of my vision to trust people. Then, a gap between this aspect of my vision and my current behavior holds the potential for creative change. The problem lies not in the gap but, as was discussed in Chapter 8, "Personal Mastery," in failing to tell the truth about the gap. Until the gap between my espoused theory and my current behavior is recognized, no learning can occur.

So the first question to pose when facing a gap between espoused theory and a theory-in-use is "Do I really value the espoused theory?" "Is it really part of my vision?" If there is no commitment to the espoused theory, then the gap does not represent a tension between reality and my vision but between reality and a view I advance (perhaps because of how it will make me look to others).

Because it's so hard to see theories-in-use, you may need the help of another person—a "ruthlessly compassionate" partner. In the quest to develop skills in reflection, we are each others' greatest assets. As the old saying goes, "The eye cannot see the eye."

Leaps of Abstraction. Our minds move at lightning speed. Ironically, this often slows our learning, because we immediately "leap" to generalizations so quickly that we never think to test them. The proverbial "castles in the sky" describes our own thinking far more often than we realize.

The conscious mind is ill-equipped to deal with large numbers of concrete details. If shown photographs of a hundred individuals, most of us will have trouble remembering each face, but we will remember categories—such as tall men, or women in red, or Asians, or the elderly. Psychologist George Miller's famous "magic number seven plus or minus two" referred to our tendency to focus on a limited number of separate variables at any one time.[11] Our rational minds are extraordinarily facile at "abstracting" from concrete particulars—substituting simple concepts for many details and then reasoning in terms of these concepts. But our very strengths in abstract conceptual reasoning also limit our learning, when we are unaware of our leaps from particulars to general concepts.

For example, have you ever heard a statement such as, "Laura doesn't care about people," and wondered about its validity? Imagine that Laura is a superior or colleague who has some particular habits that others have noted. She rarely offers generous praise. She often stares off into space when people talk to her, and then asks, "What did you say?" She sometimes cuts people off when they speak. She never comes to office parties. And in performance reviews, she mutters two or three sentences and then dismisses the person. From these particular behaviors, Laura's colleagues have concluded that she doesn't care much about people. It's been common knowledge—except, of course, for Laura, who feels that she cares very much about people.

What has happened to Laura is that her colleagues have made a leap of abstraction. They have substituted a generalization, "not caring about people" for many specific behaviors. More importantly, they have begun to treat this generalization as *fact*. No one questions whether or not Laura cares about people. It is a given.

Leaps of abstraction occur when we move from direct observations (concrete "data") to generalization without testing. Leaps of abstraction impede learning because they become axiomatic. What was once an assumption becomes treated as a fact. Once Laura's colleagues accept as fact that she doesn't care about people, no one questions her behavior when she does things that are "noncaring," and no one notices when she does something that doesn't fit the stereotype. The general view that she doesn't care leads people to treat her with greater indifference, which takes away any opportunity she might have had to exhibit more caring. The result is that Laura and her colleagues are frozen in a state of affairs that no one desires. Moreover, untested generalizations can easily become the basis for further generalization. "Could Laura have been the one behind that office intrigue? She's probably the sort who would do that sort of thing given that she doesn't care much about people . . ."

Laura's colleagues, like most of us, are not disciplined in distinguishing what they observe directly from the generalizations they infer from their observations. There are "facts"—observable data about Laura—such as the time spent in a typical performance review or looking away during a conversation. But "Laura doesn't listen much" is a generalization not a fact, as is "Laura doesn't care much." Both may be based on facts, but they are inferences nonetheless. Failing to distinguish direct observation from generalizations inferred from observation leads us never to think to test the generalization. So no one ever asked Laura whether or not she cares. If they had, they might have found out that, in her mind, she does care very much. They also might have learned that she has a hearing impediment that she hasn't told anyone about and, largely because of that, she is painfully shy in conversations.

Leaps of abstraction are just as common with business issues. At one firm, many top managers were convinced that "Customers buy products based on price; the quality of service isn't a factor." And it's no wonder they felt that way; customers continually pressed for deeper discounts, and competitors were continually attracting away customers with price promotions. When one marketer who was new to the company urged his superiors to invest in improving service, he was turned down kindly but firmly. The senior leaders never tested the idea, because their leap of abstraction had become a "fact"—that "customers don't care about service, customers buy based on price." They sat and watched while their leading competitor steadily increased its market share by providing a level of service quality that customers had never experienced, and therefore had never asked for.

How do you spot leaps of abstraction? First, by asking yourself what you believe about the way the world works—the nature of business, people in general, and specific individuals. Ask "What is the 'data' on which this generalization is based?" Then ask yourself, "Am I willing to consider that this generalization may be inaccurate or misleading?" It is important to ask this last question consciously, because, if the answer is no, there is no point in proceeding.

If you are willing to question a generalization, explicitly separate it from the "data" which led to it. "Paul Smith, the purchaser for Bailey's Shoes, and several other customers have told me they won't buy our product unless we lower the price 10 percent," you might say. "Thus, I conclude that our customers don't care about service quality." This puts all your cards on the table and gives you, and others, a better opportunity to consider alternative interpretations and courses of action.

Where possible, test the generalizations directly. This will often lead to inquiring into the reasons behind one another's actions. Such inquiry requires skills that will be discussed below. For example, just coming up to Laura and asking, "Don't you care very much about people?" is likely to evoke a defensive reaction. There are ways of approaching such exchanges, through owning up to our assumptions about others and citing the data upon which they are based, that reduce the chances of defensiveness.

But until we become aware of our leaps of abstraction, we are not even aware of the need for inquiry. This is precisely why practicing reflection as a discipline is so important. A second technique from action science, the "left-hand column," is especially useful in both starting and deepening this discipline.

Left-Hand Column. This is a powerful technique for beginning to "see" how our mental models operate in particular situations. It reveals ways that we manipulate situations to avoid dealing with how we actually think and feel, and thereby prevent a counterproductive situation from improving.

The left-hand column exercise can show managers that, indeed, they have mental models and those models play an active, sometimes unwelcome part in management practice. Once a group of managers have gone through the exercises, not only are they aware of the role of their mental models but they begin to see why dealing with their assumptions more forthrightly is important.

The "left-hand column" comes from a type of case presentation used by Chris Argyris and his colleagues. It starts with selecting a specific situation where I am interacting with one or several other people in a way that I feel is not working—specifically, that is not producing any apparent learning or moving ahead. I write out a sample of the exchange, in the form of a script. I write the script on the right-hand side of a page. On the left-hand side, I write what I am thinking but not saying at each stage in the exchange.

For example, imagine an exchange with a colleague, Bill, after a big presentation to our boss on a project we are doing together. I had to miss the presentation, but I've heard that it was poorly received.

ME: How did the presentation go?

BILL: Well, I don't know. It's really too early to say. Besides, we're breaking new ground here.

ME: Well, what do you think we should do? I believe that the issues you were raising are important.

BILL: I'm not so sure. Let's just wait and see what happens.

ME: You may be right, but I think we may need to do more than just wait.

The following page shows what the exchange looks like with my "left-hand column."

The left-hand column exercise always succeeds in bringing hidden assumptions to the surface and showing how they influence behavior. In the above example, I am making two key assumptions about Bill: he lacks confidence, especially in regard to facing up to his poor performance; and he lacks initiative. Neither may be literally true, but both are evident in my internal dialogue and both influence the way I handle the situation. My belief in his lack of confidence shows up in my skirting the fact that I have heard that the presentation was a bomb. I'm afraid that if I say it directly, he will lose what little confidence he has, or he will not be able to face the evidence. So, I bring up the subject of the presentation obliquely. My belief in Bill's lack of initiative comes up when we discuss what to do next. He gives no specific course of action despite my question. I see this as evidence of his laziness or lack of initiative: he is content to do nothing when something definitely is required, from which I conclude that I will have to manufacture some form of pressure to motivate him into action, or else I will simply have to take matters into my own hands.

The most important lesson that comes from seeing "our left-hand columns" is how we undermine opportunities for learning in con-

WHAT I'M THINKING	WHAT IS SAID
Everyone says the presentation was a bomb.	Me: How did the presentation go?
Does he really not know how bad it was? Or is he not willing to face up to it?	Bill: Well, I don't know. It's really too early to tell. Besides, we're breaking new ground here.
He really is afraid to see the truth. It only he had more confidence, he could probably learn from a situation like this. I can't believe how disastrous that presentation was to our moving ahead.	Me: Well, what do you think we should do? I believe the issues you were raising are important.
	Bill: I'm not so sure. Let's just wait and see what happens.
I've got to find a way to light a fire under this guy.	Me: You may be right, but I think we may need to do more than just wait.

flictual situations. Rather than facing squarely our problems, Bill and I talk around the subject. Instead of determining how to move forward to resolve our problems, we end our exchange with no clear course of action—in fact, with no clear definition of a problem requiring action.

Why don't I simply tell him that I believe there is a problem? Why don't I say that we must look at steps to get our project back on track? Perhaps because I am not sure how to bring up these "delicate" issues productively. Like Laura's colleagues, I imagine that to bring them up will provoke a defensive, counterproductive exchange. I'm afraid that we'll be worse off than we are now. Perhaps I avoid the issues out of a sense of politeness or desire not to be critical. Whatever the reason, the outcome is a dissatisfying exchange and I resort to looking for a way to "manipulate" Bill into a more forceful response.

There is no one "right" way to handle difficult situations such as my exchange with Bill, but it helps enormously to see first how my own reasoning and actions can contribute to making matters worse. This is where the left-hand column technique can be useful. Once I see more clearly my own assumptions and how I may be concealing them, there are several things I might do to move the conversation forward more productively. All involve sharing my own view and the "data" upon which it is based. All require being open to the possibility that Bill may share neither the view nor the data, and that both may be wrong. (After all, my informant about the presentation may have been in error.) In effect, my task is to convert the situation into one where *both* Bill and I can learn. This requires a combination of articulating my views, and learning more about Bill's views—a process which Argyris calls "balancing inquiry and advocacy."

Balancing Inquiry and Advocacy. Most managers are trained to be advocates. In fact, in many companies, what it means to be a competent manager is to be able to solve problems—to figure out what needs to be done, and enlist whatever support is needed to get it done. Individuals became successful in part because of their abilities to debate forcefully and influence others. Inquiry skills, meanwhile, go unrecognized and unrewarded. But as managers rise to senior positions, they confront issues more complex and diverse than their personal experience. Suddenly, they need to tap insights from other people. They need to learn. Now the manager's advocacy skills become counterproductive; they can close us off from actually learning from one another. What is needed is blending advocacy and inquiry to promote collaborative learning.

Even when two advocates meet for an open, candid exchange of views, there is usually little learning. They may be genuinely interested in each other's views, but pure advocacy lends a different type of structure to the conversation:

> "I appreciate your sincerity, but my experience and judgment lead me to some different conclusions. Let me tell you why your proposal won't work . . ."

As each side reasonably and calmly advocates his viewpoint just a bit more strongly, positions become more and more rigid. Advocacy without inquiry begets more advocacy. In fact, there is a systems archetype that describes what happens next; called "escalation," it's the same structure as an arms race.

The more vehemently A argues, the greater the threat to B. Thus, B argues more fiercely. Then A counterargues even more fiercely.

And so on. Managers often find escalations so grueling that, thereafter, they avoid stating any differences publicly. "It's just too much grief."

The snowball effect of reinforcing advocacy can be stopped, by beginning to ask a few questions. Simple questions such as, "What is it that leads you to that position?" and "Can you illustrate your point for me?" (Can you provide some "data" or experience in support of it?) can introject an element of inquiry into a discussion.

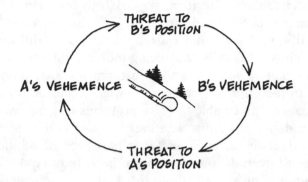

We often tape record meetings of management teams with whom we are working to develop learning skills. One indicator of a team in trouble is when in a several hour meeting there are few, if any, questions. This may seem amazing but I have seen meetings that went for three hours without a single question being asked! You don't have to be an "action science" expert to know there is not a lot of inquiry going on in such meetings.

But pure inquiry is also limited. Questioning can be crucial for breaking the spiral of reinforcing advocacy, but until a team or an individual learns to combine inquiry and advocacy, learning skills are very limited. One reason that pure inquiry is limited is that we almost always *do* have a view, regardless of whether or not we believe that our view is the only correct one. Thus, just asking lots of questions can be a way of avoiding learning—by hiding our own view behind a wall of incessant questioning.

The most productive learning usually occurs when managers combine skills in advocacy and inquiry. Another way to say this is "reciprocal inquiry." By this we mean that everyone makes his or her thinking explicit and subject to public examination. This creates an atmosphere of genuine vulnerability. No one is hiding the evidence or reasoning behind his views—advancing them without making them open to scrutiny. For example, when inquiry and advocacy are balanced, I would not only be inquiring into the reasoning behind others' views but would be stating my views in such a way as to reveal my own assumptions and reasoning and to invite others to inquire into them. I might say, "Here is my view and here is how I have arrived at it. How does it sound to you?

When operating in pure advocacy, the goal is to win the argument. When inquiry and advocacy are combined, the goal is no longer "to win the argument" but to find the best argument. This shows in how we use data and in how we reveal the reasoning behind abstractions. For example, when we operate in pure advocacy, we tend to use data selectively, presenting only the data that confirm our position. When we explain the reasoning behind our position, we expose only enough of our reasoning to "make our case," avoiding areas where we feel our case might be weak. By contrast, when both advocacy and inquiry are high, we are open to discontinuing data as well as confirming data—because we are genuinely interested in finding flaws in our views. Likewise, we expose our reasoning and look for flaws in it, and we try to understand others' reasoning.

The ideal of combining inquiry and advocacy is challenging. It can be especially difficult if you work in a highly political organization that is not open to genuine inquiry. Speaking as a veteran advocate, I can say that I have found patience and perseverence needed to move toward a more balanced approach. Progress comes in stages. For me, the first stage was learning how to inquire into others' views when I do not agree with them. My habitual response to such disagreements was to advocate my view harder. Usually, this was done without malice but in the genuine belief that I had thought things through and had a valid position. Unfortunately, it often had the consequence of polarizing or terminating discussions, and left me without the sense of partnership I truly wanted. Now, I very often respond to differences of view by asking the other person to say more about his or her view, or to expand further on how they arrived at the view.

Though we spend our lives mastering the discipline of balancing inquiry and advocacy, the rewards along the way are gratifying. Today I find that I spend very little time trying to convince people of my view, and I can honestly say that it makes life a lot easier and more fun. I'm reminded of this fact each time I find myself, usually under real stress, going back to being a one-sided advocate. What has also become obvious on repeated occasions is that, when there is inquiry and advocacy, creative outcomes are much more likely. In a sense, when two people operate in pure advocacy, the outcomes are predetermined. Either person A will win, or person B will win, or more likely both will simply retain their views. When there is inquiry and advocacy, these limitations dissolve. Persons A and B, by being open to inquire into their own views, make possible discovering completely new views.

While mastering the discipline of balancing inquiry and advocacy, it helps to keep in mind the following guidelines:[12]

When advocating your view:
* *Make* your own reasoning explicit (i.e., say how you arrived at your view and the "data" upon which it is based)
* *Encourage* others to explore your view (e.g., "Do you see gaps in my reasoning?")
* *Encourage* others to provide different views (i.e., "Do you have either different data or different conclusions, or both?")
* Actively *inquire* into others' views that differ from your own (i.e., "What are your views?" "How did you arrive at your view?" "Are you taking into account data that are different from what I have considered?")

When inquiring into others' views:
* If you are making assumptions about others' views, state your assumptions clearly and acknowledge that they are assumptions
* State the "data" upon which your assumptions are based
* Don't bother asking questions if you're not genuinely interested in the others' response (i.e., if you're only trying to be polite or to show the others up)

When you arrive at an impasse (others no longer appear to be open to inquiring into their own views):
* Ask what data or logic might change their views.
* Ask if there is any way you might together design an experiment (or some other inquiry) that might provide new information

When you or others are hesitant to express your views or to experiment with alternative ideas:

- Encourage them (or you) to think out loud about what might be making it difficult (i.e., "What is it about this situation, and about me or others, that is making open exchange difficult?")
- If there is mutual desire to do so, design with others ways of overcoming these barriers

The point is not to follow such guidelines slavishly, but to use them to keep in mind the spirit of balancing inquiry and advocacy. Like any formula for starting a learning discipline, they should be used as "training wheels" on your first bicycle. They help to get you started, and give you a feel for what it is like to ride, to practice inquiry with advocacy. As you gain skill, they can and probably should be discarded. But it is also nice to be able to come back to them periodically when you encounter some rough terrain.

However, it is important to keep in mind that guidelines will be of little use if you are not genuinely curious and willing to change your mental model of a situation. In other words, practicing inquiry and advocacy means being willing to expose the limitations in your own thinking—the willingness to be wrong. Nothing less will make it safe for others to do likewise.

As with all of the disciplines, making progress with the discipline of mental models takes time, and the signs of progress can be subtle. I remember asking Harley-Davidson President Jeff Bluestein, after several years of investing in many aspects of organizational learning work, "What do you notice that is different?" His response was simple. "I hear more and more people say, 'This is the way I am seeing things' rather than 'This is the way things are.' It may not sound like much, but the former leads to a different quality of conversation."

DOES AGREEMENT MATTER?

It's important to note that the goal in practicing the discipline of mental models is not necessarily agreement or convergence. Many mental models can exist at once. Some models may disagree.

All of them need to be considered and tested against situations that come up. This requires an organizational "commitment to the truth," which is an outgrowth of personal mastery. And it takes an understanding that we may never know the whole truth. Even after considering the mental models, as O'Brien says, "we might all wind up in different places. The goal is the best mental model for whoever happens to be out front on that particular issue. Everyone else focuses on helping that person (or persons) make the best possible decision by helping them to build the best mental model possible."

Although the goal may not be congruency, the process leads to results nonetheless when it works. "We don't mind if meetings end with people pretty far apart," O'Brien says. "People put their positions out and even if you don't agree with them, you can recognize their merit because they're well considered. You can say, 'For other reasons, I'm not going in your direction.' It's amazing, in a way; people pull together better this way than they would when they are driven to come to agreement." In particular there is little of the bitterness that typically wells up when people feel that they knew best, but never got a chance to make their case. It turns out that people can live very well with the situation where they make their case and yet another view is implemented, so long as the learning process is open and everyone acts with integrity.

"We don't have any anointed mental models," says O'Brien, "we have a philosophy of mental modeling. If we went out to the field and said, 'this is the authorized mental model for handling situation 23C,' we'd have a problem." Similarly, imposing a favored mental model on people, like imposing your vision, usually backfires. There may be a temptation for the loudest person, or the highest-ranking person, to assume that everyone else will swallow his or her mental models lock, stock, and barrel in sixty seconds. Even if his mental model is better, his role is not to inoculate everyone else with it, but to hold it up for them to consider.

Many find the de-emphasis on reaching agreement and congruency surprising. But I have often encountered statements similar to O'Brien's from members of outstanding teams. This belief that "we'll just talk it out and we'll know what to do" turns out to be a cornerstone of the alignment that is fostered through "dialogue," the heart of the discipline of team learning.

MENTAL MODELS AND THE FIFTH DISCIPLINE

I have come to believe that systems thinking without mental models is like the DC-3's radial air-cooled engine without wing flaps. Just as the Boeing 247's engineers had to downsize their engine because it lacked wing flaps, systems thinking without the discipline of mental models loses much of its power. The two disciplines go naturally together because one focuses on exposing hidden assumptions and the other focuses on how to restructure assumptions to reveal causes of significant problems.

As shown at the outset of the chapter, entrenched mental models will thwart changes that could come from systems thinking. Managers must learn to reflect on their current mental models—until prevailing assumptions are brought into the open, there is no reason to expect mental models to change, and there is little purpose in systems thinking. If managers "believe" their world views are facts rather than sets of assumptions, they will not be open to challenging those world views. If they lack skills in inquiring into their and others' ways of thinking, they will be limited in experimenting collaboratively with new ways of thinking. Moreover, if there is no established philosophy and understanding of mental models in the organization, people will misperceive the purpose of systems thinking as drawing diagrams building elaborate "models" of the world, not improving our mental models.

Systems thinking is equally important to working with mental models effectively. Contemporary research shows that most of our mental models are very often systematically flawed. They miss critical feedback relationships, misjudge time delays, and often focus on variables that are visible or salient, not necessarily high leverage. MIT's John Sterman has shown experimentally that players in the beer game, for example, consistently misjudge the delay in receiving orders once placed. Most players either don't see or don't take into account in their decision making the critical reinforcing feedbacks that develop when they panic (place more orders for beer, which wipes out their supplier's inventory, forcing them to lengthen shipping delays, which can lead to further panic). Sterman has shown similar flaws in mental models in a variety of experiments.[13]

Understanding these flaws can help to see where prevailing mental models will be weakest and where more than just "surfacing" managers' mental models will be required for effective decisions.

Eventually, what will accelerate mental models as a practical management discipline will be a *library of "generic structures"* used throughout an organization. These "structures" will be based on systems archetypes such as those presented in Chapter 6. But, they would be suited to the particulars of a given organization—its products, market, and technologies. For example, the particular "shifting the burden," and "limits to growth" structures for an oil company would differ from those for an insurance company, but the underlying archetypes would be the same. Such a library should be a natural by-product of practicing systems thinking within an organization.

Ultimately, the payoff from integrating systems thinking and mental models will be not only improving our mental models (what we think) but altering our ways of thinking: shifting from mental models dominated by events to mental models that recognize longer-term patterns of change and the underlying structures producing those patterns. For example, Shell's scenarios not only made the company's managers aware of coming changes, they helped Shell's managers take a first step up from the world of events—seeing patterns of change.

Just as "linear thinking" dominates most mental models used for critical decisions today, the learning organizations of the future will make key decisions based on shared understandings of interrelationships and patterns of change.

10

SHARED VISION

A COMMON CARING

You may remember the movie *Spartacus,* an adaptation of the story of a Roman gladiator/slave who led an army of slaves in an uprising in 71 B.C.[1] They defeated the Roman legions twice, but were finally conquered by the general Marcus Crassus after a long siege and battle. In the movie, Crassus tells the thousand survivors in Spartacus's army, "You have been slaves. You will be slaves again. But you will be spared your rightful punishment of crucifixion by the mercy of the Roman legions. All you need to do is turn over to me the slave Spartacus, because we do not know him by sight."

After a long pause, Spartacus (played by Kirk Douglas) stands up and says, "I am Spartacus." Then the man next to him stands up and says, "I am Spartacus." The next man stands up and also says, "No, I am Spartacus." Within a minute, everyone in the army is on his feet.

It doesn't matter whether this story is apocryphal or not; it demonstrates a deep truth. Each man, by standing up, chose death. But the loyalty of Spartacus's army was not to Spartacus the man. Their loyalty was to a shared vision which Spartacus had inspired— the idea that they could be free men. This vision was so compelling that no man could bear to give it up and return to slavery.

A shared vision is not an idea. It is not even an important idea such as freedom. It is, rather, a force in people's hearts, a force of impressive power. It may be inspired by an idea, but once it goes further—if it is compelling enough to acquire the support of more than one person—then it is no longer an abstraction. It is palpable. People begin to see it as if it exists. Few, if any, forces in human affairs are as powerful as shared vision.

At its simplest level, a shared vision is the answer to the question, "What do we want to create?" Just as personal visions are pictures or images people carry in their heads and hearts, so too are shared visions pictures that people throughout an organization carry. They create a sense of commonality that permeates the organization and gives coherence to diverse activities.

A vision is truly shared when you and I have a similar picture and are committed to one another having it, not just to each of us, individually, having it. When people truly share a vision they are connected, bound together by a common aspiration. Personal visions derive their power from an individual's deep caring for the vision. Shared visions derive their power from a common caring. In fact, we have to come to believe that one of the reasons people seek to build shared visions is their desire to be connected in an important undertaking.

Shared vision is vital for the learning organization because it provides the focus and energy for learning. While adaptive learning is possible without vision, generative learning occurs only when people are striving to accomplish something that matters deeply to them. In fact, the whole idea of generative learning—expanding your ability to create—will seem abstract and meaningless *until* people become excited about a vision they truly want to accomplish.

Today, "vision" is a familiar concept in corporate leadership. But when you look carefully you find that most "visions" are one person's (or one group's) vision imposed on an organization. Such visions, at best, command compliance—not commitment. A shared vision is a vision that many people are truly committed to, because it reflects their own personal vision.

WHY SHARED VISIONS MATTER

It is impossible to imagine the accomplishments of building AT&T, Ford, or Apple in the absence of shared vision. Theodore Vail had a vision of universal telephone service that would take fifty years to bring about. Henry Ford envisioned common people, not just the wealthy, owning their own automobiles. Steven Jobs, Steve Wozniak, and their Apple cofounders saw the power of the computer to empower people. It is equally impossible to imagine the rapid ascendancy of Japanese firms such as Komatsu (which grew from one third the size of Caterpillar to its equal in less than two decades), Canon (which went from nothing to matching Xerox's global market share in reprographics in the same time frame), or Honda had they not all been guided by visions of global success.[2] What is most important is that these individuals' visions became genuinely shared among people throughout all levels of their companies—focusing the energies of thousands and creating a common identity among enormously diverse people.

Many shared visions are extrinsic—that is, they focus on achieving something relative to an outsider, such as a competitor. Yet, a goal limited to defeating an opponent is transitory. Once the vision is achieved, it can easily migrate into a defensive posture of "protecting what we have, of not losing our number-one position." Such defensive goals rarely call forth the creativity and excitement of building something new. A master in the martial arts is probably not focused so much on "defeating all others" as on his own intrinsic inner standards of "excellence." This does not mean that visions must be either intrinsic or extrinsic. Both types of vision can coexist. But reliance on a vision that is solely predicated on defeating an adversary can weaken an organization long term.

Kazuo Inamori of Kyocera entreats employees "to look inward," to discover their own internal standards. He argues that, while striving to be number one in its field, a company can aim to be "better" than others or "best" in its field. But his vision is that Kyocera should always aim for "perfection" rather than just being "best." (Note Inamori's application of the principle of creative tension— "it's not what the vision is, but what it does . . .")[3]

A shared vision, especially one that is intrinsic, uplifts people's aspirations. Work becomes part of pursuing a larger purpose embodied in the organizations' products or services—accelerating learning through personal computers, bringing the world into communication through universal telephone service, or promoting freedom of movement through the personal automobile. The larger purpose can also be embodied in the style, climate, and spirit of the organization. Max de Pree, retired CEO of the Herman Miller furniture company, said his vision for Herman Miller was "to be a gift to the human spirit"—by which he meant not only Herman Miller's products, but its people, its atmosphere, and its larger commitment to productive and aesthetic work environments.[4]

Visions are exhilarating. They create the spark, the excitement that lifts an organization out of the mundane. "No matter how problematic the competition or our internal troubles," commented one manager, "my spirit always rebounds when I stroll into the building—because I know what we are doing really matters."

In a corporation, a shared vision changes people's relationship with the company. It is no longer "their company"; it becomes "our company." A shared vision is the first step in allowing people who mistrusted each other to begin to work together. It creates a common identity. In fact, an organization's shared sense of purpose, vision, and operating values establish the most basic level of commonality. Late in his career, the psychologist Abraham Maslow studied high-performing teams. One of their most striking characteristics was shared vision and purpose. Maslow observed that in exceptional teams

> the task was no longer separate from the self. . . but rather he identified with this task so strongly that you couldn't define his real self without including that task.[5]

Shared visions compel courage so naturally that people don't even realize the extent of their courage. Courage is simply doing whatever is needed in pursuit of the vision. In 1961, John Kennedy articulated a vision that had been emerging for many years among leaders within America's space program: to have a man on the moon by the end of the decade.[6] This led to countless acts of courage and daring. A modern-day Spartacus story occurred in the mid-1960s at MIT's Draper Laboratories. The lab was the lead contractor with NASA for the inertial navigation and guidance system to guide the Apollo astronauts to the moon. Several years into the project, the lab directors became convinced that their original design specifications were wrong. This posed considerable potential embarrassment, since several million dollars had already been spent. Instead of trying to jerry-rig an expedient solution, they asked NASA to disband the project and start over again. They risked not just their contract but their reputation. But no other action was possible. Their entire reason for being was embodied in one simple vision— having a man on the moon by the end of the decade. They would do whatever it took to realize that vision.

Apple Computer during the mid-1980s, when the entire small computer industry rallied behind the IBM PC, persevered with its vision of a computer which people could understand intuitively, a computer which represented the freedom to think on one's own. Along the way, Apple refused the "sure thing" opportunity to be a leading PC "clone" manufacturer. Though it never reached the volume sales of the clones, Apple's Macintosh was not only easy to use, it made "intuitiveness" and "having fun" priorities in personal computing, and became the industry standard that eventually shaped the look and feel of all operating systems.

You cannot have a learning organization without shared vision. Without a pull toward some goal which people truly want to achieve, the forces in support of the status quo can be overwhelming. Vision establishes an overarching goal. The loftiness of the target compels new ways of thinking and acting. A shared vision also provides a rudder to keep the learning process on course when stresses develop. Learning can be difficult, even painful. With a shared vision, we are more likely to expose our ways of thinking, give up deeply held views, and recognize personal and organizational shortcomings. All that trouble seems trivial compared with the importance of what we are trying to create. As Robert Fritz puts it, "In the presence of greatness, pettiness disappears." In the absence of a great dream, pettiness prevails.

Shared vision fosters risk taking and experimentation. When people are immersed in a vision, they often don't know how to do it. They run an experiment. They change direction and run another experiment. Everything is an experiment, but there is no ambiguity. It's perfectly clear why they are doing what they are doing. People aren't saying "Give me a guarantee that it will work." Everybody knows that there is no guarantee. But the people are committed nonetheless.

Lastly, shared vision addresses one of the primary puzzles that has thwarted efforts to develop systems thinking in management: "How can a commitment to the long term be fostered?"

For years, systems thinkers have endeavored to persuade managers that, unless they maintained a long-term focus, they will be in big trouble. With great vigor we have proselytized the "better before worse" consequences of many interventions, and the "shifting the burden" dynamics that result from symptomatic fixes. Yet, I have witnessed few lasting shifts to longer term commitment and action. Personally, I have come to feel that our failure lies not in unpersuasiveness or lack of sufficiently compelling evidence. *It may simply not be possible to convince human beings rationally to take a long-term view.* People do not focus on the long term because they *have* to, but because they *want* to.

In every instance where one finds a long-term view actually operating in human affairs, there is a long-term vision at work. The cathedral builders of the Middle Ages labored a lifetime with the fruits of their labors still a hundred years in the future. The Japanese believe building a great organization is like growing a tree; it takes twenty-five to fifty years. Parents of young children try to lay a foundation of values and attitude that will serve an adult twenty years hence. In all of these cases, people hold a vision that can be realized only over the long term.

Strategic planning, which should be a bastion of long-term thinking in corporations, is very often reactive and short-term. According to two of the most articulate critics of contemporary strategic planning, Gary Hamel of the London Business School and C. K. Prahalad of the University of Michigan:

> Although strategic planning is billed as a way of becoming more future oriented, most managers, when pressed, will admit that their strategic plans reveal more about today's problems than tomorrow's opportunities.[7]

With its emphasis on extensive analysis of competitors' strengths and weaknesses, of market niches and firm resources, typical strategic planning fails to achieve the one accomplishment that would foster longer range actions—in Hamel's and Prahalad's terms, setting "a goal that is worthy of commitment."

With all the attention given to this component of corporate learning, however, vision is still often regarded as a mysterious, uncontrollable force. Leaders with vision are cult heroes. While it is true that there are no formulas for "how to find your vision," there are principles and guidelines for building shared vision. There is a discipline of building vision that is emerging, and practical tools for working with shared visions. This discipline extends principles and insights from personal mastery into the world of collective aspiration and shared commitment.

THE DISCIPLINE OF BUILDING SHARED VISION

ENCOURAGING PERSONAL VISION

Shared visions emerge from personal visions. This is how they derive their energy and how they foster commitment. As Bill O'Brien of Hanover Insurance observes, "My vision is not what's important to you. The only vision that motivates you is your vision." It is not that people care only about their personal self-interest—in fact, people's personal visions usually include dimensions that concern family, organization, community, and even the world. Rather, O'Brien is stressing that caring is *personal*. It is rooted in an individual's own set of values, concerns, and aspirations. This is why genuine caring about a shared vision is rooted in personal visions. This simple truth is lost on many leaders, who decide that their organization must develop a vision by tomorrow!

Organizations intent on building shared visions continually encourage members to develop their personal visions. If people don't have their own vision, all they can do is "sign up" for someone else's. The result is compliance, never commitment. On the other hand, people with a strong sense of personal direction can join together to create a powerful synergy toward what "I/we truly want."

In this sense, personal mastery is the bedrock for developing shared visions. This means not only personal vision, but commitment to the truth and creative tension—the hallmarks of personal mastery. Shared vision can generate levels of creative tension that go far beyond individuals' comfort levels. Those who will contribute the most toward realizing a lofty vision will be those who can "hold" this creative tension: remain clear on the vision and continue to inquire into current reality. They will be the ones who believe deeply in their ability to create their future, because that is what they experience personally.

In encouraging personal vision, organizations must be careful not to infringe on individual freedoms. As was discussed in Chapter

8, "Personal Mastery," no one can give another "his vision," nor even force him to develop a vision. However, there are positive actions that can be taken to create a climate that encourages personal vision. The most direct is for leaders who have a sense of vision to communicate that in such a way that others are encouraged to share their visions. This is the art of visionary leadership— how shared visions are built from personal visions.

FROM PERSONAL VISIONS TO SHARED VISIONS

How do individual visions join to create shared visions? A useful metaphor is the hologram, the three-dimensional image created by interacting light sources.

If you cut a photograph in half, each part shows only part of the whole image. But if you divide a hologram, each part shows the whole image intact. Similarly, as you continue to divide up the hologram, no matter how small the divisions, each piece still shows the whole image. Likewise, when a group of people come to share a vision for an organization, each person sees his own picture of the organization at its best. Each shares responsibility for the whole, not just for his piece. But the component "pieces" of the hologram are not identical. Each represents the whole image from a different point of view. It's as if you were to look through holes poked in a window shade; each hole would offer a unique angle for viewing the whole image. So, too, is each individual's vision of the whole unique. We each have our own way of seeing the larger vision.

When you add up the pieces of a hologram, the image of the whole does not change fundamentally. After all, it was there in each piece. Rather the image becomes more intense, more lifelike. When more people come to share a common vision, the vision may not change fundamentally. But it becomes more alive, more real in the sense of a mental reality that people can truly imagine achieving. They now have partners, "cocreators"; the vision no longer rests on their shoulders alone. Early on, when they are nurturing an individual vision, people may say it is "my vision." But as the shared vision develops, it becomes both "my vision" and "our vision."

The first step in mastering the discipline of building shared visions is to give up traditional notions that visions are always announced from "on high" or come from an organization's institutionalized planning processes.

In the traditional hierarchical organization, no one questioned that the vision emanated from the top. Often, the big picture guiding the firm wasn't even shared—all people needed to know were their "marching orders," so that they could carry out their tasks in support of the larger vision.

That traditional top-down vision is not much different from a process that has become popular in recent years. Top management-goes off to write its vision statement, often with the help of consultants. This may be done to solve the problem of low morale or lack of strategic direction. Sometimes the process is primarily reflective. Sometimes it incorporates extensive analysis of a firm's competitors, market setting, and organizational strengths and weaknesses. Regardless, the results are often disappointing for several reasons.

First, such a vision is often a one-shot vision, a single effort at providing overarching direction and meaning to the firm's strategy. Once it's written, management assumes that they have now discharged their visionary duties. Recently, one of my Innovation Associates colleagues was explaining to two managers how our group works with vision. Before he could get far, one of the managers interrupted. "We've done that," he said. "We've already written our vision statement." "That's very interesting," my colleague responded. "What did you come up with?" The one manager turned to the other and asked, "Joe, where is that vision statement anyhow?" Writing a vision statement can be a first step in building shared vision but, alone, it rarely makes a vision come alive within an organization.

The second problem with top management going off to write their vision statement is that the resulting vision does not build on people's personal visions. Often, personal visions are ignored altogether in the search for a strategic vision. Or the official vision reflects only the personal vision of one or two people. There is little opportunity for inquiry and testing at every level so that people feel they understand and own the vision. As a result, the new official vision also fails to foster energy and commitment. It simply does not inspire people. In fact, sometimes, it even generates little passion among the top management team who created it.

Lastly, vision is not a solution to a problem. If it is seen in that light, when the "problem" of low morale or unclear strategic direction goes away, the energy behind the vision will go away also. Building shared vision must be seen as a central element of the daily work of leaders. It is ongoing and never-ending. It is actually part of a larger leadership activity: designing and nurturing "governing ideas" of the enterprise—not only its vision per se, but its purpose and core values as well.

Sometimes, managers expect shared visions to emerge from a firm's strategic planning process. But for all the same reasons that most top-down visioning processes fail, most strategic planning also fails to nurture genuine vision. According to Hamel and Prahalad:

> Creative strategies seldom emerge from the annual planning ritual. The starting point for next year's strategy is almost always this year's strategy. Improvements are incremental. The company sticks to the segments and territories it knows, even though the real opportunities may be elsewhere. The impetus for Canon's pioneering entry into the personal copier business came from an overseas sales subsidiary—not from planners in Japan.[8]

This is not to say that visions cannot emanate from the top. Often, they do. But sometimes they emanate from personal visions of individuals who are not in positions of authority. Sometimes they just "bubble up" from people interacting at many levels. The origin of the vision is less important than the process whereby it comes to be shared. It is not truly a "shared vision" until it connects with the personal visions of people throughout the organization.

For those in leadership positions, what is most important is to remember that their visions are still personal visions. Just because they occupy a position of leadership does not mean that their personal visions are *automatically* "the organization's vision." When I hear leaders say "our vision" and I know they are really describing "my vision," I recall Mark Twain's words that the official "we" should be reserved for "kings and people with tapeworm."

Ultimately, leaders intent on building shared visions must be willing to continually share their personal visions. They must also be prepared to ask, "Will you follow me?" This can be difficult. For a person who has been setting goals all through his career and simply announcing them, asking for support can feel very vulnerable.

John Kryster was the president of a large division of a leading home products company who had a vision that his division should be preeminent in its industry. This vision required not only excellent products but that the company supply the product to their "customer" (retail grocers), in a more efficient and effective manner than anyone else. He envisioned a unique worldwide distribution system that would get product to the customer in half the time and at a fraction of the cost in wastage and reshipments. He began to talk with other managers, production workers, distribution people, and grocers. Everyone seemed enthusiastic, but pointed out that many of his ideas could not be achieved because they contradicted so many traditional policies of the corporate parent.

In particular, Kryster needed the support of the head of product distribution, Harriet Sullivan, who—while technically Kryster's peer in the firm's matrix organization—had fifteen years more experience. Kryster prepared an elaborate presentation for Sullivan to show her the merits of his new distribution ideas. But for every piece of supporting data he offered, Sullivan had a countering criticism. Kryster left the meeting thinking that the doubters were probably right.

Then he conceived of a way to test the new system out in only one geographic market. The risk would be less, and he could gain the support of the local grocery chain which had been especially enthusiastic about the concept. But what should he do about Harriet Sullivan? His instincts were just not to tell her. After all, he had the authority to undertake the experiment himself, using his own distribution people. Yet, he also valued Sullivan's experience and judgment.

After a week of mulling it over, Kryster went back to ask for Sullivan's support. This time, though, he left his charts and data at home. He just told her why he believed in the idea, how it could forge a new partnership with customers, and how its merits could be tested with low risk. To his surprise, the crusty distribution chief started to offer help in designing the experiment. "When you came to me last week," she said, "you were trying to convince me. Now, you're willing to test your idea. I still think it's wrongheaded, but I can see you care a great deal. So, who knows, maybe we'll learn something."

That was many years ago. Today, Kryster's innovative distribution system is used worldwide by most of the corporation's divisions. It has significantly reduced costs and been part of broad strategic alliances the corporation is learning to forge with retail chains.

When visions start in the middle of an organization the process of sharing and listening is essentially the same as when they originate at the top. But it may take longer, especially if the vision has implications for the entire organization.

Organizational consultant Charlie Kiefer says that, "Despite the excitement that a vision generates, the process of building shared vision is not always glamorous. Managers who are skilled at building shared visions talk about the process in ordinary terms. 'Talking about our vision' just gets woven into day-to-day life. Most artists don't get very excited about the *process of* creating art. They get excited about the results." Or, as Bill O'Brien puts it, "Being a visionary leader is not about giving speeches and inspiring the troops. How I spend my day is pretty much the same as how any executive spends his day. Being a visionary leader is about solving day-to-day problems with my vision in mind."

Visions that are truly shared take time to emerge. They grow as a by-product of interactions of individual visions. Experience suggests that visions that are genuinely shared require ongoing conversation where individuals not only feel free to express their dreams, but learn how to listen to each others' dreams. Out of this listening, new insights into what is possible gradually emerge.

Listening is often more difficult than talking, especially for strong-willed managers with definite ideas of what is needed. It requires extraordinary openness and willingness to entertain a diversity of ideas. This does not imply that we must sacrifice our vision "for the larger cause." Rather, we must allow multiple visions to coexist, listening for the right course of action that transcends and unifies all our individual visions. As one highly successful CEO expressed it: "My job, fundamentally, is listening to what the organization is trying to say, and then making sure that it is forcefully articulated."

SPREADING VISIONS: ENROLLMENT COMMITMENT, AND COMPLIANCE[9]

Few subjects are closer to the heart of contemporary managers than commitment. Prodded by studies showing that most American workers acknowledge low levels of commitment and by tales of foreign competitors' committed work forces, managers have turned to "management by commitment," "high commitment work systems," and other approaches. Yet, real commitment is still rare in today's organizations. It is our experience that, 90 percent of the time, what passes for commitment is compliance.

Today, it is common to hear managers talk of getting people to "buy into" the vision. For many, I fear, this suggests a sales process, where I sell and you buy. Yet, there is a world of difference between "selling" and "enrolling." "Selling" generally means getting someone to do something that she might not do if she were in full possession of all the facts. "Enrolling," by contrast, literally means "placing one's name on the roll." Enrollment implies free choice, while "being sold" often does not.

"Enrollment is the process," in Kiefer's words, "of becoming part of something by choice." You're "committed" when you are not only enrolled but feel fully responsible for making the vision happen. I can be thoroughly enrolled in your vision. I can genuinely want it to occur. Yet, it is still your vision. I will take actions as need arises, but I do not spend my waking hours looking for what to do next.

For example, people are often enrolled in social causes out of genuine desire, for example, to see particular inequities righted. Once a year they might make a donation to help in a fund-raising campaign. But when they are committed, the "cause" can count on them. They will do whatever it takes to make the vision real. The vision is pulling them to action. Some use the term "being source" to describe the unique energy that committed people bring toward creating a vision.

In most contemporary organizations, relatively few people are enrolled—and even fewer committed. The great majority are in a state of "compliance." "Compliant" followers go along with a vision. They do what is expected of them. They support the vision, to some degree. But, they are not truly enrolled or committed.

Compliance is often confused with enrollment and commitment. In part, this occurs because compliance has prevailed for so long in most organizations, we don't know how to recognize real commitment. It is also because there are several levels of compliance, some of which lead to behavior that looks a great deal like enrollment and commitment:

POSSIBLE ATTITUDES TOWARD A VISION

Commitment: Wants it. Will make it happen. Creates whatever "laws" (structures) are needed.

Enrollment: Wants it. Will do whatever can be done within the "spirit of the law."

Genuine compliance: Sees the benefits of the vision. Does everything expected and more. Follows the "letter of the law." "Good soldier."

Formal compliance: On the whole, sees the benefits of the vision. Does what's expected and no more. "Pretty good soldier."

Grudging compliance: Does not see the benefits of the vision. But, also, does not want to lose job. Does enough of what's expected because he has to, but also lets it be known that he is not really on board.

Noncompliance: Does not see benefits of vision and will not do what's expected. "I won't do it; you can't make me."

Apathy: Neither for nor against vision. No interest. No energy. "Is it five o'clock yet?"

The speed limit in most states in the United States today is fifty-five or sixty-five miles per hour. A person who was genuinely compliant would never drive more than the official speed limit. A person formally compliant could drive five to seven miles over the limit because in most states you will not get a ticket so long as you are in this range. Someone grudgingly compliant would drive the same speed and complain continually about it. A noncompliant driver would "floor it" and do everything possible to evade troopers. On the other hand, a person who was truly committed to the official speed limit would drive that speed even if it were not a legal limit.

In most organizations, most people are in states of formal or genuine compliance with respect to the organization's goals and ground rules. They go along with "the program," sincerely trying to contribute. On the other hand, people in noncompliance or grudging compliance usually stand out. They are opposed to the goals or ground rules and let their opposition be known, either through inaction or (if they are grudgingly compliant) through "malicious obedience"—"I'll do it just to prove that it won't work." They may not speak out publicly against the organization's goals, but their views are known nonetheless (They often reserve their truest sentiments for the restroom or the bar.)

Differences between the varying states of compliance can be subtle. Most problematic is the state of genuine compliance, which is often mistaken for enrollment or commitment. The prototypical "good soldier" of genuine compliance will do whatever is expected of him, willingly. "I believe in the people behind the vision; I'll do whatever is needed, and more, to the fullest of my ability." In his own mind, the person operating in genuine compliance often thinks of himself as committed. He is, in fact, committed, but only to being "part of the team."

In fact, from his *behavior* on the job, it is often very difficult to distinguish someone who is genuinely compliant from someone who is enrolled or committed. An organization made up of genuinely compliant people would be light-years ahead of most organizations in productivity and cost effectiveness. People would not have to be told what to do more than once. They would be responsive. They would be upbeat and positive in their attitude and manner. They might also be a bit drone-like, but not necessarily. If what was expected of high performers was to take initiative and be proactive, they would exhibit those behaviors as well. In short, people in genuine compliance would do whatever they could to play by the rules of the game, both the formal and subtle rules.

Yet, there is a world of difference between compliance and commitment. The committed person brings an energy, passion, and excitement that cannot be generated by someone who is only compliant, even genuinely compliant. The committed person doesn't play by the rules of the game. He is responsible for the game. If the rules of the game stand in the way of achieving the vision, he will find ways to change the rules. A group of people truly committed to a common vision is an awesome force.

Tracy Kidder, in his Pulitzer-prize-winning book *The Soul of a New Machine,* tells the story of a product development team at Data General, brought together by a talented team leader to create an ambitious new computer. Against a business atmosphere of urgency bordering on crisis, the team turned out a ground-breaking computer in remarkable time. Visiting with the team manager Tom West in the book, and team members several years later, I learned just how remarkable their feat was. They told me of a stage in their project when certain critical software was several months behind schedule. The three engineers responsible came into the office one evening and left the next morning. By all accounts they accomplished two to three months of work that evening—and no one could explain how. These are not the feats of compliance.

What then is the difference between being genuinely compliant and enrolled and committed? The answer is deceptively simple. People who are enrolled or committed truly *want* the vision. Genuinely compliant people accept the vision. They may want it in order to get something else—for example, to keep their job, or to make their boss happy, or to get a promotion. But they do not truly want the vision in and of itself. It is not their own vision (or, at least, they do not know that it is their own vision).

Highly desired, shared commitment to a vision can be an elusive goal. One executive VP at a consumer goods company deeply desired to turn the very traditional organization into a world-class competitor by developing shared commitment to a new business vision. But after a year's effort, people continued to follow orders and do what they were told.

At this point he began to see the depth of the problem. People in his organization *had never been asked to commit to anything in their careers.* All they had ever been asked to do in their careers was be compliant. And consequently, that was all they knew how to do. That was the only mental model they had. No matter what he said about developing a real vision, or about being truly committed, it didn't matter because they could only hear it within their model of compliance.

Once he grasped this, he shifted tactics. He asked, "What might people be able to commit to?" He initiated a "wellness program," reasoning if there was anything to which people might become committed, it would be their own health. Over time, some did. They began to see that true commitment was possible in the workplace, and a near "ear" for the vision was opened.

Traditional organizations did not care about enrollment and commitment. The command and control hierarchy required only compliance. Still, today, many managers are justifiably wary of whether the energy released through commitment can be controlled and directed. So, we settle for compliance and content ourselves with moving people up the compliance ladder.

GUIDELINES FOR ENROLLMENT
AND COMMITMENT

Enrollment is a natural process that springs from your genuine enthusiasm for a vision and your willingness to let others come to their own choice.

- *Be enrolled yourself.* There is no point attempting to encourage another to be enrolled when you are not. That is "selling," not enrolling and will, at best, produce a form of superficial agreement and compliance. Worse, it will sow the seeds for future resentment.
- *Be on the level.* Don't inflate benefits or sweep problems under the rug. Describe the vision as simply and honestly as you can.
- *Let the other person choose.* You don't have to "convince" another of the benefits of a vision. In fact, efforts you might make to persuade him to "become enrolled" will be seen as manipulative and actually preclude enrollment. The more willing you are for him to make a free choice, the freer he will feel. This can be especially difficult with subordinates, who are often conditioned to feel as though they must go along. But you can still help by creating the time and safety for them to develop their own sense of vision.

There are many times when managers need compliance. They may want enrollment or commitment, but cannot accept anything below formal compliance. If that is the case, I recommend that you be on the level about it: "I know you may not agree wholeheartedly with the new direction, but at this juncture it is where the management team is committed to heading. I need your support to help it happen." Being open about the need for compliance removes hypocrisy. It also makes it easier for people to come to their choices, which may, over time, include enrollment.

The hardest lesson for many managers to face is that, ultimately, *there is really nothing you can do to get another person to enroll or commit.* Enrollment and commitment require freedom of choice. The guidelines above simply establish the conditions which are most favorable to enrollment, but they do not *cause* enrollment. Commitment likewise is very personal; efforts to force it will, at best, foster compliance.

ANCHORING VISION IN A SET
OF GOVERNING IDEAS

Building shared vision is actually only one piece of a larger activity: developing the governing ideas for the enterprise, its vision, purpose or mission, and core values. A vision not consistent with values that

people live by day by day will not only fail to inspire genuine enthusiasm, it will often foster outright cynicism.

These governing ideas answer three critical questions: "What?"
"Why?" and "How?"

- Vision is the "What?"—the picture of the future we seek to
  create.
- Purpose (or "mission") is the "Why?" the organization's
  answer to the question, "Why do we exist?" Great organizations have a larger sense of purpose that transcends providing
  for the needs of shareholders and employees. They seek to
  contribute to the world in some unique way, to add a distinctive source of value.
- Core values answer the question "How do we want to act, consistent with our mission, along the path toward achieving our
  vision? "A company's values might include integrity, openness,
  honesty, freedom, equal opportunity, leanness, merit, or loyalty. They describe how the company wants life to be on a day-
  to-day basis, while pursuing the vision.

Taken as a unit, all three governing ideas answer the question,
"What do we believe in?" When Matsushita employees recite the
company creed: "To recognize our responsibilities as industrialists,
to foster progress, to promote the general welfare of society, and to
devote ourselves to the further development of world culture,"
they're describing the company *purpose*. When they sing the company song, about "sending our goods to the people of the world,
endlessly and continuously, like water gushing from a fountain,"
they're proclaiming the corporate *vision*. And when they go to in-
house training programs that cover such topics as "fairness," "harmony and cooperation," "struggle for betterment," "courtesy and
humility," and "gratitude," the employees are learning the company's deliberately constructed *values*. (Matsushita, in fact, calls
them its "spiritual values.")[10]

I believe there is a genuine need for people to feel part of an
ennobling mission, but stating a mission or purpose in words is not
enough. Many mission statements end up sounding like 'apple pie
and motherhood.' People need visions to make the purpose more
concrete and tangible. We have to learn to 'paint pictures' of the
type of organization we want to have. Core values are necessary to
help people with day-to-day decision making. Purpose is abstract.
Visions may be long term. People need 'guiding stars' to navigate

and make decisions day to day. But core values are only helpful if they can be translated into concrete behaviors. For example, a corevalue like openness' requires the skills of reflection and inquiry within an overall context of trusting and supporting one another."

POSITIVE VERSUS NEGATIVE VISION

"What do we want?" is different from "What do we want to avoid?" This seems obvious, but in fact negative visions are probably more common than positive visions. Many organizations truly pull together only when their survival is threatened. They focus on avoiding what people don't want—being taken over, going bankrupt, losing jobs, losing market share, having a downturns in earnings, or "letting competitors beat them to market with the next new product." Negative visions are even more common in public leadership, where societies are continually bombarded with visions of "antidrugs," "antismoking," "antiwar," or "anti-nuclear energy."

Negative visions are limiting for three reasons. First, energy that could build something new is diverted to "preventing" something we don't want to happen. Second, negative visions carry a subtle yet unmistakable message of powerlessness: our people really don't care. They can pull together only when there is sufficient threat. Lastly, negative visions are inevitably short term. The organization is motivated so long as the threat persists. Once it leaves, so does the organization's vision and energy.

There are two fundamental sources of energy that can motivate organizations: fear and aspiration. The power of fear underlies negative visions. The power of aspiration drives positive visions. Fear can produce extraordinary changes in short periods, but aspiration endures as a continuing source of learning and growth.

CREATIVE TENSION AND
COMMITMENT TO THE TRUTH

In Chapter 8, I argued that personal vision, by itself, is not the key to releasing the energy of the creative process. The key is "creative tension," the tension between vision and reality. The most effective people are those who can "hold" their vision while remaining committed to seeing current reality clearly.

This principle is no less true for organizations. The hallmark of a learning organization is not lovely visions floating in space, but a relentless willingness to examine "what is" in light of our vision.

IBM in the early 1960s, for example, carried out an extraordinary series of experiments in pursuit of a daring vision, a single family of computers that would make virtually all its previous machines obsolete. In the words of a *Fortune* writer, IBM staked "its treasure, its reputation, and its position of leadership in the computer field" on a radical new concept: a series of compatible machines serving the broadest possible range of applications, from the most sophisticated scientific applications to the relatively small business needs.[11] Jay Forrester once remarked that the hallmark of a great organization is "how quickly bad news travels upward." IBM's capacity to recognize and learn from its mistakes proved pivotal during this period. One of the most discouraging was an early attempt at a high-end machine called "Stretch," introduced in 1960. IBM CEO Tom Watson, Jr., effectively killed the project in May 1961, after only a few had been sold. (Watson cut Stretch's hefty $13.5 million price tag almost in half, thereby making it uneconomical to produce.) To him, there was little choice: the machine did not satisfy its customers, never achieving more than 70 percent of its promised specifications. A few days later, Watson spoke candidly to an industry group. "Our greatest mistake in Stretch," he said, "is that we walked up to the plate and pointed at the center field stands. When we swung, it was not a homer but a hard line drive to the outfield. We're going to be a good deal more careful about what we promise in the future."

Indeed they were. Under the direction of many of the same men who had learned from Stretch, IBM introduced the System 360 three years later, which proved to be the platform for its extraordinary growth over the next ten years.

SHARED VISION AND THE FIFTH DISCIPLINE

WHY VISIONS DIE PREMATURELY

Many visions never take root and spread—despite having intrinsic merit. Several limits to growth structures can come into play to arrest the building of momentum behind a new vision. Understanding these structures can help considerably in sustaining the visioning process.

Visions spread because of a reinforcing process of increasing clarity, enthusiasm, communication and commitment. As people talk, the vision grows clearer. As it gets clearer, enthusiasm for its benefits builds.

And soon, the vision starts to spread in a reinforcing spiral of communication and excitement. Enthusiasm can also be reinforced by early successes in pursuing the vision (another potential reinforcing process, not shown on this diagram).

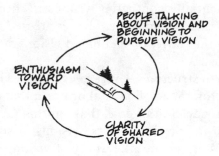

If the reinforcing process operated unfettered, it would lead to continuing growth in clarity and shared commitment toward the vision, among increasing numbers of people. But any of a variety of limiting factors can come into play to slow down this virtuous cycle.

The visioning process can wither if, as more people get involved, the diversity of views dissipates focus and generates unmanageable conflicts. People see different ideal futures. Must those who do not agree immediately with the emerging shared vision change their views? Do they conclude that the vision is set in stone and no longer influenceable? Do they feel that their own visions do not even matter? If the answer to any of these questions is "yes," the enrolling process can grind to a halt with a wave of increasing polarization.

This is a classic limits to growth structure, where the reinforcing process of growing enthusiasm for the vision interacts with a balancing process that limits the spread of the visions, due to increasing diversity and polarization

Reading clockwise around the balancing circle on the following page, from the top: As enthusiasm builds, more people are talking about the vision and the diversity of views increases, leading to peo-

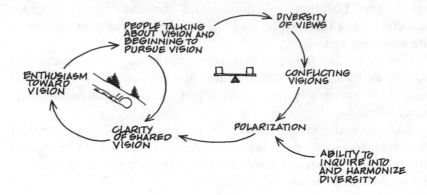

ple expressing potentially conflicting visions. If other people are unable to allow this diversity to be expressed, polarization increases, reducing the clarity of the shared visions, and limiting the growth of enthusiasm.

In limits to growth structures, leverage usually lies in understanding the limiting factor, the implicit goal or norm that drives the balancing feedback process. In this case, that limiting factor is the ability (or inability) to inquire into diverse visions in such a way that deeper, common visions emerge. Diversity of visions will grow until it exceeds the organization's capacity to "harmonize" diversity.

The most important skills to circumvent this limit are the reflection and inquiry skills developed in Chapter 9, "Mental Models." In effect, the visioning process is a special type of inquiry process. It is an inquiry into the future we truly seek to create. If it becomes a pure advocacy process, it will result in compliance, at best, not commitment.

Approaching the visioning as an inquiry process does not mean that I have to give up my view. On the contrary, visions need strong advocates. But advocates who can also inquire into others' visions open the possibility for the vision to evolve, to become larger than our individual visions. *That* is the principle of the hologram.

Visions can also die because people become discouraged by the apparent difficulty in bringing the vision into reality. As clarity about the nature of the vision increases so does awareness of the gap between the vision and current reality. People become disheartened, uncertain, or even cynical, leading to a decline in enthusiasm. The limits to growth structure for "organizational discouragement" looks like the following figure.

In this structure, the limiting factor is the capacity of people in

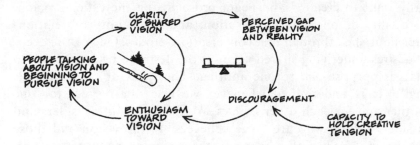

the organization to "hold" creative tension, the central principle of personal mastery. This is why we say that personal mastery is the bedrock for developing shared vision—organizations that do not encourage personal mastery find it very difficult to foster sustained commitment to a lofty vision.

Emerging visions can also die because people get overwhelmed by the demands of current reality and lose their focus on the vision. The limiting factor becomes the time and energy to focus on a vision:

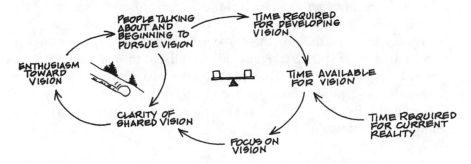

In this case, the leverage must lie either in finding ways to focus less time and effort on fighting crises and managing current reality, or breaking off those pursuing the new vision from those responsible for handling "current reality." In many ways, this is the strategy of "skunk works," small groups that quietly pursue new ideas out of the organizational mainstream. While this approach is often necessary, it is difficult to avoid fostering two polar extreme "camps" that no longer can support one another.

Lastly, a vision can die if people forget their connection to one another. This is one of the reasons that approaching visioning as a joint inquiry is so important. Once people stop asking "What do we really want to create?" and begin proselytizing the official vision, the quality of ongoing conversation, and the quality of relationships nourished through that conversation, erodes. One of the deepest desires underlying shared vision is the desire to be connected, to a larger purpose *and* to one another. The spirit of connection is fragile. It is undermined whenever we lose our respect for one another and for each other's views. We then split into insiders and outsiders—those who are "true believers" in the vision and those who are not. When this happens, the visioning conversations no longer build genuine enthusiasms toward the vision:

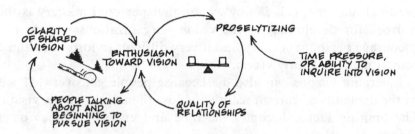

The limiting factor when people begin proselytizing and lose their sense of relationship can be time or skills. If there is great urgency to "sign up" for the new vision, people may just not perceive that there is time to really talk and listen to one another. This will be especially likely if people are also unskilled in how to have such a conversation, how to share their vision in such a way that they are not proselytizing, but are encouraging others to reflect on their own visions.

THE MISSING SYNERGY: SHARED VISION AND SYSTEMS THINKING

I believe that the discipline of building shared vision lacks a critical underpinning if practiced without systems thinking. Vision paints the picture of what we want to create. Systems thinking reveals how we have created what we currently have.

In recent years, many leaders have jumped on the vision bandwagon. They've developed corporate vision and mission statements. They've worked to enroll everyone in the vision. Yet, the expected surges in productivity and competitiveness often fail to arrive. This has led many to become disaffected with vision and visioning. The fad cycle has run its course, and the baby is about to be thrown out with the bath water.

The problem lies not in shared visions themselves, so long as they are developed carefully. The problem lies in our reactive orientation toward current reality. Vision becomes a living force only when people truly believe they can shape their future. The simple fact is that most managers do not *experience* that they are contributing to creating their current reality. So they don't see how they can contribute toward changing that reality. Their problems are created by somebody "out there" or by "the system."

This attitude can be elusive to pin down because in many organizations the belief "We cannot create our future" is so threatening that it can never be acknowledged. There is a strong espoused view that being a good manager and leader means being proactive, being in charge of your own future. A person who questions publicly whether the organization can achieve what it has set out to do is quickly labeled as "not on board" and seen as a problem.

Yet, this "can do" optimism is a thin veneer over a fundamentally reactive view, because most organizations are dominated by linear thinking, not systems thinking. The dominance of the event mentality tells people that the name of the game is reacting to change, not generating change. An event orientation will eventually drive out real vision, leaving only hollow "vision statements," good ideas that are never taken to heart.

But as people in an organization begin to learn how existing policies and actions are creating their current reality, a new, more fertile soil for vision develops. A new source of confidence develops, rooted in deeper understanding of the forces shaping current reality, a place where there is leverage for influencing those forces. I'll always remember a manager emerging from an extended "microworld" computer simulation session at one of the companies in our research program. When asked what he had learned, he replied: "I discovered that the reality we have is only one of several possible realities."

11

TEAM LEARNING

THE POTENTIAL WISDOM OF TEAMS

"By design and by talent," wrote basketball player Bill Russell of his team, the Boston Celtics, "[we] were a team of specialists, and like a team of specialists in any field, our performance depended both on individual excellence and on how well we worked together. None of us had to strain to understand that we had to complement each other's specialties; it was simply a fact, and we all tried to figure out ways to make our combination more effective. . . . Off the court, most of us were oddballs by society's standards—not the kind of people who blend in with others or who tailor their personalities to match what's expected of them."[1]

Russell is careful to tell us that it's not friendship, it's a different kind of team relationship that made his team's work special. That relationship, more than any individual triumph, gave him his greatest moments in the sport: "Every so often a Celtic game would heat up so that it became more than a physical or even mental game," he wrote, "and would be magical. The feeling is difficult to describe, and I certainly never talked about it when I was playing. When it happened I could feel my play rise to a new level . . . It would surround not only me and the other Celtics but also the players on the other team, and even the referees . . . At that special level, all sorts of odd things happened. The game would be in the white heat of competition, and yet I wouldn't feel competitive, which is a miracle in itself . . . The game would move so fast that every fake, cut, and pass would be surprising, and yet nothing could surprise me. It was almost as if we were playing in slow motion. During those spells, I could almost sense how the next play would develop and where the next shot would be taken . . . To me, the key was that *both* teams had to be playing at their peaks, and they had to be competitive. . . ."

Russell's Celtics (winner of eleven world championships in thirteen years) demonstrate a phenomenon we have come to call "alignment," when a group of people function as a whole. In most teams, the energies of individual members work at cross purposes. If we drew a picture of the team as a collection of individuals with different degrees of "personal power" (ability to accomplish intended results) headed in different directions in their lives, the picture might look something like this:[2]

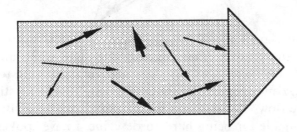

The fundamental characteristic of the relatively unaligned team is wasted energy. Individuals may work extraordinarily hard, but their efforts do not efficiently translate to team effort. By contrast, when a team becomes more aligned, a commonality of direction emerges, and individuals' energies harmonize. There is less wasted energy. In fact, a resonance or synergy develops, like the "coherent" light of a laser rather than the incoherent and scattered light of a light bulb. There is commonality of purpose, a shared vision, and understanding of how to complement one another's efforts. Individuals do not sacrifice their personal interests to the larger team vision; rather, the shared vision becomes an extension of their

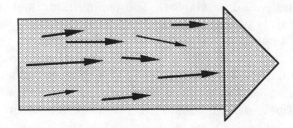

personal visions. In fact, alignment is the *necessary condition* before empowering the individual will empower the whole team. Empowering the individual when there is a relatively low level of alignment worsens the chaos and makes managing the team even more difficult:

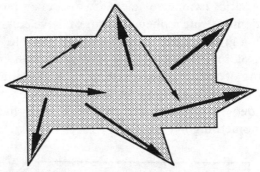

Jazz musicians know about alignment. There is a phrase in jazz, "being in the groove," that suggests the state when an ensemble "plays as one." These experiences are very difficult to put into words—jazz musicians talk about them in almost mystical terms: "the music flows through you rather than from you." But they are no less tangible for being hard to describe. I have spoken to many managers who have been members of teams that performed at similarly extraordinary levels. They will describe meetings that lasted for hours yet "flew by," not remembering "who said what, but knowing when we had really come to a shared understanding," of "never having to vote—we just got to a point of knowing what we needed to do."

Team learning is the process of aligning and developing the capacity of a team to create the results its members truly desire. It builds on the discipline of developing shared vision. It also builds on personal mastery, for talented teams are made up of talented individuals. But shared vision and talent are not enough. The world is full of teams of talented individuals who share a vision for a while, yet fail to learn. The great jazz ensemble has talent and a shared vision (even if they don't discuss it), but what really matters is that the musicians know how to *play* together.

There has never been a greater need for mastering team learning in organizations than there is today. Whether they are management teams or product development teams or cross-functional task forces—teams, "people who need one another to act," in the words of Arie de Geus, are becoming the key learning unit in organizations. This is so because almost all important decisions are now made in teams, either directly or through the need for teams to translate individual decisions into action. Individual learning, at some level, is irrelevant for organizational learning. Individuals learn all the time and yet there is no organizational learning. But if teams learn, they become a microcosm for learning throughout the organization. Insights gained are put into action. Skills developed can propagate to other individuals and to other teams (although there is no guarantee that they will propagate). The team's accomplishments can set the tone and establish a standard for learning together for the larger organization.

Within organizations, team learning has three critical dimensions. First, there is the need to think insightfully about complex issues. Here, teams must learn how to tap the potential for many minds to be more intelligent than one mind. While easy to say, there are powerful forces at work in organizations that tend to make the intelligence of the team less than, not greater than, the intelligence of individual team members. Many of these forces are within the direct control of the team members.

Second, there is the need for innovative, coordinated action. The championship sports teams and great jazz ensembles provide metaphors for acting in spontaneous yet coordinated ways. Outstanding teams in organizations develop the same sort of relationship—an "operational trust," where each team member remains conscious of other team members and can be counted on to act in ways that complement each other's actions.

Third, there is the role of team members on other teams. For example, most of the actions of senior teams are actually carried out through other teams. Thus, a learning team continually fosters other learning teams through inculcating the practices and skills of team learning more broadly.

Though it involves individual skills and areas of understanding, team learning is a collective discipline. Thus, it is meaningless to say that "I," as an individual, am mastering the discipline of team learning, just as it would be meaningless to say that "I am mastering the practice of being a great jazz ensemble."

The discipline of team learning involves mastering the practices of dialogue and discussion, the two distinct ways that teams converse. In dialogue, there is the free and creative exploration of complex and subtle issues, a deep "listening" to one another and suspending of one's own views. By contrast, in discussion different views are presented and defended and there is a search for the best view to support decisions that must be made at this time. Dialogue and discussion are potentially complementary, but most teams lack the ability to distinguish between the two and to move consciously between them.

Team learning also involves learning how to deal creatively with the powerful forces opposing productive dialogue and discussion in working teams. Chief among these are what Chris Argyris calls "defensive routines," habitual ways of interacting that protect us and others from threat or embarrassment, but which also prevent us from learning. For example, faced with conflict, team members frequently either "smooth over" differences or "speak out" in a no-holds-barred, "winner take all" free-for-all of opinion—what my colleague Bill Isaacs calls "the abstraction wars." Yet, the very defensive routines that thwart learning also hold great potential for fostering learning, if we can only learn how to unlock the energy they contain. The inquiry and reflection skills introduced in Chapter 9 begin to release this energy, which can then be focused in dialogue and discussion.

Systems thinking is especially prone to evoking defensiveness because of its central message, that our actions create our reality. Thus, a team may resist seeing important problems more systemically. To do so would imply that the problems arise from our own policies and strategies—that is "from us"—rather than from forces outside our control. I have seen many situations where teams will say "we're already thinking systemically," or espouse a systems view, then do nothing to put it into practice, or simply hold steadfastly to the view that "there's nothing we can do except cope with these problems." All of these strategies succeed in avoiding serious examination of how their own actions may be creating the very problems with which they try so hard to cope. More than other analytic frameworks, systems thinking requires mature teams capable of inquiring into complex, conflictual issues.

Lastly, the discipline of team learning, like any discipline, requires practice. Yet, this is exactly what teams in modern organizations lack. Imagine trying to build a great theater ensemble or a great symphony orchestra without rehearsal. Imagine a championship sports team without practice. In fact, the process whereby such teams learn is through continual movement between practice and performance, practice, performance, practice again, perform again. We are at the very beginning of learning how to create analogous opportunities for practice in management teams—some examples are given below.

Despite its importance, team learning remains poorly understood. Until we can describe the phenomenon better, it will remain mysterious. Until we have some theory of what happens when teams learn (as opposed to individuals in teams learning), we will be unable to distinguish group intelligence from "groupthink," when individuals succumb to group pressures for conformity. Until there are reliable methods for building teams that can learn together, its occurrence will remain a product of happenstance. This is why mastering team learning will be a critical step in building learning organizations.

THE DISCIPLINE OF
TEAM LEARNING

DIALOGUE AND DISCUSSION[3]

In a remarkable book, *Physics and Beyond: Encounters and Conversations,* Werner Heisenberg (formulator of the famous "Uncertainty Principle" in modern physics) argues that "Science is rooted in conversations. The cooperation of different people may culminate in scientific results of the utmost importance." Heisenberg then recalls a lifetime of conversations with Pauli, Einstein, Bohr, and the other great figures who uprooted and reshaped traditional physics in the first half of this century. These conversations, which Heisenberg says "had a lasting effect on my thinking," literally gave birth to many of the theories for which these men eventually became famous. Heisenberg's conversations, recalled in vivid detail and emotion, illustrate the staggering potential of collaborative learning—that collectively, we can be more insightful, more intelligent than we can possibly be individually.

The IQ of the team can, potentially, be much greater than the IQ of the individuals.

Given Heisenberg's reflections, it is perhaps not surprising that a significant contributor to the emerging discipline of team learning was a contemporary physicist, the late David Bohm. Bohm, a leading quantum theorist, worked to develop a theory and method of "dialogue," when a group "becomes open to the flow of a larger intelligence." Dialogue, it turns out, is a very old idea revered by the ancient Greeks and practiced by many "primitive" societies such as the American Indians. Yet, it is all but lost to the modern world. All of us have had some taste of dialogue—in special conversations that begin to have a "life of their own," taking us in directions we could never have imagined or planned in advance. But these experiences come rarely, a product of circumstance rather than systematic effort and disciplined practice.

Bohm's later work on the theory and practice of dialogue represents a unique synthesis of the two major intellectual currents underlying the disciplines discussed in the preceding chapters: the systems or holistic view of nature, and the interactions between our thinking and internal models and our perceptions and actions. "Quantum theory," said Bohm, "implies that the universe is basically an indivisible whole, even though on the larger scale level it may be represented approximately as divisible into separately existing parts. In particular, this means that, at a quantum theoretical level of accuracy, the observing instrument and the observed object participate in each other in an irreducible way. At this level perception and action therefore cannot be separated."

This is reminiscent of some of the key features of systems thinking, which calls attention to how what is happening is often the consequence of our own actions as guided by our perceptions. Similar questions are raised by the theory of relativity, as Bohm suggested in a 1965 book, *The Special Theory of Relativity*[4] In this book, Bohm started to connect the systems perspective and mental models more explicitly. In particular, he argued that the purpose of science was not the "accumulation of knowledge" (since, after all, all scientific theories are eventually proved false) but rather the creation of "mental maps" that guide and shape our perception and action, bringing about a constant "mutual participation between nature and consciousness."

However, Bohm's most distinctive contribution, one which leads to unique insights into team learning, stems from seeing thought as "largely as collective phenomenon." Bohm became interested fairly early in the analogy between the collective properties of particles (for example, the system wide movements of an "electron sea") and the way in which our thought works. Later, he saw that this sort of analogy could throw an important light on the general "counter-productiveness of thought, as can be observed in almost every phase of life. "Our thought is incoherent," Bohm asserts, "and the resulting counterproductiveness lies at the root of the world's problems." But, Bohm says, since thought is to a large degree collective, we cannot just improve thought individually. "As with electrons, we must look on thought as a systemic phenomenon arising from how we interact and discourse with one another."

There are two primary types of discourse, dialogue and discussion. Both are important to a team capable of continual generative learning, but their power lies in their synergy, which is not likely to be present when the distinctions between them are not appreciated.

Bohm points out that the word "discussion" has the same root as percussion and concussion. It suggests something like a "ping-pong game where we are hitting the ball back and forth between us." In such a game the subject of common interest may be analyzed and dissected from many points of view provided by those who take part. Clearly, this can be useful. Yet, the purpose of a game is normally "to win" and in this case winning means to have one's views accepted by the group. You might occasionally accept part of another person's view in order to strengthen your own, but you fundamentally want your view to prevail." A sustained emphasis on winning is not compatible, however, with giving first priority to coherence and truth. Bohm suggests that what is needed to bring about such a change of priorities is "dialogue," which is a different mode of communication.

By contrast with discussion, the word "dialogue" comes from the Greek *dialogos*. *Dia* means through. *Logos* means the word, or more broadly, the meaning. Bohm suggests that the original meaning of dialogue was the "meaning passing or moving through . . . a free flow of meaning between people, in the sense of a stream that flows between two banks."[5] In dialogue, Bohm contends, a group accesses a larger "pool of common meaning," which cannot be accessed individually. "The whole organizes the parts," rather than trying to pull the parts into a whole.

The purpose of a dialogue is to go beyond any one individual's understanding. "We are not trying to win in a dialogue. We all win if we are doing it right." In dialogue, individuals gain insights that simply could not be achieved individually. "A new kind of mind begins to come into being which is based on the development of a common meaning . . . People are no longer primarily in opposition, nor can they said to be interacting, rather they are participating in this pool of common meaning, which is capable of constant development and change."

In dialogue, a group explores complex difficult issues from many points of view. Individuals suspend their assumptions but they communicate their assumptions freely. The result is a free exploration that brings to the surface the full depth of people's experience and thought, and yet can move beyond their individual views.

"The purpose of dialogue," Bohm suggests, "is to reveal the incoherence in our thought." There are three types of incoherence. "Thought denies that it is participative." Thought stops tracking reality and "just goes, like a program." And thought establishes its own standard of reference for fixing problems, problems which it contributed to creating in the first place.

To illustrate, consider prejudice. Once a person begins to accept a stereotype of a particular group, that "thought" becomes an active agent, "participating" in shaping how he or she interacts with another person who falls into that stereotyped class. In turn, the tone of their interaction influences the other person's behavior. The prejudiced person can't see how his prejudice shapes what he "sees" and how he acts. In some sense, if he did, he would no longer be prejudiced. To operate, the "thought" of prejudice must remain hidden to its holder.

"Thought *presents* itself (stands in front) of us and pretends that it does not *represent*." We are like actors who forget they are playing a role. We become trapped in the theater of our thoughts (the words "theater" and "theory" have the same root—*theoria*—"to look at"). This is when thought starts, in Bohm's words, to become "incoherent." "Reality may change but the theater continues." We operate in the theater, defining problems, taking actions, "solving problems," losing touch with the larger reality from which the theater is generated.

Dialogue is a way of helping people to "see the representative and participatory nature of thought [and] . . . to become more sensitive to and make it safe to acknowledge the incoherence in our thought." *In dialogue people become observers of their own thinking.*

What they observe is that their thinking is active. For example, when a conflict surfaces in a dialogue people are likely to realize that there is a tension, but the tension arises, literally, from our thoughts. People will say, "It is our thoughts and the way we hold on to them that are in conflict, not us." Once people see the participatory nature of their thought, they begin to separate themselves from their thought. They begin to take a more creative, less reactive, stance toward their thought.

People in dialogue also begin to observe the collective nature of thought. Bohm says that "Most thought is collective in origin. Each individual does something with it," but originates collectively by and large. "Language, for example, is entirely collective," says Bohm. "And without language, thought as we know it couldn't be there." Most of the assumptions we hold were acquired from the pool of culturally acceptable assumptions. Few of us learn truly to "think for ourselves." He or she who does is sure, as Emerson said long ago, "to be misunderstood."

They also begin to observe the difference between "thinking" as an ongoing process as distinct from "thoughts," the results of that process. This is very important, according to Bohm, to begin correcting the incoherence in our thinking.

If collective thinking is an ongoing stream, "thoughts" are like leaves floating on the surface that wash up on the banks. We gather in the leaves, which we experience as "thoughts." We misperceive the thoughts as our own, because we fail to see the stream of collective thinking from which they arise.

In dialogue, people begin to see the stream that flows between the banks. They begin to "participate in this pool of common meaning, which is capable of constant development and change." Bohm believes that our normal processes of thought are like a "coarse net that gathers in only the coarsest elements of the stream. In dialogue, a "kind of sensitivity" develops that goes beyond what is familiar, what we normally recognize as thinking. This sensitivity is "a fine net" capable of gathering in the subtle meanings in the flow of thinking. Bohm believes this sensitivity lies at the root of real intelligence.

So, according to Bohm, collective learning is not only possible but vital to realize the potentials of human intelligence. "Through dialogue people can help each other to become aware of the incoherence in each other's thoughts, and in this way the collective thought becomes more and more coherent [from the Latin *cohaerere*—"hanging together"]. It is difficult to give a simple definition of coherence, beyond saying that one may sense it as order, consistency, beauty, or harmony.

The main point, however, is not to strive for some abstract ideal of coherence. It is rather for all the participants to work together to become sensitive to all the possible forms of *incoherence*. Incoherence may be indicated by contradictions and confusion but more basically it is seen by the fact that our thinking is producing consequences that we don't really want.

Bohm identifies three basic conditions necessary for dialogue:

1. all participants must "suspend" their assumptions, literally to hold them "as if suspended before us";
2. all participants must regard one another as colleagues;
3. there must be a "facilitator" who "holds the context" of dialogue.

These conditions contribute to allowing the "free flow of meaning" to pass through a group, by diminishing resistance to the flow. Just as resistance in an electrical circuit causes the flow of current to generate heat (wasted energy), so does the normal functioning of a group dissipate energy. In dialogue there is "cool energy, like a superconductor." "Hot topics," subjects that would otherwise become sources of emotional discord and fractiousness become discussable. Even more, they become windows to deeper insights.

Suspending Assumptions. To "suspend" one's assumptions means to hold them, "as it were, 'hanging in front of you,' constantly accessible to questioning and observation." This does not mean throwing out our assumptions, suppressing them, or avoiding their expression. Nor does it say that having opinions is "bad," or that we should eliminate subjectivism. Rather, it means being aware of our assumptions and holding them up for examination. This cannot be done if we are defending our opinions. Nor, can it be done if we are unaware of our assumptions, or unaware that our views are based on *assumptions*, rather than incontrovertible fact.

Bohm argues that once an individual "digs in his or her heels" and decides "this is the way it is," the flow of dialogue is blocked. This requires operating on the "knife edge," as Bohm puts it, because "the mind wants to keep moving away from suspending assumptions . . . to adopting non-negotiable and rigid opinions which we then feel compelled to defend."

For example, in a recent dialogue session involving a top management team of a highly successful technology company (reported in detail below), people perceived a deep "split" in the organization between R&D and everyone else, a split due to R&D's exalted role at the company. This split had its roots in the firm's thirty year history of innovation: they literally pioneered several dramatic new products that in turn became industry standards. Product innovation was the cornerstone of the firm's reputation in the marketplace. Thus, no one felt able to talk about the split, even though it was creating many problems. To do so might have challenged the long-cherished value of technology leadership and of giving highly creative engineers the autonomy to pursue their product visions. Moreover, the number-two person in R&D was in the meeting.

When the condition of suspending all assumptions was discussed, the head of marketing asked, "*All* assumptions?" When he received an affirmative answer, he looked perplexed. Later, as the session continued, he acknowledged that he held the assumption that R&D saw itself as the "keeper of the flame" for the organization, and that he further assumed that this made them unapproachable regarding market information that might influence product development. This led to the R&D manager responding that he too assumed that others saw him in this light, and that, to everyone's surprise, he felt that this assumption limited his and the R&D organization's effectiveness. Both shared these assumptions *as assumptions,* not proven fact. As a result, the ensuing dialogue opened up into a dramatic exploration of views that was unprecedented in its candor and its strategy implications.

Suspending assumptions is a lot like seeing "leaps of abstraction" and "inquiring into the reasoning behind the abstraction," basic reflection and inquiry skills developed in Chapter 9, "Mental Models." But in dialogue, suspending assumptions must be done collectively. The team's discipline of holding assumptions suspended allowed the team members to see their own assumptions clearly because they could be held up and contrasted with each others' assumptions. Suspending assumptions is difficult, Bohm maintains, because of "the very nature of thought. Thought continually deludes us into a view that 'this is the way it is.'" The discipline of suspending assumptions is an antidote to that delusion.

Seeing Each Other as Colleagues. Dialogue can occur only when a group of people see each other as colleagues in mutual quest for deeper insight and clarity. Thinking of one other as colleagues is important because thought is participative. The conscious act of thinking of one other as colleagues contributes toward interacting as colleagues. This may sound simple, but it can make a profound difference.

Seeing each other as colleagues is critical to establish a positive tone and to offset the vulnerability that dialogue brings. In dialogue people actually feel as if they are building something, a new deeper understanding. Seeing each other as colleagues and friends, while it may sound simple, proves to be extremely important. We talk differently with friends from the way we do with people who are not friends. Interestingly, as dialogue develops, team members will find this feeling of friendship developing even towards others with whom they do not have much in common. What is necessary going in is the *willingness* to consider each other as colleagues. In addition, there is a certain vulnerability to holding assumptions in suspension. Treating each other as colleagues acknowledges the mutual risk and establishes the sense of safety in facing the risk.

Colleagueship does not mean that you need to agree or share the same views. On the contrary, the real power of seeing each other as colleagues comes into play when there are differences of view. It is easy to feel collegial when everyone agrees. When there are significant disagreements, it is more difficult. But the payoff is also much greater. Choosing to view adversaries as "colleagues with different views" has the greatest benefits.

Bohm expressed doubts about the possiblity of dialogue in organizations because of the condition of colleagueship: "Hierarchy is antithetical to dialogue, and it is difficult to escape hiearchy in organizations." He asks: "Can those in authority really 'level' with those in subordinate positions?" Such questions have several operational implications for organizational teams. First, everyone involved must truly *want* the benefits of dialogue more than he wants to hold onto his privileges of rank. If one person is used to having his view prevail because he is the most senior person, then that privilege must be surrendered in dialogue. If one person is used to withholding his views because he is more junior, then that security of nondisclosure must also be surrendered. Fear and judgment must give way. Dialogue is playful; it requires the willingness to play with new ideas, to examine them and test them. As soon as we become overly concerned with "who said what," or "not saying something stupid," the playfulness will evaporate.

These conditions cannot be taken lightly, but we have found many organizational teams consistently up to the challenge if everyone knows what will be expected of him in advance. Deep down, there is a longing for dialogue, especially when focused on issues of the utmost importance to us. But that doesn't mean dialogue is always possible in organizations. If all participants are not willing to live by the conditions of suspending assumptions and colleagueship, dialogue will not be possible.

A Facilitator Who "Holds the Context" of Dialogue. In the absence of a skilled facilitator, our habits of thought continually pull us toward discussion and away from dialogue. This is especially true in the early stages of developing dialogue as a team discipline. We take what "presents itself in our thoughts as literal, rather than as a representation. We believe in our own views and want them to prevail. We are worried about suspending our assumptions publicly. We may even be uncertain if it is psychologically safe to suspend "all assumptions"—"After all, aren't there some assumptions that I must hold on to or lose my sense of identity?"

The facilitator of a dialogue session carries out many of the basic duties of a good "process facilitator." These functions include helping people maintain ownership of the process and the outcomes—we are responsible for what is happening. If people start to harbor reservations that "so-and-so" won't let us talk about this, that constitutes an assumption not held in suspension. The facilitator also must keep the dialogue moving. If any one individual should start to divert the process to a discussion when a discussion is not actually what is called for, this needs to be identified, and the group asked whether the conditions for dialogue are continuing to be met. The facilitator always walks a careful line between being knowledgeable and helpful in the process at hand, yet not taking on the "expert" or "doctor" mantle that would shift attention away from the members of the team, and their own ideas and responsibility.[6]

But, in dialogue the facilitator also does something more. His understanding of dialogue allows him to influence the flow of development simply through participating. For example, after someone has made an observation, the facilitator may say, "But the opposite may also be true." Beyond such reminders of the conditions for dialogue, the facilitator's participation demonstrates dialogue. The artistry of dialogue lies in experiencing the flow of meaning and seeing the one thing that needs to be said now. Like the Quakers, who enjoin members to say not simply whatever pops into their heads but only those thoughts that are compelling (and which cause the speaker to *quake* from the need to speak them), the facilitator says only what is needed at each point in time. This deepens others' appreciation of dialogue more than any abstract explanation can ever do.

As teams develop experience and skill in dialogue, the role of the facilitator becomes less crucial and he or she can gradually become just one of the participants. Dialogue emerges from the "leaderless" group once the team members have developed their skill and understanding. In societies where dialogue is an ongoing discipline, there usually are no appointed facilitators. For example, many American Indian tribes cultivated dialogue to a high art without formal facilitators. Shamans and other wise men had special roles, but the group was capable of entering a dialogue on its own.

Balancing Dialogue and Discussion. In team learning, discussion is the necessary counterpart of dialogue. In a discussion, different views are presented and defended, and as explained earlier this may provide a useful analysis of the whole situation. In dialogue, different views are presented as a means toward discovering a new view. In a discussion, decisions are made. In a dialogue, complex issues are explored. When a team must reach agreement and decisions must be taken, some discussion is needed. On the basis of a commonly agreed-upon analysis, alternative views need to be weighed and a preferred view selected (which may be one of the original alternatives or a new view that emerges from the discussion). When they are productive, discussions converge on a conclusion or course of action. On the other hand, dialogues are diverging; they do not seek agreement, but a richer grasp of complex issues. Both dialogue and discussion can lead to new courses of action; but actions are often the focus of discussion, whereas new actions emerge as a by-product of dialogue.

A learning team masters movement back and forth between dialogue and discussion. The ground rules are different. The goals are different. Failing to distinguish them, teams usually have neither dialogue nor productive discussions.

A unique relationship develops among team members who enter into dialogue regularly. They develop a deep trust that cannot help but carry over to discussions. They develop a richer understanding of the uniqueness of each person's point of view. Moreover, they experience how larger understandings emerge by holding one's own point of view "gently." They learn to master the art of holding a position, rather than being "held by their positions." When it is appropriate to defend a point of view, they do it more gracefully and with less rigidity, that is without putting "winning" as a first priority.

Moreover, to a large degree, the skills that allow dialogue are identical to the skills that can make discussions productive rather than destructive. These are the skills of inquiry and reflection, originally discussed in Chapter 9, "Mental Models." In fact, one of the reasons that dialogue is so important is that it offers a safe environment for honing these skills and for discovering the profound group learning that they can lead to.

Reflection, Inquiry, and Dialogue. In David Bohm's thinking we hear deep echoes of the "action science" approach discussed in Chapter 9—the importance of making one's views open to influence; and the problem of confusing our mental models with reality. What makes Bohm's work distinctive is that he is articulating a "new" vision of what can happen in a group that transcends the disabilities identified by the action scientists. Moreover, Bohm's dialogue is a *team discipline.* It cannot be achieved individually.

Part of the vision of dialogue is the assumption of a "larger pool of meaning" accessible only to a group. This idea, while it may appear radical at first, has deep intuitive appeal to managers who have long cultivated the subtler aspects of collective inquiry and consensus building.

Such managers learn early on to distinguish two types of consensus: a "focusing down" type of consensus that seeks the common denominator in multiple individual views, and an "opening up" type of consensus that seeks a picture larger than any one person's point of view. The first type of consensus builds from the "content" of our individual views—discovering what part of my view is shared by you and the others. This is our "common ground," upon which we can all agree.

The second type of consensus builds more from the idea that we each have a "view," a way of looking at reality. Each person's view is a unique perspective on a larger reality. If I can "look out" through your view and you through mine, we will each see something we might not have seen alone.

If dialogue articulates a unique vision of team learning, reflection and inquiry skills may prove essential to realizing that vision. Just as personal vision provides a foundation for building shared vision, so too do reflection and inquiry skills provide a foundation for dialogue and discussion. Dialogue that is *grounded in* reflection and inquiry skills is likely to be more reliable and less dependent on particulars of circumstance, such as the chemistry among team members.

DEALING WITH "CURRENT REALITY": CONFLICT AND DEFENSIVE ROUTINES

Contrary to popular myth, great teams are not characterized by an absence of conflict. On the contrary, in my experience, one of the most reliable indicators of a team that is continually learning is the visible conflict of ideas. In great teams conflict becomes productive. There may, and often will, be conflict around the vision. In fact, the essence of the "visioning" process lies in the gradual emergence of a shared vision from different personal visions. Even when people share a common vision, they may have many different ideas about how to achieve that vision. The loftier the vision, the more uncertain we are how it is to be achieved. The free flow of conflicting ideas is critical for creative thinking, for discovering new solutions no one individual would have come to on his own. Conflict becomes, in effect, part of the ongoing dialogue.

On the other hand, in mediocre teams, one of two conditions usually surrounds conflict. Either, there is an appearance of no conflict on the surface, or there is rigid polarization. In the "smooth surface" teams, members believe that they must suppress their conflicting views in order to maintain the team—if each person spoke her or his mind, the team would be torn apart by irreconcilable differences. The polarized team is one in which managers "speak out," but conflicting views are deeply entrenched. Everyone knows where everyone else stands, and there is little movement.

For more than forty years, Chris Argyris and his colleagues have studied the dilemma of why bright, capable managers often fail to learn effectively in management teams. Their work suggests that the difference between great teams and mediocre teams lies in how they face conflict and deal with the defensiveness that invariably surrounds conflict. "We are programmed to create defensive routines," says Argyris, "and cover them up with further defensive routines . . . This programming occurs early in life."[7]

Defensive routines, as noted in Chapter 9, "Mental Models," are entrenched habits we use to protect ourselves from the embarrassment and threat that come with exposing our thinking. Defensive routines form a sort of protective shell around our deepest assumptions, defending us against pain, but also keeping us from learning about the causes of the pain. The source of defensive routines, according to Argyris, is not belief in our views or desire to preserve social relations, as we might tell ourselves, but fear of exposing the thinking that lies behind our views. "Defensive reasoning," says Argyris ". . . protects us from learning about the validity of our reasoning."[8] For most of us, exposing our reasoning is threatening because we are afraid that people will find errors in it. The perceived threat from exposing our thinking starts early in life and, for most of us, is steadily reinforced in school—remember the trauma of being called on and not having the "right answer"—and later in work.

Defensive routines are so diverse and so commonplace, they usually go unnoticed. We say, "That's a very interesting idea," when we have no intention of taking the idea seriously. We deliberately confront someone to squash an idea, to avoid having to consider it. Or, in the guise of being helpful, we shelter someone from criticism, but also shelter ourselves from engaging difficult issues. When a difficult issue comes up, we change the subject—ostensibly out of respect for the "manners" of good behavior.

One forceful CEO recently lamented to me about the absence of "real leaders" in his organization. He felt his company was full of compliant people, not committed visionaries. This was especially frustrating to a man who regards himself as a skilled communicator and risk taker. In fact, he is so brilliant at articulating *his* vision that he intimidates everyone around him. Consequently, his views rarely get challenged publicly. People have learned not to express their own views and visions around him. While he would not see his own forcefulness as a defensive strategy, if he looked carefully, he would see that it functions in exactly that way.

The most effective defensive routines, like that of the forceful CEO, are those we cannot see. Ostensibly, the CEO hoped to provoke others into expressing their thoughts. But his overbearing behavior reliably prevented them from doing so, thereby protecting his views from challenge. If expressed as a conscious strategy, the defensiveness is transparent: "Keep people on the defensive through intimidation, so they won't confront my thinking." If the CEO saw his strategy presented in such bald terms, he would almost certainly disavow it. The fact that it remains hidden keeps it operative.

Problems caused by defensive routines compound in organizations where to have incomplete or faulty understanding is a sign of weakness or, worse, incompetence. Deep within the mental models of managers in many organizations is the belief that managers must know what's going on. It is simply unacceptable for managers to act as though they do not know what is causing a problem. Those that reach senior positions are masters at appearing to know what is going on, and those intent on reaching such positions learn early on to develop an air of confident knowledge.

Managers who internalize this mental model find themselves in one of two binds. Some actually internalize this air of confidence and simply believe that they know the answers to most important problems. But, to protect their belief, they must close themselves to alternative views and make themselves uninfluenceable. Their bind is that to remain confident they must remain rigid. Others believe they are expected to know what is causing important problems but, deep down, recognize the uncertainty in their solutions. Their bind is that to maintain a facade of confidence they must obscure their ignorance. Whichever bind they find themselves in, managers who take on the burden of having to know the answers become highly skillful in defensive routines that preserve their aura as capable decision makers by not revealing the thinking behind their decisions.

Such defensiveness becomes an accepted part of organizational culture. Argyris says, "Whenever I ask individuals . . . what leads them to play political games in organizations? They respond that that's human nature and the nature of organizations. . . . We are the carriers of defensive routines, and organizations are the hosts. Once organizations have been infected, they too become carriers."[9]

Teams are microcosms of the larger organization, so it is not surprising that the defensive patterns characteristic of the larger organization become embedded in the team. In effect, defensive routines block the flow of energy in a team that might otherwise contribute toward a common vision. To the members of a team caught in their defensive routines, they feel very much like walls—blocks and traps that prevent collective learning.

To see how subtle team defensive routines become, consider the case of ATP products: a young division of an innovative, highly decentralized corporation. (The company and individual names are disguised.) Jim Tabor, the thirty-three-year-old division president, was deeply committed to the corporate values of freedom and local autonomy. He believed strongly in ATP's products, which were based on a new printed circuit board technology. He was tremendously enthusiastic, a natural cheerleader for his people. In turn, the members of his management team worked long hours and shared his enthusiasm for their prospects.

Their efforts were rewarded with several years of rapid (30 to 50 percent per year) growth in bookings, reaching $50 million in sales in 1994. However, 1995 witnessed a disastrous collapse in bookings.[10] Two major minicomputer manufacturers had become so convinced of ATP's technology that they had designed the ATP circuit boards into new lines of hardware. But when the 1995 downturn in the minicomputer industry hit, the manufacturers suspended work on the new lines, leaving ATP with a 50 percent shortfall on projected bookings. The business did not bounce back in 1996. Jim Tabor was eventually removed as division president, although he stayed on as engineering manager.

What went wrong at ATP? Through their enthusiasm, the ATP management had locked itself into a strategy that was internally inconsistent. The team had set aggressive growth targets, in part to please the corporate management, but also because of belief in their product. Meeting these targets had created strong pressures on the sales force, to which they had responded by building major business relationships with a few key customers, customers upon whom ATP had become highly dependent. When some of those customers ran into their own business troubles, ATP was doomed.

Why had ATP's management team sanctioned a strategy that left the division so vulnerable? Why did the corporate leadership not intervene to insist that the young division managers diversify their customer base? At the heart of their problem was a set of defensive routines, embedded in a "shifting the burden" structure.

As Argyris says, defensive routines are a response to a problem; here, the problem is a need to learn, arising from a "learning gap" between what is known and what needs to be known. The "fundamental solution" is inquiry that results eventually in new understanding and new behavior—that is, learning. But the need for learning also creates a threat. Individuals and teams respond defensively to the threat. This leads to the "symptomatic solution": defensive routines that eliminate the learning gap by reducing the *perceived need* for learning.

All the key players at ATP were caught in their own particular defensive routines. Several of ATP's managers had expressed con-

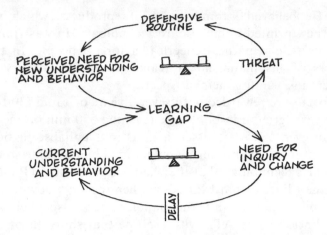

cern about their reliance on a narrow customer base. When the issue was raised in team meetings, everyone agreed it was a problem. But no one did anything about it because everyone was too busy. Driven by their challenging growth targets, ATP's managers had expanded capacity aggressively and created powerful pressures for new order bookings, regardless of where they came from.

The corporate managers to whom Tabor reported were caught in a similar bind. Here too there was concern about ATP's narrow customer base. Privately, some of the corporate managers had questions regarding Tabor's ability to build for long-term growth. But these same executives also believed strongly in a corporate philosophy of not undermining division presidents' authority to run their own businesses. They were uncertain how to raise their qualms without seeming unsupportive of Tabor's leadership, so they made only oblique comments or kept quiet.

On the other side of the table, Jim Tabor had questions himself, which he was reluctant to raise in meetings with his superiors. He had never been a division president before. He was eager to prove his abilities. He believed deeply in the business's potential and he felt committed to his fellow managers at ATP. He didn't want to let them down, just as he didn't want to let down his superiors. So he didn't talk about his own uneasiness concerning the aggressive growth targets ATP had set.

The conflicts among ATP's management, corporate management, and Tabor were submerged under a surface of defensive routines and thus were never resolved. Within the team, qualms about the basic business strategy were lost in the pressures to meet the targets dictated by the strategy. Tabor's corporate superiors wanted to offer help but didn't want to appear unsupportive. Tabor needed help but he didn't want to appear unconfident. Behind the surface of mutual support, camaraderie, and "all for one" spirit, lay ways of dealing with conflict that ultimately resulted in outcomes contrary to everyone's intentions.

The more effective defensive routines are, the more effectively they cover up underlying problems, the less effectively these problems are faced, and the worse the problems tend to become. The real need to learn didn't go away at ATP. By avoiding the real problems—how to build up a broad customer base—the team allowed the problems to get worse. As in all shifting the burden structures, the more teams turn to defensive routines, the more they come to rely on them. "The paradox," writes Argyris, "is that when [defensive routines] succeed in preventing immediate pain they also prevent us from learning how to reduce what causes the pain in the first place."[11]

As Argyris also says, defensive routines are "self-sealing"—they obscure their own existence. This comes in large measure because we have society-wide norms that say that we *should* be open and that defensiveness is bad. This makes it difficult to acknowledge defensive routines, even if we know that we are being defensive. If Tabor's corporate superiors had stated their strategy explicitly, it would have sounded something like the following: "We are avoiding questioning Jim's abilities, to avoid having to face the conflict that would ensue and to maintain an appearance of support." If such a strategy were stated, they would surely have disavowed it. Likewise, if Tabor had said, "I am avoiding expressing my doubts about how we are managing because I am afraid that it will make me look weak or incompetent," his defensive strategy would have been unsustainable. But no one voiced these feelings because of the same basic fears that made everyone take up the defensive routines in the first place.

If you can't easily state defensive routines, where is the leverage for reducing them? In most shifting the burden structures, there are two possible areas of leverage: (1) weaken the symptomatic solution and (2) strengthen the fundamental solution. One way of weakening the symptomatic solution is diminishing the emotional threat that prompts the defensive response in the first place. For example, if Tabor had felt comfortable about acknowledging his own uncertainty in front of his corporate superiors, or if they had felt comfortable raising their questions, each would have been less inclined to avoiding fundamental questioning of ATP's strategy.[12] Learning how to deal with defensive routines when they arise would also weaken the symptomatic solution. To retain their power, defensive routines *must remain undiscussable.* Teams stay stuck in their defensive routines only when they pretend that they don't have any defensive routines, that everything is all right, and that they can say "anything."

But how to make them discussable is a challenge. Trying to "fix" another person's defensive routine is almost guaranteed to backfire. For example, try asking someone why he has been behaving defensively. Universally, the first response is a protest: "Me? I'm not behaving defensively!" By focusing attention on the other person, the "confronter" has taken no responsibility for the situation. It *always* takes two (or more) to dance. If we perceive a defensive routine operating, it is a good bet that we are part of it. Skillful managers learn to confront defensiveness without producing more defensiveness.

They do so by self-disclosure and by inquiring into the causes of their own defensiveness. For example, they might say something such as, "I notice that I am feeling threatened by this new proposal. You may be also. Could you help me in seeing where this uneasiness is coming from?" Or, "Is what I am saying making sense? I think that the way I am communicating makes me seem closed and adamant on this point. But I'd like to hear your view so that we can get a more objective picture." (Obviously, it is the spirit of the statements not their specifics that matter.) Both of these statements acknowledge the speaker's experience of uneasiness and invite a joint inquiry into its causes.

The skills for defusing defensive routines are essentially the same skills used for strengthening the "fundamental solution" in the shifting the burden structure—the skills of reflection and mutual inquiry. By inquiring effectively into the causes of the problems at hand—that is, by inquiring in such a way as to reveal your own assumptions and reasoning, make them open to influence, and encourage others to do likewise—defensive routines are less likely to come into play.[13]

While defensive routines can become especially pernicious in a team, on the other hand, teams have unique capabilities for transcending defensiveness—if there is genuine commitment to learning. What is required, not surprisingly, is a vision of what we really want, both in terms of business results and how we want to work together, and a ruthless commitment to telling the truth about our current reality. In this sense, team learning and building shared vision are sister disciplines. They naturally go together to build creative tension in a team.

In the presence of a genuinely shared vision, defensive routines become just another aspect of current reality. Like the structural conflicts discussed in the chapter on personal mastery, they derive their power from being unrecognized. A team committed to the truth has unique powers to surface and acknowledge their own defensiveness. Then the defensive routines can actually become a source of energy rather than inertia.

Defensive routines can become a surprising ally toward building a learning team by providing a signal when learning is not occurring. Most of us know when we are being defensive, even if we cannot fully identify the source or pattern of our defensiveness. If you think about it, one of the most useful skills of a learning team would be the ability to recognize when people are *not* reflecting on their own assumptions, when they are *not* inquiring into each other's thinking, when they are *not* exposing their thinking in a way that encourages others to inquire into it. When we are feeling defensive, seeking to avoid an issue, thinking we need to protect someone else or ourselves—these are tangible signals that can be used to reestablish a climate of learning. But we must learn to recognize the signals and learn how to acknowledge the defensiveness without provoking more defensiveness.

Defensive routines may signal especially difficult and especially important issues. Often, the stronger the defensiveness, the more important the issue around which people are defending or protecting their views. If these views can be brought out productively, they may provide windows onto each other's thinking. When defensiveness is met by self-disclosure and inquiry balanced with advocacy, team members begin to see more of each other's thinking.

Lastly, as team members learn how to work with rather than against their defensive routines, they start to build confidence that "we are senior to our defensiveness." Defensive routines pull down team members. They drain energy and sap people's spirit. When a team sees itself transcend blocks that have been preventing learning, blocks which many felt were inevitable—as Argyris observed, "the nature of organizations"—they gain tangible experience that there may be many aspects of their reality that they have the power to change.

In medieval times, alchemy was a symbol for transformation of what is most common (lead) into what is most precious (gold). So, too, do learning teams practice a special form of alchemy, the transformation of potentially divisive conflict and defensiveness into learning. They do this through their vision and skill. Through dialogue, team members gain tangible experience of the larger intelligence that can operate. This experience strengthens the team members' vision of how they might operate. But unless the team also builds the skills for seeing rather than obscuring current reality, their capacity for learning will be unreliable. Without reflection and inquiry skills, they will get thrown off course when defensiveness arises—their learning will depend on circumstances.

It is not the absence of defensiveness that characterizes learning teams but the way defensiveness is faced. A team committed to learning must be committed not only to telling the truth about what's going on "out there," in their business reality, but also about what's going on "in here," within the team itself. To see reality more clearly, we must also see our strategies for obscuring reality.

The power and insight that start to emerge when this happens are considerable. In effect, defensive routines are like safes within which we "lock up" energy that could be directed toward collective learning. As defensiveness becomes "unlocked," that insight and energy are released, becoming available for building shared understanding and advancing toward what the team members truly want to create.

THE MISSING LINK: PRACTICE

It cannot be stressed too much that team learning is a *team skill*. A group of talented individual learners will not necessarily produce a learning team, any more than a group of talented athletes will produce a great sports team. Learning teams learn how to learn together.

If anything, team skills are *more* challenging to develop than individual skills. This is why learning teams need "practice fields," ways to practice together so that they can develop their collective learning skills. The almost total absence of meaningful practice or rehearsal is probably the predominant factor that keeps most management teams from being effective learning units.

What exactly is "practice"? In *The Reflective Practitioner*, Donald Schon identifies the essential principles of practice as experimentation in a *"virtual world."* A virtual world is a "constructed representation of the real world." It can be as simple as the architects' sketchpad:

> Here they can draw and talk their moves in a spatial-action language, leaving traces which represent the forms of buildings on the site. Because the drawing reveals qualities and relations unimagined beforehand, moves can function as experiments . . . [discovering] that building shapes do not fit the slope and that . . . classrooms are too small in scale.[14]

The essence of a virtual world is the freedom it allows for experimentation. The pace of action can be slowed down or speeded up. Phenomena that occur very rapidly can be stretched out over time to study more carefully. Phenomena that stretch out over very long periods can be speeded up to see more clearly the consequences of particular actions. No move is irreversible. Actions that cannot be reversed or taken back and redone in the real setting can be redone countless times. Changes in the environment can be eliminated, either completely or partially. Complexity can be simplified by uncoupling variables that are interlocked in reality.

The manipulations that Schon describes in the virtual worlds of the architects and other professionals match precisely what happens when the basketball team or the symphony orchestra practices. They vary the pace of the action—by slowing down the music, by running plays in slow motion. They isolate components and simplify the complexity—by playing individual sections, by running plays without a competitor. They reverse what is, in the real performance, irreversible—they replay the same section over and over, they rerun the play over and over.

Interestingly, the few examples in business of teams which learn consistently over a long period of time seem to be exactly those settings where effective virtual worlds operate. For instance, modern advertising practice is based on the concept of a creative team, where an account supervisor, art director, and copywriter work closely together, often for years. So close are these teams that teammates often switch agencies together, rather than break apart. What makes advertising teams special is that they practice together, as consistently and intensively as the members of a basketball team do. They brainstorm ideas, and then experiment with them, testing them in storyboards or mock-ups, and eventually presenting them—first to higher-ups in the agency, then to the client.

Team learning requires that type of regular practice. But management teams, by and large, are bereft of it. True, they have the abstract, intellectual debates of ideas, and many team members come to learn each others' intellectual opinions, often only too well. But there is nothing akin to a storyboard or a rehearsal. The main product of the team's work is decisions about specific situations, often debated and decided under great time pressure, and each decision is final as soon as it is made. There is no experimentation with decisions; worse still, there is little opportunity to form reasoned assessments of the wisdom of different decisions, and there is no opportunity to step back, as a team, and reflect on how we might arrive at better decisions together.

LEARNING HOW "TO PRACTICE"

Today, the discipline of team learning is, I believe, poised for a breakthrough because we are gradually learning how "to practice." This starts with creataing distinct "practice fields" so that a team can begin to develop its *joint skill* in fostering a team IQ that exceeds individual IQs. It can also involve creating "learning laboratories" and "micro-worlds," computer-supported environments where team learning confronts the dynamics of complex business realities. (See Chapters 14 and 15 for more on practice fields and learning infrastructures.)

Dialogue sessions allow a team to come together to "practice" dialogue and develop the skills it demands. The basic conditions for such a session include:

1. having all members of the "team" (those who need one another to act) together
2. explaining the ground rules of dialogue
3. enforcing those ground rules so that if anyone finds himself unable to "suspend" his assumptions, the team acknowledges that it is now "discussing" not "dialoguing"
4. making possible, indeed encouraging, team members to raise the most difficult, subtle, and conflictual issues essential to the team's work

We think of dialogue sessions as "practice" because they are designed to foster team skills. Yet, the practical results of such sessions can be significant.

Recently, the management team at DataQuest Drives, a leading manufacturer of disk drives and related computer peripherals held such a session.[15] As mentioned earlier, DataQuest is a firm with a well-established market image for technological innovation. In addition to being dominated internally by R&D, DataQuest's charismatic founder recently retired after shepherding the firm's successful growth for more than thirty years. After a year of spotty business success with the new management in place, things were rocky. DataQuest's new president, John MacCarthy, faced the daunting challenge of filling the shoes of a legend, facing more difficult business conditions than the legend ever had to worry about (the entire market was overbuilt), and with a team of strong players who had not yet begun to work as a whole.

On the heels of a tumultuous reorganization, MacCarthy's management team came together for two days with the following invitation from the president:

MEMO TO:

FROM John MacCarthy
SUBJECT *Special Meeting*

As you are well aware, we are accelerating change and I need your input prior to finalizing our strategies and implementation plans. I believe there is opportunity for us to improve our understanding and the way we implement change.

The session is intended to be the first in a series of dialogues to help us clarify the assumptions, programs, and responsibilities underlying the implementation of our key strategies. We have the view that only through the input from a larger group can we execute our changes and programs in a coherent and unambiguous way. The purpose of this two-day session is to gain understanding of each other's view by thinking through the major issues facing us at this time.

This session is not an attempt to make decisions as much as a setting to examine directions and the assumptions underlying them.

We have a second goal. This is to be together as colleagues, leaving all our roles and positions at the door. In this dialogue we should consider ourselves equals who still have substantive knowledge of the situations we are considering.

We see this meeting as the first step toward establishing ongoing substantive dialogue among us. Our experience begins to show that to engage in dialogue takes practice, and we should expect to be learning how to do this in this session. Several ground rules are helpful and we invite you to participate by following these as much as you can.

Suggested Ground Rules
1. Suspension of assumptions. Typically people take a position and defend it, holding to it. Others take up opposite positions and polarization results. In this session, we would like to examine some of our assumptions underlying our direction and strategy and not seek to defend them.
2. Acting as colleagues. We are asking everyone to leave his or her position at the door. There will be no particular hierarchy in this meeting, except for the facilitator, who will, hopefully, keep us on track.
3. Spirit of inquiry. We would like to have people begin to explore the thinking behind their views, the deeper assumptions they may hold, and the evidence they have that leads them to these views. So it will be fair to begin to ask other questions such as "What leads you to say or believe this?" or "What makes you ask about this?"

Over the two days, many previously closed subjects became open, blocks to communication came down, and rifts were healed. None was more important for the organization than the healed rift between R&D and marketing and sales.

Joe Grauweiler, the head of R&D, and Charlie Smyth, the head of marketing and sales have had a friendly albeit distant relationship for over ten years. Both are deeply proud of what DataQuest has achieved. Both believe deeply in its commitment to "participative management" and its related ideals about people and the organization. Yet, both are caught in a conflict that epitomizes the forces that are restraining DataQuest Drives' continuing growth. R&D is viewed as artists, designers, creators. Marketing sees itself, and is seen by others, as "the great unwashed," dealing in the messy world of sleazy dealers' bargain making (who have no particular loyalty to DataQuest), price discounting, and irate customers.

The "two cultures" of R&D and Marketing are reflected in numerous organizational conflicts. For example, both Grauweiler and Smyth have their own product budgets. Grauweiler's is for new development. Smyth's is for acquisitions, buying smaller companies whose products round out DataQuest's and make the firm, in Smyth's eyes, more competitive in the marketplace. There is no integrated product plan uniting the two. Marketing felt compelled to this "end run" because they saw R&D as being unresponsive to the full range of customer needs. R&D, it turns out, saw, itself being cut out of important product decisions. As the dialogue unfolded, Grauweiler expressed a level of concern that came as a surprise, because people assumed that R&D valued its autonomy:

GRAUWEILER: Let me offer a way to look at the issue of product strategy, which I submit today is being viewed as sort of an arm wrestle. We have, in effect, amassed a two pronged product strategy. We've not been overt or clear about it. My evidence is that we've not really brought the full competencies of the organization together to understand what amounts really to Data Quest's make/buy decision on product. That being the case, we have one group of people spending money on some product programs with a certain level of confidence and another group of people spending money on product programs with a different view. And "never the twain shall meet." That's just insane to me. There should be a singular, overriding product strategy that supports R&D and marketing. And, beneath that, come any number of make/buy decisions . . ."

MACCARTHY: I think we all fundamentally agree with that.

GRAUWEILER: Could I submit that we are telegraphing the opposite.

OTHERS: Yes.

GRAUWEILER: It's more acute than just not doing it well. We're being perceived as doing the opposite.

SMYTH: I was trying to get back and think of the rationale for why the make versus buy decision is a different and separated decision. At this point, it appears disjointed . . . One is, in my view, problem-solving, research-driven focus. The DataQuest label . . . On the other hand, in other products that DataQuest has not directed resources to, we are doing that through "buy." We're acquiring the access to that in a way other than Data-Quest's research . . . because it is more market reactive than fundamental problem-solution driven. And we don't want to pollute, you might say, the purity of what it is we want to do with research. . . .

PHILLIPS (HUMAN RESOURCE VP): I think that has put us in conflict.

GRAUWEILER: Absolutely! That's the problem. That's the prejudgment that I don't tolerate. How about the people who you're depending upon having some say in it? And don't protect my purity for me.

SMYTH: Well . . . I'm not uncomfortable with the rationale for what we have done. There may be a better way to do it. But I do think that, at some point in our history here, we decided not to invest in vertical storage disk files . . . just conventional junk that the market will buy that's not innovative. It's not interesting . . . And we wanted to allocate our finite resources and talent to what DataQuest's image is, which is research, innovative, product-driven . . . So we went out and acquired the more pedestrian stuff.

PHILLIPS: If we are just blue-skying it today, let me tell you what has always confused me. And I'm laying that on both marketing and R&D. "Research-driven product company" is how we've always talked about ourselves. And when we talk that way, it kind of puts us to say that any product that doesn't have the DataQuest investment in innovative research is outside Data-Quest. Somehow or another, we've structured ourselves that way and become in competition . . .

MACCARTHY: That's one definition of research-based. Do you know the other definition? The other definition is that nobody else in DataQuest does any research and development if it's not on a new product.

GRAUWEILER: I don't like that one either.

PHILLIPS: You hit point number two, because I was saying to myself . . . if you take the overriding direction statement as it is on the board, whether or not your decision is to make or buy, it still has to be research- and development-driven. It's got to be innovative . . .

MACCARTHY: I think we're onto something here. What we're saying is that the company in the past has been locked in. The only thing that made us great was product research and development. So we're having this incredible tension here. I would suggest that we bought subsidiaries to launch us . . . I think the dilemma that you're [Grauweiler] helping us to see is that . . . we should be offering whatever products the customer fundamentally needs. But then there's the other side that says, "But if it come out of DataQuest's research, it has to carry a DataQuest label." What you're saying is that's not true. That [what label to put on] ought to be a marketing decision based on what positioning you're trying to do. That's very helpful . . . because most of us have felt that if a product is not going to have a DataQuest label on it, you won't develop it in the first place.

HADLY (MANUFACTURING VP): But that's also making a statement that the entire company is research-driven, not just R&D, that other innovative ideas including product can come from other sides of the company. It doesn't all have to funnel through R&D.

GRAUWEILER: That's fine, but I don't know why that needs to be said. I'm not challenging you at all. But I think there's an inference here again that troubles me. I feel saddled representing the R&D legacy of the past, which I don't buy into. And I find it ironic that the more I work desperately to move our organization forward to the new reality, the more you're convinced to hold us back where we used to be! And I find that a strange dilemma.

HADLY: And conversely, there's a feeling here that that's the same on the other side.

ALL: Yes.

HADLY: We try to move the organization forward . . . we seem to be held back because you can't be research-driven and innovative unless it comes through R&D.

GRAUWEILER: I never said that! . . . Now, could I play it a different way? I think the statement of a research-driven product company is a correct statement. I firmly believe that the company's success will, in part . . . always be governed by our prowess with products. Anything that I see that starts to erode that orientation scares me to death. You have to have good stuff . . . good services and good products. I don't say that implies how you get them. Or that there's only one way to get good product . . . We don't have a very concerted or collaborative process in place to get that, but I know we have to.

MACCARTHY: Now the other side would be this—I believe some of the work that Charlie [Smyth] has done in marketing and in distribution [developing a new network of exclusive DataQuest dealers] is as much "R&D effort" as what goes on in R&D.

GRAUWEILER: I totally believe that.

MACCARTHY: And yet we suffer that, if the investment made there doesn't become instantaneously converted into a return, there's an incredible criticism of the organization.

GRAUWEILER: Welcome to the world of R&D.

SMYTH: There are two points I want to make from this. It looks to me like your efforts could be put to developing a product that could be manufactured outside . . . it looks to me that we've thrown away some development efforts that could have been licensed to other companies even . . . I've always thought it was crazy that, in order to get a product out of R&D, you had to put a DataQuest label on it.

GRAUWEILER: That's been a constraint on our program . . .

SMYTH: Now, the other thing is that we're not communicating in any kind of rich way between marketing and R&D. As a matter of fact, it's getting more separate . . . If we're going to work on the total needs of the customer . . . there has to be a way that that's seen in a lot of different places in the company.

HADLY: You started off by asking why is there this tension between R&D and marketing. You also have the tension between manufacturing and finance . . . To me it comes down to two words: "Empowerment versus Control." We tend to be a very control-oriented organization overall . . . Because they've got control and won't let me in, I'm going to go over here and do my own thing because I feel powerless to affect that at all. That's where I think some of it comes in—not by anything we necessarily want to have happen, but it's happening all over the company.

The results of this dialogue were nothing short of remarkable for DataQuest. First, a thirty-year rift between R&D and marketing started to be healed. Second, the "end run" that marketing had been doing to augment product lines was no longer necessary. R&D was interested and wanted to participate in studying acquisitions as well as developing products that could be marketed under other labels, as part of one coordinated product plan. The sacrosanct DataQuest label was not limited to products developed by DataQuest's own R&D but should be used based on "market considerations." The R&D head made it clear that he did not want to be fit into an old stereotype that R&D alone was responsible for innovation. The other functions, in his view, were equal partners in innovation, by innovating in processes, in understanding customer needs, and in business management. Moreover the R&D head was angry that he was even being saddled with an old stereotype.

TEAM LEARNING AND THE FIFTH DISCIPLINE

Both the perspective and the tools of systems thinking figure centrally in team learning.

David Bohm's work on dialogue is informed throughout by a systemic perspective. In fact, an integrating thread throughout Bohm's work has been to continue to advance the perspective of "wholeness" in physics. Bohm's primary critique of contemporary thought, the "pollution" in the stream of collective thinking, is "fragmentation," the "tendency of thought to break things apart."

Likewise, the approach taken by learning teams to defensive routines is intrinsically systemic. Rather than seeing the defensiveness in terms of others' behavior, the leverage lies in recognizing defensive routines as joint creations and to find our own role in creating and sustaining them. If we only look for defensive routines "out there," and fail to see them "in here" our efforts to deal with them just increase the defensiveness.

The tools of systems thinking are also important because virtually all the prime tasks of management teams—developing strategy, shaping visions, designing policy and organizational structures—involve wrestling with enormous complexity. Furthermore, this complexity does not "stay put." Each situation is in a continual state of flux.

Perhaps the single greatest liability of management teams is that they confront these complex, dynamic realities with a language designed for simple, static problems. Management consultant Charles Kiefer says it this way: "Reality is composed of multiple-simultaneous, interdependent cause-effect-cause relationships. From this reality, normal verbal language extracts simple, linear cause-effort chains. This accounts for a great deal of why managers are so drawn to low leverage interventions." For example, if the problem is long product development times we hire more engineers to reduce times; if the problem is low profits we cut costs; if the problem is falling market share we cut price to boost share.

Because we see the world in simple obvious terms, we come to believe in simple, obvious solutions. This leads to the frenzied search for simple "fixes," a task that preoccupies the time of many managers. John Manoogian, director of Ford's "Project Alpha," says, "The find and fix mentality results in an endless stream of short-term fixes, which appear to make problems go away, except they keep returning. So, then, we go off and fix them again. The find and fix experts will go on forever."

The problems compound in a diverse, cross-functional team such as a management team. Each team member carries his or her own, predominantly linear mental models. Each person's mental model focuses on different parts of the system. Each emphasizes different cause-effect chains. This makes it virtually impossible for a shared picture of the system as a whole to emerge in normal conversation. Is it any wonder that the strategies that emerge often represent watered-down compromises based on murky assumptions, full of internal contradictions, which the rest of the organization can't understand, let alone implement? The team members genuinely resemble the proverbial blind men and the elephant—each knows the part of the elephant within his grasp, each believes the whole must look like the piece he holds, and each feels that his understanding is the correct one.

This situation is unlikely to improve until teams share a new language for describing complexity. Today, the only universal language of business is financial accounting. But accounting deals with detail complexity not dynamic complexity. It offers "snapshots" of the financial conditions of a business, but it does not describe how those conditions were created. Today, there are several tools and frameworks that provide alternatives to traditional accounting as a business language. These include competitive analysis, "Total Quality," and, though much less widely used, scenario methods such as those developed at Shell.[16] But none of these tools deals with dynamic complexity very well or at all.

The systems archetypes offer a potentially powerful basis for a language by which management teams can deal productively with complexity. As teams such as the one at ATP master the basic archetypes, their conversations will naturally become more and more conversations about underlying structures and leverage and less and less predominated by crises and short-term "fixes."

If the ATP management team had been fluent in the language of the systems archetypes, the implications of their narrow-minded focus on meeting monthly and quarterly sales targets would have been inescapable. In particular, they would have realized that *when they increased pressures to meet sales targets,* they communicated very clearly to the salesforce the message: "When push comes to shove, it's better to pursue the low-risk additional sale to a current customer than the high-risk effort to create a new customer." This "shifted the burden" from building their customer base to making more sales to existing customers, thereby making them more dependent on a few key customers.

If the corporate managers had likewise been able to see and discuss this structure, they would have been able to surface their concerns about Jim Tabor's management more effectively. Rather than wrestling with how they could raise issues that might appear critical of Tabor's management skills and unsupportive, they could have simply laid out the two feedback processes and inquired into how *any of them* could be more confident that the fundamental solution of broadening the customer base was receiving adequate attention.

When the systems archetypes are used in conversations about complex and potentially conflictual management issues, reliably, they "objectify" the conversation. The conversation becomes about "the structure," the systemic forces at play, not about personalities and leadership styles. Difficult questions can be raised in a way that does not carry innuendos of management incompetence or implied criticism. Rather, people are asking, "Is the burden shifting to selling to current customers versus broadening our customer base?" "How would we know if it was?" This, of course, is precisely the benefit of a *language for complexity*—it makes it easier to discuss complex issues objectively and dispassionately.

Without a shared language for dealing with complexity, team learning is limited. If one member of a team sees a problem more systemically than others, that person's insight will get reliably discounted—if for no other reason than the intrinsic biases toward linear views in our normal everyday language. On the other hand, the benefits of teams developing fluency in the language of the systems archetypes are enormous, *and* the difficulties of mastering the language are actually reduced in a team. As David Bohm says, language *is* collective. Learning a new language, by definition, means learning how to converse with one another in the language. There is simply no more effective way to learn a language than through use, which is exactly what happens when a team starts to learn the language of systems thinking.

PART IV

Reflections
From Practice

INTRODUCTION

The ideas in the following pages synthesize some twenty conversations with people I admire greatly, gifted exponents of "the art and practice of the learning organization." They come from diverse organizational contexts—from business, governmental and nongovernmental organizations, primary and secondary education, and community organizations. In turn, they represent a much larger number of organizational learning practitioners I have learned from and been inspired by over many years.

In the introduction to Part IV of the original edition of *The Fifth Discipline*, I offered "prototypes" as a metaphor for the journey of creating learning organizations. In 1903, when the Wright brothers flew at Kitty Hawk, the airplane was "invented." Between then and 1935, when the DC-3, the first commercially successful plane, was introduced, there were countless prototypes. (Another two decades passed before the know-how and infrastructure reached the critical scale that allowed commercial air travel to become a major industry.) In the introduction, I suggested that the journey from invention to successful innovation in technology represents a search for synergies among diverse developments, which only together enable something new to be viable. When this happens, prototypes, if I may mix metaphors, take off. And, I suggested then, the five disciplines might be the basis for such a synergy in management innovation.

While much has happened since this book was first written in 1990, the basic metaphor of prototypes still seems apt to me. There are no answers or magic pills. There is no alternative to learning through experimentation. Benchmarking and studying "best practices" will not suffice—because the prototyping process does not involve just incremental changes in established ways of doing things, but radical new ideas and practices that together create a new way of managing. Fortunately, what has changed is that there are now many examples of successful prototypes in many different industry and cultural contexts.

Physical engineering prototypes usually get tested in laboratory settings, whereas organizational prototypes quickly find themselves facing harsh realities. This is hardly made easier by the profoundly conflicting forces, "things getting better" and "things getting worse," that characterize the present era. While on one hand, the basic ideas espoused in *The Fifth Discipline* fifteen years ago have gained widespread credibility, on the other, the organizational climate for most practitioners is more difficult.

"There is no doubt that the importance of learning and continual knowledge creation has been accepted by mainstream management," commented Marv Adams, chief information officer and head of strategy for Ford. "But that's different than saying that it's widespread and practiced in a consistent way during good times and bad in most companies." David Marsing, formerly responsible for much of Intel's global manufacturing, observed that "While many organizations have increased their understanding of culture and its role in performance, and have intentionally designed processes that recognize culture, the level of skill and sophistication is still low." The challenges differ little outside the private sector. Barbara Stocking, formerly a regional director of the British National Health Service and now president of Oxfam GB (Great Britain), observed that she was always a "developmentally oriented manager; helping people to evolve their organization was my natural style. But over the years I've come to appreciate that the common change model is to drive goals from the top down, and that there are few people in senior leadership positions who are interested in developing people or organizations."

Yet, as the stories that follow show, it is in the middle of these complex crosscurrents that innovators somehow find space for leading change. Although they come from very different organizational circumstances, they draw their inspiration from a common idea that there must be a more human, more productive, and ultimately more creative way for people to work together. And though they still represent a small minority of managers and organizations, they demonstrate that a growing cadre of sophisticated leaders are beginning to transform the prevailing system of management around the world. How could the journey of changing deeply held assumptions and practices unfold in any other way?

12

FOUNDATIONS

What struck me most from the interviews we conducted for the revision of this book was the ways that its core ideas, many of which seemed radical in 1990, had become deeply integrated into people's ways of seeing the world and into their managerial practices. The ideas that follow seem now to be accepted almost universally among serious practitioners of organizational learning, constituting a new foundation upon which future work will build.

In one way or another, everyone we spoke with had sought to create more reflective work environments where dialogue and seeing taken-for-granted mental models were possible. The idea of growing organizations through growing people permeated all the stories. Many interviewees spoke of the shift in mindset from "fixing parts" to appreciating organizations as living systems that have immense capabilities, typically untapped, to learn, evolve, and heal themselves.

SHAPING A CULTURE OF REFLECTIVENESS AND DEEPER CONVERSATION

CHANGE THROUGH CONVERSATION

"BP often feels like a performance-driven machine, and I was trained by that machine," says Executive VP Vivienne Cox. "When I first took responsibility for a business unit almost fifteen years ago, I was eager to try some new ideas. My colleagues John and Gene (who had responsibility for, respectively, a closely related business and both businesses together) and I had a simple idea—we wanted to foster greater cooperation across organizational boundaries, and to share information and knowledge so we could make better decisions.

"We weren't sure how to get this new organizational model to work, but eventually we decided that the best way was just to get people talking to one another. If each person could better understand what others did, we would begin to get a sense of the possibilities, and the right structure and design would flow from that. We set up a series of workshops, most of which focused on various problems we had and options for dealing with them. What gradually emerged from these conversations was an idea for a different way of organizing the business. I was absolutely astonished that the ideas that came out of those workshops were not the ideas that I'd started with. Indeed, my own ideas were the wrong ones. Just the act of getting people together and talking with one another created a whole set of possibilities that led to a better business."

The new ideas the groups generated were fairly complex and difficult to implement, but they proved to be the genesis of a structure for a much larger organization, which Cox runs today. "The themes from those conversations have proven to be fundamental and enduring, and have led to considerable competitive advantage for BP. That work was also the most fun I had ever had in business. John and Gene and I provoked courage in one another to do things we wouldn't have done by ourselves. We learned things about how cultures can change that you never find out in the huge programmed culture changes driven from the top.

"In my subsequent jobs here I had different types of bosses, including strong command-and-control types, which led me to reflect on the contrast between the experiences. I knew what it felt like to work for a person who managed through performance targets and denied any possibility of real life occurring in conversation. When I moved into new jobs where I had more freedom, I continued to experiment with how to get people together to talk with one another."

Cox, who today is the highest-ranking woman in BP, articulates a simple but still largely unappreciated view in mainstream management. Though virtually everyone advocates better communication, the spirit of openness required to lead projects like Cox's remains rare, in part because it is still poorly understood.

REFLECTIVE OPENNESS

Part IV of the original edition of *The Fifth Discipline* discussed distinctions between participative openness and reflective openness. Participative openness, which might also be called expressive openness, concerns speaking openly about one's views. While it is an important element of creating a more learning-oriented work environment, it is also dangerously incomplete. It started to come into vogue in the 1980s, an outgrowth of the philosophy of "participative management." Some organizations even tried to institutionalize formal procedures for open communication. But many of these eventually fell out of favor because they and their organizational proponents were simply not very effective.[1] In a classic 1994 *Harvard Business Review* article, Chris Argyris criticized "good communication that blocks learning," arguing that formal communication mechanisms like focus groups and organizational surveys in effect give employees mechanisms for letting management know what they think without taking any responsibility for problems and their role in doing something about them. These mechanisms fail because "they do not get people to reflect on their own work and behavior. They do not encourage individual accountability. And they do not surface the kinds of deep and potentially threatening or embarrassing information that can motivate learning and produce real change." But, as Argyris implies, moving beyond participative openness may be difficult, especially for managers seeking to maintain control.

Roger Saillant used organizational learning methods for many years at Ford Motor Company, where he was one of the organization's most effective managers. For most of the 1980s and 1990s, he was moved from one daunting manufacturing site to another, in Northern Ireland, Eastern Europe, China, and Mexico. In some cases, he succeeded in transforming operations that were among Ford's poorest performers into some of the best. In other cases, he started up new plants that became best-in-class in settings with no comparable history of manufacturing excellence. Many are still among Ford's top-performing manufacturing operations a decade after his tenure.

What most surprised Saillant over the years was not what he accomplished, but how his bosses in the Ford system reacted to what he did. "I always felt that so long as I respected the company's core values and business objectives, I could try to do things in ways that were more consistent with who I am and what I care about," Saillant reflects. "Of course, gradually my bosses would grasp that I was engaging people differently in order to achieve these results. But they never asked me *how* I was accomplishing the results—I mean, no one *ever* asked. I was always puzzled by that because you'd think they'd have an interest in getting similar results elsewhere. They would just say to me, 'You should do this [go to this new site] because we need you to go do this,' or, 'You'll make a difference if you go here.' They always shrank from the conversation that would start by asking, 'How did you really do that?'

"I think it's because they sort of knew how I did it, but didn't want to know. At some level, they were not prepared to be that vulnerable. Maybe they were a little frightened by what it meant to challenge themselves, to be that exposed, that human. Somehow, I had learned that if you can get connected with what's inside of you, you can be fearless in your openness. That can be scary as a leader."

Participative openness is inadequate because it fails to generate the commitment and shared understanding needed for real change. As one disgruntled executive put it, "The implicit assumption around here is that the solution to all problems is sharing our views." The core problem is that learning together starts when we actually listen to one another rather than just talk at one another. And listening is not easy. Reflective openness leads to looking inward, allowing our conversations to make us more aware of the biases and limitations in our own thinking, and how our thinking and actions contribute to problems.

Reflective openness is the cornerstone of the discipline of mental models. None of us has a company in our heads, or a family, or a country. But our life experience shapes a rich mix of assumptions, feelings, and at best some well-formed hypotheses about these systems. Nurturing reflective openness leads to a willingness to continually test these views. It is characterized by true open-mindedness, the first step toward deeper listening and real conversation. This is easy to say but not so easy to do—because, as master practitioners like Cox or Saillant know, building an environment of reflectiveness starts with our own willingness to open ourselves, to be vulnerable, to be "exposed," as Saillant put it. This is unlikely to happen in any organizational environment that does not have a deep commitment to helping people grow, and to creating the trust and spirit of mutuality this requires.

GROWING PEOPLE

As I look back now, perhaps the most radical of the five disciplines was personal mastery, the idea that an organizational environment could be created in which people could truly grow as human beings. Most companies today espouse some variation on the philosophy that "people are our most important asset" and invest considerable sums in work force development, largely through training programs. But truly committing to helping people grow requires much more than this. I've listened to people like Vivienne Cox and Roger Saillant share their experiences for many years, and the emotional center of their stories is always the same. Through diverse life experiences they have formed an unshakable conviction of the power inherent in releasing and aligning human spirit—and they are on a lifelong journey to discover what this means and how to do it.

In 2005, a group of business leaders in Worcester, Massachusetts, initiated the first William J. O'Brien Memorial Lecture Series. The aim was to honor and extend Bill O'Brien's legacy through an annual speech given by a business leader who exemplified O'Brien's conviction that "the best way to grow financial capital is through growing human capital." The first speaker in this series was Rich Teerlink, former CEO of Harley-Davidson and one of the founders of the SoL network. "Being truly committed to growing people is an act of faith," says Teerlink. "You have to believe in your heart that people want to pursue a vision that matters, that they want to contribute and be responsible for results, and that they are willing to look at shortfalls in their own behavior and correct problems whenever they are able. These beliefs are not easy for control-oriented managers, and that is why there remains a big gap between the 'talk' and the 'walk' regarding developing people."

A PURPOSE WORTHY OF COMMITMENT

Creating an environment where people can grow starts with "having a purpose worthy of people's commitment," says Goran Carstedt, former president of Volvo Sweden and IKEA North America (and SoL's first managing director). "Business leaders often ask their people to be committed to the organization's goals," says Carstedt. "But the real question is what is the organization committed to, and is that worth my time?" Despite much literature on organizational purpose, and ubiquitous vision and values statements, "there is a lot of cynicism," says Saillant, among employees about where their company's real commitment lies. And a lot of confusion—starting with the idea that the purpose of a company is, by definition, to maximize return on invested capital. Years ago, Peter Drucker said that "making money for a company is like oxygen for a person; if you don't have enough of it you're out of the game." In other words, profitability is a performance requirement for all businesses, but it is not a purpose. Extending Drucker's metaphor, companies who take profit as their purpose are like people who think life is about breathing. They're missing something.

Ironically, equating a business's purpose with the economic bottom line also dooms the enterprise to financial mediocrity, as countless studies of long-term business performance have shown.[2] In a world where more people have more choices about where and how they work, it matters that an organization stand for something. A company that lacks a purpose worthy of commitment fails to foster commitment. It forces people to lead fragmented lives that can never tap the passion, imagination, willingness to take risks, patience, persistence, and desire for meaning that are the cornerstones of long-term financial success.

"I just wanted my work life and personal life to be one life," says Brigitte Tantawy-Monsou of Unilever. After a career in supply chain management, R&D, and business excellence, Tantawy-Monsou says her introduction to organizational learning, personal mastery, and mental models in 2002 "helped me to make sense of my past experiences. Because I am very analytical and scientific, it also gave me a new dimension, a 'soft' dimension. It helped me see that you can understand an organization or team as a social system, and that there is a more integrated way of looking at problems." She found that the systems view also applied to her personally. "I was especially interested in the idea of alignment between a person and [his or her] company's goals and values. This was a new management concept, and it spoke to my personal desire for alignment."

Gradually, Tantawy-Monsou found herself drawn into projects truly worthy of her commitment, applying organizational learning tools to Unilever's sustainability agenda. Eventually she was even able to redefine her job so that she could work full-time on sustainability. "I wanted to contribute more, both inside the organization and beyond, to issues that really mattered, and organizational learning helped me build my capabilities to have more influence. It's coincided with a step in my career, and in my life as a whole." But this would not have been possible had not Unilever's top management, several years earlier, begun to recognize that historic environmental changes threatened the future of their businesses. As one of the largest sellers of fish products (food products made with fish) in the world, they realized by the mid-1990s that, in the words of one top executive, "We won't have a fish business worth being in if there aren't fundamental changes toward sustainable fishing."[3] Today, in addition to working on business-related sustainability initiatives within Unilever, Tantawy-Monsou is an organizer of the European SoL Sustainability Consortium, an extension of the U.S.–based SoL Sustainability Consortium. "I've almost always enjoyed my work, but for the first time I feel now that I am able to work on what really matters to me as a person," she says.

TRANSFORMATIVE RELATIONSHIPS

As Tantawy-Monsou's story illustrates, growing as a human being starts with a commitment to something that truly matters. It unfolds within what the people at Roca call networks of "transformative relationships."

Roca (Spanish for "rock") is an organization whose purpose is to build a safe and healthy community for young people. Chelsea, Massachusetts, where Roca is based, is less than two miles from

Boston's financial center, but it is a world away culturally. It is inhabited mostly by Latino, Southeast Asian, and Central African immigrants. "As an immigrant, you have lost your friends, your job, your standards, and your standing in your community," says Saroeum Phoung, former director of the Roca street workers. "Families become dysfunctional. Typically, the father cannot speak the language, so he cannot hold a job. Because he no longer can be a provider, he becomes an abuser. Usually the second generation has even more difficulty, because they grow up without any family stability. They have no drive to advance because they have no hope that advancing is possible. So they, as I did, join gangs."

Recruiting former teenage gang members, young parents, and community members to work on the streets to help others and to rebuild community, Roca has become an interface between police, courts, schools, and a host of social service agencies. In the eighteen years since Roca's founding, Chelsea has seen dramatic decreases in crime rates and violence, and increases in graduation rates. Many young people who probably would not have survived their teens have ended up in community and four-year colleges and are holding jobs and living productive lives. "What Roca has accomplished is nothing short of amazing," says Harry Spence, director of the Department of Social Services (DSS) for the Commonwealth of Massachusetts. "If we had a half-dozen Rocas, it would make a huge impact on our work across the state."

I've spent a fair amount of time with the youth leaders of Roca, and I continue to learn from their deep understanding of how to help people grow. "Creating transformative relationships is the basis of our work," Tun Krouch told me during one of my visits with a group of street workers. "The young people we're dealing with need a relationship that can help them to live," says founder Molly Baldwin. "Our first job is simply to show up for them. Many have never had someone they could count on to be consistent, to be with them in a relationship of complete support for who they really are as human beings. Over time, they then start to do that for one another."

Roca's core method and continual training ground for this "showing up for one another" is what the group calls "peacekeeping circles," a type of collective reflective practice based on Native American traditions of learning and healing. "We learn to truly listen to each other in circles," says Omar Ortez.

Marina Rodriguez tells a typical circle story: "Recently, we had a young woman who had gotten pregnant, and she didn't know how to tell her mom. She was afraid. In a more typical situation, the girl might have run away, or some family friend might have intervened, but instead we decided that the best way to support her was to create a circle. The street worker had a good relationship with her, and formed a small circle with a few people the girl and the mother trusted. We dealt with the situation together, which is wholly different than the girl and the mom just yelling at each other. The key was to create a conversation that would let the mother listen to her daughter, and let them accept one another. The whole idea is to enlarge your circle to build the support that you need."

"It becomes about cooperative learning," Susan Ulrich adds. "A circle conversation is where you can all sit together and figure out what is going on and how we're going to deal with it. You see that a problem is not just one person's problem, it is [everyone's] problem. In circle, we are equals, we all have problems and we learn by helping one another."

"We have a saying we learned from a chief justice of a Navajo tribal court," adds Baldwin. "He says, 'You can't get to a good place in a bad way.' Circles keep us grounded in our connectedness and create community day by day as we confront whatever we have to confront together."[4]

IT STARTS WITH ME

The commitment to personal growth is important—and it is most important for those in positions of leadership. "I always have to be willing to work on my own stuff," says Baldwin. "If we are in a disagreement with the cops, I have to look at what I have invested in maintaining that battle—there are so many times that I would just rather go out and yell at somebody than remain calm and look at my part in perpetuating whatever is going on."

"It all starts with personal mastery," says Saillant. "It all starts with my willingness to see the shortcomings that are all too evident to those around me. I can never expect the people around me in an organization to be more open and willing to learn and improve than I am."

ORGANIZATIONS AS LIVING SYSTEMS

There are two distinct intellectual traditions behind the systems viewpoint as it has emerged in modern science. The engineering theory of systems provides practical tools like systems archetypes and computer simulation models for making sense of complex, interdependent problems. An understanding of living systems helps us appreciate the capacities of teams, organizations, and larger systems to learn and evolve. When I was writing in 1990, I emphasized the former because, as Ford's Marv Adams says, "there are so many crucial problems in the world that are not being addressed because leaders are not good systems thinkers." It appears to me that the two in concert may provide both the tools and the leadership principles needed to go forward. I've come to this understanding because I now see that this living system view subtly pervades the thinking of virtually all effective practitioners of organizational learning.[5]

MACHINE-AGE THINKING

My appreciation of the importance of living systems for how we think about businesses was catalyzed by Arie de Geus's book *The Living Company*. Seeing a business as a living system simply means seeing it as a human community, an idea de Geus makes pointedly through the question, "How do we see a business—as a human community or as a machine for making money?" While almost everyone would decry the latter image, our contemporary language and managerial practices tell a different story.

In fact, machine images pervade management jargon. We have managers who "run" a company, much the way you would run a machine. We have the "owners" of the company, which is perfectly appropriate terminology for a machine but somewhat problematic when applied to a human community. And of course there are leaders who "drive change." As with these other images, I often wonder if people ever think about what they are saying when using such language. If they did, they might stop and question themselves, even for a moment. After all, most of us "drive" a car. But we also know what happens when we try to "drive" our spouse or teenage children—usually the opposite of our intended outcome! It is interesting how readily we gravitate to such language when talking about what it takes for organizations to change—which, of course, is de Geus's point: we all tend to think of our organizations as being more like machines than living systems.

De Geus came to appreciate the difference between seeing companies as machines and seeing them as human communities as a result of pursuing a very practical question, "What features characterize long-lived companies?" Shell's famous study of corporate longevity (see Chapter 2), which de Geus directed, found that the average life expectancy of Fortune 500 firms was less than forty years, but the study also found some twenty companies around the world which had survived two centuries or longer. Looking for common features that transcended differences in history, national culture, industry context, and technology, the study's authors concluded that the long-lived companies tended to think of themselves more as human communities than as financial institutions. In the words of the original Shell study, they "had a sense of who they were that transcended what they did," giving them capabilities to evolve and adapt—to learn—not matched by their contemporaries.

The living system view is assuming ever more relevance in today's world of global interdependence and complexity—as illustrated by the "secret" story of the world's largest business. Despite revenues that are some ten times those of Wal-Mart and a market value that is, conservatively speaking, more than double that of General Electric, Visa is one of the business world's best-kept secrets. It is certainly not that its product is little known, nor that it is the leader of an obscure industry. There are few other companies that could claim one-sixth of the world's population as its customers last year! Yet over the past decade, there have been well over a thousand feature articles in *Business Week*, *Fortune*, and *Forbes* on Microsoft, more than three hundred and fifty on GE—and about thirty-five on Visa. Why? Because Visa simply doesn't look like a typical global corporation. It has no publicly traded stock because it is owned by its twenty thousand member organizations. It has no large corporate headquarters because it is a network governed by those members and a written constitution that spells out its purpose and operating principles and the decision-making authority vested in its elected governing boards. It lacks a typical high-profile CEO who guides its strategy (and pulls down an astronomical compensation) because its strategy is in fact many strategies that arise from the thousands of autonomous businesses in the network.

Visa doesn't look or work like most other large corporations because it was inspired by an image different from the machine imagery accompanying most corporations. In the midst of the massive overshoot and financial collapse in the early years of the credit card industry, Visa's founding CEO Dee Hock had a realization. He saw clearly that it was "beyond the power of reason to design an organization" capable of coordinating a global network of financial transactions of the sort that had started to develop.[7] Yet, he also knew that nature regularly achieves just that. Why, he wondered, couldn't "a human organization work like a rain forest?" Why couldn't it be patterned on biological concepts and methods? "What if we quit arguing about the structure of a new institution and tried to think of it as having some sort of genetic code?" In short, Visa was inspired by abandoning our "old perspective and mechanistic model of reality" and embracing principles of living systems as a basis for organizing. Eventually Hock even coined a term for the type of organizing he envisioned, "chaordic," because in nature "order continually emerges from seeming chaos, while in management we always try to impose order because we fear that chaos will take over."

The biologist Gregory Bateson said, "The source of all our problems today comes from the gap between how we think and how nature works."[8] The "DNA" of our dominant institutions is based on machine thinking, for example, "all systems must have someone in control." We know that in healthy living systems, like the human body or a wetlands, control is distributed. But we are so habituated to the "someone must be in control" mindset—what Hock calls "the closet Newtonian" inside us—that we fail to imagine real alternatives. Yet, those alternatives appear all around us if we learn how to see them.

HOW THE WORK GETS DONE

"We just wanted to understand how the work gets done," says Hewlett-Packard's Anne Murray Allen, former head of IT and strategy for the Ink Supply Organization (ISO), HP's largest and most profitable division for more than a decade. "I can't remember when I first got started looking at things from a systems point of view, but it goes way back—something about the way I am wired. When *The Fifth Discipline* first came out, I devoured it. I was already a practitioner of dialogue, coaching clients on the power of listening and what it took to come together and do extraordinary things, even before I came to HP. At HP, I got involved in strategy, and especially the strategic role of IT, which naturally led into knowledge management when that started to become a big focus. But all the 'lessons learned' databases and the like never seemed to me to be very high-leverage, nor the whole idea that knowledge is somehow floating all around us and all we have to do is capture and codify it. That notion has become a lot less popular now because companies have spent a lot of money on 'knowledge management systems' and don't have a lot to show for it.

"The problem starts with not understanding knowledge, how it is created and how it operates in practical settings—because knowledge is social. Knowledge is what we know how to do, and we do things with one another. That is how the work gets done. Collaboration is the flip side of knowledge management. You can't talk about one without the other. So, to manage knowledge you need to address collaboration and tools that help people collaborate. Today, much of our work is on knowledge networks, which we also call networks of collaboration: how people work together to create value and to create new sources of value. This is a very organic process, but there are ways to understand it and ways to help rather than hinder it."

Several years ago, Allen began working with a social network researcher at the University of Oregon, Dennis Sandow, on a series of studies. "We soon learned two things: it was possible to identify different social networks associated with different key technical capabilities, and people enjoyed being part of the studies. The beauty of Dennis's approach, unlike [that of] most academics, was that he did not do the analysis for people, he taught the engineers how to become their own network analysts."

"My real aim," says Sandow, "was to help people reflect on how they did their work. People are naturally interested in understanding how their own work occurs and explaining it to others—especially to managers who are fond of reorganizing and reassigning people without any real understanding of the repercussions. Today, those engineers have a whole new language for communicating with managers."[9]

Allen and Sandow's work has developed a novel bridge connecting the practice of reflection, the importance of relationships, and an understanding of organizations as living systems. "Over time we've learned that networks of knowledge expand and become stronger through reflection," says Allen. "When we think about who we collaborate with, and together reflect on our process of collaboration, we legitimize one another." For example, the ISO was facing important problems that required a new understanding in material chemistry. ISO worked together with two highly competitive vendors to develop a social-network map of the HP-vendor system. The map not only clarified who knew what, it contributed to trust and a sense of mutuality: "People felt seen, and their concerns and contributions were equally clear to all. By building trust and openness early on, this network reduced new ink-jet cartridge development time by sixteen weeks after just a few weeks of collaboration. Today we have many examples like this, and gradually the pragmatic value of fostering reflection on our knowledge networks is being recognized."

Looking back on their work, Allen and Sandow concluded, "As the philosophy of the physical sciences dominated the Industrial Age, the philosophy of the biological sciences is beginning to dominate the Knowledge Age. This philosophy views knowledge, people, and organizations as living systems . . . [which represents a shift from] (1) focusing on parts to focusing on the whole, (2) focusing on categorization to focusing on integration, (3) focusing on individuals to focusing on interactions, and (4) focusing on systems outside the observer to focusing on systems that include the observer."[10]

Allen and Sandow's view of social systems was influenced by the Chilean biologist Humberto Maturana, who is famous for his pioneering studies of cognition in living systems. Maturana says that intelligent action is created in social systems where all the members of a network accept the others as legitimate participants in the network. In 2000, the management of ISO hosted the first of two two-day seminars given by Maturana. It was a memorable experience, as more than one hundred engineers listened to him talk about love as the recognition of the other as a legitimate other—and the "emotion that expands intelligence." His comments made me recall something I had learned in writing the foreword for de Geus's book. The English word "company" comes from the French *compaigne*—the sharing of bread, the same root as "companion." Interestingly, the oldest Swedish term for business, *narings liv*, means "nourishment for life," and the oldest Chinese symbol for business translates as "life meaning." Perhaps when we rediscover organizations as living systems, we will also rediscover what it actually means to us as human beings to work together for a purpose that really matters.

13

IMPETUS

Building learning-oriented cultures is hard work in any setting. It takes months and years—indeed, it is a never-ending journey. It is fraught with risks, either of failing to realize true cultural change, or of succeeding in doing so and thus becoming a threat to those who want to keep things as they are. Building learning-oriented cultures is demanding because learning stretches us personally, and it is always easier to stay in our comfort zone. Nothing in the past fifteen years has lessened my appreciation of these challenges. Given all that, what would compel people to embark on such an undertaking?

There seem to be three overlapping but distinct motivations that compel people to take on the difficult work of building learning organizations. Some seek a better model for how to manage and lead change. Some are trying to build an organization's overall capacity for continual adaptation to change. All seem to believe that there is a way of managing and organizing work that is superior in both pragmatic and human terms, that significantly improves performance and creates the types of workplaces in which most of us would truly like to work.

A DIFEERENT APPROACH
TO CHANGE

"Before coming to the World Bank I'd been in organizations that were going through dramatic, but what you might call mechanistic, change," says Dorothy Hamachi-Berry, VP of human resources at the International Finance Corporation (IFC), the part of the World Bank that invests in private enterprise in developing countries. "Typically, a new leader would come in and there would be a 'burning platform,' some compelling reason that you had to destroy everything and start again. This approach never seemed to work in any of the places I knew. When I first came to the Bank in 1996, we had a new leader, and we were sending hundreds of our top managers through university executive development programs. They were all being exposed to the same change model, but, lo and behold, nothing was changing. That's when I started to ask, is there a different model? I knew the alternative had to start from aspiration, and the aspiration of our clients."

At the time, the Bank was trying to address organizational problems that had long limited its effectiveness. For example, rather than having "country managers" based in Washington, the Bank was relocating people in such positions to the actual countries. The idea was to get managers "on the ground" and thus more in tune with their clients' needs, desires, and goals. At the same time, professional networks were created to deepen the Bank's global knowledge base, and a new matrix organization was put in place.

In 1989, a learning project began with the Bank's Mexico team (at this time Hamachi-Berry was still human resources VP for the whole World Bank) and the human development team, those working on health and education. "We had a great country team but they were struggling with this new way of doing business in the matrix." she recalls. After a two-day foundational workshop, the team worked for several months with learning tools like dialogue, systems thinking, and personal mastery, with the overall aim of helping clients clarify their development aspirations. One of the long-standing problems at the Bank was its inability to work across its own internal boundaries to get funding through to innovative on-the-ground projects. "In Mexico, we got the clients, country team, and network people working together in a new collaborative way, which had happened infrequently in the past. As a team they worked together to develop solutions to problems, rather than the Bank coming in with a prescriptive approach. The results were exciting projects where you could see impact, like a new way of delivering education and health services to children in remote mountainous areas. It was a great prototype showing what could happen if Bank staff worked with clients to enable clients to drive their own development process, rather than the other way around. And pretty soon we had demand for more projects."

About this time Hamachi-Berry moved from the World Bank to the IFC, because there was an opportunity for similar innovations within the top management. She built on what she had learned in Mexico. "We never used terms like 'organizational learning' or talked about *The Fifth Discipline* because it sounded too academic and the ideas would lose their power. Instead we talked about building aspiration—our own and our clients'— and the capacity for dialogue and inquiry."

Initially, there was little demand for work with the learning tools from the investment officers. It was simply not the way they worked. "Our investment officers were deal makers, and dialogue and inquiry were not their style. It was like pulling teeth. But Peter Woicke, the IFC's CEO, recognized the value of this sort of approach, so we concentrated on working with his management team. Peter was patient, and it took a couple of years but eventually you could see the results in how people interacted and what they could do together. People learned to be candid, to openly disagree, and to be intentional about surfacing conflicts rather than skating around them." The first turning point came when several of Woicke's direct reports wanted to undertake similar development processes with their own teams. "Gradually a lot of the basic learning practices started to show up in how people worked. The IFC is the one part of the Bank group that has a bottom-line focus: commercial success and having a development impact are both important. Because people could track business impact, the value of the work was more readily apparent. Today, the work is totally demand-driven, and we get lots of requests for capacity-building help from line managers themselves."

Hamachi-Berry and her colleagues got another test of the longer-term impacts of their cultural change efforts when Woicke retired a year ago. "What would happen when the CEO champion for this approach was gone? We knew that many very successful innovations like this get shot down or fail to spread despite their success. But this work has influenced policy and strategy changes, and our business has doubled in the last six years.[1] In fact, we've had three consecutive years of record growth and profitability—we've never done so well in our history. I think our success has been helped a lot by having so many line managers who embody a spirit of vision and who have included others in building a learning environment. Once you have a few of these people in an organization you build momentum, and everything gets much easier.

"Our ability to work together and with our clients is leading to better investment decisions, which are building more successful businesses, which can have more impact on sustainable development. This alignment between business and development success has been our aim all along. It's clear, looking back, that it took real patience, the sort that is often missing in change efforts, and a willingness to lead by example rather than just sending everybody 'off to the program.' Peter's extensive management experience outside the Bank seemed to have convinced him that inquiry and real aspiration mattered, and he was willing to take the time needed for him and his team to develop their own capacities. And that dovetailed with the patience it took [before] people could see evidence of practical results and then want to build their own capacities."

BUILDING ADAPTIVE ORGANIZATIONS

THE FUTURE OF IT

Ford's Marv Adams stands in a long line of people drawn to learning organization work not only as a way to lead change, but also as a way to build organizations with greater capacity to deal with ongoing change, what he calls "adaptive organizations."

"As a CIO, you have a unique perspective from which to see a business as a whole," says Adams. "Today, two things stand out: the extraordinary level of connectedness of the organizations we are creating, and the interdependent and volatile environments we are operating in. In Ford today we have over three hundred thousand

IT users, in twenty basic business functions, interacting through two thousand four hundred application programs, developed by six thousand IT professionals in ten different IT development groups, working with two hundred different IT vendors. And all this is exploding with the proliferation of hand-held and embedded computational devices: there are now some 35 billion microcontrollers, 750 million smart sensors, and 1.5 billion mobile IT devices in operation in the world and the numbers are growing exponentially. This higher connectivity brings greater volatility and nonlinear effects where changes arise suddenly that could not be predicted from the past. In the four years following 2000, worldwide financial damage from intentionally dangerous 'malware' grew tenfold to over $200 billion.

"This connectivity and volatility mean that we have to manage in a very different way. Keeping pace with the pace of change is essential to succeed. We can't do that through our traditional top-down control mentalities, but we also can't do it with no structure and total chaos. Continually finding the right balance between too much and too little structure will be a key to having the adaptive capabilities to survive."

Adams believes that increased adaptive organizational capabilities represent the future of IT within organizations. "Because we are involved with infrastructures that knit together the enterprise, IT professionals have a powerful window onto how the organization succeeds or fails in operating holistically." While these professionals' technical responsibilities will continue, a whole new way to contribute is emerging: "helping people see patterns and manage complexity," says Adams. "People are overwhelmed with information. This cannot be solved by just building better IT systems. It requires collaboration and systems thinking in the context of pervasive computing and real-time systems."

Today, Adams is developing a new generation of IT staff who consult with business managers on a host of strategic, operational, and cultural change issues, using a novel synthesis of ideas from systems thinking and complexity science. They employ systems thinking tools to help people in visualizing systemic patterns, and draw on ideas from complexity theory to frame strategic change options, such as reducing variability, changing measures, and creating new "interaction patterns."[2]

For example, Ford recently faced the daunting task of converting a host of legacy financial control systems to comply with the new

U.S. Sarbanes-Oxley mandates. "Sarbanes-Oxley defined a set of financial controls that companies will be held accountable for. If they don't comply they'll fail the Sarbanes-Oxley certification, and it will affect the reputation of the company and the perceived risk for investors," Adams says. "Company officers are also personally accountable for problems that come from lack of controls—so it's a big deal. We thought it would be impossible to achieve certification within the first year, because we not only have many different control systems developed over forty years at Ford but we have still others embedded within acquired companies like Jaguar, Volvo, and Land Rover."

Adams formed a working group from the different business units, and they looked at the audit data and discovered "patterns of vulnerabilities." These patterns were further clarified through systems diagrams and dialogue sessions, which showed in particular how the IT system contributed to vulnerability. For example, the group realized that one source of problems was too much variability in reporting policies. So they defined a policy baseline and used it to replace a hodgepodge notebook of policies that had built up over decades. The company also had too much variability in how assets were defined, so the group came up with a new, simpler classification system, along with a simpler and more focused measurement system. They then trained "certified masters" to work with people around the world to check for classification consistency and share best practices, thereby creating a set of interactions that had never before existed. Before long, "we had 11,000 people across the globe using a common language to identify and work on all the control issues, and within two weeks we had most of them identified. It was amazing to see the release of energy across the organization that came with simply helping people see the systems that they were stuck in, then finding the right amount of structure to enable change."

Adams continues, "We're applying similar approaches to a host of problems, and learning how to build capacity so that the organization can keep pace with and hopefully improve its position in its ecosystem. Building this capacity into the culture takes time, but nature points us toward basic methods that work, such as sensing or seeing patterns; recombining ideas; and 'mutation,' that is, experimentation and feedback. Systems modeling, collaboration and dialogue, and looking for instances of too much variability are the analogs in the organizational system. If they can all be combined effectively, they foster innovations."

AN ADAPTIVE POLICE FORCE

Over the past decade, I've been fascinated to see a small number of public-sector organizations around the world embrace learning tools and principles in service of the same need for continual learning and adaptation. None have been more diligent in the effort than the Singapore Police Force (SPF). "We live in a fast-moving world and increasingly find ourselves inundated with issues that are complex and laden with uncertainties," says Commissioner Khoo Boon Hui.[3] "We've seen recently how the influx of new designer drugs, illegal immigrants, and new forms of crime and terrorism threaten the safety and security of numerous communities that are ill-prepared to deal with them. We have to develop the capacity to identify trends and deal with potential problems before they adversely affect the lives of the people we serve. It is my fervent belief that this capability can only come about through the management of knowledge in an organizational culture that promotes learning."

Khoo and the SPF were drawn, along with a number of other organizations, into a movement Singapore began more than a decade ago to become "a learning nation."

"When I assumed command of the Singapore Police Force, I saw trends that concerned me. The work of the police officer was often perceived to be unchallenging, routine, and menial, unbefitting the new generation of knowledge workers. We were unable to recruit the people we needed. The SPF was also run as a command-and-control organization. Our officers had to follow standard operating procedures strictly, and this meant that they could not cope with the rapidly evolving nature of threats to law and order that required making decisions quickly with little or no time to seek guidance from their supervisors. But 'empowering' people is easier said than done. So in 1997, we initiated a transformation of both the nature of our officers' work through a radical change in our business model, and a change in our culture toward one of trust and openness through investing in organizational development. We knew this would be difficult and take time, so we visited organizations [that] were working on these issues, including SoL member companies in the U.S."

Cultures are not built from scratch, but instead evolve, as they conserve and improve upon what is working and let go of what is not. "Since the early 1980s we had successfully developed our community policing, and our officers were familiar faces in the communities they served. Though they were no longer feared but trusted, they were not adequately equipped in terms of knowledge or skills to identify and deal with the underlying issues that were of concern to the community. We therefore enlarged their job scopes to include engaging the community to help them identify and resolve localized safety and security issues. Police officers began [helping] community members take greater ownership of safety and security issues within their own neighborhoods.

"As their work became more knowledge intensive, the officers picked up learning organization skills so that they could better engage the community in generative dialogue and problem solving through systems thinking. They also needed to build up networks of stakeholders for resolving longer-term issues," Khoo explains. This dovetailed with the equally new concept of teamwork in policing functions, "leveraging the power of collective thinking." Last, they emphasized developing leadership capabilities at all levels and inculcating core values, "so as to entrust our officers with greater discretion, confident that they would decide and act in alignment with our shared vision."

As the officers dealt with a wider range of issues, they also needed to be more connected across the entire organization. "They needed to draw from the SPF's vast store of knowledge, including other officers' and their colleagues' personal experiences. We embarked on capturing the tacit knowledge of experience through the use of narratives and storytelling—making available the personal accounts of officers involved in resolving critical incidents." To encourage knowledge transfer, they also set up special experience-sharing sessions that helped frontline police officers learn how to deal with difficult situations and customers, and implemented After Action Reviews (AARs) to further increase local reflection and to broaden awareness across the system. This effort also led to an electronic bulletin board, where police officers could log on and share their views about almost anything. "It surprises many people to know that the discussion threads are not moderated and what you read is what our police officers actually feel and think. What makes the bulletin board tick is the passion of the contributors who feel safe and concerned enough to be utterly candid in expressing their views and sharing their knowledge and experiences." Lastly, Khoo and his team shifted the traditional emphasis on rigid SOPs; many of them were "rewritten to stress principles rather than prescriptive instructions, so as to facilitate the exercise of discretion based on best practices."

These changes have been especially important in dealing with new challenges like those posed by global terrorism. "With little experience of our own to draw upon, the SPF had to establish relationships with as many people and organizations as possible who could contribute to our store of knowledge." The force now works with counterparts from all over the world to learn from their experiences. It has also tapped into a network of academics, religious experts, and community leaders to obtain a diverse range of perspectives. "As with other core problems, our interest is in not only reacting but diagnosing the sources of these problems through working closely with our community partners.

"At the end of the day, it is the people who are the drivers of any organizational transformation. Trust and focusing on how people in the organization relate to one another form the basis of our core theory of success. As the quality of relationships strengthens, the quality of thinking improves. As the members of a team consider more facets of an issue and share a greater number of different perspectives, the quality of their actions improves, which ultimately improves the results we can achieve." And the results have been encouraging. Singapore's annual crime rate is now about eight hundred crimes per one hundred thousand population—less than two-thirds the figure recorded in the mid-1990s and about one-third of Japan's. The efforts have also dramatically increased the number of crimes solved, which currently stands at about 60 percent, compared to 32 percent a decade ago and Japan's 25 percent. More importantly, "we have managed to improve our bonds with the community by securing their trust, cooperation and, dare I say, respect," Khoo reports. Today, the police force recruits more than a fair share of highly educated job seekers.

PERFORMANCE AND HAPPINESS

It is not accidental that Commissioner Khoo's story illustrates dramatic increases in achievement in concert with creating a more meaningful and personally rewarding work environment. Recall Vivienne Cox's remark as she looked back on her experience in getting people to talk with one another in order to rethink a complex organizational structure: "That work was also the most fun I had ever had in business." Although their ways of expressing it differ, I can think of few skillful practitioners of organizational learning who do not harbor similar aims. "I think the quality of relationships has improved a lot around here," says Hamachi-Berry.

"People feel more creativity and the satisfaction of accomplishment in situations where they previously felt there was no way to change the systems," says Ford's Adams.

"It's all about 'productivity,' personal and organizational productivity," says HP's Allen. "By that, I do not mean people having to work twelve hours a day instead of eight. I mean that people's jobs increase in meaning, and it becomes dramatically easier to impact business results."

Allen's comment brings to mind a powerful story from the early days of the SoL network. In the early-1990s, Dave Marsing was responsible for the ramp-up of Fab 9, a factory that was the lead facility for Intel's "486" microprocessor. It was an enormously challenging and stressful undertaking, and midway through he had a heart attack. He was fortunate that he was rushed to the emergency room and there was no long-term damage to his heart. But when he returned to his job several weeks later, he had a clear message to deliver to his colleagues. "I wanted them to know that I would no longer be working the insanely long hours that I had previously, and that I would be leaving in time for dinners with my family. They would know how to reach me on the weekends in case they needed me, but only for emergencies. I told them we would be taking more time to talk and reflect as we worked to meet our deadlines. I don't think any of them thought I was serious, but gradually they realized I was.

"The culture we created with this shift was core to the formation of the values and principles that were at the heart of the design and development of the new Fab 11 factory, which we started a few years later. In the end we broke all records at Intel for the ramp-up of Fab 11, achieving full-scale operation nine to twelve months faster than the most aggressive estimate. This saved the company several billion dollars in cost, not to mention the market benefits of having the new chips we were making available that much sooner and designed into more new products for customers. The facility is still the world's largest and highest performing factory in the world.

"What had become very clear to me was that we had been substituting working harder for working smarter. I mean, we had people being taken away in ambulances periodically, and it was just regarded as normal. When I made the commitment to stop working so intensely, it created space for others to choose likewise, and the result was we started working together differently, achieving what we never could have through just long hours and superhuman effort."

Obviously, the happiness that people like Marsing seek does not imply a life without challenge or difficulties. In fact, when people become more engaged in and committed to their work, they are usually willing to confront more difficult issues. They are willing to risk doing things beyond their comfort zone. They are even willing to fail in pursuit of goals that really matter to them, rather than being trapped in avoiding shortfalls like "those cold and timid souls who know neither victory nor defeat," as Theodore Roosevelt put it.

Bill O'Brien used to define happiness as "the general sense that your life is headed in the right direction and that you have the opportunity to make a difference." I have always thought of it as one of those odd qualities we value but cannot achieve by direct effort. Have you ever known anyone working to be happy? In my experience such people have one thing in common: they are not very happy. On the other hand, if we live our lives in pursuit of what matters most to us, and we do our work with people whose friendship we value, we will have all the happiness we need. In this sense, happiness is simply a by-product of a life well lived. This is what motivates practitioners of organizational learning.

14

STRATEGIES

It has always been clear that there are no magic bullets for building learning organizations: no formulas, no three steps, no seven ways. Yet, much has been learned and continues to be learned about creating work environments that produce inspired results and generate fun while doing so. The interviews we conducted for this edition provided a wonderful opportunity to check in with master practitioners on the state of the art and the core strategies they employ in service of that art. This chapter begins with an overview of what it means to think strategically—what the basic aims are and where to put your focus—and then lays out and illustrates eight different strategies that people follow in diverse settings.

THINKING AND ACTING STRATEGICALLY

What does it mean to think and act strategically in building learning organizations? For *The Fifth Discipline Fieldbook*, my colleagues and I developed a simple picture of a framework that helped readers understand strategic leadership at any level in building learning organizations. The framework addressed two sets of questions. One, what are our aims? What are the fundamental areas of growth and innovation that define a learning culture and make it robust? How would we know it if we saw it? Two, where do leaders focus their attention and efforts to create such a culture? How can we do it? The former we called the "deep learning cycle." The latter we called the "strategic architecture." Today the circle-triangle figure provides an overall perspective for appreciating the strategies that diverse leaders employ.[1]

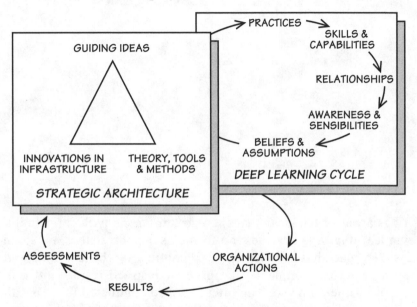

While this framework has several elements, the primary distinctions arise from basic insights about learning. Learning always has two levels. At one level, all learning is judged by what the learner can do, the results he or she produces, as shown at the bottom of the figure. But we wouldn't say we had learned to ride a bicycle if we succeeded in riding only once. On the deeper level, learning is about developing a capacity to reliably produce a certain quality of results. It is about becoming a "bicycle rider" not just riding one time, and this capacity is what grows as a result of the deep learning cycle. The learning environment needed to sustain this deep learning cycle is the focus of the strategic architecture.[2]

The deep learning cycle encompasses five elements, each of which skillful leaders pay attention to in building a healthy learning culture: beliefs and assumptions, established practices, skills and capabilities, networks of relationships, and awareness and sensibilities. These five cultural elements are always influencing one another. Start with beliefs and assumptions (you could start anywhere in the cycle).[3] While these taken-for-granted ways of seeing the world are often invisible to those who hold them, they shape organizational practices, guide how people do things, and, in turn, determine what skills and capabilities people develop based on those organizational practices.[4] For example, if people believe real listening matters, they establish practices like "check-ins" in daily work that encourage reflecting on our ways of listening.[5] Similarly, our practices and skills and capabilities influence networks of relationships and shape awareness. For example, when people develop skillful practices of dialogue, they become more appreciative of who they depend on and who depends on them, and this strengthens social networks. Or, when people become skillful in systems languages like systems archetypes, they start to see patterns of interdependencies that were previously invisible to them. In turn, "seeing is believing"—our experience is the most direct source of reinforcement for our beliefs and assumptions.

It is common to talk of an organization's culture as if it is simply "the way things are." But no culture is static. It is continually reinforced by how we live with one another day to day. By connecting these elements as part of a deep learning cycle, this framework expresses the important assumption that all these elements can and do change (albeit slowly)—and when they do, they tend to evolve together. The deep learning cycle can either reinforce the culture as it exists now or reinforce what is emerging. When we operate differently with one another, we also set in motion possibilities for changing all of these elements.

People naturally want to know where to intervene in order to influence this deep learning cycle. Many approaches are possible, but coherent strategies have three elements: (1) guiding ideas; (2) theory, tools, and methods; and (3) innovations in organizational infrastructure. Guiding ideas constitute the governing concepts and principles that define why an organization exists, what we seek to accomplish, and how we intend to operate. It is the domain of purpose, vision, and values. Theory, tools, and methods refers to explicit ideas about how things work (for example, a systems map of the procurement process or a simulation model of why "fire fighting" characterizes new product launches), and the practical means by which people apply those theories, solve problems, negotiate differences, and monitor progress. Tools are crucial to any deep learning process. Buckminster Fuller used to say that "you cannot change how someone thinks," but you can give them a tool "the use of which leads them to think differently." Organizational infrastructures such as formal roles and management structures, like their physical counterparts, shape how energy and resources flow. Many of the important innovations described in this chapter take the form of new learning infrastructures, implemented in concert with clear guiding ideas and appropriate tools and methods.

The overarching viewpoint behind this framework is known in social theory as "structuration," or the theory of "enacted systems." Chapter 3 presented the central principle of systems thinking, that structure influences behavior and that the leverage for change increases as we learn to focus on underlying structures, rather than events or behaviors. These structures are made up of beliefs and assumptions, established practices, skills and capabilities, networks of relationships, and awareness and sensibilities—in other words, the elements of the deep learning cycle. The second key element of the systems view is that the structures that govern social systems arise through the cumulative effects of the actions taken by the participants in those systems. In other words, as Winston Churchill put it, we shape our structures and then they shape us.

How do these systemic structures change? We have created the structures that currently dominate by virtue of how we have operated in the past, and they can change if we see them and start to operate differently. This is a big statement, and its credibility rests on evidence, such as the stories and examples in the preceding chapters and those that follow. But in a sense, it is also quite intuitive.

The streets of a city constitute a physical structure that shapes how traffic flows. It is very hard to drive your car where there are no streets. In Boston, the streets in the oldest part of the city follow no pattern whatsoever, and the joke is that it is the fault of the seventeenth-century cows. The paved streets of the twentieth century were laid on top of cart paths that had developed in the two preceding centuries, which sensible cart drivers had established by following the well-worn trails their cows had been making for a century before that. Now, presumably the cows had little ability to see the patterns of their trails, nor did they likely care. But people might look at this structure and decide there could be a better way, something that Bostonians' love of the past apparently precluded.

When the story of Boston's cows and streets is transposed onto our organizations, it raises two questions. What does it take to see the structural patterns we are enacting? And are we operating more like cows or people—like cows, doing what we have been doing because we have been doing it, or, like people, stepping back and attempting to see the deeper patterns and then choosing to do things differently? Obviously, any conceptual framework of this sort is abstract, and real understanding of how it all works must be gained through concrete experience, for which no book is a substitute. Nonetheless, the eight strategies and examples that follow should give a sense of the state of practical know-how today.

1. INTEGRATING LEARNING AND WORKING

Fragmentation, or making learning an "add-on" to people's regular work, has probably limited more organizational learning initiatives than any other factor. Over the years, many people have translated the imperative to "become a learning organization" into new programs to train people in mental models or systems thinking. Unfortunately, there was usually little opportunity to apply these tools to daily work, and, even if managers had similar training, the work environment was hardly conducive to reflecting, thinking more deeply about problems, and building shared visions. It was even worse when initiatives were driven by CEOs giving speeches on becoming a learning organization. Indeed, given the common mindset that big cultural changes needed to be driven from the top, it took many years for people to learn that such speeches were usually not a very good idea. Gradually, they realized that it was like waving a large flag that said "fad," "here we go again," or, in the carefully chosen language of managers at SoL corporate member Harley-Davidson, "AFP" (translated in polite company as "another fine program").

REFLECTION AND ACTION

The main flaw in these situations is the absence of effective infrastructures to help people integrate learning and working. Doing this well starts with appreciating the realities of people's work and identifying where and how specific learning approaches such as improved reflection can make a practical difference. It also helps people in roles where they can offer ongoing quality support to line management groups.

"Reflection gets a bad rap in business because we don't have the discipline to connect reflection and action," says Ilean Galloway, one of the senior managers in the organizational development department at Intel's New Mexico site. "People say they don't have time to just sit around and talk, and they're right. But we also often don't have time to think. I live in a very networked, interconnected work setting. In a global organization, people are literally working around the clock, solving problems by e-mail at midnight with a colleague on the other side of the world. But I think physiologically, technology has gone beyond what we as human beings are capable of doing. I am not sure how much real understanding is being developed through the use of e-mail, pagers, and cell phones. These devices are great for communicating and generating actions on routine issues. But when complex challenges confront us, they can seduce us into thinking we understand the situation. In reality, complex challenges require a different approach, one that allows us to pursue deeper, often hidden, meanings; surface underlying assumptions; and make connections between parts of the entire system. Then we can make sense of the situation and achieve shared meaning before taking action."

To counteract this decline in critical thinking, Galloway regularly gets together with different teams she supports, often for a day or longer. Although she sometimes has to "force people to take the time, afterward they are always grateful for the opportunity."

Making these sessions valuable, she has learned, comes from "discipline on the back end of it." She explains, "We have one consultant who said, 'Peter Senge has got it all wrong, people don't have time to sit around talking.' I don't really agree with that. What we don't have time for is reflection for its own sake. Reflection that [isn't] connected to action is what [makes] people think they don't have time for this. Part of my job has been to help teams develop more discipline on seeing where we have arrived and making sure we all follow through. Then, people have plenty of energy for reflection. One team I worked with went to a bed-and-breakfast for three different one-week meetings. The place had a train caboose on the property, where we would meet at critical points. The time there became symbolic for them. Later on, people would call me and say 'We've got to go to the caboose' when they knew they had some important thinking to do."

Galloway's colleagues at Intel have also learned that reflection does not mean agreement on everything. She says, "Our aim is to build real shared understanding and commitment to what we say we will do. What reflection says is that we hear everything. It does not say we're going to attend to everyone's needs. This is something that is a big part of Intel's culture—we call it 'disagree and commit.' When I was at another company you committed but you couldn't tell your team that you didn't agree with the decision the team was being asked to implement. At Intel, when you represent your team in a decision making forum, you can go back to your team and say, 'Look, we talked about this, and I had a different perspective. They heard my perspective and we've agreed to do this. We are committed to implement the decision, but we'll have a checkpoint to make sure these actions are achieving the results we intend. If they aren't, the decision and actions can be revisited.'"

LEARNING OVER TIME

A culture that integrates action and reflection arrives at better decisions to which people can genuinely commit, and its people have a more prepared mental state. The latter means having a richer set of perspectives about issues that concern you, a crucial capability in today's turbulent organizational environments. In fact, most of the time, things do not turn out as we expect. But the potential value of unexpected developments is rarely tapped. Instead, when things turn out contrary to our expectations, we go immediately into problem-solving mode and react, or just try harder—without taking the time to see whether this unexpected development is telling us something important about our assumptions.

"This more prepared mental state is really where a lot of the longer-term payoff is," says Galloway. "Part of our disagree-and-commit discipline is establishing a monitoring process to track the consequences of decisions." This involves an explicit time frame after which participants in Galloway's groups come back to key questions and assess whether "things are working like we thought or we're learning something we weren't expecting. Either way, those who disagree know they are providing useful perspectives that shape our ongoing learning.

"For example, we had a scenario planning process in '99, with the management team of one of our fabs. We looked at possible futures that were far from people's normal mindset, like a major collapse in the tech market or the effects of a disruptive technology. We forced ourselves to think through how we would respond. This occurred at the height of the bull market. We couldn't build capacity fast enough. But we hadn't even gotten all our scenario stories written and circulated to everyone when the tech market bust suddenly started." Because they had thought through this possibility, the Intel management team had a big advantage, Galloway says, and they were "able to take corrective actions quickly. These included some things that were difficult to do, like offering redeployment, moving resources to areas where they were more needed, and changing our fab strategies. We responded quickly and with a clear picture of our new direction because we had reflected on potential actions.

"We take this reflective work very seriously," she adds. "There is no point in doing it if you do not take the time and resources to do it well. Sometimes it takes a year before people see the value in some of our dialogues."

Galloway has learned to keep good records, using graphic facilitation and more conventional types of recording—"anything that helps people see that their thoughts were heard. I've had people ask 'Can I look at those meeting reports?' two years later because now these issues are coming up again and they remember some important ideas. It all comes down to helping people at the time they really need help. You have to be patient."

And you have to make reflection part of the way work is done. One simple method that has found broad application within the SoL network is "After Action Reviews," a tool developed by the U.S. Army. It can be used after an elaborate two-day war game simulation or after a one-hour meeting. In its simplest form, an AAR consists of three questions:

- What happened?
- What did we expect?
- What can we learn from the gap?

Having simple protocols like AARs for connecting action and reflection matters, but having a supportive management environment is essential. In the Army, AARs took root as part of a long-term journey, as one general put it, "from a culture of reports to a culture of review: we were always good at writing reports for our superiors but not necessarily at learning from our experience." The same management commitment is needed in companies.

AFTER ACTION REVIEWS[6]

Within minutes after the lights went out on August 14, 2003, everyone at DTE Energy, the parent of Detroit Edison, knew that something big was happening. Within those few moments, the power grid had failed for fifty million Americans and Canadians. But, for DTE, the blackout of 2003 was not just a freak occurrence. Rather, it was an extreme case of the emergency response which defines the essence of their business, and from which they would learn how to improve. Within 24 hours of the blackout, a series of After Action Reviews were called to assess how well DTE managed excess capacity to restore service, deployed personnel, communicated with the public, and met basic infrastructure needs. Such reviews have become standard practice during emergency responses at DTE—even as they work to restore power as quickly as possible, people are thinking about how they are responding and how they could do it better in the future. Even during the crisis, CEO Tony Earley said, "I must have seen at least five, maybe ten people, holding pads with the heading 'AAR Observations' on them. Right in the middle of the crisis, without any prompting. People just assumed there was going to be an AAR. It was great to see."

The integration of AARs into the culture took several years and was guided by four specific strategies:

1. Leadership by request and example. Help managers at all levels appreciate the importance of deep learning and ongoing discipline versus one-time events and quick fixes, and help them develop a learning practice that reflects their own priorities and challenges.
2. Events seen as learning opportunities. Develop the organization's ability, at senior, middle, and grassroots levels, to recognize day-to-day events, as well as major crises, as opportunities to learn, and help teams link past and present so that lessons from the past can be applied to improving current results.
3. Grassroots exposure to AARs. Introduce teams to the tool by demonstrating its ability to provide a safe environment

for learning their own priorities and challenges, but don't mandate its use, and don't insist on perfection.

4. A cadre of trained facilitators. Develop specialists who understand both how to facilitate AARs and how to help guide teams toward "high-yield" applications (tangible return for the investment).

The intention of these four strategies is local ownership for learning that matters. Most departments and teams know what practices they need to improve. The simple question, "If you could improve performance in one area that would make a significant difference for the enterprise, what would that be?" points them toward their most natural local learning practice. The AAR approach potentially makes the work team the first, best customer for its own learning, in sharp contrast to the "capture-and-disseminate" model of most knowledge-management practices.

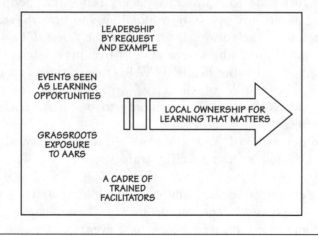

2. STARTING WHERE YOU ARE WITH WHOEVER IS THERE

To recap, integrating learning and working is the first core strategy used by those who build learning organizations, and fragmentation is its main obstacle. A problem closely related to fragmentation comes up when people believe that there is little they can do without the support of top management. It is easy to think that the deep learning strategic framework only applies to top management. But in fact, thinking strategically is imperative for leaders at all levels.

"I often hear people say 'We can't initiate change without top managers driving it,'" says Intel's Galloway. "If we waited around for top managers to drive every change that is needed, we would wait a long time. That's one of my hot buttons, I must admit. Part of it has to do with my background. When I started in graduate school in 1986, I felt like I had come home. I knew this organizational learning and change work was my calling. But I also heard all my professors continually saying 'organizational change has to start at the top.' At that time, as an African-American woman, I knew I was not going to get a job with the head of [an] organization. So, I had to think long and hard about whether I believed I was going to get a chance to make a difference. Two things helped me. One, I started to look at the social changes in the U.S. The civil rights movement, and the feminist movement were reshaping lives and the nation. They were not initiated by elected officials; these were grassroots movements. Second, I ran across an article by John H. Johnson, the late publisher of *Ebony* magazine. In the '50s when he tried to start the magazine, the white establishment said he wouldn't have anybody to put in the magazine—there were no middle- or upper-class African Americans, no black celebrities. He couldn't get any money to publish it. But he said, 'There is no defense against an excellence that meets a pressing public need,' and proved them wrong. I have the quote on my wall, and that became my strategy."

THE "IMPOSSIBLES"

Galloway translated this dictum into what is a guiding principle for many of the most talented leaders of learning initiatives: focus on problems that people believe cannot be solved. "I try to find a pressing public need, something the organization has given up hope of ever resolving, something people have learned to just live with. I call these 'the impossibles.' Each year I try to work on at least one impossible, something that scares me to death, that I can't even figure out how to approach. The key is just to get started. Once we do, people say 'Oh, that was easy.'

"I know I won't get a lot of support for projects like this. The fact that I can't get support tells me it is the right project. I believe

Einstein's statement that the consciousness that created the problem cannot be the one that solves it. I try to start looking at this problem and say, 'What is this problem trying to tell us? What can I see that's different about this? Once I start to figure that out, then I can enroll people. I start talking with people who will say, 'Oh, I have an extra hour. I'm willing to do this for you.' My boss will say, 'If you want to work on that, OK. Let me know what you need from me.' Then it gradually starts to build from there.

"For example, last year we started working on reducing the mean time to solve highly technical problems. Many of the organization's leaders thought that a significant reduction was impossible, but one of our senior organizational development consultants saw the opportunity to 'do the impossible.' She partnered up with a senior engineer to challenge the thinking and structures limiting faster problem solving. They utilized rapid learning cycles with testing and reflection to apply new approaches which ultimately dispelled the belief that faster results meant less quality. The results they achieved were dramatic. Problems that had taken months to solve were now being solved in four weeks.

"The irony is that if we were only working at the top of the organization we might never have been aware of some of these problems and thus might never have attempted to solve them. But when you build a team that believes that change from any place in the system is possible, significant change can sprout from even the tiniest of seeds."

OF THE PEOPLE, BY THE PEOPLE

Tackling the "impossibles" happens only when you are able to tap people's talents and deepest aspirations. I never cease to be amazed how steadfast master learning practitioners are in their conviction that this is always possible, even in very difficult circumstances.

In 1986, Roger Saillant became the first plant manager for a startup electronic-components plant in Chihuahua, Mexico, the first state-of-the-art facility of its kind for Ford in the country. It was not an assignment many of his peers in the company would have sought. According to business writer Ann Graham, "few at (Ford) headquarters believed a plant in a developing country could meet a tightly timed launch and sustain quality production."[7]

But Saillant quickly discovered that people there "cared a lot about their community and had never been given the chance to take real responsibility for an operation like this." He also discovered traditional power dynamics that would make his task difficult. A year after he arrived, and only two months before their launch date, a group of senior technicians tried to put their own appointee into a key position. This directly challenged a set of values and an open promotion system Saillant had worked to establish collaboratively. When one of the Mexican managers came to him and told him this was happening, "I knew that he really didn't expect me to do anything about it. Ford managers had been told for years that we had to work with this sort of thing if we wanted to have a smooth relationship with local political leaders."

Instead Saillant asked the entire technician group to leave when they admitted what they were doing. "I will never forget standing outside the plant as they left. Many of the other employees were watching, probably wondering what would happen now. And the truth is, I had no idea." He also knew he would "get a lot of crap immediately from my bosses, but the new personnel policies would not mean a thing if the old boy network continued.

"I knew that something had shifted about two months later when we were preparing for a visit from Dearborn [Ford's corporate headquarters] for the grand opening of the plant. There was a forecast for a big storm the evening before the site tour. I was lying in bed at two in the morning and started to hear the rain falling. It was pouring. All I could think about was the roofing work that was not quite done. Finally, I just got out of bed and headed down to the plant. I went inside and it was dark but I could hear this drip, drip, drip—not slow, mind you. I started walking around looking for the leaks and then I saw someone moving. To the end of my days, I will never forget seeing Alfego Torres positioning these huge leafy plants we had gotten for the opening ceremonies under the leaks to soak up the water. I almost started to cry. He was one of the hourly workers who had been promoted through our new personnel system, someone the old bosses would never have promoted. I knew in that moment that the community of people in this facility had turned the corner. It was now their plant."

The next day, the weather cleared for the big visit. The visit went fine, although the Ford execs were at first taken aback when they saw the finished plant. It was painted blue and pink, colors that the

Mexicans love and that the team had picked, along with lots of other architectural and decorative features native to the country. (There were also many features that had never been included in similar plants, things like an outdoor family activity center, a local school, and family health facilities.) "This isn't a Ford plant," one of the execs complained to Saillant. "No," he said, "It's the Chihuahua Ford plant."

Saillant continues, "On their walking tour, one of the hourly assembly workers went up to the executive VP, who I had known for many years, and asked him to put out his cigarette. Charlie was a chain smoker, and I doubt anyone had ever told him that he couldn't smoke in one of his own plants. But here was this small Mexican woman looking up at this six-foot-three Ford executive, and asking him to either stop smoking or go outside. What could he do? We had all agreed that one of our ground rules, part of our commitment to a healthy and clean working environment for everyone, was no smoking, and she was just doing what we had all agreed we would do. After that, my bosses didn't harass me much, especially since we launched six weeks early and the plant eventually became the number-one of its type in the world." In 1994, the plant received a presidential award as Mexico's most outstanding business.[8]

3 . BECOMING BICULTURAL

A subtle area of attitude and skill, one that seems to distinguish serial innovators like Saillant and Galloway, involves never losing touch with the larger organizational environment—something we call "becoming bicultural." While this sounds easy, failing to consider the greater environment has proven to be the undoing of many otherwise successful learning initiatives. One of the most painful lessons of the first ten years of the SoL network was discovering that success did not always lead to success. We lived through many examples of small-scale or local applications of learning tools that accomplished a great deal but did not spread in the larger corporate environment. Indeed, these successes often got the innovators into trouble.

One of the best documented examples of this phenomenon was a pioneering product development effort, "AutoCo's Epsilon team," that enabled a new model-year car development team to effectively shave a year off a five-year development cycle, return more than $50 million in allocated but unspent overrun costs, and achieve what many observers called "the smoothest new model launch in company history."[9] Still, when a major reorganization unfolded during the waning months of the project, the senior leaders on the team were not offered positions they considered attractive and all took early retirement. This experience came as something of a shock to many of us at that time, but it was an important awakening.

It turns out there is a rich history of successful innovations that fail to spread. For example, in *The Age of Heretics*, Art Kleiner documented early adopters of team- and process-oriented manufacturing processes in the mid-1960s, two decades before such practices became widely accepted, who were driven out of their companies.[10] "Corporate heretics," as Kleiner calls them, may play a key role in the larger patterns of innovation but often suffer personally for their efforts. The "build a better mousetrap" theory—"if we innovate successfully, the world will beat a path to our doorway"—provides a poor guide to the complex political dynamics of large organizations and how they respond to innovation.

But such fates are not inevitable. As we came to understand these problems, we discovered that one source of the trouble lay in the very enthusiasm and passion of the innovators themselves.[11] Without this passion they would never take the risks involved in doing something truly new. Without this passion they would not have the patience and perseverance required to succeed. Nor would they attract others who shared their passion. But their passion can also get them in trouble. It can blind them to how they are being perceived by those who are not part of their effort, and it can make them uninterested in how their efforts affect others.

Fundamental innovations that produce significant leaps in performance can be threatening to people and teams performing closer to the norm. When such improvements are achieved through significantly different methods—methods that are poorly understood by others—the threat increases. And when the advocates for those methods describe them with an air of jargon-laden mystery, their group can easily be labeled a "cult." "Whenever I met with [the managers of the team] they talked about 'ladders of inference' and 'systems thinking,'" said the VP of product development at AutoCo. "It was all quite incomprehensible to me."

"They were having too much fun," said another team leader bluntly. "Nobody enjoys work that much." Assessing performance is always complex, and enthusiastic advocates are usually prejudiced. They see what is improving and may be inclined to disregard other aspects of their performance that cynics or skeptics consider substandard. Eventually we dubbed this host of problems the "true believers syndrome" and realized it is a primary reason that promising innovations often fail to spread.

The other side of the coin to "starting where you are," the second strategy we discussed, is becoming adroit at working with the political forces within an organization. Innovators intent on building cultures of learning and openness sometimes feel that they are living in two worlds—the open, learning-oriented world of the team or organization they are working to develop, and the more traditional world of the mainstream organization. As we came to understand the problems of innovators who ran afoul of the corporate immune system, we started to see that sustaining innovation requires leaders who become bicultural, moving back and forth effectively between the two different worlds, respecting the ground rules in each.

STEALTH TRANSFORMATION

One strategy that works for some leaders is to simply keep their innovations below the radar of senior management. When Intel's Dave Marsing first shared his story at a SoL meeting of the breakthrough accomplishments in the ramp-up of Fab 11, he framed the whole effort as a "stealth transformation." His focus was on how to transform the working environment of an organization while not drawing the attention of the larger corporation; he did so in part by avoiding jargon and conversational styles that would not communicate well within the larger system. "We made no efforts to hide what we were doing," he said, "but at the same time we did not make a big deal about it. If people asked, we were happy to share and do our best to explain."

When we interviewed Marsing for this book, he said that he felt that stealth transformation strategies are still needed. "If anything, today you need to be even more savvy about power politics, not because senior managers are more power hungry but because of the intense financial pressures everyone is under. You need to be able to innovate and not trigger red flags. Your strategies have to be skillfully designed, culturally and linguistically. If I were doing Fab 11 ramp-up today, I would still do the same thing. We were able to show levels of performance that were much better than 'best in market,' and corporate management in companies like Intel are always looking for these sorts of comparisons. But I would do everything I could to communicate changes I was trying to achieve in ways that management would get. For example, Intel is a very measurement-oriented culture. If I were in an operating job today, I would work with my bosses on ways to measure technological agility and the ability to deal with market shifts in ways that preserve high ROI. I would look for ways to align these strategic concerns with building a more fluid and flexible operating environment."

Marsing believes these abilities are going to become even more important because the environment for companies is changing at an accelerating rate. This shows up in a higher turnover of senior managers and a "continual need to re-educate your bosses. It is like playing in an ensemble when the beat of the music is continually changing. It's an enormous challenge to stay in sync when the beat keeps changing. If you're innovating within a business operation, part of your job today is to work more closely with your bosses to stay aligned—even though the instincts of many innovators are to want more autonomy."

WORKING IN THE LANGUAGE OF THE INCUMBENT

Echoing Marsing, Roger Saillant has learned "that you need to work in the language of the incumbent. This means being very clear about where formal organizational power resides and how it is used. A big part of my job in places like Mexico was connecting the language of the incumbent—which was usually about numbers—with a language based on deep values that my people understood. The people in the plant were not indifferent to what Ford management wanted, but they could not always understand and relate it to their own concerns. When they could, I could tell them very straight that if we deliver what management expects of us, we will be able to create what really matters to us also. I would then work very hard to have clear agreements with my management and full transparency. Usually they didn't care much about how we did things, but I wanted to make sure they never felt that I was less than forthcoming or spoke to them in ways that intentionally obscured things."

In dealing with his bosses, Saillant also adopted as a managerial credo "under-promise and over-deliver," a very careful strategy for managing expectations. "I believe strongly in delivering what you commit to, but it is easy for people enthusiastic about a more trusting work environment to make claims that skeptics will have an investment in eventually disproving. You've got to craft goals in the language and worldview of the hierarchy, and then help people make sense of those goals in their own terms. Often, they will also want to go for other things or bigger stretches, which is fine for the working team, but [it's] best to keep it to themselves."

4 . C R E A T I N G   P R A C T I C E   F I E L D S

The fourth of our eight strategies for building learning organizations, one that often evolves into more established learning infrastructures, involves creating "practice fields." The idea of practice fields comes from a simple fact: it is very difficult to learn anything new without the opportunity for practice. While a classroom is often the first image that comes to people when they hear the word "learning," the typical classroom does not evoke much of the spirit or practice of learning. Classroom learners are usually passive. The classroom concerns mostly listening and thinking, not doing. For many people, classroom imagery evokes strong feelings of the need to avoid errors and the importance of getting "right answers." Real learning processes, in contrast, are defined by trying something new and making many mistakes. Practice fields or rehearsal halls offer a very different environment from traditional classrooms. People are actively doing what they want to be able to do well. They are making mistakes, stopping, trying again, talking about what's working and what isn't, and gradually developing a greater ability for effective action in the "performance fields," where results matter. For this reason, creating practice fields and establishing a regular rhythm of practice and performance has become a common strategy among practitioners of learning organization development.

THE CAMP AND THE HIERARCHY

Similar to Ilean Galloway and her reflective meetings, Roger Saillant has adopted a simple strategy based on the work of organizational psychologist Bruce Gibbs that he has used around the world, "the camp" and "the hierarchy." First, he wants to get people used to distinguishing the formal management system—what gets measured, formal roles and accountabilities, and agreed-upon goals—from "when we take time to really talk and get to know one another more deeply." He came to the term "camp" because many people had experiences going to camps as children and he wanted to identify a place where people could "play and relax, but also deal with difficult issues and emotions." Like Galloway, Saillant has found that introducing the camp idea can be tricky, because people are busy and taking time "away from work" can initially seem non-productive. But, eventually, "camps become a part of how we manage, as people learn how invaluable they can be to see what is really going on."

For example, Saillant had a plant in Northern Ireland that was deeply mired in the conflicts of the region. The plant manager was Catholic, but the majority of those in the work force were Protestant. "There were two guys who had not spoken for ten years because one of them once cut the other off coming out of the parking lot." Gradually, the camp process in this setting became a way of exposing "the real truths about what people valued beyond maintaining the conflicts." For many this turned out to be their children. "I discovered that they wanted a future for their children. I went back to my boss and told him that I was going to hire twenty-two sons and daughters of people in the plant and place them in apprenticeship programs, even though the plant hadn't met its financial targets, and even though there was a head-count control in Ford at the time. The camp meetings convinced me that we needed to do this as an act of trust." Eventually, the plant made a turnaround and became quite successful, "because we had gotten to what really mattered underneath all the bickering, and acted upon it."

THE SWIRL AND THE WALL OF FIRE

Some organizations make the rhythm of practice and performance part of their organizational design. At Harley-Davidson, for example, there is a distinction between the "management system" and "the swirl." The former includes business objectives, formal roles and accountabilities, and controls. The latter refers to the host of issues and ideas that are continually being debated, experimented with, and tested throughout the organization. In typical Harley fashion, the barrier that separates the two is called "the Wall of Fire." An idea or goal that has passed through the wall of fire is one that enough people believed was worth pursuing to make it an organization-wide commitment.

Many potentially important ideas may stay "in the swirl" for years, even if they have senior-level champions. When the president of Harley-Davidson, while hosting a SoL Sustainability Consortium meeting, explained, "Sustainability is not one of our management objectives today," it came as something of a shock to many there whose lives were devoted to the topic. But as he talked, it became evident that he took the subject of sustainability seriously. The VP of strategy chaired the company's "informal" sustainability task force. They were doing a lot that was relevant: the company's core business strategy is marketing the "Harley experience," not just bikes (which tends to create a huge demand for used bikes and significantly extends their productive lifetime); Harley is building up a major business in remanufactured parts to service older bikes (which keeps old parts out of landfills); and the company is now building a new energy-efficient product development center.

Gradually, it became clear that "the swirl" was important business, a sort of incubator for the new and a way to legitimate ongoing exploration and practice.

After the Harley-Davidson president had spoken, a Fortune 50 company representative (one of the long-standing members of the Consortium) said, "Maybe I've been following the wrong strategy, trying to get my management to officially embrace sustainability. We could set a few targets and create some new metrics, but it might only produce a superficial buy-in. Until people see that these issues are critical to the future of the business, maybe it's better that they stay 'in the swirl.' The problem is, right now we don't have any way to legitimate the exploration of potentially significant but radical new ideas. That might be our real limitation."

Practice fields come in many shapes and sizes, from Saillant's camp meetings to Galloway's reflective retreats to Harley's organizational swirl. We are probably at the beginning of an evolution of increasingly sophisticated practice fields, such as the simulated microworlds that Ford now develops and uses. I believe these advances hold a key to developing learning capabilities in the future.

But the journey of development starts when managers embrace the simple principle "no practice, no learning." No sports team would expect to be successful if the players showed up only for games, any more than a theater troupe or orchestra could imagine just performing and never rehearsing. Yet, this is exactly what we expect in most organizations. Is there any wonder learning is so limited?

5. CONNECTING WITH THE CORE OF THE BUSINESS

Respect for the mainstream organization can motivate people to become bicultural in their language and strategies, and to develop practice fields that will help them minimize conflict with formal management structures. But our fifth strategy involves a deeper level of connection, one that ultimately proves pivotal in developing guiding ideas and intentions. For radical new ideas and practices to take root within an organization there must be fertile soil. How to find this may not be apparent at the outset. Successful learning practitioners intent upon having a large-scale impact learn how to connect with the core of the organization—at the deepest levels of individual and collective identity—and how the organization most naturally creates value.

GETTING STARTED: FINDING OUT WHO WE ARE

There is no fixed formula for connecting the core identity of an organization to something that has no precedent in its history. But the approach starts with believing such an identity exists—that the organization is not just about making money, or whatever products or services it currently makes or provides. This requires a real spirit of discovery, of being willing to be guided by your heart and being prepared to see what has always been there, unseen.

Over the past decade, Nike has evolved an extraordinary "design for environment" network of product managers and designers. It started when Darcy Winslow, who was heading Nike's advanced R&D, began thinking, "there must be more to this business than the next cool gadget." About that time, environmental designers Michael Braungart and Bill McDonough, after designing Nike's European headquarters, studied one of Nike's shoes against their toxicity measures for product components and processes. The results, according to Winslow, "really opened up my eyes. I thought, 'Do we really understand the products we—and our whole industry—are creating?'" Her question eventually led to the creation of a new position, general manager of sustainable business strategies. "Sustainability was something that Nike management was starting to talk about, but it was still primarily from a compliance standpoint, in terms of policies and working with manufacturing partners around labor practices. I told them, 'If we are really serious about sustainability, it has to happen within product creation. We have to find a way to eliminate waste and toxicity in our products. Consumers experience Nike through our products.'[12] They said, 'Great, go do it,' and we created this new job."

As is the case with many people in new jobs focused on emerging issues, Winslow had a big mandate but not a lot of authority. None of the product development teams actually reported to her, and she was working with large, amorphous questions, like "What would it take to embed sustainability into what we do as a company?" and "How do we communicate that to our customers?" But the whole idea of sustainability, she says, "connected with me so deeply, so personally. It was not like I needed to think about whether this was important to me. I just knew 'We have to do this.' It became one of the most energizing and complicated challenges in my work."

About that time she read Malcolm Gladwell's *The Tipping Point*. "Gladwell says that if you can get 20 percent of the population moving in the same direction, you've reached the tipping point. So, I was thinking, 20 percent of twenty-five thousand people in Nike— that's going to be tough." But she was not alone. Together with a few other women in parallel but different jobs in the company, she hosted a two-day meeting for about two hundred of Nike's key managers, and brought in Braungart and McDonough, along with other business leaders and luminaries in the sustainability field, just to get sustainability into everyone's awareness.

"I watched people's reactions to our initial efforts and was so encouraged; I was getting in touch again with why I love this company. We have all the problems of any big company, but as I rediscovered 'who' Nike is, I realized that we are people who innovate. This company is all about innovation. That is what really turns people on, and we were all seeing that the whole sustainability arena offers untold opportunities for innovation."

Would-be change leaders often limit themselves through encountering two subtle barriers that they fail to recognize: They do not go deeply enough into themselves to discover what is truly calling them, and they do not go deeply enough into the organization to discover what it stands for. When people fail to go deeply enough into themselves, they pursue "good ideas" that fail to tap their own passions. When they do not go deeply enough into what the company stands for, they end up trying to "push" their ideas into the organization.

It may seem a bit odd to talk about "who" an organization is, or what an organization "stands for," but it is not odd if you look at it as a human community. As a community, the organization came into being because there were enough people who cared about something to pursue it together. Nike, for example, was created by runners who were passionate about running and about creating better shoes for runners. As time went on, the business evolved beyond running, and it became necessary to reach down to a deeper level to connect with a core or essence that included but was not limited by this original vision. Today, Nike has eleven maxims; the first is "It is in our nature to innovate." When Winslow could see how her passion for sustainability was really all about innovation, her whole change strategy shifted.

FIELDWORK: DISCERNING THE SOURCE OF AN ORGANIZATION'S CREATIVITY

As the connection to "who we are" starts to become clear, the next question arises: how a new vision can tap into the organization's creative process, how new sources of value are generated most naturally in the organization. This is the journey from vision to reality, discovering how compelling new ideas most naturally shape organizational action and results. At Nike, this meant going to product designers and product managers.

Once she rediscovered the importance of innovation for Nike, Winslow knew that she "had to go upstream and connect with our designers and product managers." Nike has about three hundred key designers, so she asked herself, "How could I connect with 20 percent of our most influential designers?" The answer was by going out and talking with them, one by one. "It was very organic:

I went knocking on doors. When there was a connection, I just went deeper. The emerging leaders, people who were going to take the idea and run with it, just presented themselves.

"This was very different from other sustainability initiatives. For example, we had a mandate from the Corporate Responsibility team to be 'PVC-free,' to get PVCs out of our shoes.[13] But that came across as 'Stop, you can't do that.' To designers, this basically closes a door. We wanted to open doors by saying, 'Think about it this way: there are basically untold opportunities for creating completely new products without compromising performance or aesthetics.' It took a lot of time, and I didn't speak to people just once. [I] had to go back and pursue it again. But it was like finding diamonds in the rough—people who were just waiting to have this conversation.

"In these conversations I felt like I was connecting with who Nike really is and what drives this company, the heart of our self-image and the heart of what has made us successful," says Winslow. "The more I did this, the more I could see that the ideas of zero waste and toxicity were natural goals for us." Although Nike hasn't yet "cracked the nut" of embedding sustainability into the business and communicating that to customers, the company has made substantial gains. "Over the past five years, we have [developed] long-range sustainability goals of 'zero waste, zero toxins, 100 percent closed loop' [all manufacturing by-products and materials in products are either reused or biodegradable] and some new products that actually meet these goals—no glues and cements so you can take it apart at the end of its use, and woven so that we don't create waste from cutting materials. We have an entire line of organic cotton products [Nike helped create the Organic Cotton Exchange to bring more organic cotton to market worldwide]; an internal sustainable materials group that informs designers about materials choices; and many take-back and recycling initiatives." Recently, one of the company's top three management goals became "to deliver sustainable products and innovation." Winslow says, "It's clear that more and more customers get the story. Who knows, this might be our greatest possibility. When you think about it, Nike is one of the few companies that could make this sustainability stuff 'cool.'"

6. BUILDING LEARNING COMMUNITIES

As Darcy Winslow discovered, when our own deep questions and aspirations connect with an organization's essence, community develops. Attunement to new learning communities, networks of relationships based on common aims and shared meaning, becomes both a strategy and an outcome for leaders. And there is nothing that limits this process to businesses.

CONVERSATIONS WITH HEART AND MEANING

"Our single greatest discovery has probably been the power of simply getting people asking, 'What is good for the kids?'" says Les Omotani, the superintendent of West Des Moines public schools for ten years and now superintendent of the Hewlett-Woodmere system in Long Island. "Gradually, this has evolved into building learning communities as the core strategy for change."

When Omotani first came to West Des Moines, he found "a pretty typical school system." Parts of the community were very affluent because much of the suburban growth in the city had spread to the west. But it also had three Title I schools (schools that receive state funding because of low income levels), and significant achievement gaps existed between different schools. Development was also skewed. "We tended to build our new schools in the west, following the population trends, but I also learned that people cared about all the schools and students doing well.

"When we started to organize regular community dialogues, lots of people showed up, not just teachers and administrators or parents, but local business people and town officials. Gradually, we started asking questions about things that are what people in the education mainstream refer to as 'immovable walls.' Why are we limited to a one hundred and eighty-day school year? There are a lot of kids who could really benefit from thirty more days of instruction. Are we not putting enough attention on schools in the oldest part of the community? Why is kindergarten only a half day, when we know kids can benefit from a whole day? It wasn't me pushing my agenda. It took some time, but these questions just arose naturally as the types of issues that were being neglected."

At the same time, Omotani had teams of teachers and administrators and community members who were working together on the details of different ideas. The two processes, dialogue and implementation—again, reflection and action—were moving in parallel, and feeding each other. "Gradually we were able to hold community forums where we weren't afraid of introducing new ideas that were still taking shape. We said, 'Why don't we show that we trust people enough to say there really are choices? We don't have to build the next school in the west. The money could go elsewhere. We could fix up an older school. What would happen if we did it differently?'"

Eventually, they did do a lot of things differently. One Title I school and its feeder school became a 'Leonard Bernstein model,' one with an arts-based approach to integrated learning. "To say that 'music and the arts are profoundly important in addition to academic success' in a school with the greatest number of Title I students is pretty striking when schools everywhere in America have cut the arts back or out entirely," says Omotani. Today, the newest elementary school is in the oldest part of the town. The second Title I school is being completely refurbished. And this will be the sixth year the school system will offer an extended-year program, approximately two hundred and ten days long, for students throughout the system who need it. "After I left, the community committed to maintaining the early childhood learning center we had started [that offered] daylong kindergarten, which was a real sign to me that these ideas had taken root." Overall, many of the achievement gaps have been reduced and overall student performance throughout the system is better than it was.

"It's very hard to explain to people how this all worked," says Omotani. "It wasn't any one thing that happened that enabled this or that innovation to occur. It was definitely the result of those conversations. It was all about developing a capacity to talk together in very diverse groups, developing a collaborative network of people who were supportive of one another, and through this tapping people's deep caring for kids.

"I was brought up as a Japanese-Canadian in Alberta, Canada, and I've also spent a lot of time in Hawaii and with our native peoples. In those cultures, when a child comes up to a group of adults, the adults will always stop their conversation to see what the child needs. One of the first things I became aware of when I moved to this part of the U.S. was that adults tended to ignore kids. I noticed that here people mostly just go right on talking.

"Now, I don't think we are so different as human beings, but something about how we live seems to have cut us off a bit from our innate caring for kids. As the community became what dialogue researchers call 'a safe container,' this innate caring just started to come out more, and the conversations and thinking became profoundly different from what was going on elsewhere. We came to a simple phrase: 'As the community, so the schools; as the schools, so the community.' If you say that enough, the meaning becomes clear. People start to remember it and start to repeat it themselves."

"Communities grow from people pursuing questions that have heart and meaning to them," says Juanita Brown, founder of the World Café method for organizing large meetings as genuine dialogues. Like Darcy Winslow, Les Omotani and his colleagues created a space for the deeper conversations. When this is done, learning communities arise as a by-product. It is important that this "social space" be created consciously and be maintained. But it is also important to realize that the creation of learning communities is a natural process that does not need to be controlled or manipulated—indeed, attempts to control it can easily backfire.

7. WORKING WITH "THE OTHER"

The shadow side of community is clique or even cult, when people gravitate toward people like themselves and with whom they mostly agree, excluding others. For this reason, embracing diversity, our seventh strategy, becomes a key guiding idea for leaders, beyond political correctness or mere sentiment.

Several years ago, Margaret Wheatley, a long-time student of living systems and organizations,[14] was studying the then-new phenomenon of "Internet communities" and made a surprising comment. "The more I look at these, the more they seem like anticommunities," she said. When I asked her what she meant, she observed, "On the Internet there is zero cost of exit. If people get tired of each other or turn off to what others are saying, they can simply disconnect. That's it. The result is 'communities' where everyone mostly agrees with one another. It's made me realize that real community is something that can only happen when we are stuck with one another."

BUILDING BRIDGES TO TRADITIONAL
NONPARTNERS

Partnering with those who are different is a core strategy at Roca, the Chelsea, Massachusetts, service organization. Roca focuses on "building bridges across boundaries" that otherwise trap young people in systems ill-attuned to their realities and needs. "Our work is always about building networks of transformative relationships, so we can start to understand the patterns behind problems in our community," says Omar Ortez. "These networks of relationships start with kids on the streets, but they have also extended gradually to other organizations like police, the courts, the schools, and DSS [the Massachusetts Division of Social Services]. This starts to create new systems that can work in favor of the kids."

"We used to give organizations like the police a hard time because we were always trying to protect the kids," says Molly Baldwin. "Then I discovered something remarkable. When you start to see the system from the viewpoint of people who are in very different parts of it, you become more responsible. You start to see that your prejudice, your attachment to your point of view, was really a way of protecting yourself. It also helps others look at themselves and their biases.

"Sometimes little miracles happen. Officer Pete was a cop who came to one of our circle trainings. During the training someone told a story about starfish. The story goes that someone sees an old man standing on the beach among hundreds of starfish that have been stranded by the tide going out. When the old man picks up a ⸺fish and throws it back into the sea, [the person] yells at the old mai. 'What difference will that make? It's just one starfish.' And the old ma. ⸺lls back, 'It made a difference for that starfish.'"

"Two d⸺ later I was walking up the street," continues Roca staffer Anisha ⸺ablani, "and I bumped into one of the detectives and he said, 'Wha⸺ did you guys do to Pete? He keeps talking about some story about starfish.' Unbelievable. I almost died. Officer Pete! It was the coolest thing I ever heard."

CONNECTING ACROSS THE SECTORS

Building relationships across boundaries between very different types of organizations is becoming a key strategy for influencing larger systems as well. "We're discovering that partnering to increase diversity of viewpoint is a key lever for strategic change," says Andre van Heemstra, a member of the management board at Unilever.

Recently, Unilever completed a historic joint study with Oxfam of Unilever's poverty reduction efforts in Indonesia.[15] Both organizations had a lot at risk. Unilever, as a leading multinational consumer goods company and champion of corporate responsibility, had to prepare for a critical assessment of its efforts to positively impact the developing world. Oxfam, as a leading global NGO that criticized international trade guidelines for unfairly favoring large global corporations, had to prepare for attacks for working with just such an organization. "Big companies like ours obviously are working hard to increase internal diversity, but we also need to increase external diversity," says van Heemstra. "It is difficult. But what Oxfam and Unilever can do together greatly exceeds what we can do on our own." Barbara Stocking, Oxfam's president, was also a champion of the project. "We all know the problems with the big multinational companies, but we need to go beyond just throwing bricks. We run campaigns to raise public awareness about real problems, but it's not enough to solve those problems that go beyond one company's behavior. Creating more systemic solutions will require working together."

THE NEXT STAGE OF DIVERSITY

The imperative to build more diverse and inclusive communities will only grow in an increasingly networked world. "One of the big changes I've seen," says Ilean Galloway, "is the need to work with people who are very different from you. Because of the increasingly networked way in which work is getting done, our ability to work with diverse people is so much more important than in the past." Galloway says that not long ago, people tended to work "in small homogeneous circles—people from the same workgroup, or same location— but now the circles include people from around the world on a routine basis. This bigger circle includes people who are different from us in many ways. Many organizations' diversity initiatives include establishing the business case for diversity, aligning human resource guidelines and policies, and hiring diverse people. With this groundwork laid, the real challenge for creating an inclusive work environment shifts to each and every employee. We have to look at who we pick to work with on our teams, the choices we all make, and whether those choices are really in line with what it will take to get the work done. If I am uncomfortable working with my Chinese colleague, or he with me, the networks that form might preclude good solutions to our problems."

Galloway pointed out that traditional approaches to dealing with diversity put people into categories. "The real issues here are much more personal, and more developmental, than the way most corporations have been looking at diversity. It is about our ability to understand and appreciate how [others] think, communicate, and relate. It's about living together."

8. DEVELOPING LEARNING INFRASTRUCTURES

Many of the above examples show how innovations in learning infrastructures are often a key element of effective learning strategies. When organizations like Intel or Ford or DTE Energy or Nike create or redefine management roles to support reflection or systems thinking, they create learning infrastructures. So do managers who establish regular practice fields or invest in technologies for sharing information and enabling working groups to connect with each other more easily. Yet, this area is often overlooked—perhaps because innovations in infrastructures are not as dramatic as articulating new guiding ideas, or as concrete as new tools and methods. But it makes little sense to articulate guiding ideas that do not align with how resources are allocated, nor is it helpful to introduce people to tools and methods that they have little opportunity to use.

Learning infrastructures do not leave learning to chance. The history of how the quality movement in Japan took off provides a compelling example of the importance of learning infrastructures. In the 1950s and early 1960s, experts like W. Edwards Deming and Joseph Juran taught top managers basic principles (guiding ideas). Afterward, many people were trained in basic tools like statistical process control. But several years later, a few companies like Toyota realized that they needed to train frontline workers in these tools, and, most importantly, redefine their job responsibilities so they had the authority to analyze and improve their own processes. Without these changes in job responsibilities, quality control would have remained the responsibility of experts—not the workers themselves—and working and learning would not have become integrated.

A PIONEER IN LEARNING INFRASTRUCTURES

We have learned the most about learning infrastructures from the U.S. Army, a long-time strategic partner in the SoL network. I have seen no corporation with comparable sophistication in this area.

For the Army, learning infrastructure includes:

- Training and Formal Education: this includes entry-level training institutions like the Military Academy at West Point all the way up to the Army War College, where colonels go for twelve-month educational programs prior to being promoted to the most senior positions.
- Practice: ways that various types of simulations (computer-based and physical) are carried out and tools like After Action Reviews (AARs) are used to debrief and learn from simulated experience. This category includes institutions like the National Training Center, where large-scale multiple-day simulations are carried out.
- Research: study of real and simulated engagements to analyze successful and unsuccessful practices; includes institutions like the Army Center for Lessons Learned, which is responsible for distilling insights and lessons to shape future education and training, new simulation practices, and ultimately doctrine.
- Doctrine: the highest level of policy, articulating core assumptions and beliefs about successful command; this is the responsibility of the Office for Doctrine, directed by one of the most senior generals.

In many ways, the Army's continual investment in learning infrastructure rests on a deep conviction in learning the lessons from history. For several years, the Army Chief of Staff hosted executives from SoL companies for a walking tour of the Gettysburg battlefield, guided by the Army's "chief historian." Two things immediately struck the corporate people about this: the fact that there was such a role and that the person in it held the rank of general, as has often been the case since the role's inception. As we walked and talked, it became apparent that the other Army officers in the group also had a deep knowledge of details of the famous Gettysburg battle (widely seen as a turning point in the U.S. Civil War), and that they could quickly relate the lessons from that battle to current challenges they faced. This was no academic history, but a rather stunning example of "oral history" that had deep meaning for people. The officers knew the stories of individuals who had led different skirmishes, and who had been injured or died in particular places (over 60,000 perished as a result of the three-day battle). This history was personal, connecting directly to their own experience as commanders and soldiers, and to the costs of mistakes in judgment or execution—and the imperative to learn.

Most of the executives leave this experience with an acute sense that learning requires much more than good intentions and a few tools. It has to become deeply embedded in the fabric of how an organization works if it is to have a real impact. Many conclude that it borders on dereliction that their organizations invest so few resources in studying what has succeeded and failed in their past strategies, operational changes, and leadership approaches. Instead, they more or less "make it up as they go along," with little serious theory to guide leaders at different levels. It's no wonder that a new CEO typically sees his or her job as pushing a whole new strategy, almost as if there were no history.

ARE OTHER ORGANIZATIONS PREPARED TO TAKE THIS SERIOUSLY?

Of the U.S. Army's many types of infrastructures, the one most common in other organizations is formal education and training, and even that is often cut back quickly under financial stress. Yet, without the other three—practice, research, and doctrine—training is likely to be neither well-focused nor effectively translated into work practices. And that is not likely to change until there is a management philosophy that recognizes the crucial role of learning infrastructures. Perhaps the real reason learning infrastructures remain largely unappreciated is that most managers still focus narrowly on achieving near-term results, not building capacity for future results. As one CEO lamented, "We have lots of infrastructures for decision making, but none for learning."

I personally believe that a gradual awakening is occurring—evident in DTE's investment in AARs, and in Intel's investment in reflective coaches like Ilean Galloway. And, if the term "learning organizations" is to become more than a slogan, I believe this awakening holds a key.

A small but growing number of executives, like Ford's Marv Adams, see it the same way. "By and large, corporations do a poor job at systemic understanding of problems," says Adams. "This is easy to understand given the time pressures people are under and the fragmentation of management responsibilities. But, interdependency is growing dramatically, and those organizations that make even modest progress in developing capacity to understand and work with complexity will have real advantages. We have already seen many occasions where seeing systemic patterns and adopting sound complex systems strategies have paid off in intelligent and adaptive solutions to otherwise intractable business problems."

The key, Adams says, "is building these learning capacities into the organization," not making them a matter of episodic learning. "The next generation of learning infrastructures," Adams believes, "will take advantage of distributed computing, simulation, and sophisticated internal consulting resources. There is a long way to go, but the payoffs will be considerable."

WHAT'S IN A NAME?

Part of the fun of the past few years has been seeing how many different ways people describe their work in creating more learning-oriented organizational cultures. Marv Adams of Ford talks of building "the adaptive enterprise." For Anne Murray Allen at HP, it is all about "understanding how work really gets done and how collaboration evolves knowledge networks." Commissioner Khoo in Singapore speaks of the importance of "managing knowledge in a culture that promotes learning." Dorothy Hamachi-Berry focuses on "aspiration" and "inquiry and dialogue skills" at the IFC. Roger Saillant and his colleagues at Plug Power, the small fuel cell company he joined after leaving Ford, talk of "learning to become a learning organization" (one of my favorites). Les Omotani expressed the view of many, saying, "When you care and serve and lead by listening and paying attention to all people in the community, including children and the elderly, you don't have to call it anything. The culture starts to change [through] just being present with people, because that's what they want."

When my colleagues and I initially chose to adopt the term "learning organization," we did it with some trepidation, knowing that the term would likely become a fad, and knowing that the ensuing fad cycle would be relatively short-lived.[16] Still, the simple image of the "learning organization" seemed consistent with building organizations based on reflectiveness, deep aspirations, and the desire to see systemic barriers and enact systems more in line with what people wanted to create.

In the later years of his life, Dr. Deming claimed that the terms "TQM," "QM," and "quality management" were worthless because they had come to mean "whatever people want them to mean." But his work was remarkably consistent at its core and continually evolved throughout his lifetime.

Watching the inevitable journey of faddishness and post-faddishness of "the learning organization," I have formed one conclusion. People need to find their own language for describing the intent of their efforts in ways that work in their own context, as part of developing their own strategies and leadership practices. How we talk about our work matters. But the key lies in our personal journey of reflection, experimentation, and becoming more open, not the words we use. It is the reality we create, not how we label it, that matters.

15

THE LEADER'S NEW WORK

O f all the material in Part IV of the original *Fifth Discipline*, the most widely read was the chapter that bore this title.[1] Looking back, I believe that was because we all know that bringing about the sorts of changes needed in the creation of learning organizations is enormously challenging work and requires real leadership. The chapter started by quoting Hanover's Bill O'Brien: "I talk with people all over the country about learning organizations and 'metanoia,' and the response is always very positive. If this type of organization is so widely preferred, why don't people create such organizations? I think the answer is leadership. People have no real comprehension of the type of commitment that's required to build such an organization."

At SoL's 2005 annual Executive Champions Workshop (ECW), Roger Saillant (now at Plug Power) and Mieko Nishimizu, the World Bank's recently retired vice president for Southeast Asia, served as mentors for the attending group of senior managers. While at the Bank, Nishimizu was widely respected not only for her innovative work with many countries but also as a developer of younger leaders, several of whom are now in key positions within the Bank. On the last day, the group requested some additional time to learn how the two of them had developed as leaders.

At Nishimizu's suggestion, the three of us sat in the center of a circle of the other participants, and the two of them started to inquire about the experiences that had shaped each of them. Saillant told stories about his experiences in Mexico, Northern Ireland, and China, where people who had never had a voice became gifted leaders. Nishimizu talked about her journey from being trained as an economist to coming to terms with the reality of poverty.

At one point Saillant suddenly asked, "Mieko, when did it shift for you?" I sensed that many who were listening were uncertain what he meant. But, sitting opposite Nishimizu, I could see that she understood exactly. She looked straight at him and answered, "I was in Cairo. I had been through two days of World Bank meetings at an expensive hotel. I wanted to get away and went to the 'City of the Dead,' a cemetery on the outskirts of Cairo where homeless people had settled. The people were very poor, living in the sort of urban squatters' camps that are common in the developing world. I sat with one woman whose young daughter was very sick. She was dehydrated from a simple diarrhea. They were waiting for some medicine that had not arrived, but all she needed was good clean water with salts. I could tell, from looking at the baby, that it might not make any difference. I asked if I could hold the little girl, and the mother gave her to me." As Nishimizu told this story, her eyes filled with tears, and the group became very quiet. "A few minutes later, she died," she said, and paused. After a moment she added, "I knew it was not necessary. I knew that this little girl did not have to die. That is when it shifted for me."

WHAT DO WE MEAN BY "LEADERS"?

"To become a leader, you must first become a human being," said Confucius, more than twenty-five hundred years ago. In the famous *Great Learning*, Confucius lays out a developmental theory in terms of seven "meditative spaces" of leadership cultivation. These ideas find parallels in wisdom traditions around the world. Indeed, wisdom itself is one of the oldest ideas associated with leadership.

Unfortunately, this perspective on leading has almost been lost today. The very word "leader" has come to refer largely to positional authority, a synonym for top management—as when people say, "Change will only happen if it is driven by the leaders," or "The problem here is our leadership." Regardless of the accuracy of such statements, there is a deeper message. Such statements point to particular people in top management jobs and refer to them as "the leaders." Why not just say "our senior management" or "our executive managers"? Certainly that would be less ambiguous. But we encode a broader message when we refer to such people as the leaders. That message is that the only people with power to bring about change are those at the top of the hierarchy, not those further down. This represents a profound and tragic confusion. First, it declares that all others are not leaders and have little power to bring about change. Second, it oversimplifies a much more complex and important subject, how to understand the diverse roles of leaders at many levels and how to develop networks of leaders capable of sustaining deep change.

Recognizing this confusion some years ago, we began to think in terms of an "ecology of leadership" and how local line leaders, internal network leaders, and executive leaders contributed to this ecology. As we looked across diverse efforts at building learning cultures within the SoL network, it was clear that all three types of leaders were vital, albeit in different ways. Eventually, this view of distributed leadership was presented in *The Dance of Change* fieldbook, which examined ten recurring challenges in initiating and sustaining profound change and the interdependencies among leaders addressing these challenges.[2]

Local line leaders, like Dave Marsing of Intel or Roger Saillant, formerly of Ford, are vital for integrating innovative practices into daily work: for testing the efficacy of systems thinking tools and for working with mental models, for deepening conversations and for building shared visions that connect to people's reality, and for creating work environments where learning and working are integrated. Without effective local line leaders, new ideas—no matter how compelling—do not get translated into action, and the intentions behind change initiatives from the top can easily be thwarted.

Network leaders, like Brigitte Tantawy-Monsou of Unilever or Ilean Galloway of Intel, are helpers, seed carriers, and connectors. They often work closely with local line leaders in building local capacity and integrating new practices. They are vital for spreading new ideas and practices from one working group to another and between organizations, and for connecting innovative line leaders with one another. They build larger networks that diffuse successful innovations and important learning and knowledge.

Executive leaders, like Vivienne Cox of BP and Les Omotani, formerly of the West Des Moines school system, shape the overall environment for innovation and change. They lead in developing guiding ideas about purpose, values, and vision for the enterprise as a whole. They do not have to be the sole source of these ideas; such ideas may come from many places. But they must take responsibility for ensuring the existence of credible and uplifting guiding ideas in the organization. Executive leaders are also vital for dealing with structural impediments to innovation, such as poorly designed measurement and reward systems. And they are role models who must embody values and aspirations if these are to be credible. In many ways, it is this symbolic impact of hierarchical authority that is most important for change, and most neglected. Effective executive leaders embrace the old dictum "Actions speak louder than words," knowing that in any organization it applies especially to those who are most visible.

Each of these types of leaders needs the others. Local line leaders need executive leaders to understand and address larger systemic barriers to change, and network leaders to prevent isolation and to enable learning from peers. Network leaders need local line leaders to test ideas in practice, and executive leaders to translate local insights into broader organization-wide guidelines and standards. Executive leaders need local line leaders to move strategic aims from concept to capability, and network leaders to build larger networks for learning and change.

Cutting across these different organizational positions from which leaders operate are three fundamental roles that characterize all leaders' work. In the original edition of *The Fifth Discipline*, I wrote, "Our traditional views of leaders—as special people who set the direction, make the key decisions, and energize the troops—are deeply rooted in an individualistic and nonsystemic worldview. Especially in the West, leaders are heroes—great men (and very occasionally women) who 'rise to the fore' in times of crisis. So long as such myths prevail, they reinforce a focus on short-term events and charismatic heroes rather than on systemic forces and collective learning. At its heart, the traditional view of leadership is based on assumptions of people's powerlessness, their lack of personal vision and inability to master the forces of change, deficits which can be remedied only by a few great leaders.

"The new view of leadership in learning organizations centers on subtler and more important tasks. In a learning organization, leaders are designers, teachers, and stewards." Today, I see these fundamental roles as being more important than ever, but I've also come to appreciate the difficulties and personal challenges they pose.

LEADER AS DESIGNER

If people imagine their organization as an ocean liner and themselves as the leaders, what is their role? For years, the most common answer I received when posing this question to groups of managers was "the captain." Others might say, "The navigator, setting the direction." A few would say "The helmsman, actually controlling the direction," or "the engineer down below stoking the fire, providing energy," or even "the social director, making sure everybody's enrolled, involved, and communicating." While these are legitimate leadership roles, there is another which, in many ways, eclipses them all in importance. Yet, rarely do people think of it.

The neglected leadership role is that of the designer of the ship. No one has a more sweeping influence on the ship than the designer. What good does it do for the captain to say, "Turn starboard thirty degrees," when the designer has built a rudder that will turn only to port, or that takes six hours to turn to starboard? It's fruitless to be the leader in an organization that is poorly designed.

Translating the role of designer from the context of an engineering system to that of a social system is tricky. As leaders in organizational contexts, we are not designing a thing, something separate from ourselves. When we think of ourselves as designers, it might even be tempting to think of the organization as a sort of machine, one that somehow needs to be redesigned. But, we are participants in the system not outsiders, and you do not redesign a living system as you would redesign an automobile.

Leaders who appreciate organizations as living systems approach design work differently. They realize that they can create organizational artifacts like new metrics, or formal roles and processes, or intranet Web sites, or innovative meetings—but it is what happens when people use the artifacts or processes or participate in the meetings that matters.

ITERATIVE DESIGN AND LEARNING INFRASTRUCTURES

Learning infrastructures that effectively integrate working and learning do not emerge wholly formed. Rather, they develop over time in ways that depend on leaders who appreciate and are comfortable with an open, iterative design process.

New infrastructures start with the willingness to experiment. In 2003, the engineering and operations services business line of Saudi Aramco, the state oil company of Saudi Arabia, decided to utilize a radical new method called "the world café" for organizing large business meetings. For several years, the leadership group and small working teams within the organization had been using systems thinking and related learning tools to improve problem solving and for clarifying business strategy, but they had not managed to effectively engage the larger organization. Now their innovations were beginning to make them feel "that we were alone," says Senior VP Salim Al-Aydh. "What we were doing was not linked with the rest of the corporation. We were not in rhythm and couldn't take our new thinking to different levels."

In the spring of 2002, when Al-Aydh participated in the SoL Executive Champions Workshop in Egypt, he saw firsthand the world café method and began to think about how it could be used for larger-scale learning. Developed by Juanita Brown and David Isaacs, long-time members of the SoL network, the process provides a simple but powerful structure for larger group dialogue.[3] It starts by having people sit at small café tables, focused on a common question or topic that has important meaning for them. As people rotate to different tables, these small, intimate conversations begin to get connected to one another. Over a few hours, people participate in multiple small conversations and simultaneously gain a sense of how the larger group as a whole is thinking. "The café process helped me a lot," says Al-Aydh. "In the ECW, we found that all these different people from different backgrounds and different businesses were facing very similar issues. The café process helped improve understanding by exposing multiple points of view."

At the same time, Saudi Aramco's senior management was rethinking its business strategy in the context of the realities of the Saudi economy: a large demographic bubble of teenagers and young adults entering the work force; unemployment rates hovering around 30 percent; a declining per capita GDP (it has fallen 50 per-

cent in real terms since the mid-1970s); and an unsustainable
dependency on oil. "For the first time in our history, we developed
a strategic direction as a team, and the dialogue expanded our perspective. Like every business, we have to please our shareholders,
but in order to thrive we also have to promote the local economy. I
asked myself, 'How do we communicate these issues with our work
force, take this thinking to different levels in the organization?'
Most people will tell you that one of our weaknesses as an organization is how to communicate with people. I had been looking
around for a tool that would overcome this weakness, and the session in Egypt really sparked my imagination."

In 2003, Al-Aydh and his colleagues held "Café '03," bringing
together supervisors, managers, general managers, executive directors, and executive management in one room, about six hundred
people all together. Using the café process, they attempted to communicate these larger issues about why change was needed in the
company's strategy. "We gave people a chance to talk all together, to
raise questions and to help us surface and understand alternative
viewpoints."

Café '03 was a step in a new direction, but it was just a first step.
"We did a survey afterwards, to find out how much of this had
really influenced people's thinking and behavior. Although the
results were much better than with more traditional attempts to
communicate, we were still not satisfied with the level of engage-
ment. Unless you spend enough time to answer the question 'What
does this mean to me?'—at the end of the day, people don't really
see how it affects them."

Al-Aydh and his colleagues then designed "line of sight" meetings, bringing different organizations together to talk about how
these issues were linked to their day-to-day businesses and activities.
Then came "clarity of sight," a series of small group sessions
involving fifteen to twenty-five participants. Through these efforts,
Al-Aydh personally met and engaged over one thousand employees
in conversations around the need for change.

"Those sessions were very helpful. At one point, we talked about
our GDP falling to $735 per capita, or $2 per day. People would
then ask, 'Is it true that we will be living on $2 per day if we don't
change?' And I said, 'Yes,' and explained to them why I think that is
possible. That phrase, '$2 per day,' became famous in our company.
People started saying, 'If we don't help the local economy, if we
don't develop businesses [other] than oil, if we don't outsource more

to local contractors, create more jobs, and train and hire more local people, then we will end up living on $2 per day. Our kids will have no jobs. We will be poor."

As this questioning and rethinking started to build momentum, the café process evolved. "Over time we developed a better understanding and learned how to engage people, how to connect stakeholder's concerns and their work. We also saw that communicating differently internally was great, but what about the other people around us, inside and outside the company?" This question led to Café '04, which brought together internal and external customers. With Line of Sight '04 and Clarity of Sight '04, Aramço people were no longer just talking among themselves. In Café '05, they extended the process to include contractors and service providers, bringing more than a thousand people together in a café format in a huge airplane hangar. "We conducted the café in early January, so we could talk about these major issues in the context of our operating plan for the coming year. Before this, most employees had never participated in the planning process. But we recognized that if we are going to work together on these major issues, people need to know how we as a company are planning on moving forward."

The new learning infrastructure involved only Al-Aydh's engineering and operations services business unit and its network of business partners, but others started to notice. A 2004 survey showed that people in Al-Aydh's business unit were well ahead of others in their understanding of the corporate strategy and how it related to their own work. "I think the bottom line is that our efforts worked. The corporation identified that there is a need to do more to improve communication in other business areas. Now the cafés are starting to spread around the company."

The world café is a useful method, but it is not a magic bullet. Just as important is what the story of Saudi Aramco's cafés illustrates in regard to what it means to be a "designer" of learning infrastructures. First, one must recognize that an important need for communication and learning is not being met. Then, have the courage and imagination to break the mold, to do something very different to meet that need. That is followed by being open to look critically at what is being achieved and to modify and adjust the approach, using patience and determination to persevere, and not expecting to get it all right the first time. Finally, in the role of designer, a leader must be willing to allow others to continue to evolve the infrastructures to suit their own situations and not to feel the need to control the process.

IT INFRASTRUCTURES

The same leadership in iterative design comes into play with more popular communication infrastructures like Web sites and portals. For years, it was assumed that these functioned as was intended by their technical designers. But, in fact, the opposite can happen. For example, when the first "groupware" was introduced, companies invested in it seeking to boost collaboration. Often this intent was completely overwhelmed by established organizational cultures that were based on internal competition. My MIT colleague, Wanda Orlikowski, found that people in consulting firms that had installed Lotus Notes used it mostly to do things they had been doing all along, like sending e-mails and scheduling meetings, rather than sharing new client or technical information.[4] In a culture where what I know determines my status and pay, it is naive to suppose that a new computer infrastructure will lead people to start collaborating. It is much more likely to be used in ways that reinforce the existing culture than in ways that change it.

Leadership in designing IT-based infrastructures starts with designing the composition of the team responsible for implementation. "When I led the SAP implementation for HP's printing group," says Anne Murray Allen, "80 percent of the team was from business—finance, procurement, manufacturing—and the entire team worked in one physical space. You couldn't tell who was from IT or from the business. We were not installing a new tool. We were transforming the way we did work. Years later, when I took on the work of leading the HP employee portal intranet and knowledge management project, we approached the work the same way. The guiding strategy was to focus on how the technology could enable people throughout HP to find one another and to help one another—to build and expand knowledge networks across organizational boundaries. This was much more important than the technology itself."

The same thinking needs to guide more novel learning infrastructures, like microworlds. When I originally wrote this book, I envisioned these simulated learning environments as a key learning infrastructure for the future, and boldly proclaimed them "the technology of the learning organization" in the chapter subtitle. Although simulation has become much more common in the intervening years, my hopes for the impact of microworlds have not yet been realized. The culprit, I believe, is too much emphasis on the technology (simulation models in this case) and too little on a patient iterative design process that focuses on real learning and change.

"I think the idea of microworlds as laid out in *The Fifth Discipline* was ahead of its time," says Ford's Jeremy Seligman, a senior member of Marv Adams's staff. "But the pervasiveness of computers and increasing advances in computing power are starting to make the difference. We are seeing more and more instances of management flight simulators and microworlds as meaningful drivers of business strategy development and decision making." One Ford plant manager has taken more than one thousand employees through a plant floor/manufacturing flight simulator that lets people at all levels of the manufacturing process experience possible scenarios and outcomes before they happen, making them more adaptive, and certainly more understanding of the whole system of which they are a part. "This led to significant increases in productivity on the plant floor, and I expect to see similar projects in other plants," says Seligman. "We've also had success in sales planning. One microworld that transformed the thinking of a leadership team in a very large regional business changed sales plans, metrics, and core strategic assumptions. This is such a step ahead of endless conference room marathons based on insufficient data and unarticulated views of possible futures.

"You have to be patient and keep looking for where and how to engage people with their real needs. The design paradigm is evolving rapidly. Gradually, I think we are getting to a more refined view of the critical success factors for implementing microworlds in organizational contexts." Seligman and Adams's continuing experimentation and refinement are based on a deep conviction that, as Seligmans says, "as we learn how to embed these sorts of learning tools in work settings, hold a critical difference between survival and extinction for companies in the current hypercompetitive marketplace."

GUIDING IDEAS

Seeing design as part of a living system applies equally to more subtle design tasks, like the "design" of guiding ideas. "Organization design is widely misconstrued as moving around boxes and lines," Bill O'Brien used to say. "The first task of organizational design concerns designing the governing ideas—the purpose, vision, and core values by which people will live." But while it is common for management teams to come up with vision and mission statements, understanding that people interpret and behave with such statements in many different ways leads to different strategies.

When you approach the design of guiding ideas with this in mind, several things happen. First, you worry less about getting the words right and more about using the words to engage people. "We used to think we had to fully bake the pie before we served it to the community," said Les Omotani, the school superintendent in Long Island. "As our teams of teachers, administrators, and community members became used to learning and working together, we weren't afraid to go to them with half-baked ideas and visions, because they were the ones who would come together to work the details out. We got to the point where we said, you know, why don't we show some trust here and go out to the community and say, 'We have choices and we need to find together what we are committed to.'"

Second, you are prepared to take longer to develop statements of guiding ideas. In 2001, Darcy Winslow became the leader of the women's footwear division at Nike, the company's first division devoted exclusively to women's products. She and her management team took a year to come up with four guiding principles for how they wanted to relate to their customer.[5] "What mattered was that we were looking for principles that expressed who we were in terms of our commitments. Coming to appreciate and to start to live by these principles was a core process that built our team. Though they will surely evolve, they've stuck now for four years, even after I had to move on to another job. People can still look at them and say, 'Are we making our decisions for the right reasons?'"

Third, as Winslow's last comment suggests, you focus on how the guiding ideas are used. Bill O'Brien used to use his "BS meter" to determine whether visions and values were real or just "feel good" statements. "At the end of the day, you just ask yourself, 'How did our vision and values influence decisions I made today?' If they did not, then they are pretty much BS." At heart, this is the difference between a guiding or governing idea, as discussed in the previous chapter, and just another good idea. At a meeting of the SoL Sustainability Consortium in spring 2002, one of the founders, Bernie Bulkin from BP, showed us a new T-shirt he had just picked up. On the back were four words: Respect, Integrity, Communications, Excellence. Then he showed us the front of the shirt, which read "Enron."

This last point illuminates one of the most basic misunderstandings about guiding ideas. People can obsess about getting the words right. Even the question "Is this the right vision?" is the wrong question. A focus on getting the words right leads to beautiful, even inspiring, vision statements that produce little or no change. On the other hand, artful designers in the domain of guiding ideas know that, in my colleague Robert Fritz's words, "It's not what the vision is, it's what the vision does." They see visions and other guiding ideas as tools for mobilizing and focusing energy. They judge the ideas by their impact, not by how they sound. And they never forget that guiding ideas are always works in progress.

THE DESIGNER'S ACKNOWLEDGMENT

While the ramifications of leaders' design work can be sweeping, it is important to appreciate that very often, little credit goes to the designer. This is why the ship designer's work is unrecognized as leadership. The consequences of good design that appear today may be the result of work done long in the past, and work today may show its benefits far in the future. The hallmark of good design is the absence of crisis—not a good way to get attention in a "leaders are heroes" organization culture. Those who aspire to lead out of a desire to control, to gain fame, or simply to be at the center of the action will find little to attract them to the quiet design work of leadership. "You can get a great deal done from almost any position in an organization if you focus on small wins and you don't mind others getting the credit," says Roger Saillant.

In the extreme, masterful design may be all but invisible, a point made eloquently by Lao Tzu some 2,500 years ago:

> The wicked leader is he whom the people revile.
> The good leader is he whom the people revere.
> The great leader is he of whom the people say, "We did it ourselves."

This type of leadership is not without its rewards. Those who practice it find deep satisfaction in being part of an organization capable of producing results that people truly care about. In fact, they find these rewards more enduring than the power and praise granted to more traditional leaders.

LEADER AS TEACHER

A great teacher is someone around whom others learn. Great teachers create space for learning and invite people into that space. By contrast, less-masterful teachers focus on what they are teaching and how they are doing it. The spirit of the leader as a grower of people was beautifully articulated by Robert Greenleaf, who after a career working with many talented leaders at AT&T from the mid-1920s to the mid-1960s, identified the desire to serve as the core motivation for great leaders, and the growth of people as the chief indicator of such leaders, whom he called "servant leaders." "The best test [of the servant leader] is: Do those served grow as persons? Do they become healthier, wiser, freer, more autonomous, more likely themselves to become servants?"[6]

SEEING GAPS IN ORGANIZATIONAL CAPACITY

Just as design work is often catalyzed by the recognition of an important need for communication or coordination that is not being met, leaders' work as teachers often starts with their recognition of an important capacity that is lacking in an organization. In 2001, Vivienne Cox started organizing "salons" to enable BP managers to think together about the future. She says, "As I rose to more senior positions in BP, I began to see that a core issue for us was collective leadership. We have a lot of very competent individual leaders within BP, but we also have a culture that stresses individual accountability and often promotes excessive competition between people.

"I started with the notion of convening a set of conversations that had no agenda. I invited twenty or thirty people for a day and a half, and invited them to take the conversation wherever they wanted to take it. The groups were very diverse. They included a complete cross-section of grades from within BP, senior and more junior managers, including new graduates who had just entered the organization. About one-third of the people were from outside BP; the first one included a headmaster, a ballet dancer, someone from a charity, and people from other businesses. The rule was that everybody had to know at least one other person in the room.

"In a way I didn't care about specific outcomes from the conversations. I was more interested in the conversation itself. I picked very broad subjects in order to stretch us in important directions: issues around globalization, about how we managed and our impact in the world. For example, we had a session with Tom Johnson on the tyranny of numbers, the way we tend to run our businesses based on obsessive focus on what we can measure, while we all know very well that much of what matters cannot be measured.[7] That was a fascinating conversation. People loved the fact that they were given space to talk about what they were concerned about. It didn't really matter what the topic was that we started with; the conversation always took on a life of its own."

The impacts of such efforts to build new capacities are always difficult to gauge. One indication of success is simply whether or not people show up. In the case of Cox's salons, despite the conflict with BP's performance-oriented culture, people kept coming. One of her senior management peers commented to me, "Viv's meetings drive me crazy." But he also kept making room in his very full calendar to come as often as possible. Cox herself was unsure of the impact, because the salons didn't continue on their own without her convening them. "I was quite disappointed until I realized that the salons had seeded things which had many of the same elements. Maybe people didn't feel they had the positional power, or the right to do exactly what I'd done, or maybe they simply didn't want to. Eventually I saw that there were people who really had been influenced by these conversations and were holding meetings, or organizing workshops or exploring issues in new and different ways. "

The salons also taught Cox valuable lessons in creating environments for learning that can close important capacity gaps, lessons that have been especially important as she has been promoted into more senior jobs. "How do you lead an organization of this scope and scale when you cannot be involved in everything directly? For me, the secret is to focus on a very few, carefully considered interventions and a way of conducting myself that is personally consistent with that. For example, when we bring people together for a strategy conversation, the only thing I control is the construction of the space, and the construction of the intention, what I feel is the real imperative. The rest of it, I don't control. It is controlled by the people who are there through their conversations and interactions."

THE TEACHER'S DILEMMA

In the original edition of this book, I talked about the fundamental need to help people develop a more "empowering view of current reality." By this I meant a way of seeing current reality that reinforced rather than undermined our sense of confidence in shaping the future. "Reality" as perceived by most people in most organizations means pressures that must be borne, crises that must be reacted to, and limitations that must be accepted. Given such ways of defining reality, vision is an idle dream or a cynical delusion at worst—but not an achievable end. How, then, do leaders help people see reality as a medium for creating their visions rather than as a source of limitation? This is a core task of the "leader as teacher."

One way is to help people see problems in terms of underlying systemic structures and mental models rather than just short-term events. This can help in appreciating the forces shaping reality, and how we are part of those forces and can affect them (see Chapter 3, "Prisoners of the System, or Prisoners of Our Own Thinking?"). But developing systems thinking capabilities takes time and patience, and leaders committed to this path invariably face a dilemma, one familiar to any teacher attempting to help learners develop difficult new skills.

"We have been pretty successful in applying systems thinking to solve some important problems," says Marv Adams, "but I've also become concerned because I can see limits as to how we've done it. For example, we had to take nearly a billion dollars out of a $3.5 billion IT budget across the globe. A small group of us met and sketched out ten systems thinking diagrams that represented the highest-leverage opportunities to cut costs without losing capacity. Instead of revealing those systems diagrams to the organization, we just kicked off ten work streams and made sure that the interventions people were pursuing were rooted in the insights we had from those ten diagrams. We succeeded in cutting out the billion dollars, but I personally struggled with not sharing that insight and not having more people do the systems thinking. We used the technique behind the scenes. It almost felt manipulative to me. I feel like if I can see a picture, I need to explain it to people and say, 'This is why we're intervening here, and this is why we're not intervening here.'"

Adams realized there were two problems with his otherwise successful intervention. First, few people had had to build their capacity themselves to see the systemic forces. Second, he knew that he had been successful in this intervention because he controlled the resources to make the needed changes. By contrast, for most business problems, Adams and his systems thinking staff operate more as "influencers," because different people have to take different actions based on new ways of seeing the situation. "We need to paint the picture so other people can see it, or better help them to paint the picture for themselves," he says.

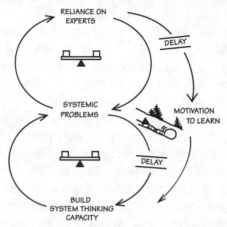

As Adams knows, if this dilemma is not addressed, a "shifting the burden" dynamic will develop, in which the pressure to solve important problems will lead to expert groups who can analyze the situation and come up with insights. But by so doing, they make it unnecessary to build broader organizational capacity. Moreover, people get used to having experts who can solve their problems for them; people can then easily lose motivation to develop their own capacities. Over time, reinforcing pressures will develop that cause people to rely even more on the experts. Problems may get solved, but the organization will be no smarter.

As with most shifting the burden situations, the successful strategy is to respond to short-term opportunities in ways that build longer-term capacity, to connect "event-driven systems thinking" with "developmental systems thinking."

BEING A LEARNER FIRST

To be a true teacher, you must be a learner first. Indeed, teachers' own passion for learning inspires their students as much as their expertise does. So, too, must managers who are committed to organizational learning tools and principles be practitioners, not just "advocates" or preachers.

This was eloquently expressed by Greg Merten shortly after he retired as general manager and vice president of the Ink Supply Organization, for many years Hewlett-Packard's largest and most profitable division. According to Merten, learning is the very source of leading. "If I look back over my career at HP, I've been around many very skillful people, but those who ultimately became the most effective leaders, at whatever level or role, were inevitably real learners. Whatever they had accomplished in the past seemed to figure little in their self-image. They were always aware of their needs to grow as people, and knew that the 'learning game' requires a relentless commitment to discovering what is effective here and now. It is very clear to me that when the company thrived it was because many in key positions had this orientation of learners, and when that was not the case, we struggled."

While Merten's point that leaders need to be learners seems obvious, its implications can take time to hit home—especially for highly committed people, whose very commitment can blind them to their own need to learn. "Forty people came to our first training in peacekeeping circles: young people, police and probation officers, community members, and friends," says Roca's Molly Baldwin. "Halfway through the opening session, several of us sat and talked in the middle of a circle formed by the full group. Within three minutes everything blew up. People were screaming, the kids were swearing, everyone was saying, 'See! This is never going to work!' Watching the session break down was wrenching, but eventually I understood how committed I was to divisiveness and not unity, how far I was from being a peacemaker. I understood on a visceral level the problems with 'us and them' thinking, and how I perpetuated that, personally and for the organization. Continuing to insist, 'I'm right, you're wrong! The issue is you, not us, because we hold the moral high ground!' was a big source of our problems."[8]

LEADER AS STEWARD

In *Servant Leadership*, Greenleaf says that "the servant leader is servant first . . . It begins with the natural feeling that one wants to serve . . . Then the conscious choice brings one to aspire to lead. That person is sharply different from one who is leader first, perhaps to assuage an unusual power drive or to acquire material possessions."[9]

The idea of leaders who serve those they lead may seem idealistic, but I am convinced it is also pragmatic. I once asked a Marine Corps colonel why servant leadership was widely embraced in the Corps. He said: "It has been shown again and again in combat that when people's lives are at stake, they will only reliably follow commanding officers who they trust, who they perceive as having their well-being at heart."

Stewardship is also about serving a larger purpose. As Bill O'Brien used to say, "All genuine commitment is to something larger than oneself." In 1990 I wrote about the "purpose story" that seems to guide natural leaders at all levels, commenting on how very different people "draw their own inspiration from the same source . . . a deep story and sense of purpose, a larger 'pattern of becoming' that lies behind their individual visions . . . Many otherwise competent managers in leadership positions are not leaders of the same ilk precisely because they have no larger story . . . [that] connects them to a larger undertaking . . . [and] brings a depth of meaning to their visions, a larger landscape upon which personal dreams and goals stand out as landmarks on a longer journey."

Looking back on these words today, I see hidden within them two paradoxes. The first concerns certainty and commitment. The second, conservation and change.

THE PARADOXES OF STEWARDSHIP

Knowing one's purpose story can easily suggest a sense of certainty about what one's life is all about, and even a sort of closed-ness. Conversely, those who lack this certainty could conclude that they have no such larger purpose and therefore are limited as leaders.

I have come to believe that certainty regarding our purpose, and equally regarding our goals, carries its own dangers, dangers we see frequently displayed in today's world. In a penetrating analysis, *The True Believer*, philosopher Eric Hoffer asks what ultimately distinguishes the committed person from the fanatic.[10] His conclusion is "certainty." The fanatic is certain that he is right. By Hoffer's definition, whenever we act with certainty that we have the answer we act as fanatics, regardless of the cause. There is a part of us that is closed, that sees a world of black and white. Genuine commitment, on the other hand, always co-exists with some element of questioning and uncertainty. In this sense, commitment is truly a choice, rather than a compulsion.

The second paradox of stewardship, conservation and change, comes from the fact that in one sense, leadership is always about change. Leaders, individually and collectively, work to bring about a different order of things. Their focus is invariably on the new, on what is trying to emerge. I believe one of the reasons a deep sense of purpose is so important for leaders is that it also provides an anchor. While pursuing what is new and emergent, they are also stewards for something they intend to conserve. Yet what they seek to conserve, paradoxically, is a key to enabling change. You can see this, for example, in stories like Darcy Winslow's. She wanted to "connect to the core" of Nike's identity as an innovator: in doing so, she freed up energy for change. It also showed up when Dorothy Berry helped the IFC's managers connect with their aspiration to align successful private enterprises with sustainable development, or when Dave Marsing of Intel discovered that he and his colleagues truly wanted to conserve healthy living.

Chilean biologist Humberto Maturana says evolution is a process of "transformation through conservation." Nature, according to Maturana, conserves a few basic features, and in so doing frees everything else to change. A simple example is "bilateral symmetry" in the animal world: two eyes, two ears, four legs, and so on. But what is important is the extraordinary evolutionary variety that occurs within the constraints of bilateral symmetry. Change leaders often forget to ask a powerful question: "What do we seek to conserve?" Change naturally induces fear in us all: fear of the unknown, of failure, of not being needed in a new order of things. When we obsessively focus only on what needs to be changed, and not on what we intend to conserve, we reinforce these fears. But when we can clarify what we intend to conserve, some of this fear can be released. When leaders consciously apply this principle, they usually discover that people seek to conserve identity and relationships, such as their identity as innovators, their partnership in reducing poverty, or their support of one another's mental and physical well-being.

POWER AND THE NATURE OF AMBITION

Sadly, such examples of genuine stewardship also highlight a very different leadership reality more evident to many today: breakdowns in stewardship, exemplified by abuse of power. "In my view the greatest evil in the world today is ever-increasing power and wealth in ever-fewer hands," says Visa founder Dee Hock.

Much is made today of how information technologies enable increasing distribution of power where "[people] dispersed physically but connected by technology are now able, on a scale never before imaginable, to make their own decisions using information gathered from many other people and places."[11] Yet, the potential distribution of power and authority often clashes with deeper personal drives, especially within senior managers. HP's Ann Murray Allen puts it this way: "The nurturing and support of social networks—when it occurs—happens mostly at the business unit level, where products and services are more directly tied to customers. Unfortunately I too often see these networks of collaboration give way to networks of ambition at the corporate headquarters level."

Barbara Stocking of Oxfam sees a connection between ambition, results, and the traditional male domination of the executive suite. "There are a lot of studies now that show that women's ways of leading are different regarding competition and ambition. When management teams are so caught up in jockeying for status and position that they don't actually deliver results, then the women on those teams will stand back and say, 'Frankly, I can't be bothered. I've got a family to look after and the rest of my life to manage, and I'm not going to devote enormous quantities of my time to a whole load of infighting.' I don't know whether it's because so many women have other responsibilities or it's just a woman's nature. But they tend to pull back and say, 'If it's not achieving something, then I'm not going to waste my time on it.' On the whole, women in senior positions tend to be more ambitious about the thing itself rather than their own future and career."

Stocking's comments suggest a secret appreciated by all too few managers: having a larger life might actually help managers maintain a sense of perspective and be better managers. Several years ago, when she was to be promoted to a senior management position at BP, Vivienne Cox had also just had her first baby. She went to one of the most senior managers at BP and told him, "I just want you to know that BP is not the most important thing in my life. My daughter is. If you think this will be in conflict with these new responsibilities, then it would be better to not promote me." Cox reflects today, "While my job is very demanding, being clear about my personal priorities has really helped me, and maybe others in the organization as well."

SUSTAINABLE RESULTS

The business world's current obsession with ethical breakdowns arising from untempered personal ambition misses a more important point: how personal ambition can compromise results achieved whether or not there is outright management malfeasance. I think it is no coincidence that leaders like Stocking and Cox have been able to achieve significant long-term results. It starts with focus. When positional authority leads managers to invest energy in protecting or expanding turf, it comes at the expense of focusing on, as Stocking said, "the thing itself," the actual results people are trying to achieve. But there is another matter of time horizon. If managers focus only on short-term results, they are often justified in continuing to intervene to sustain results. Whether this is done consciously or inadvertently, it creates a shifting the burden dynamic and a self-reinforcing dependency on management intervention. In this way, focusing on short-term results becomes a strategy for further concentrating power.

"I reflected a lot on this when I worked with the National Health Service," Stocking says.[12] "I would watch managers fix immediate problems, like 'waiting list targets,' by not attending to anything else. But if you've done nothing to fundamentally change how the whole system is working, once you take your eye off it, the problems come right back. If you take the time to figure out with people how you can get a system that is going to continue to deliver better results, it takes a lot longer but when you've got it, it doesn't walk away from you. I would say, 'It may take me a bit longer to get there, but when I get there I know what I've got is more sustainable.' Eventually, we developed a principle to guide us. When we have to go in and intervene, say, in a hospital, then we should do it in a way that enables the people there to know better how to help themselves in the future. The whole point is to try to improve so we don't have to intervene again.

"Now, in Oxfam, we have a similar challenge. In humanitarian work there is enormous psychological reward, kudos and personal satisfaction, in stepping into a humanitarian crisis and doing it well. You know, 'the white men in shorts flying in and delivering.' Now we're trying to reach the point where we never have to go into a country and deliver humanitarian relief. If we've done our work well, we've helped local people develop to the point where they are able to help themselves. In the world of aid, I would say the motivation is not personal power in the sense of control, but a subtler sense of power that comes from feeling needed. Regardless, the dynamics are the same, a reinforcing need for the person in power."

BEING A STEWARD OF YOUR VISION

Stewardship is, in the words of one of the young Roca street workers, ultimately about "doing what is right for the whole." This commitment brings with it a shift in our relationship to our personal vision. It ceases to be a possession, as in "this is my vision." We become a steward of the vision. We are "its" as much as it is ours. George Bernard Shaw, as noted earlier, expressed the relationship succinctly when he spoke of "being used for a purpose recognized by yourself as a mighty one."

Slightly different in tone and focus, but no less evocative, are the words of Lebanese poet Kahlil Gibran, who, in speaking of parents and children, captured the special sense of responsibility without possessiveness felt by leaders as stewards of their vision:

> Your children are not your children.
> They are the sons and daughters of life's longing for itself.
> They come through you, not from you.
> And though they are with you, they belong not to you.
> You may give them your love but not your thoughts,
> For they have their own thoughts.
> You may house their bodies but not their souls,
> For their souls dwell in the house of tomorrow, which you cannot
> visit, not even in your dreams. You may strive to be like them, but strive
>   not to make them like you.
> For life goes not backward nor tarries with yesterday. You are the bows
>   from which your children as living arrows are
> sent forth. The archer sees the mark upon the path of the infinite, and
>   he

bends you with his might that the arrows may go swift and
   far.
Let your bending in the archer's hand be for gladness; For even as he
   loves the arrow that flies, so he loves the bow that
is stable.[13]

HOW CAN SUCH LEADERS BE DEVELOPED?

The English verb "lead" comes from an Indo-European root, *leith*, which means "to cross a threshold," an image also often associated with dying. So, it is no surprise that extraordinary leaders, like Mieko Nishimizu and Roger Saillant, often have deep personal stories of moments of awakening, when some old part of them died and a new part emerged. Interestingly, a widely used but poorly understood term, "charisma," conveys a related idea.

The word "charismatic" typically suggests a strong and forceful, even magnetic, personality, someone who commands attention. Unfortunately, this is usually taken to be a result of certain idiosyncratic features that make the person "special," like striking looks and a deep voice. But most of the outstanding leaders I have had the privilege to know possess neither striking physical appearance nor forceful personality. What distinguishes them is the clarity and persuasiveness of their ideas, the depth of their commitment, and the extent of their openness to continually learning more. They do not "have the answer," but they seem to instill confidence in those around them that, together, "we can learn whatever we need to learn in order to achieve the results we truly desire."

In fact, the word *charism* comes from the Catholic church, where it means one's distinctive personal "gifts," given by the Holy Spirit. To be charismatic, then, means to develop one's gifts. In short, we develop as true charismatic leaders to the extent that we become ourselves. Herein lies the secret of real leadership development.

Watching what this has meant to different leaders, I've been struck by the variety of their developmental aims and approaches. Some work to develop conceptual and communication skills. Others strive to listen to and appreciate others and their ideas. Some use the five disciplines as a developmental framework. Some use other approaches. But all are committed to working on their own development, to "struggling to become a human being," as Saillant says.

There also seems to be one commonality that transcends differences in how these leaders go about their work and their development. This is the principle of creative tension. Despite all their
many differences, truly effective leaders seem to come to a shared
appreciation of the power of holding a vision and concurrently
looking deeply and honestly at current reality. I have never seen an
effective leader who did not recognize this principle, whether he or
she had thought about it consciously or not.

We did not invent the principle of creative tension through the
organizational learning work; indeed, many others have described it
in the past. Imprisoned in the Birmingham, Alabama, jail after a
historic antisegregation protest march, Martin Luther King Jr.
wrote, "Just as Socrates felt that it was necessary to create a tension
in the mind, so that individuals could rise from the bondage of
myths and half truths . . . so must we . . . create the kind of tension
in society that will help men rise from the dark depths of prejudice
and racism."[14] While Dr. King is famous for his "dream" of equal-
ity, his leadership, like Gandhi's before him, was grounded in
helping people see current reality, "to dramatize the present situation," as he put it. He knew that the juxtaposition of the two, the
dream and the present reality, was the real force for change.

I've been surprised to discover that the term "leader" is generally
an assessment made by others. People who are truly leading seem
rarely to think of themselves in that way. Their focus is invariably
on what needs to be done, the larger system in which they are operating, and the people with whom they are creating—not on themselves as "leaders." Indeed, if it is otherwise, there is probably a
problem. For there is always the danger, especially for those in leadership positions, of becoming "heroes in their own minds," as long-
time colleague and co-author Bryan Smith puts it.

A Hewlett-Packard employee studying the company's history
once asked co-founder David Packard about his theory of leadership. She reported that after a long pause, he said simply, "I don't
know about theories of leadership. Bill [Hewlett, the co-founder]
and I were just doing what we loved and were so delighted that people wanted to join us."

16

SYSTEMS CITIZENS

In the fall of 2002, Mieko Nishimizu of the World Bank was asked to deliver a keynote address in her home country, as part of a celebration of the fifty-year anniversary of Japan entering the "Bretton Woods Accord," the post-World War II international monetary regime. In the speech, Nishimizu shared her personal story of coming to terms with the reality of poverty and her perspective on our global situation. Near the end, she eloquently summarized the poignancy of the historic times in which we live

> The future appears alien to us. It differs from the past most notably in that the earth itself is the relevant unit with which to frame and measure that future. Discriminating issues that shape the future are all fundamentally global. We belong to one inescapable network of mutuality: mutuality of ecosystems; mutuality of freer movement of information, ideas, people, capital, goods and services; and mutuality of peace and security. We are tied, indeed, in a single fabric of destiny on Planet Earth.

The impetus for building organizational learning capabilities has traditionally come from people who want to find more effective approaches to organizational change; who want to build more adaptive enterprises; and who believe in growing human and social capital in order to grow financial capital. But today, a new set of external motivations are starting to form, as we wake up to our "single fabric of destiny" and realize that we face profound societal and organizational learning challenges. Today I believe that the real possibilities for creating learning organizations may arise from the intertwining of these two forces for change.

All organizations sit within larger systems—industries, communities, and larger living systems. In one sense, it is illogical to think that the well-being of a company can be advanced independent of the well-being of its industry, its society, and the natural systems upon which it depends. For a long time, businesses have taken these larger systems mostly for granted, but it is now increasingly evident that businesses, individually and collectively, influence these systems and that the consequences of that relationship are becoming significant. Some of these influences are clear, such as when a manufacturing facility relocates, leaving half of a town unemployed, or when a power plant discharges nitrous and sulfuric oxides into the air. But many of the influences arise through larger systemic connections that remain invisible to most.

As I am writing this, yet another devastating hurricane has just hit the Gulf Coast in the southeastern United States. Like many other people, I am concerned for the safety and well-being of those affected—but I am also worried that we will not focus on more than emergency relief: once the immediate crisis has passed, the deeper systemic issues will remain. The pictures of entrenched poverty that the hurricanes have revealed have shocked many. But in fact many people in the United States live in Third World conditions. The states hardest hit by the hurricane—Arkansas, Mississippi, and Louisiana—have, respectively, the first-, third-, and fifth-highest percentages of residents living below the poverty line in the United States.[1] And the increased frequency and strength of the hurricanes in the last seasons is not just bad luck. Climate experts have been warning for years that as the oceans heat up, weather instability will grow; in particular, they have warned us that tropical storms moving over these warm waters have more energy to draw into them, leading to more and more severe hurricanes.

I believe climate change and entrenched poverty coexisting with economic prosperity are as much the icons of our age as are the Internet and global markets. As individuals and as businesses, we have never had to be concerned about how day-to-day decisions like the products we buy and the energy we use affect people who live thousands of miles away, or on the other side of the planet. This is the human side of globalization, and it is, indeed, an alien place for all of us. We've never been here before—and the future is watching.

SEEING SYSTEMS

Systems citizenship starts with seeing the systems that we have shaped and which in turn shape us. As the players in the beer game learned, being stuck in a system that is not working invariably leads to feeling frustrated and trapped—until we see the larger patterns and our own part in creating these patterns. Once we do, new alternatives become evident.

There are two fundamental aspects to seeing systems: seeing patterns of interdependency and seeing into the future. The ability to see interdependencies can be aided by tools like systems diagrams, but can also arise from stories, pictures, and songs. Seeing into the future starts with knowing how to interpret signs that are present today but go unrecognized by those without a systems perspective.

Seeing interdependencies that have been invisible to us leads to a particular kind of awakening, "knowing what we knew but didn't know that we knew." Several years ago, two different engineering specialty groups within a large product development team created the following diagram showing how they inadvertently created problems for one another.[2]

When one group (the NVH [noise-vibration-harshness] engineers) had a vibration problem and applied a quick fix, like "adding reinforcements," rather than working with the other group on a more integrated solution, the side effects, such as the added weight of the reinforcements, often affected the second group. The second development group (who were responsible for the total weight of the vehicle) then followed suit: eschewing a collaborative solution with the NVH engineers, they simply took out the weight elsewhere and compensated with their own quick fix, such as specifying a higher tire pressure to meet safety requirements. But the higher tire pressure had the side effect of increased harshness, which then

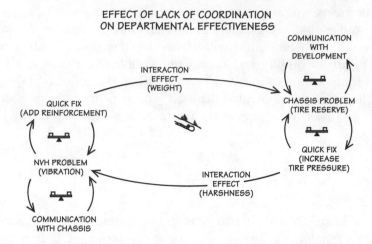

EFFECT OF LACK OF COORDINATION
ON DEPARTMENTAL EFFECTIVENESS

became a whole new problem for the NVH engineers. When both groups saw the diagram together, they recognized a pattern that had plagued them for years, a reinforcing reliance on quick fixes caused by schedule pressures and an unwillingness to take the time to work out integrative solutions—and they knew how it had arisen. As they sat there, shaking their heads, they also saw what this pattern meant for their future: escalating hostilities and inferior overall product designs. Finally, someone said, "Look what we're doing to ourselves."

My experience is that when people truly see a systemic pattern that they have created and comprehend the suffering it will create in the future, they invariably discover ways to change the pattern. For these engineers, changing the pattern meant simply developing trust and working more closely together to achieve their goals, and they did just that. Spurred by several other similar awakenings, the larger team eventually finished the major new model car they were developing one year in advance, and returned over $60 million in allocated but unneeded "overrun budget."

SEEING THE GLOBAL CLIMATE CHANGE SYSTEM

Seeing global systems in ways that mobilize change may seem more difficult, but I believe the basic principles are not fundamentally different. Following is a simple systems diagram to help people see the system influencing global climate change.[3] As with the beer game, our first need is to expand our personal boundaries of awareness beyond just managing our own position. In this case, the traditional focus of business and of society has been on economic activity, and its growth through reinforcing processes involving income, demand, and capital investment. What we have not seen, until very recently, is one of the physical by-products of economic growth: greenhouse gases like CO_2 released into the atmosphere.

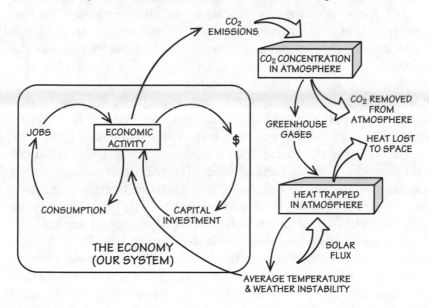

These emissions flow into a stock of CO_2 in the atmosphere (CO_2 concentration), just like the orders placed in the beer game flow into the supplier's backlog.[4] (See page 49.) As the stock of CO_2 in the atmosphere rises, more heat is trapped in the atmosphere. The resulting temperature increases have largely unknown effects on natural systems and ultimately on economic activity. Some claim that warmer climates will be good for business and economic growth. But many question these optimistic scenarios, and the simple truth is that immense uncertainties lie ahead—including weather instability, the spread of tropical diseases, the effects of added freshwater in the oceans from melting glaciers and polar ice, and shifting ocean currents.

In recent years, people around the world have begun to see this system, but they have sharply divided views about the implications for the next few decades and consequently the urgency of curtailing CO_2 emissions. Enough countries eventually approved the 1994 Kyoto Protocol, designed to curtail greenhouse gas emissions, that it finally went into effect in 2003. But the two largest producers of

CO_2 emissions, the United States (approximately 25 percent of global emissions) and China (approximately 11 percent), refused to join. A small but growing number of global corporate leaders believe even more aggressive actions are needed, including BP's John Browne, who first broke ranks with other oil company CEOs in 1997, speaking out about the dangers of climate change in a historic speech at Stanford University.[5] Still, for many citizens of the world, climate change remains a disquieting but distant concern. As an American friend said to me recently, "Well, it will probably be a problem for people in a hundred years or so."

These sharply diverging views are a tragic testimony to our inability to apply even the most rudimentary systems thinking to look at the facts we have today in ways that allow us to see their implications for the future. The following graphs show historical data from the last one hundred and fifty years that correspond to the parts of the systems diagram, CO_2 emissions and average temperature, at the periphery of our mental models.[6] The lower curve shows a slight rise—a bit less than 1 degree—in average annual temperature, not likely to invoke great concern, especially given the many short-term fluctuations. But patterns in the top two curves are much less ambiguous: CO_2 concentration in the atmosphere has increased about 30 percent over the last one hundred and fifty years (middle graph) and CO_2 emissions from combustion of fossil fuels (top graph) has grown dramatically from virtually zero.[7]

I first showed these graphs at a major business conference on sustainable development in Europe in 2004. The five hundred or so attendees were knowledgeable and involved in a host of sustainability initiatives, including climate change. Eager to gauge their ability to interpret these curves systemically, I asked, "How would an 8-year-old child make sense of this situation and what would they want to know?" I suggested to the group that they start by thinking of a bathtub and the water flowing into the bathtub. People quickly saw that CO_2 emissions are like the water flowing into the tub and CO_2 concentration is like the current water level. When I asked what other information the child would want to know, several realized that the future also depended on the size of the outflow, the rate at which CO_2 is coming out of the atmosphere. Having realized that this missing piece of data was important to know, I asked how many people knew what the level of this outflow, "carbon sequestration," was in relation to the level of the inflow of emissions. I was shocked to find only about ten hands raised. At that moment I understood

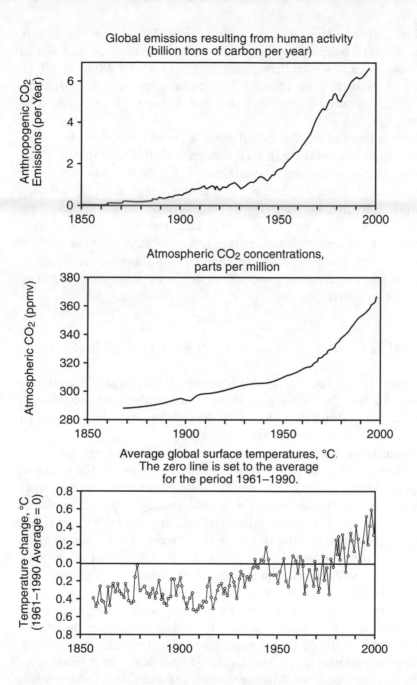

Global emissions resulting from human activity
(billion tons of carbon per year)

Atmospheric CO₂ concentrations,
parts per million

Average global surface temperatures, °C.
The zero line is set to the average
for the period 1961–1990.

why we were in trouble. Only a few people in a group of this caliber knew that CO₂ is coming out of the atmosphere at far less than one-half the rate at which it is going in![8]

Gradually the significance of this figure dawned on the group. Even if every country in the world met the targets of the Kyoto Protocol tomorrow (stabilizing global emissions at 1990 levels), CO_2 would continue to grow forever! A 50 percent,[9] or greater, reduction in CO_2 emissions worldwide is beyond anyone's most aggressive plans.[10]

No one knows how the global climate system will react to a continuing dramatic increase in CO_2 concentration. More importantly, no one knows what we as denizens of Earth will choose to do to reduce emissions. As the ancient Chinese adage goes, "If we keep heading as we are, we are likely to get where we are going." And we do know that the "we" will be our children and grandchildren. Despite all the uncertainties, it is safe to say that we have not yet seen the real effects of climate change, but the next generations will—unless we can learn to see the system we are creating and head in a different direction.

LIVING AS IF WE *ARE* THE SYSTEM

It is easy to get lost in thinking about global issues like climate change, to feel that there is nothing you can do, and maybe even that there is nothing anyone can do. But global systems are not just global. They are also right here.

Herein lies a secret of the systems worldview. The system is not only out there, it is in here. We are the seed carriers of the whole in the sense that we carry the mental models that pervade the larger system. We are all actors in the global energy system, the global food system, and the global industrialization process. We can either think and act in ways that reinforce the system as it currently operates, or think and act in ways that lead in different directions. Because the systems that shape our lives manifest themselves at multiple levels, we can work at multiple levels.

This does not mean that any one of us as individuals, or any one organization, can unilaterally shift these larger systems overnight. In fact, a good rule of thumb is that no one can do this unilaterally. Neither the president of the United States nor the president of China has the power to shift the world's present dependence on fossil fuels, even though their nations are the two largest users. They too are but actors in a larger system, often far more constrained than we imagine. Yet, the global energy system is enacted by humans and human institutions. It is not based on the laws of physics. Alternative systems can also be enacted.

We are all novices in understanding how systemic change can occur at the scale that matters. But the experience of many in the SoL network over the past fifteen years suggests that it can begin when enough people and institutions start to see the present system and their part in how it operates. In terms of greenhouse gases, this awareness seems to be growing among a number of leaders, especially some of the large multinational corporations and large NGOs that truly must think globally. "If I reflect on what many organizations have been going through," says Andre van Heemstra of Unilever, "the awareness of sustainability has been growing because systems thinking, in different forms, is enabling us to see more interdependencies than we have seen in the past. It is those interdependencies which make you conclude that it is more than stupid, it is reckless to think of commercial sustainability in isolation, [without thinking of] either social or environmental sustainability."[11]

This seeing must eventually encompass a critical mass of the players that sustain the present system—what we have come to call a "strategic microcosm." In a company, this strategic microcosm represents a meaningful cross-section of people and teams that shape the present system, as when enough managers and engineers in the product development team of the auto engineering group saw the patterns of dysfunctions they were creating that thwarted their goals. Similar strategic microcosms can enable change in industries, in complex global supply networks, and perhaps even in societies. It is here that organizations grounded in systems thinking and the related learning disciplines can make a difference, by fostering collective rethinking and innovation and serving as a convener for microcosms of larger systems.

BUSINESS AS INCUBATOR: THE SEEDS OF A NEW ENERGY SYSTEM

As businesses, we must be the change we want to see in the world. This will mean that most everything is up for change: our products, our process, our business models, how we manage and lead, and how we are with one another. It is not likely that we can change just bits and pieces and shift the whole.

– Roger Saillant, Plug Power

Buckminster Fuller used to be fond of saying that we must learn to operate our societies on our "energy income," the steady energy from the sun, not our "energy capital," deposits in the earth's crust formed from life the sun's light nurtured millions of years ago. Creating such an energy system that can meet the needs of modern society will require many new technologies, one of which will probably be a new generation of fuel cells. By using hydrogen and oxygen as inputs, fuel cells generate electricity through an electrochemical reaction, with heat and water as the only by-products. For years, fuel cells have been hailed as a key element for an environmentally sound energy system, but they have never reached competitive price and reliability levels for most commercial applications.[12]

Roger Saillant understood all this very well when, after 30 years in the auto industry, he left Visteon, a Ford Motor Company spin-off, to become CEO of a small fuel cell manufacturer of about five hundred employees (less than one-twentieth the number of employees he had previously been responsible for) that had never made a profit, and had seen its stock fall from $150 a share to less than $10 in the dot-com stock market crash, also wiping out much of the personal wealth of many employees. But, as a Ph.D. who had done four years of post-doctoral work in chemistry, Saillant had been thinking about the transition to a hydrogen economy for many years, and knew how important it could be for the state of the world. He also knew he was bringing his experience in organizational learning and world-class manufacturing operations to an industry that had often suffered from a surplus of hype and a deficit of management skill.

At Plug Power, Saillant not only found a demoralized work force but one that lacked a larger picture for why their work might matter. They were a technology company, and people were focused on the technical problems of designing and building workable fuel cells. But they had never thought much about the larger problems of sustainability, nor about creating a learning-oriented work culture. "It had never occurred to people to try and match our technical innovations with innovations in how we treated one another and [innovations] related to our larger world," says one engineer. Soon, however, a leadership group formed, including not only senior managers but engineers and local managers, that set out to build one of the best operated fuel cell businesses in the world, and to do this "though implementing learning organization principles with sustainability principles as the basis for our organization."

Today, Plug Power has a "Who We Are" statement developed by

all its employees. It begins: "Plug Power is a tightly knit community passionately driven by the common goal of achieving the triple bottom line: People, Planet and Profit. Our success is based on the balance of our drive to transform the energy industry, our involvement in the community and the love of our families. We lead by example and engage our work with a singular determination and an unstoppable resolve."

In the five years since Saillant arrived, Plug Power has come a long way toward being a successful fuel cell business.[13] Equally important, the company is moving toward setting a standard for sustainable "zero-to-landfill" product design that will shape the fledgling fuel cell industry. "We believe we can demonstrate that it is technically possible and economically advantageous to design fuel cells for complete reuse," says Senior Technology Officer John Elter. (Elter was nominated for the U.S. National Medal of Technology for his work in leading the famous "Lakes" team at Xerox that produced a revolutionary new copier platform in the late 1990s that was 94 percent re-manufacturable and 96 percent recyclable.) "In the future, customers who buy fuel cell products will expect to return them at the end of their service life, and the manufacturers will want them back because their components will be much too valuable to ever dump into a landfill."[14]

While many criticize U.S. wastefulness in energy, Saillant sees the country as having a significant leadership opportunity. "Americans consume 25 percent of the world's energy and generate about the same proportion of greenhouse gases, with only 5 percent of the world's population. How we design and produce products sets global norms, but today our manufacturing model causes us to waste nearly one million pounds of material per person per year, or more than one ton per person per day. The United States is a dominant force in the Western culture. The Western culture is dominant in the world. How we hold ourselves accountable for our use of our dominance and advantage in the world can profoundly accelerate or retard the changes we want to see."

Lessons Saillant learned around the world shape his sense of how to change things. "Living and working in north-central Mexico, Northern Ireland, eastern Europe, and Asia, I learned a lot about being a guest. I believe we must learn to be better guests in all our relationships, in our communities, and in our planet setting. We need to grow spirituality and catch up to our technology. We have powerful minds, and we're capable of creating visions and allowing

these visions to pull us forward. First, however, we must see ourselves as just one part of the global system and play out our roles
accordingly."

SoL researcher Katrin Kaeufer, who has been doing studies of
many corporations moving toward more sustainable products and
processes, says, "Plug is the only company we have yet studied
where becoming a sustainable business and becoming a learning
organization seem inseparable. When I interviewed people about the
company and their work, they used 'sustainability' and 'learning to
become a learning organization' almost interchangeably. People
seemed to have internalized the idea that building a sustainable
enterprise is not possible without creating a learning culture."

SUPPLY NETWORKS: THE SYSTEM SEEING ITSELF

The innovations that will have the big impact will be ones that
integrate complete value chains around securing long term viabil-
ity for social and ecological as well as economic systems.
                                            – Darcy Winslow, Nike

Today's businesses sit within complex supply networks that often
span the world. In recent years, leaders have focused on managing
supply chains for efficiency improvements, cost reductions, and
more rapid response. But these are small steps compared to the
changes needed to create truly sustainable supply networks that will
remain viable into the future. Creating such networks will require
engaging organizations across entire supply chains in seeing the
larger system that they are creating and innovating new ways of
operating together.

No global supply networks affect more people than those for
food. Food production and distribution is the world's largest industry, employing over a billion people. For most of those living in
wealthy northern countries, global food systems seem to be working
fine. After all, a consumer in New York or Paris can buy a can-
taloupe in the middle of winter for $1.50. But behind affordable
prices and high availability for well-off consumers sits a system that
is one of the most powerful generators of poverty, political and economic instability, and local environmental destruction in the world.

Over the last fifty years, prices of agricultural commodities like
soy, maize (corn), wheat, cotton, and potatoes have fallen between

60 and 80 percent, while production for these same products has increased by factors of two to ten. Falling prices may be a boon to rich consumers, but they are a tragedy for rural families worldwide who depend on farm incomes. For example, the average selling price of coffee today equals roughly half what it costs coffee growers to produce.[16] In effect, today's global food system produces cheap food for the rich and expensive food for the poor, a condition that more and more global businesses are starting to see.[17] Addressing a conference of advertising executives, the VP of marketing for Unilever Europe, Chris Pomfret, said "the security of our global food supply chains [is] absolutely critical to the future of our business. 'Can sustainability sell?' is the wrong question. The real question is: 'Can a business like ours survive in the long term without sustainability?'"[18]

Seeing the System Together. Still, the number of people and key institutions that truly see the global food system is far too small and far too non-integrated to make much difference. Although Unilever is one of the largest sellers of food products in the world, what it can accomplish acting alone is negligible. "Doing something about sustainable agriculture will require bringing parties together that normally do not cooperate," says van Heemstra. For systems like global agriculture, this means that not only diverse businesses but also governmental and nongovernmental organizations must learn how to see the system together.

In 2004, Unilever and Oxfam were joined by over thirty multinational food companies, global and local NGOs, major foundations, and government representatives from the Netherlands, the European Commission, and Brazil in a novel experiment called the Sustainable Food Lab. The aim was to bring "sustainable food supply chains into the mainstream," using a new process to foster collaborative learning across the supply chain.[19]

As the Sustainable Food Lab project began to develop, it became clear that the participants shared many understandings of the interdependencies of the present system and a poignant image of where it is headed. In their words, they were trapped in a "race to the bottom," going faster and faster toward where no one wanted to go. Three interacting sets of reinforcing forces are continuing to drive this race:[20]

1. Reinforcing growth in supply driven by rising production and rising profits, leading to capital investment and further increases in capacity (food producers)

2. Reinforcing growth in demand driven by supply increases that lower prices and raise availability, leading to further increase in supply as producers see more market opportunities (food companies, retailers, and consumers)
3. Further increases in capacity driven by falling prices, spurring investments in increased efficiency and land use in order to maintain farm incomes (local and larger food producers)

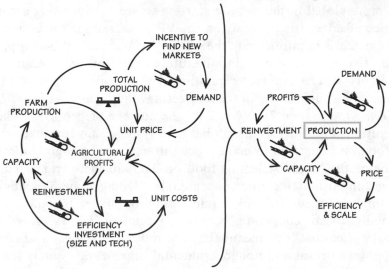

The first and second sets of forces drive growth in capacity, production, and demand in many industries, not just food. They grow stronger as large multinational corporations with access to financial capital and advanced technology enter and come to dominate industries. But there are at least two novel features of food production that make these basic economic forces problematic. In general, as rising production and falling prices turn products into commodities, producers search for lower-cost ways to produce, until profits are so low that there is little incentive for businesses to expand further. But the farmers and small farming companies in poorer countries who face falling prices often continue increasing production even when there is zero profit or even loss. Farmers do so because their only other option is to abandon their farms and traditional life, and pursue an even more uncertain future by migrating to cities. Instead, they attempt to maintain their incomes by boosting production through efficiency increases like use of fertilizers and pesticides, or by farming more marginal land (the third set of reinforcing forces). In short, the reality of our food systems is that production continues to rise and prices to fall even when economic conditions are adverse. Or, as the members of the Sustainable Food Lab put it, "When incomes are up, production rises, and when incomes are down, production rises."

This leads to the second distinctive reality of food systems: production cannot be driven up indefinitely without exceeding environmentally sustainable yields. Forced into relentless increases in production, farmers find themselves in a vicious cycle of pursuing short-term production increases that reduce the longer-term fertility of their land and lead to still more desperate measures to keep up production and incomes. Worldwide trends of overproduction have resulted in the loss of more than a billion hectares (an area the size of China and India combined) of topsoil in the last fifty years.

Driving the system are different and conflicting mental models. "Global food production is a classic case of a system out of control," says Hal Hamilton, director of the Sustainability Institute and co-director of the Sustainable Food Lab project. "No one intends their decisions to result in a system that is unsustainable. Individuals make the best decisions possible, but they are doing so in a system that is critically fragmented. Most companies think the answer is to use technology to increase productivity. On the other side of the street, many activists are dedicated to fighting big corporations [that] they see as destroying local farming communities and ecologies. Governments get caught in the middle between corporate pressures to boost production and the political instability of farmers displaced from their lands by falling prices. Rich country governments respond by spending $500 billion a year for farm subsidies, but poor governments don't have this option. What is lacking is any way for all of these groups to think together on behalf of the long term and their common interests."

The Sustainable Food Lab is attempting to provide the missing piece through collaborative "sensing," "presencing," and "realizing"—a particular way to link together the different learning disciplines for complex problems involving diverse stakeholders. (See Appendix 3.)

Collaborative sensing ("co-sensing") requires looking outward and looking inward. For the Sustainable Food Lab team, looking outward started with systems maps and other conceptual tools, but also included "learning journeys" in rural Brazil to experience parts of the system firsthand that most had never seen. Facing the reality of a system which we have all played a part in creating can generate powerful forces for change—if there is time to allow the meaning of this reality to penetrate our habitual ways of thinking and feeling, thus catalyzing deeper visions, individually and collectively. Between understanding the system forces conceptually and seeing the system more viscerally through the learning journeys, the Sustainable Food Lab members knew the "race to the bottom" was a tragic competition with no winners.[21] "It is so obvious that the whole agricultural system is sick," comments one business member.

In a six-day retreat, two months after the learning journeys, each person spent two days and nights on a "solo" in a wilderness setting, one of the oldest methods of gently lifting us out of our normal mindsets and incubating new visions. Rather than forcing very different personal visions into a single shared vision, team members then formulated different "prototype" initiatives reflecting their unique perspectives and areas of influence. These ranged from focusing on specific supply chains, to researching how to communicate the realities of the whole system to consumers, to building a broad-based business coalition of food businesses that could potentially shift the rules of the game affecting all agricultural commodities.[22]

Building Shared Visions That Can Shift Larger Systems. Though it is too early to gauge the impact of any of these specific initiatives, I believe these efforts provide four important lessons that can be used by others attempting to see and shift larger systems.

First, because the most intractable systemic issues cross geographic and institutional boundaries, the strategic microcosm needed to address the system must likewise be a cross-sector group representing business, government, and civil society. Forming groups of people from these different worlds who are willing to work together rather than just throw bricks at one another can itself be a major task. It took more than two years to assemble the initial group for the Sustainable Food Lab, starting with the commitment of Unilever and Oxfam to work together.

Second, seeing systems collectively entails a multifaceted journey of thinking and feeling. You will know you are starting to see the system when people begin to move beyond blame to recognize that we are all part of the problem. The global food system is driven by (1) companies pursuing "business-as-usual" models with little regard for the effects on farming families, farming communities, and environmental systems; (2) farmers being unable to moderate pressures for continual production growth; and (3) all of us as consumers when we buy food at the cheapest price with little thought as to where the food comes from.

The third lesson is that the quality of collective seeing and the shared commitment that it can engender are shaped by the quality of relationships people develop. The transformation of larger systems will not arise from the transactional relationships that characterize most business, government, and NGO activities. "The relationships among leaders across normal boundaries might be the most crucial ingredient to major change," says Hamilton. The Food Lab participants found themselves developing deep connections, trust, and respect for each other—and recognizing that their strength as a team lay as much in their differences as in their similarities.

Finally, enacting new systems is not about getting "the answer," it is about developing networks of engaged and trusting people who are guided by a common understanding of the current system and a commitment to create new systems. "If I learned anything . . . it is the notion that we need to be working on all different parts of the system in order to successfully change the whole system," comments one Lab team member. Echoing Les Omotani's comment on bringing change to large school systems, another adds, "[To get started,] you don't have to have the answers for everything that needs to be done to solve the problem. In fact, if you did have all the answers, you might not have the best answer."

As we develop our capacity to see large global systems, deeper patterns will become clearer. When I attended a daylong session on international manufacturing at MIT, I listened to a representative of a leading labor rights NGO talking about the problems with multinational apparel manufacturers. and heard a tale remarkably similar to that of global food production—a tale of falling prices, relentless expansion, and lower-than-living-wage conditions for workers. Then, to my amazement, not once but several times, the labor advocate talked of a "race to the bottom" in global apparel manufacturing. I left wondering whether the Sustainable Food Lab might not be just about food, but about learning how to shift the forces driving many global supply chains toward where nobody wants to go.

SOCIETY: TALKING ACROSS THE BOUNDARIES

It is time for all of us to come together and think about the future we want to create. If we do nothing, our children could be living on $2 a day.

– Salim Al-Aydh

In an increasingly interdependent world, it is ironic that many of our societies are becoming more fragmented and polarized. In one sense, this is understandable. When one is facing complex issues that engender considerable fear, there is security in being able to pull back into a particular ideology, a one true answer. But one group's ideology is rarely shared by others, and consequently walls develop between groups. After a while, ideology becomes identity, and polarization becomes self-reinforcing.

Our interconnected world confronts all societies with a mandate to revive the capacity to talk together and live together. Nowhere are the stakes higher than in the Middle East. Building on its know-how with dialogue in general and the world café process in particular, in the fall of 2004 Saudi Aramco convened a dialogue meeting in Hawar, the first in an unusual series of gatherings. In many ways, it was the next logical step in the process that began when Aramco expanded to include key business partners in its strategic dialogues on the core problems confronting Saudi society. But this went farther in terms of the range of participants. It was convened by Gulf SoL, a SoL network that included over twenty companies from throughout the Gulf region (Kuwait, Dubai, the United Arab Emirates, and Bahrain, in addition to Saudi Arabia). The group was, on average, more senior than participants in the earlier meetings, with many heads and founders of companies, along with founders of influential NGOs and schools, and leading thinkers and academics. And it included both men and women—for many, it was the first time in their lives that they had attended such a meeting with both sexes.

As with the earlier sessions Aramco convened, this dialogue started with a presentation that surveyed the current economic condition of the Gulf region countries. Nearly all of these countries have the same core problems seen in Saudi Arabia: large and rapidly expanding numbers of unemployed young people, stagnant or falling GDP per capita, and economies overly dependent on oil. This presentation catalyzed two days of passionate conversation about the area's traditional culture, its schools, its oil-dependent economy, and its possibilities for change.

In my experience, when people are able to engage authentically in discussions on subjects that matter deeply to them, there is almost no limit to their energy, courage, and willingness to step into foreign territory. During breaks in this gathering, traditionally dressed Arab gentlemen repeatedly came up to me in states that ranged from bewilderment to anxiety and said things like, "In all my life, I have never talked about subjects like this with a lady." My sense was that, in some ways, the women were more ready for serious dialogue. Excluded by law from professional activities in many of the Gulf countries, they form networks to mentor and support one another. Like other excluded groups finally invited to the table, they had been waiting for this day, and they were not shy. They spoke with fire and conviction, articulate about the pressing issues facing their societies, and relentlessly positive about possibilities for change.

As I listened, I also saw the universality of the issues with which participants wrestled. Their core questions were similar to those of people everywhere: How do we preserve what we care deeply about in our traditions while allowing those traditions to evolve in harmony with today's world? How can we be responsible to our children, to create conditions in which they can have an authentic Arab identity and yet be able to thrive in a globalizing society? What would healthy twenty-first-century Islamic Gulf societies look like?

A second gathering similar to the Hawar dialogue was held six months later, and as I write this, a third is being planned. Several initiatives have started to form—including a job training center for young Saudis to assist in the school-to-work transition, a national mentoring network connecting successful business leaders with young people, and a variety of education initiatives involving promising innovations in the traditional school system, widely recognized as an area of pivotal change. Many young leaders are joining the conversations. One participant, for example, has started a women's college in Jeddah, which, unlike the traditional universities, works closely with Saudi businesses to ensure an education that addresses real needs for social change and innovation.

As I sat in the closing circle at the Hawar dialogue, an older mentor to many of the Saudi women, listening to one person after another share what the conversation had meant to him or her, leaned over to me and whispered, "This is historic." I just nodded—knowing the truth of her words and knowing also that I had only the dimmest comprehension of what this really meant for her, for the other women in the circle, and for everyone else.

When she said this, two thoughts came to mind. The word "politics" comes from the Greek *polis*, the gathering place where citizens came to talk about the issues of the day. What I saw in Hawar, and what I see happening in projects like the Sustainable Food Lab, is a rebirth of the polis, people coming together, reaching toward one another across their differences rather than being driven apart by those differences. It is hard for me to imagine effectively confronting the host of imbalances in our present way of living together on the planet without recovering this capacity for dialogue.

Second, I had a powerful sense of having been there before. I suddenly recalled being in South Africa, fifteen years earlier. My good friend and colleague, Adam Kahane, who has led successful civic dialogue work in South Africa, Guatemala, and elsewhere,[23] once commented that he did not see the possibility for this happening in Israel and Palestine, because, in his view, "both sides still think they can stick to the way they have been doing things. They have not yet seen that they have no future without changing their own thinking and strategies." By contrast, in the mid-1980s, cultural polarization started to shift in South Africa. People started to see into the future; they started to recognize the simple fact that their current path was leading in a direction that no one wanted. When this happens in a society, those who have been polarized, the excluded and the included, start to talk with one another—as citizens with a common destiny. They see their interdependency in creating a different future, and new forces for change are set free.

Business finds itself in an awkward position of being, in a sense, the most global institution in the world today. Large multinational corporations, like BP, Unilever, and Saudi Aramco, arguably have a more comprehensive view of global economic, cultural, and environmental trends than do most national governments. Because of this, they can play a pivotal role in convening people to see larger systems that transcend national boundaries, and to confront deep issues that political partisanship may obscure. Corporations will be most effective in doing so to the degree that they advocate for the health of the whole, and use methods for collective inquiry, systems thinking, and the building of shared visions that they have tested and refined on their own problems—indeed businesses' practical experience with such methods may be one of their greatest contributions. In political climates dominated by fragmentation, polarization, and distrust, the best leaders will be those with practical experience in the power of reflective conversation and an understanding of how transformative relationships can solve complex problems. For these reasons, in the coming years, I expect "business as usual" to change quite a bit.

EDUCATION FOR THE 21ST CENTURY

The real systems citizens are mostly under the age of twenty. More and more children growing up today have a perspective and awareness of the world as a whole that did not exist in the past. More than any previous generation, they see what is happening around the world, and they naturally relate to other people and cultures differently. And they have deep concerns about their future.

Several years ago we began including children and young people in SoL dialogues, especially when we were talking about the future of education and global systemic issues. I will never forget hearing a 12-year-old girl in one of these sessions say very matter-of-factly to a forty-five-year-old executive, "We feel like you drank your juice and then you drank ours."

Schools could play a pivotal role in transforming young people's concerns about the future into the foundations for productive systems citizens if they could see this as their role and think of themselves as part of a global system. Former dean of the MIT Engineering School Gordon Brown, a champion of systems thinking in schools in the later years of his life, used to say, "To be a teacher is to be a prophet. We are not preparing children for the world we have lived in but for a future that we can barely imagine." Unfortunately, around the world, schools are caught up in the pressures to preserve a traditional system that finds itself under increasing stress, unable to innovate. So while children grow up today with the instincts to be systems citizens, there is little to encourage them in this direction.

This is especially ironic given the mounting evidence that children are natural systems thinkers; if given a chance to cultivate these innate talents, they can develop sophisticated critical thinking skills much more quickly than one might expect. In schools where systems thinking is woven throughout the curriculum, and students and teachers work together as learners and mentors rather than passive listeners and all-knowing experts, these innate skills can truly flower. If we can succeed in moving toward a learner-centered, systems-based education system, I believe we will see just how readily systems citizenship develops—and how ineffective the traditional classroom, teacher-centric model of learning actually is.[24]

I also believe one key in this shift will be accepting that innovations needed in education represent a bigger task than educators can accomplish in isolation; they will need to be co-created by a microcosm of the whole system, including business and the students themselves. Les Omotani, superintendent of Hewlett-Woodmere district in Long Island, says, "I have found that one of the most reliable ways to get people thinking freshly about becoming a genuine learning community is to elevate the student voice and the role of students in our conversations, our planning, and our decision making. Last year, for example, we ran a 'wellness café' with the students—a big meeting organized as a world café on the theme of wellness. Fifty students volunteered to be table hosts and facilitators, and two hundred people from the community came, including some faculty members. Kids here are hungry for this sort of more responsible and active leadership role. I also believe this could develop into a national movement. Our schools are paralyzed. Overstressed teachers and administrators try desperately to fend off pressures from dissatisfied business leaders and fearful parents. Yet we all know the education for the twenty-first century must change profoundly from education for the nineteenth and twentieth centuries. This requires space for innovation, not just pressures for performance. Young people feel this acutely. They know they need to grow up as citizens of the world. They need to understand the world's problems and they need to know how to work productively on them. Schools that fail to address these needs will be increasingly marginalized and irrelevant for kids. And, the young people are eager to be part of this. The real question is, 'Are we?'"

17

FRONTIERS

We stand at the frontier of the reinvention of the prevailing system of management. What has been developing for centuries cannot be reversed in a few years. Nor is there any basis for being sanguine that the new will steadily supplant the old. Deep habits of thought and action drive ways of operating that make managers feel the need to maintain control, investors demand that businesses grow at any cost, and the whole private-sector system operate in a way that often "privatizes" profits and "socializes" costs like deteriorating environmental and social capital. Nevertheless, powerful forces for change are also at play: the Internet is breaking down traditional information monopolies, increasingly networked organizations cannot be controlled from the top, and awareness of the costs of global industrial development patterns is growing.

In the preceding chapters, I have tried to share innovations emerging around the world and across diverse organizational settings. The emphasis has been on what is already occurring, including ways that the foundational elements of learning cultures are being integrated into businesses, schools, and governmental, non-governmental, and community organizations. As I look at these all together, it seems to me that something wholly new is emerging, something that could not have been grasped fifteen years ago, when *The Fifth Discipline* was first published.

DISCOVERING AND EMBODYING NATURE'S PATTERNS

For many years, the common definition of learning within the SoL network has been learning is a process of enhancing learners' capacity, individually and collectively, to produce results they truly want to produce. This definition has been helpful because it emphasizes two crucial features of learning that are often misunderstood: (1) the building of capacity for effective action, as opposed to intellectual understanding only; and (2) the fact that this capacity builds over time, often over considerable time. We had considered many alternative definitions, but found none as simple and useful. So it came as a surprise when, a couple of years ago, I encountered a very different definition of learning, one that was even simpler.

The source of this new definition was H. Thomas Johnson, one of the world's leading accounting theorists. Johnson is co-inventor of activity-based costing (ABC) and co-author of *Relevance Lost: The Rise and Fall of Management Accounting*, cited by *Harvard Business Review* as one of the seminal management books of the past 75 years.[1] Though ABC was considered a significant contribution, Johnson himself thought of it only as a first step in radically rethinking performance management, and devoted himself in the following decade to in-depth study of a small number of industry-leading firms. One of these was Toyota, whose approach to cost management he documented in *Profit Beyond Measure*,[2] a heretical book that suggested that Toyota's extraordinary long-term success was due in part to carefully limiting the use of performance metrics by managers. In particular, Johnson argued that when performance metrics are reported to those at higher levels in the management hierarchy, managers are induced to use them to set numerical targets and drive change—what W. Edwards Deming called "meddling." Johnson, like Deming, claimed that continual learning and superior performance actually depend on connecting metrics and target setting with in-depth process knowledge at the front lines.

This directly contradicts what many managers consider their primary task—setting numerical targets and driving results—which may be why so few competitors have been able to match Toyota's long-term performance.[3]

But sensing and acting locally is exactly how complex living systems work—indeed, it was through studying living systems that Johnson came to understand Toyota's approach to cost management. No one is "in charge" of a forest. Your body does not wait for orders from the brain to flow coagulants to a cut in your finger. Whatever "centralized" control does exist in nature is possible precisely because of complex networks of local control. We have no idea how we walk, but once this "body knowledge" is developed, the body responds to our conscious directives; without that body knowledge, all the central directives in the world would be ineffectual. Johnson realized that Toyota's approach to performance management embodied the essence of living systems: company managers were engaged in continually building and deploying locally embedded know-how and then trusting frontline workers to manage and improve cost performance. In effect, Toyota's approach to localized performance management amounted to discovering and embodying nature's patterns, and that is why Toyota's team were superior learners.

This simple definition of learning illuminates a wide range of potentially profound changes in social systems, from how we work together to the nature of industrial systems as a whole. For example, Plug Power's "zero-to-landfill" vision for manufacturing fuel cells is inspired by a transcendent law of living systems, zero waste. Or, put differently, "waste equals food." Every by-product of one natural system is a nutrient for another natural system. I've just returned from China, where the president and prime minister regularly talk now about the "circular economy" based on this principle. Designing all products, packaging for products, and processes used in making products to eliminate all waste would represent a profound transformation for industrial economies, and any country aspiring to this vision faces a long road. But the basic concept of a circular economy is clear, as are its distinctions from industrial economies as they have developed over the past two hundred years (see figure that follows).[4]

In many ways, the same spirit of learning to come into harmony with nature guides the Sustainable Food Lab—in this case, harmony at a global scale. The members of the Sustainable Food Lab under-

WHY INDUSTRY PRODUCES WASTE

LIVING SYSTEMS FOLLOW CYCLES

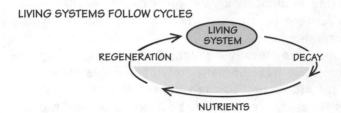

INDUSTRIAL-AGE SYSTEMS DO NOT

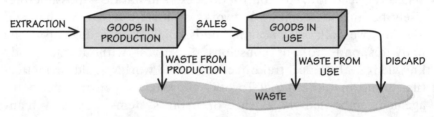

HOW INDUSTRY CAN REDUCE WASTE BY MIMICING NATURE

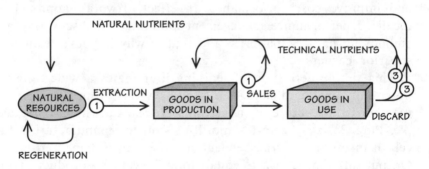

stand that no economic system can remain viable that systematically destroys the social and ecological systems upon which it
depends. How we organize the production and distribution of food
could be considered humankind's first system. So, it is fitting that it
should also be the first of our global systems that we bring back
into harmony with social and ecological reality.

This spirit of learning as discovering and embodying nature's
patterns subtly infuses all the other innovations discussed in the
preceding chapters. When managers are committed to growing people in order to grow the enterprise or committed to utilizing conversation as the core process for change, their practices reflect insights
into human nature—our innate desire to grow as human beings and
to be in relationship with one another. Similarly, consider the new

understanding of self-creating social networks as a natural pattern of organizing—"how work actually gets done," as Anne Murray Allen put it. And remember Dee Hock's generative question that gave rise to Visa's radical decentralized governance structure: "Why couldn't an organization work like a rain forest?"

Eventually, H. Thomas Johnson's definition of learning led me to realize that the first principle underlying our work on organizational learning is simply to develop a system of management consistent with nature—human nature and the nature of the larger social and natural systems in which we always operate. I remember my first conversation with a young woman from China as to why *The Fifth Discipline* had become so popular in her country. She answered in a surprising way. "We see it as a book about personal development," she said. "So much of management theory from the West contradicts our basic belief in developing our deepest nature as human beings. Your book reinforces this belief and gives us hope that this can be consistent with building successful organizations." Anthropologist Edward Hall calls the drive to learn the "most basic drive in the human species." What is this drive to learn other than our own innate personal quest to discover and embody nature's patterns in all aspects of our lives?

THE NEXT GENERATION OF LEADERS

I also now believe that many of the most important leaders in the coming decades will not be those we have been assuming they would be. A new order of things must be brought forward by a new order of leaders. It is no surprise that wherever we see a new system of management starting to take root, we see leaders emerging from the periphery—people who do not come from the traditional centers of power but from the cultural, economic and demographic periphery: women, the poor, and the young.

WOMEN LEADING AS WOMEN

The percentage of women in diverse leadership positions has been rising for several decades. But often the first or second generation of women in senior positions have to "be more like men than the men," in order to prove that they are "real leaders" by the masculine criteria that are still dominant. Conversely, in the words of researcher Joyce Fletcher, women leading "as women" often become labeled as "good team players" or, worse, as "nice," the kiss of death when promotion decisions are made. Fletcher argues that when women lead in their most natural ways in most organizations, they disappear from the attention of their co-workers and their male-oriented leadership models.[5]

In this light, one of the most interesting projects to develop within the SoL Sustainability Consortium has been the "Women Leading Sustainability" initiative.[6] The genesis of this project was the discovery that a disproportionate number of the highest-impact initiatives within this network had been instigated by women leaders, such as Darcy Winslow of Nike, Barbara Stocking of Oxfam, Brigitte Tantawy-Monsou of Unilever, and Dorothy Berry and Mieko Nishimizu of the World Bank. This led to the obvious questions, "What is it about women's sensibilities that have made them step forward regarding sustainability issues, and what is it about their ways of leading that have made them effective?"

Many answers to these questions are implied in the preceding chapters. Barbara Stocking described herself as "a developmentally oriented manager," and said that women don't have the time for corporate politics and infighting. Women tend to be less ambitious about personal advancement, and more ambitious "about the thing itself," she added. When Ilean Galloway realized in graduate school that, as a black woman, she "was not going to get a job with the head of [an] organization," she began a journey of discovering the distinctive power of being an internal network leader in a network-oriented organization—her credibility comes from her knowledge and integrity, not from her position.

It is also clear that women gravitate toward longer-term issues that lie at the periphery of most businesses' attention, like sustainability, and approach these from a standpoint of collaboration and discovery rather than solutions and plans. For example, Simone Amber, formerly one of the senior financial managers in the global oil services company Schlumberger, now coordinates an Internet-based education initiative (Schlumberger Excellence in Educational Development, or SEED) that engages some fifteen hundred Schlumberger volunteers mentoring over two hundred thousand children in thirty-five developing countries. How did one woman do this with no formal mandate and (initially) no budget? By connecting with the core of the corporation's values and traditional commitment to the communities in which it did business, and by tapping people's desire to be more directly involved in the lives of children. SEED's state-of-the art Web site (in all seven major languages of the world) is impressive, but what makes the project succeed is the extraordinary SEED volunteer network.[7] "There exists an untapped potential goodwill in companies that we can help manifest by avoiding the politics and internal competition in favor of people's hearts," she says.

LEADERS FROM THE ECONOMIC PERIPHERY

Countless leaders from the economic periphery are applying the same learning principles and methods used by their counterparts in the world of established organizations. Bringing vision and deep listening to on-the-ground settings, these community leaders catalyze forces for systemic change that larger organizations cannot access. "The essence of my capacity to serve as a leader," says Sayra Pinto of Roca, "is that people know that I am one of them, that I have traveled the road they have traveled, suffered the fears they suffer, and that I know just how smart and capable they really are."

The community leader I have probably known the longest is Mwalimu Musheshe, who started the Uganda Rural Development and Training project (URDT) in the early 1980s with the idea of using learning principles and practices to stimulate rural development.[8] Working in what was then one of the poorest parts of the country, Musheshe and his colleagues taught people how to formulate their visions and how to build shared visions, how to recognize mental models that held them back and how to resolve differing views through listening to one another, and how to think about their villages as systems. They combined all of this with practical on-the-ground projects like digging better wells and building more secure granaries. "Most of all we had to help people shed their inherited sense of fatalism," says Musheshe. "The attitude that we could do nothing about our future was in fact our biggest obstacle." Today the area where they have concentrated their efforts is one of the most prosperous rural regions of the country, and URDT is starting the first women's university in Uganda so that women have opportunities for leadership on a larger scale because they have been limited by the lack of higher education.

By tapping and nurturing local leadership capacities, leaders like Pinto and Musheshe establish a foundation for enduring development, something that has eluded countless wealthy northern countries in their efforts to help poorer countries. "The development sector is still engaged in a large-scale mechanistic and hierarchical approach to addressing the challenges of poverty and so-called under-development," writes Marianne Knuth, founder of Kufunda Village, a demonstration site and learning network dedicated to sustainable agriculture in Zimbabwe.[9] "In the name of material development, villages and communities have to adopt less communal ways of relating to each other. In the name of development, problems are fixed for a community without recognizing the need for ownership in the development initiative by the community itself . . . And so it often is that many of the larger-scale development initiatives fix a problem for a short term, only to have the problem return years later (abandoned boreholes, broken-down toilets, or community pumps for which no one has taken ownership after the intervener has left)."

Interestingly, Knuth does not see that Kufunda is doing something unique. "We are one of a great many experiments around the world, a growing movement of people and organizations, in education, business, design, architecture," she says, pursuing "a shared inquiry around how we can come back to a more life-giving way of working."

YOUTH LEADERSHIP

Increasingly, the leadership needed for systemic change is coming from young people. Often ignored as leaders, teenagers and young adults have a strong stake in the future, perhaps the strongest. They are also the least invested in the past, giving them a distinctive ability to see the flaws in current mental models and institutional patterns and the courage to create something new. When young people develop basic leadership and collaborative learning skills, they can be a formidable force for change.

Marianne Knuth has been an activist for a long time. She left Zimbabwe at the age of 16 in order to pursue her education in Europe (her father is Danish). Ten years later, she co-founded "Pioneers for Change," a global network of young leaders, committed, in their terms, to "be themselves, do what matters, start now, engage with others, and never stop asking questions." Over the past few years, I have gotten to know many of these young people and have been deeply moved by their calm centeredness, their imagination in confronting difficult issues, and their accomplishments.

I recently joined several members of the Pioneers for Change at a major conference on global change in Sweden. The participants were mostly senior corporate and government executives, and leading experts on different global issues. At my request, the organizers agreed to set up a special session where the Pioneers could talk about their approaches to leadership in large-scale organizational change—a conversation which revealed several interesting differences between the Pioneers and the more experienced leaders.

First, the young people saw their lack of knowledge as an asset. "We don't know much, so it's easy for us to ask lots of questions," stated Christel Scholten, a co-founder of the Pioneers network who was instrumental in the formation of a major sustainable development program at ABN AMRO Bank, a program which she now heads. The program came into existence through Scholten's continually raising issues until people saw their relevance. As we talked, many of the more experienced managers at the conference began to see how their past knowledge and accomplishments could actually be an impediment in leading change. One seasoned manager realized that not only did his knowledge bias his views but "people can easily relate to me based on their expectations of how I see problems, and before I know it, I am defending views I may not even care that strongly about." By contrast, the young leaders were able to remain open, and, through their genuine inquiry, often enabled shared understanding and commitment in ways that strong advocacy can impede.

Second, these young leaders are remarkably connected around the world. When they run into difficulties, they may turn to partners in Bangladesh, India, South Africa, the Philippines, or Croatia for help. By continually sharing with and helping one another, they develop eclectic views of problems and can draw forth surprising resources for change. For example, when Scholten was struggling with her new job at the bank, she drew encouragement and help from fellow Pioneers working in global finance in Asia and Europe.

Lastly, the young people work at remaining unattached to their views. Several years ago, a group of the Pioneers founded The Hypocrites Club. "The way it works," says Knuth, "is that whenever we meet, we have a little competition. Each of us gets to tell a story about how we have given up on our beliefs or sold out or just caved in—to avoid conflict or just smooth things over, or when we acted one way but thought another. Sometimes these are things that might have been weighing on me. Sometimes, it is something that I might have barely noticed at the time. But the stories can be funny, and by the time we get going, we're working hard to show that each of us is hypocritical as the other. It makes for a great evening."

THREE OPENINGS

There is one remaining question. Over the last quarter-century, I have watched many people in many different settings work with tools and principles for fostering vision and purposefulness, deeper conversation and reflectiveness, and systemic thinking. It is clear that some attain remarkable results and some accomplish very little. Why is this? I do not think the difference lies in intelligence or even commitment. It certainly does not stem from organizational position or power. But it seems to have to do with where people are "coming from." As Bill O'Brien observed near the end of his life, "The primary determinant of the outcome of an intervention is the inner state of the intervenor."

My colleague and co-author of *Presence*, Otto Scharmer, explains a shift in orientation and intention that arises from three "thresholds," or openings through which we must pass in leading profound change: opening the head, opening the heart, and opening the will.[10]

The first involves opening ourselves to see and hear what is in front of us but we have not yet been able to see. This is the threshold of "suspension"—suspending taken-for-granted assumptions that have shaped our perceptions in the past. The second threshold involves seeing with the heart—opening it to see our connection to what is around us, the pain, the suffering, and the problems, as well as the joy. Here we move beyond our comfortable stories that blame outside forces or people for what is not working and see that we too are part of the problem. The third threshold involves letting go of the last remnants of what Scharmer call "our small 's' self" and letting whatever may arise come through us. Here we connect "with the future that comes into being through us and with what we are here to do." Passing through this third threshold does not mean that all our questions about the meaning of our lives are suddenly answered, but that "we are alive in the heart of this question and it carries us forward."

I believe that faced with the profound challenges of the present, more leaders of all sorts are starting to appreciate these three shifts. They have a new awareness of the profound challenges we face—the growing gap, as Ford's Marv Adams says, between "accelerating interdependency and our institutions' inability to think and act systemically." But this new awareness is also arising from specific experiences. For example, as more people are working with mental models and fostering more inquiry-oriented conversations for change, the power of opening our minds becomes clear. "I know we are starting to move to a deeper and more productive level of conversation when I notice people being less inclined to treat their opinions as facts," says BP's Vivienne Cox. "They become less strident. They become less certain about things. They start to have a sense of humor. They lighten up. Even though we may be discussing serious subjects, we become a bit less serious, more playful and exploratory. That's when I know a sense of real inquiry is developing."

Scharmer's second and third shifts are catalyzed by seeing, cognitively and emotionally, and by connecting with our deepest aspirations. Salim Al-Aydh opens each of the dialogues in the Gulf SoL network with pictures of children and talks about his grandchildren. This way, when people then look at the economic prospects for the region, they are not just looking at numbers; they are imagining the lives that their children and children's children will be living. "We cannot start to talk together seriously about the future we truly want to create, and the changes that may be needed, without opening our hearts, and we will never undertake the actions needed without this," he says.

This opening of the heart turns on the readiness to be vulnerable, a quality few managers have cultivated traditionally. Reflecting on his career of remarkable turnaround stories in the 1980s and 1990s at Ford, Roger Saillant commented that his bosses never asked him how he accomplished his results. He concluded that this was because, at some level, they knew it entailed a degree of vulnerability, of being human, that is never comfortable, and most of them were not prepared to feel that exposed.

As we move through the third opening, we become willing to let go of our agendas and predetermined goals, to allow our intentions and strategies to be molded by forces larger than our own individual wills. This is the hardest of the three to talk about in the abstract, but it is very clear when it happens.

The whole progression of three openings is beautifully illustrated in Marianne Knuth's reflections on how Kufunda Village works. "We bring together community organizers from across Zimbabwe regularly to learn from each other; and to become more conscious of unconscious assumptions (both inherited and cultural) that may hold them back and how they can work with those. But, we can only do this by being likewise open ourselves, knowing that we do not have the answers, that we do not know what they must do to realize their dreams."

The power that starts with opening minds builds through the "magic of connecting with one another," Knuth says. "I am easily moved to tears, in fact, so much that it used to embarrass me. I have, however, come to recognize it as an indicator of my being connecting with something of essence—be it deep felt joy, compassion, grief, inspiration. Sometimes those feelings are my own, telling me something, at other times it is the joy or pain of another that reaches out and touches me deeply. I have also realized that if in my speech I am moved to tears, it is okay—in fact it often brings the people I am communicating with closer to me. We meet in another place—outside of mere intellect. We meet . . . through the doors of our hearts, not the doors of our minds."

The third opening started to unfold for Knuth when she returned to Zimbabwe after attending school in Denmark, with no clear plan, just knowing that it was "a call that I simply had to heed: How we might create—and recreate—healthy vibrant communities in the midst of a country and continent viewed by the rest of the world as poor, as lost. I believe each one of us is here for a reason, and when you find it, and embrace it, your heart will sing, and you will be carried along by life as you follow her desire for you."

When leaders at any level and in any setting move through these three openings, there are few limits to what is possible. "If you can achieve real innocence in what you do," says Saillant, "become truly insignificant in the sense that you're not trying to lay claim to it for yourself or trying to be recognized for the outcome—and that's very tough to do—gifts arrive. They may take the form of influence, of strength, of will, of a sense of purpose, of energy, or just all sorts of things happening that aid the cause. When people can find that inside themselves, when they can get connected to what we all kind of sense is there, when they can get to that light, it's one of the greatest gifts. It's the place where miracles come from."

Reflecting on her journey, Knuth says simply, "In the beginning was the meeting . . . How we meet people determines all else. Do we meet people assuming the best we can about them? Do we meet each person curious about the miracle of a human being that we are about to connect with? Or do we meet a poor person that we are about to help?

"I met Anna Marunda again yesterday, one of the community organizers in the Kufunda network. She is a widow of 46. She lives on a $2 per month pension from her late husband, but must pay $20 every three months in children's school fees. In the past year, Anna has set up a women's crochet cooperative; has recently started teaching knitting to women in her area, has built her own compost toilet, and is teaching others how to build their own; is running an AIDS dialogue group, and has been providing home care for AIDS patients. We had a conversation about the wonders she had discovered about herself in the past year. She said, 'I have learned that I have been an example in my community for being a widowed woman who overcame severe hardship. I have learned that I am a strong woman. I have learned that I can find peace of mind within myself. I have learned that I am a good listener, and I am trustworthy and so people are coming to me, inviting me to join different community organizations.'

"I do not understand how all of these things are happening. But I do know that we met Anna in her wisdom. Not in her poverty."

Knuth writes in her journal the simple comment, "Life is sacred and should be met in that way." She adds, "I guess it is simply the experience of slowing down enough to really appreciate the beauty that surrounds us—the stunning colors of an evening sky, the gentle beauty of a flock of cows, the miracle of a seedling pushing its way through the earth, the grounding experience of settling down on one of the huge granite rocks that mark the Zimbabwean countryside, the magic of connecting deeply with another human being whether in joy or in sorrow . . . Each time I notice and appreciate the miracle of these seeming simple acts of creation, I also feel more certain that life is infinitely rich and full of magic and love, and that the being that manages to stay connected to that sense is richer than the one which does not."[11]

I cannot read these words of Roger Saillant's or Marianne Knuth's without being deeply moved. Without doubt, the thing I struggle most to communicate is the factual knowledge of what is possible when we open ourselves in these ways. I have seen so many miracles—situations with impossible problems that were somehow resolved. I have seen so many people grow into who they truly are and then rise up to face the next difficult problem, lighter and more joyful. And through the journey, they grow closer, to themselves, to one another, and to life.

There are as many ways to characterize the essence of this work as there are people doing it: it is a system of management consistent with nature, human nature, and the nature of larger living systems; it is working together in ways that realize our highest aspirations; it is being the change we seek to create. Or, as Marianne Knuth so beautifully says, it is staying connected to the being that never stopped being connected.

PART V

Coda

18

THE INDIVISIBLE
WHOLE

When I was young I always wanted to be an astronaut. I even studied aeronautics and astronautics in college to prepare. But then I got hooked on "systems theory" and a new, earthbound career was born.

But I still remained deeply fascinated with the experience of being in space, a fascination that was heightened by the first Apollo pictures of the earth. So it was with great interest that I finally had an opportunity to get to know astronaut Rusty Schweickart who attended one of our leadership programs several years ago.

I learned from Rusty that many of the astronauts struggle when they return to earth, trying to put into words their feelings of what it meant to them to hover above their home planet. Rusty struggled for five years (he flew on Apollo 9, which tested the lunar module in earth orbit in March 1969) before words adequate to the task began to form.

In the summer of 1974, he had been invited to speak to a gathering on "planetary culture" at Lindisfarne, a spiritual community on Long Island. After considering and discarding many ways of sharing his experience he realized that he couldn't tell it as his story.

Because it was our story. He realized that he and the other astronauts represented an "extension of the sensory apparatus of the human species. Yes, I was looking out from my eyes and feeling with my senses but it was also our eyes and our senses. We who were the first to leave and look back at the earth were looking back for all of humankind. Though there were only a few of us, it was our responsibility to report back what we experienced." Realizing this, he decided simply to describe what it was like—as if you and I, the listeners, were there as well.[1]

Up there you go around every hour and a half, time after time after time. You wake up usually in the mornings. And just the way that the track of your orbits go, you wake up over the Mideast, over North Africa. As you eat breakfast you look out the window as you're going past and there's the Mediterranean area, and Greece, and Rome, and North Africa, and the Sinai, the whole area. And you realize in one glance that what you're seeing is what was the whole history of man for years—the cradle of civilization. And you think of all the history you can imagine looking at that scene.

And you go around down across North Africa and out over the Indian Ocean, and look up at that great sub-continent of India pointed down toward you as you go past it. And Ceylon off to the side, Burma, Southeast Asia, out over the Philippines, and up across that monstrous Pacific Ocean, vast body of water—you've never realized how big that is before. And you finally come up across the coast of California and look for those friendly things: Los Angeles, and Phoenix, and on across El Paso and there's Houston, there's home, and you look and sure enough there's the Astrodome. And you identify with that, you know—it's an attachment.

And down across New Orleans and then looking down to the south and there's the whole peninsula of Florida laid out. And all the hundreds of hours you spent flying across that route, down in the atmosphere, all that is friendly again. And you go out across the Atlantic Ocean and back across Africa.

And that identity—that you identify with Houston, and then you identify with Los Angeles and Phoenix and New Orleans and everything. And the next thing you recognize in yourself, is you're identifying with North Africa. You look forward to that, you anticipate it. And there it is. That whole process begins to shift what it is you identify with. When you go around it in an hour and a half you begin to recognize that your identity is with the whole thing. And that makes a change.

You look down there and you can't imagine how many borders and boundaries you crossed again and again and again. And you don't even see 'em. At that wake-up scene—the Mideast—you know there are hundreds of people killing each other over some imaginary line that you can't see. From where you see it, the thing is a whole, and it's so beautiful. And you wish you could take one from each side in hand and say, "Look at it from this perspective. Look at that. What's important?"

And so a little later on, your friend, again those same neighbors, the person next to you goes to the moon. And now he looks back and sees the Earth not as something big where he can see the beautiful details, but he sees the Earth as a small thing out there. And now that contrast between the bright blue and white Christmas tree ornament and that black sky, that infinite universe, really comes through.

The size of it, the significance of it—it becomes both things, it becomes so small and so fragile, and such a precious little spot in the universe, that you can block it out with your thumb, and you realize that on that small spot, that little blue and white thing is everything that means anything to you. All of history and music, and poetry and art and war and death and birth and love, tears, joy, games, all of it is on that little spot out there that you can cover with your thumb.

And you realize that that perspective . . . that you've changed, that there's something new there. That relationship is no longer what it was. And then you look back on the time when you were outside on the EVA [extravehicular activity] and those few moments that you had the time because the camera malfunctioned, that you had the time to think about what was happening. And you recall staring out there at the spectacle that went before your eyes. Because now you're no longer inside something with a window looking out at the picture, but now you're out there and what you've got around your head is a goldfish bowl and there are no boundaries. There are no frames, there are no boundaries.

Floating in space, Rusty discovered the first principles of systems thinking. But he discovered them in a way that few of us ever do—not at a rational or intellectual level but at a level of direct experience. The earth is an indivisible whole, just as each of us is an indivisible whole. Nature (and that includes us) is not made up of parts within wholes. It is made up of wholes within wholes. All boundaries, national boundaries included, are fundamentally arbitrary. We invent them and then, ironically, we find ourselves trapped within them.

But there was something more. In the years following that first talk at Lindisfarne, Rusty found himself drawn into a whole new series of insights and personal changes. He found himself drawn into new work, leaving his post as commissioner of the California Energy Commission and becoming more active in joint projects involving U.S. astronauts and Soviet cosmonauts.[2] He listened and learned about others' experience. He began to involve himself in activities that seemed congruent with his new understandings.

One that had a special impact was learning about the "Gaia" hypothesis—the theory that the biosphere, all life on earth, is itself a living organism.[3] This idea, which has deep roots in many preindustrial cultures, such as American Indian cultures, "struck a deep chord in me," says Rusty. "For the first time it gave the scientist in me a way to talk about aspects of my experience in space that I couldn't even articulate to myself. I had experienced the earth in a way that I had no way to describe. I had experienced the aliveness of it—of it all."

At the conclusion of the leadership workshop, someone asked spontaneously, "Rusty, tell us what it was like up there?" He paused for a long time. When he finally spoke, he said only one thing. "It was like seeing a baby about to be born."

Something new is happening. And it has to do with it all—the whole.

APPENDIX 1:
THE LEARNING
DISCIPLINES

Each of the five learning disciplines can be thought of on three distinct levels:

- practices: what you do
- principles: guiding ideas and insights
- essences: the state of being of those with high levels of mastery in the discipline

The practices are activities upon which practitioners of the discipline focus their time and energy. For example, systems thinking entails using the "systems archetypes" in order to perceive underlying structures in complex situations. Personal mastery entails "clarifying personal vision," and "holding creative tension," simultaneously focusing on the vision and current reality and allowing the tension between the two to generate energy toward achieving the vision. Working with mental models involves distinguishing the direct "data" of experience from the generalizations or abstractions that we form based on the data.

The practices are the most evident aspect of any discipline. They are also the primary focus of individuals or groups when they begin to follow a discipline. For the beginner, they require "discipline" in the sense of conscious and consistent effort because following the practices is not yet second nature. In a heated debate, the novice at working with mental models will have to make an effort to identify the assumptions he is making and why. Often the beginner's efforts in a discipline are characterized by time displacement: only *after* the debate, does one see one's assumptions clearly and distinguish them from the "data" and reasoning upon which they are based. However, eventually, the practices of a discipline become more and more automatic and active in "real time." You find yourself spontaneously thinking of systems archetypes, re-creating (which is different from recalling) your vision, and recognizing your assumptions as they come into play, while confronting pressing problems.

Equally central to any discipline are the underlying principles. These represent the theory that lies behind the practices of the disciplines. For example, "structure influences behavior" is a central principle underlying systems thinking, as is "policy resistance," the tendency of complex systems to resist efforts to change their behavior. The former implies that the ability to influence reality comes from seeing structures that are controlling behavior and events. The latter implies that efforts to manipulate behavior, for example through well-intentioned programs such as building new houses for disadvantaged urban dwellers, will generally improve matters only in the short run and often lead to still more problems in the long run. Similarly, the power of vision is a principle of personal mastery, as is the distinction between "creative tension" and "emotional tension."

The principles behind a discipline are important to the beginner as well as to the master. For the beginner, they help him in understanding the rationale behind the discipline and in making sense of the practices of the discipline. For the master, they are points of reference which aid in continually refining the practice of the discipline and in explaining it to others.

It is important to recognize that mastering any of the disciplines requires effort on both the levels of understanding the principles *and* following the practices. It is tempting to think that just because one understands certain principles one has "learned" about the discipline. This is the familiar trap of confusing intellectual understanding with learning. Learning always involves new understandings and new behaviors, "thinking" and "doing." This is the reason for distinguishing principles from practices. Both are vital.

The third level, the "essences" of the disciplines, is different. There is no point in focusing one's conscious attention and effort on these essences in learning a discipline, any more than it would make sense to *make an effort* to experience love or joy or tranquillity. The essences of the disciplines are the *state of being* that comes to be experienced naturally by individuals or groups with high levels of mastery in the disciplines. While these are difficult to express in words, they are vital to grasp fully the meaning and purpose of each discipline. Each of the disciplines alters its practitioner in certain very basic ways. This is why we refer to them as *personal* disciplines, even those that must be practiced collaboratively.

For example, systems thinking leads to experiencing more and more of the interconnectedness of life and to seeing wholes rather than parts. Whenever there are problems, in a family or in an organization, a master of systems thinking automatically sees them as arising from underlying structures rather than from individual mistakes or ill will. Likewise, personal mastery leads to an increased sense of "beingness," awareness of the present moment, both what is happening within us and outside of us, and to heightened experience of "generativeness," of being part of the creative forces shaping one's life.

At the level of essences, the disciplines start to converge. There is a common sensibility uniting the disciplines—the sensibility of being learners in an intrinsically interdependent world. Yet, there are still differences between the disciplines. But the differences become increasingly subtle. For example, "interconnectedness" (systems thinking) and "connectedness" (personal mastery) are subtle distinctions. The former has to do with awareness of how things interrelate to one another; the latter with awareness of being part of rather than apart from the world. So, too, is the distinction between "commonality of purpose" (shared vision) and "alignment" (team learning) a fine one. While the former has to do with a common direction and reason for being, the latter has to do with "functioning as a whole" when we actually work together. Though subtle, these distinctions are important. Just as the connoisseur of fine wines makes distinctions that the novice would not, so do individuals and groups who develop high levels of mastery in the disciplines see distinctions that might be obscure to beginners.

Lastly, the disciplines of building shared vision and team learning differ from the other three in that they are inherently collective in nature. The practices are activities engaged in by groups. The principles must be understood by groups. And the essences are states of being experienced collectively.

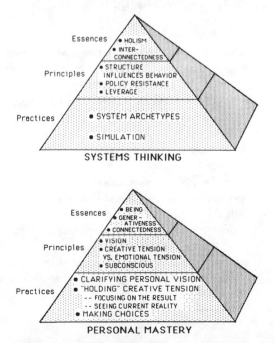

SYSTEMS THINKING

PERSONAL MASTERY

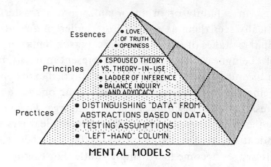

MENTAL MODELS

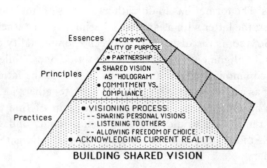

BUILDING SHARED VISION

One does not master a discipline all at once. There are distinct stages of learning that we all go through. Diana Smith has devised a three-stage continuum for developing new capacities that is helpful in approaching all the learning disciplines:

New Values and Assumptions	**Stage Three: Values and Operating Assumptions**
	People can string together rules that reflect new action values and operating assumptions. They can enact these rules under stress and ambiguity, continuing to aid their own and others' learning. By this stage, people will have adapted the rules into their own particular model, speaking in their own voice.
New Action Rules	**Stage Two: New Action Rules**
	As old assumptions "loosen" in response to the cognitive insights of Stage One, people begin to experiment with action rules based on new assumptions so they can see what they yield. They may need to rely on the new language to produce new actions, and they will find it difficult to access or string together new rules when under stress.

Stage One: New Cognitive Capacities

People see new things and can speak a new language. This allows them to see more clearly their own and others' assumptions, actions, and consequences of both. Typically, they find it hard to translate these new cognitive and linguistic competencies into fundamentally new actions. They may begin to behave differently, but the basic rules, assumptions, and values are the same.

New Cognitive, Linguistic Capacities

A P P E N D I X 2:
S Y S T E M S
A R C H E T Y P E S [1]

BALANCING PROCESS WITH DELAY

Structure:

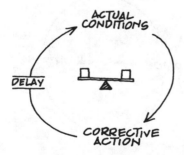

Description: A person, a group, or an organization, acting toward a goal, adjusts their behavior in response to delayed feedback. If they are not conscious of the delay, they end up taking more corrective action than needed, or (sometimes) just giving up because they cannot see that any progress is being made.

Early Warning Symptom: "We thought we were in balance, but then we over-shot the mark." (Later, you may overshoot in the other direction again.)

Management Principle: In a sluggish system, aggressiveness produces instability. Either be patient or make the system more responsive.

Business Story: Real estate developers keep building new properties until the market has gone soft—but, by then, there are already enough additional properties still under construction to guarantee a glut.

Other Examples: A shower where the hot water responds sluggishly to changes in the faucet positions; production/distribution glut and shortage cycles (such as that of the beer game); cycles in production rates and in-process inventory due to long manufacturing cycle times; the Tiananmen Square massacre, in which the government delayed its reaction to protest, and then cracked down unexpectedly hard; sudden, excessive stock market soars and crashes.

LIMITS TO GROWTH

Structure:

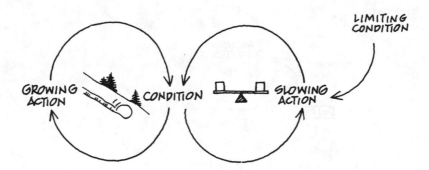

Description: A process feeds on itself to produce a period of accelerating growth or expansion. Then the growth begins to slow (often inexplicably to the participants in the system) and eventually comes to a halt, and may even reverse itself and begin an accelerating collapse.

The growth phase is caused by a reinforcing feedback process (or by several reinforcing feedback processes). The slowing arises due to a balancing process brought into play as a "limit" is approached. The limit can be a resource constraint, or an external or internal response to growth. The accelerating collapse (when it occurs) arises from the reinforcing process operating in reverse, to generate more and more contraction.

Early Warning Symptom: "Why should we worry about problems we don't have? We're growing tremendously." (A little later, "Sure there are some problems, but all we have to do is go back to what was working before." Still later, "The harder we run, the more we seem to stay in the same place.")

Management Principle: Don't push on the reinforcing (growth) process, remove (or weaken) the source of limitation.

Business Story: A company instituted an affirmative action program, which grew in support and activity as well-qualified minority employees were successfully introduced into work teams throughout the company. But eventually resistance emerged; the new staffers were perceived as not having "earned" their positions over other qualified aspirants. The harder individual teams were pressured to accept the new members, the more they resisted.

Other Examples: Learning a new skill, such as tennis, you make rapid progress early on as your competence and confidence builds, but then you begin to encounter limits to your natural abilities that can be overcome only by learning new techniques that may come "less naturally" at first.

A new startup that grows rapidly until it reaches a size that requires more professional management skills and formal organization; a new product team that works beautifully until its success causes it to bring in too many new members who neither share the work style nor values of the founding members; a city that grows steadily until available land is filled, leading to rising housing prices; a social movement that grows until it encounters increasing resistance from "nonconverts"; an animal population that grows rapidly when its natural predators are removed, only to overgraze its range and decline due to starvation.

SHIFTING THE BURDEN

Structure: See figure on following page.

Description: A short-term "solution" is used to correct a problem, with seemingly positive immediate results. As this correction is used more and more, more fundamental long-term corrective measures are used less and less. Over time, the capabilities for the fundamental solution may atrophy or become disabled, leading to even greater reliance on the symptomatic solution.

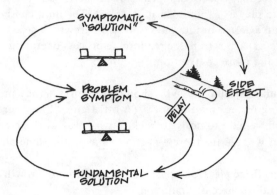

Early Warning Symptom: "Look here, this solution has worked so far! What do you mean, there's trouble down that road?"

Management Principle: Focus on the fundamental solution. If symptomatic solution is imperative (because of delays in fundamental solution), use it to gain time while working on the fundamental solution.

Business Story: A dramatic new circuit board technology can be used to develop unique functionality and cost savings in a great many new product applications, but it can also be substituted for existing boards in current products. Salespeople can try to sell to "specialty customers" who appreciate the special properties of the technology and will eventually design new products which exploit it fully (the "fundamental solution") or sell to "commodity customers" who do not care about its special properties and will simply substitute it for other boards (the "symptomatic solution"). Given management pressures to meet quarterly sales targets, salespeople sell to whoever is ready to buy, which usually will be commodity customers since there are more of them and delays in the selling cycle are shorter. Over time, the dramatic new technology fails to develop a loyal customer base and becomes subject to the price and margin pressures that characterize commodity products.

Other Examples: Selling more to existing customers rather than broadening the customer base (The "ATP case" from Chapter 11); paying bills by borrowing, instead of going through the discipline of budgeting; using alcohol, drugs, or even something as benign as exercise to relieve work stress and thereby not facing the need to control the workload itself; and any addiction, anywhere, to anything.

SPECIAL CASE: SHIFTING THE BURDEN TO THE INTERVENOR

Structure:

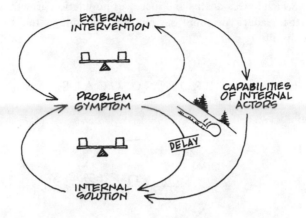

One area where shifting the burden structures are so common and so pernicious that it warrants special notice is when outside "intervenors" try to help solve problems. The intervention attempts to ameliorate obvious problem symptoms, and does so so successfully that the people within the system never learn how to deal with the problems themselves.

Management Principle: "Teach people to fish, rather than giving them fish." Focus on enhancing the capabilities of the "host system" to solve its own problems. If outside help is needed, "helpers" should be strictly limited to a one-time intervention (and everyone knows this in advance) or be able to help people develop their own skills, resources, and infrastructure to be more capable in the future.

Business Story: An innovative insurance company was committed to the concept of independent local offices that would call on headquarters staff only for occasional help. Initially the concept worked well, until the industry went through a crisis. Facing sudden severe losses, the local offices called in the more experienced central management for help in rewriting rate structures—a process which took months. Meanwhile, the local managers focused their attention on managing the crisis. The crisis was resolved, but the next time rate structures were called into question, the local offices had lost some of their confidence. They called in the central managers as "insurance." After several years of this behavior, the local offices found themselves without underwriters who could manage rate structure changes independently.

Other Examples: Dependence on outside contractors instead of training your own people. Numerous forms of government aid that attempt to solve pressing problems only to foster dependency and need for increasing aid: welfare systems that foster single-family households; housing or job training programs that attract the needy to cities with the best programs; food aid to developing countries which lowers deaths and increases population growth; social security systems that reduce personal savings and encourage the breakup of the extended family.

ERODING GOALS

Structure:

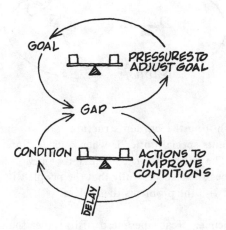

Description: A shifting the burden type of structure in which the short-term solution involves letting a long-term, fundamental goal decline.

Early Warning Symptom: "It's okay if our performance standards slide a little, just until the crisis is over."

Management Principle: Hold the vision.

Business Story: A high-tech manufacturer finds itself losing market share, despite a terrific product and ongoing improvements. But the firm, oriented toward its design "geniuses," had never gotten production scheduling under control. An outside investigator discovered that customers were increasingly dissatisfied with late schedules, and were turning to competitors instead. The company stood on its record: "We've maintained a consistent 90 percent success in meeting the delivery time quoted to the customer." It therefore looked elsewhere for the problem. However, every time the company begin to slip its schedules, it responded by making the quoted delivery time a little longer. Thus, the quoted delivery time to customers was getting lengthier, and lengthier, and lengthier . . .

Other Examples: Successful people who lower their own expectations for themselves and gradually become less successful. Firms that tacitly lower their quality standards by cutting budgets rather than investing in developing new higher quality (and perhaps lower cost) ways of doing things, all the while proclaiming their continued commitment to quality. Lowered government targets for "full employment" or balancing the federal deficit. Sliding targets for controlling dangerous pollutants or protecting endangered species.

ESCALATION

Structure:[2]

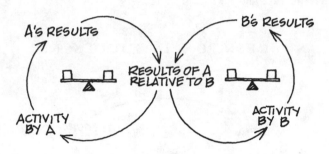

Description: Two people or organizations each see their welfare as depending on a relative advantage over the other. Whenever one side gets ahead, the other is more threatened, leading it to act more aggressively to reestablish its advantage, which threatens the first, increasing its aggressiveness, and so on. Often each side sees its own aggressive behavior as a defensive response to the other's aggression; but each side acting "in defense" results in a buildup that goes far beyond either side's desires.

Early Warning Symptom: "If our opponent would only slow down, then we could stop fighting this battle and get some other things done."

Management Principle: Look for a way for both sides to "win," or to achieve their objectives. In many instances, one side can unilaterally reverse the vicious spiral by taking overtly aggressive "peaceful" actions that cause the other to feel less threatened.

Business Story: A company developed an ingenious design for a stroller, which carried three toddlers at once, yet was light and convenient for travel. It was an immediate hit with families with several young children. Almost simultaneously, a competitor emerged with a similar product. After several years, jealous of the other company's share of the market, the first company lowered its price by 20 percent. The second company felt a decline in sales, and lowered its price too. Then the first company, still committed to boosting share, lowered its prices still further. The second company reluctantly did the same, even though its profits were beginning to suffer. Several years later, both companies were barely breaking even, and survival of the triple carriage was in doubt.

Other Examples: Advertising wars. Increasing reliance on lawyers to settle disputes. Gang warfare. The breakup of a marriage. Inflating budget estimates: as some groups inflate their estimates, others find themselves doing likewise in order to get "their piece of the pie," which leads to everyone inflating his estimates still further. Battle for the "ear" of the president of a company. And, of course, the arms race and the war on terror.

SUCCESS TO THE SUCCESSFUL

Structure:

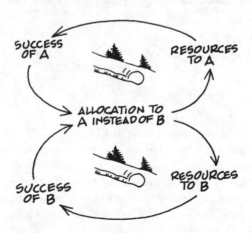

Description: Two activities compete for limited support or resources. The more successful one becomes, the more support it gains, thereby starving the other.

Early Warning Symptom: One of the two interrelated activities, groups, or individuals is beginning to do very well and the other is struggling.

Management Principle: Look for the overarching goal for balanced achievement of both choices. In some cases, break or weaken the coupling between the two, so that they do not compete for the same limited resource (this is desirable in cases where the coupling is inadvertent and creates an unhealthy competition for resources).

Business Story: A manager has two proteges, and wishes to bring both along equally in the firm. However, one of the two ends up getting preferential treatment because the other is out sick for a week. When the second protege returns to work, the manager feels guilty, and avoids the person, thereby giving still more opportunity to the first protege. The first protege, feeling the approval, flourishes, and therefore gets more opportunity. The second protege, feeling insecure, does less effective work and receives even fewer opportunities, although the two people had equal ability in the beginning. Eventually, the second protege leaves the firm.

Other examples: Balancing home and work life, in which a worker gets caught working overtime so much that relationships at home deteriorate and it gets more and more "painful" to go home, which, of course, makes the worker even more likely to neglect home life in the future. Two products compete for limited financial and managerial resources within a firm; one is an immediate hit in the marketplace and receives more investment, which depletes the resources available to the other, setting in motion a reinforcing spiral fueling growth of the first and starving the second. A shy student gets off to a poor start in school (perhaps because of emotional problems or an undetected learning disability), becomes labeled a "slow learner," and gets less and less encouragement and attention than his or her more outgoing peers.

TRAGEDY OF THE COMMONS

Structure:

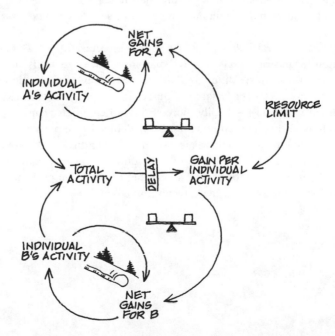

Description: Individuals use a commonly available but limited resource solely on the basis of individual need. At first they are rewarded for using it; eventually, they get diminishing returns, which causes them to intensify their efforts. Eventually, the resource is either significantly depleted, eroded, or entirely used up.

Early Warning Symptom: "There used to be plenty for everyone. Now things are getting tough. If I'm going to get any profit out of it this year, I'll have to work harder."

Management Principle: Manage the "commons," either through educating everyone and creating forms of self-regulation and peer pressure, or through an official regulating mechanism, ideally designed by participants.

Business Story: Several divisions of a company agreed to share a retail salesforce. Each district manager was initially concerned that the shared salesforce wouldn't give enough attention to his or her particular business, and that volume would decline. One particularly aggressive manager advised all his account managers to set higher sales targets than were truly needed, so that the salesforce would at least give them the minimum support they needed. The other divisions saw this division pushing for extra work, and decided to employ the same strategy. The new salesforce's managers wanted to accommodate all of their "clients," so they continued to accept the higher requests from the divisions. This created a tremendous overburden of work, lowered performance, and increased turnover. Pretty soon, joining the retail salesforce was only slightly more popular than joining the French Foreign Legion, and each division had to go back to maintaining its own salesforce.

Other Examples: Exhaustion of a shared secretarial pool. Deteriorating reputation for customer service after customers have had to listen to six different salespeople from six different divisions of the same corporation pitching competing products. (The "shared resource" in this case was the firm's positive customer reputation.) A highly successful retail chain gives up on joint sales promotions with manufacturers after being deluged with proposals by enthusiastic manufacturers, or establishes terms for joint ventures that leave little profit for the manufacturers. Depletion of a natural resource by competing companies which mine it. And, of course, all manner of pollution problems from acid rain to ozone depletion and the "greenhouse effect."

FIXES THAT FAIL

Structure:

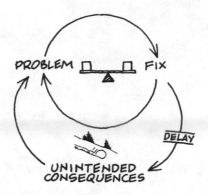

Description: A fix, effective in the short term, has unforeseen long-term consequences which may require even more use of the same fix.

Early Warning Symptom: "It always seemed to work before; why isn't it working now?"

Management Principle: Maintain focus on the long term. Disregard short-term "fix," if feasible, or use it only to "buy time" while working on long-term remedy.

Business Story: A manufacturing company launched a new set of high-performance parts, which were wildly successful at first. However, the CEO was driven by maximizing his ROI, so he deferred ordering expensive, new production machines. Manufacturing quality suffered, which led to a reputation for low quality. Customer demand fell off dramatically over the ensuing year, which depressed returns and made the CEO even more unwilling to invest in new production equipment.

Other Examples: People and organizations who borrow to pay interest on other loans, thereby ensuring that they will have to pay even more interest later. Cutting back maintenance schedules to save costs, which eventually leads to more breakdowns and higher costs, creating still more cost-cutting pressures.

GROWTH AND UNDERINVESTMENT

Structure: See figure on following page

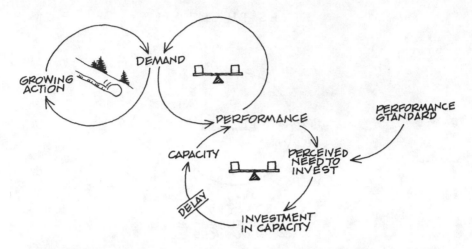

Description: Growth approaches a limit which can be eliminated or pushed into the future if the firm, or individual, invests in additional "capacity." But the investment must be aggressive and sufficiently rapid to forestall reduced growth, or else it will never get made. Oftentimes, key goals or performance standards are lowered to justify underinvestment. When this happens, there is a self-fulfilling prophecy where lower goals lead to lower expectations, which are then borne out by poor performance caused by underinvestment. (This is the Wondertech structure described in Chapter 7.)

Early Warning Symptom: "Well, we used to be the best, and we'll be the best again, but right now we have to conserve our resources and not over-invest."

Management Principle: If there is a genuine potential for growth, build capacity in advance of demand, as a strategy for creating demand. Hold the vision, especially as regards assessing key performance standards and evaluating whether capacity to meet potential demand is adequate.

Business Story: People Express Airlines found itself unable to build service capacity to keep pace with exploding demand. Rather than putting more resources into training or growing more slowly (for example, through raising prices somewhat), the firm tried to "outgrow" its problems. The result was deteriorating service quality and increased competition, while morale deteriorated. In order to keep up with the continued stress, the company relied more and more on the "solution" of underinvesting in service capacity, until customers no longer found flying People Express attractive.

Other Examples: Companies which let service quality or product quality of any sort decline, simultaneously blaming competition or their sales management for not pushing hard enough to maintain sales. People with grand visions who never realistically assess the time and effort they must put in to achieve their visions.

APPENDIX 3:
THE U PROCESS

The U process was developed by C. Otto Scharmer, Joseph Jaworski, Adam Kahane, and many of their colleagues as a way to design and lead deep collective learning processes.[1] In effect, it can provide a framework for organizing how the five disciplines are used in time (see Figure 1).

The U process helps a group collaboratively undertake:

1. sensing: deep inquiry into their mental models through seeing reality beyond their filters
2. presencing: moving from there to a deep process of connecting with purpose and visioning, individually and collectively
3. realizing: then moving into rapid prototyping to translate visions into concrete working models from which feedback can be garnered and further adjustments made.

While the five disciplines may be used in all three phases of the U, they are naturally emphasized in different areas. Moving "down the U" especially concerns suspending established mental models and engaging in a process of collective inquiry based on directly experiencing the system, as well as dialogue involving many points of view regarding reality. Personal and shared visioning are central to the bottom of the U, and team learning, along with continual reflection on mental models and visions, characterizes moving "up the U."

For example, for members of the Sustainable Food Lab, sensing involved, in addition to reflection on individual ways of seeing global food systems, the five-day learning journey in Brazil. This meant talking directly with struggling farmers and their families, farmer cooperatives, multinational commodity producers, environmental NGOs, and government agencies. The experience was especially powerful for those from the corporations who had never encountered the actual system "on the ground."

"In most of Latin America the farmer has stopped being a development agent and is now a client, a recipient of poverty-reduction programs," said one team member. Another asked, "What are we going to do about young people [displaced from traditional rural communities] with no future?" The experience was powerful also as a way of seeing how different people encountering the same reality make sense of it in very different ways. After a visit with a small farmers' cooperative, a list of observations from the team included: hardworking, very political, not sustainable, very sustainable, needs to be modernized, needs time to mature, an excellent model. "I am so amazed that [we] can look at the same thing and see something so different . . . There is so much I don't understand about others' perspectives," said one lab team member.

At the bottom of the U, there is silence and listening to what is seeking to emerge and to our own part in creating the new. Relative to the five disciplines, the U process offers a distinctive approach to visioning, by placing it at the bottom of the U, after the extended process of sensing. First, this sequencing guarantees that people are deeply grounded in the reality of their situation, including recognition of the different realities for different people. Second, visioning becomes grounded in a sense of larger purpose. Although visions at the outset may be important for motivating the whole process, they invariably evolve and take on more depth and significance after the sensing phase. This does not mean that people somehow "derive" their vision from assessing present reality. Quite the opposite. At the bottom of the U, allowing time for true quiet and deep reflection tends to evoke genuine caring and a sense of calling. In terms of the principle of creative tension, connecting strongly with the current reality enables new choices for telling the truth about what we really want.

For the thirty members of the core Sustainable Food Lab team, the six-day retreat enabled synthesizing the learning journey experiences, deepening their sense of purpose in creating alternative systems, and developing the initial prototyping initiatives. The two-day wilderness "solo" enabled quiet and a more direct connection with nature, both the living systems within which they sat and their own nature. Economist Brian Arthur, who helped prepare the team members for their solo experience and worked with them when they returned, observed that the energy in the group had shifted to "stillness and good-heartedness." Out of this stillness came a quality of imaginativeness that led to prototyping initiatives no one had thought of before.

Moving up the right side of the U can likewise involve all the disciplines, but team learning is especially important because a group is learning together how to create alternative ways for a complex system to operate that are both practical and radical. Pervading the whole realizing phase are systems thinking, working with mental models, and visions, because the sensing and presencing processes continually repeat. This occurs for two reasons: (1) new members enter the prototyping initiatives (and must go through their own sensing and presencing); (2) people discover new facts about the reality of the system through attempting to bring about change and continually revisiting their visions, and may discover that the vision has changed. Following the principle of creative tension, changes in visions moving up the U do not represent "lowering the vision" to lessen emotional tension but rather represent truly seeing what people truly want to create.

So, the realizing phase is not only creating successful alternatives to the present system but also continually deepening shared understanding and clarifying visions. Some of the efforts to realize alternative systems will succeed and some will fail. Those that succeed quite often succeed in ways that no one anticipated or evolve in new and unexpected directions. The real point in moving up the U, and the point of the whole U process, is building capacity in large and diverse communities to see "what is" and to enact new social systems. It is learning how to learn for complex intra- and inter-organizational networks. "I have never seen a process quite like this," said Oran Hesterman, head of agricultural programs for the Kellogg Foundation, the Sustainable Food Lab's major sponsor, "for bringing a very diverse group to a profound place of connection, with one another and with what it is we are here to do."

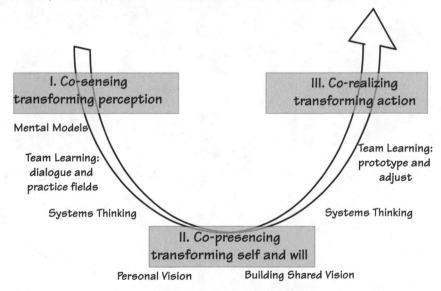

Figure 1. The U Process and the Five Disciplines

NOTES

INTRODUCTION TO REVISED EDITION

1. This list was developed by a group of business and education innovators convened by SoL (Society for Organizational Learning) and the Change Leadership Group of the Harvard Graduate School of Education. (Booth Sweeney, Senge, Wagner, 2002).

CHAPTER 1
"GIVE ME A LEVER LONG ENOUGH...AND SINGLE-HANDED I CAN MOVE THE WORLD"

1. Daniel Yankelovich, *New Rules: Searching for Self-fulfillment in a World Turned Upside Down* (New York: Random House), 1981.
2. I am indebted to my MIT colleague Alan Graham for the insight that basic innovation occurs through the integration of diverse technologies into a new ensemble. See A. K. Graham, "Software Design: Breaking the Bottleneck," *IEEE Spectrum* (March 1982): 43–50; A. K. Graham and P. Senge, "A Long-Wave Hypothesis of Innovation," Technological Forecasting and Social Change (1980): 283–311.
3. Arie de Geus, "Planning as Learning," *Harvard Business Review* (March/April 1988): 70–74.

4. Although semi-conductor and software producers like Intel and Microsoft eventually came to dominate the computer industry financially, Apple pioneered the commercialization of the "graphical user interface," which brought friendly, easy-to-use computers to the mainstream public.

5. Edward Hall, *Beyond Culture* (New York: Anchor), 2007, 207.

CHAPTER 2
DOES YOUR ORGANIZATION HAVE
A LEARNING DISABILITY?

1. Arie de Geus, "Planning as Learning," *Harvard Business Review* (March/April 1988): 70–74.

2. These figures come from the United States Department of Commerce, *U.S. Industrial Outlook,* in 1962 (pp. 58-59), 1970 (p. 355), 1975 (p. 355), 1979 (p. 287), 1981 (p. 320), and 1989 (pp. 34–35), and U.S. Congress Office of Technology Assessment, *Technology and the American Economic Transition: Choices for the Future Washington:* (U.S. Government Printing Office), 1988 (p. 326).

3. Draper Kauffman, Jr. *Systems 1: An Introduction to Systems Thinking* (Minneapolis: Future Systems Inc.), 1980 (available through Innovation Associates, P.O. Box 2008, Framingham, MA 01701).

4. Chris Argyris, *Overcoming Organizational Defenses* (New York: Prentice-Hall), 1990.

5. Barbara Tuchman, *The March of Folly: From Troy to Vietnam* (New York: Knopf), 1984.

6. Ibid.

7. Jared Diamond, *Collapse: How Societies Choose to Fail or Succeed* (New York: Penguin), 2004.

CHAPTER 3
PRISONERS OF THE SYSTEM, OR
PRISONERS OF OUR OWN THINKING?

1. Directions for the interactive game can be obtained from the System Dynamics Group at MIT Sloan School of Management, Cambridge MA 02139. http://www.systemdynamics.org/Beer.htm.

2. In the actual decision-making simulation there are four positions, one of which (a distributor) is omitted to simplify the story—which is complicated enough as it is.

3. But, of course, any simulation is a simplification. You might wonder if changing any of the details of the game would change the results. Wondering the same thing, we've tinkered often over the years. Sometimes, as in the story told

here, there are three players. Usually, we play with four. We've varied the penalties imposed for excess inventory and for backlogs. Sometimes we use a computer simulation to make the calculations; most times we set up a big board game on long tables, moving pennies from square to square to represent beer deliveries. Players have been given different amounts of advance information about the range of consumer demands that retailers can expect. Different patterns of consumer demand have been tried. Some of these variations make the crisis slightly more extreme; some make it slightly milder. But none affect the overall pattern of crises.

4. U.S. Congress Office of Technology Assessment: *Technology and the American Economic Transition: Choices for the Future* (Washington: U.S. Government Printing Office), 1988, 324.

5. Steven Burke, "Chip Manufacturers Find a Pot of Gold in DRAM Shortage," PC Week, May 31, 1988, 107; Steven Burke and Ken Sieg-mann, "Memory-Board Prices Surging in the Wake of Growing Chip Shortage," *PC Week,* March 1, 1988, 1.

6. J. Rhea "Profits Peak as Semiconductor Sales Boom," *Electronic News* 18:1 (August 6, 1973); "Boom Times Again for Semiconductors," *Business Weekly,* April 20, 1974, 65-68; "Semiconductors Take a Sudden Plunge," Business Week, November 16, 1974, 64-65; F. Pollare, "Inventory Buildup: Semiconductor Distress Sales Emerge," *Electronic News* 20:45 (February 10, 1975).

7. Joseph B. White and Bradley A. Stertz, "Auto Industry Battens Down for a Slump," *Wall Street Journal,* May 30, 1989, sec. A.

8. "MacNeil-Lehrer Newshour," video documentary on the beer game and business cycles (interview with John Sterman at MIT), aired November 1989, Public Broadcasting System.

9. Donella H. Meadows, "Whole Earth Models and Systems," *Co-Evolution Quarterly* (Summer 1982): 98-108.

10. Leo Tolstoy, *War and Peace* (Constance Garnett translation).

11. Ibid.

12. Janice T. Gibson and Mika Haritos-Fatouros, "The Education of a Torturer," *Psychology Today,* November 1986, 50. Also: "The Mind is a Formidable Liar: A Pirandellian Prison," *New York Times Magazine,* April 8, 1973.

13. Similar amplification is characteristic of real business cycles, where raw material producing industries typically fluctuate far more than retail and service industries. See Gottfried Haberler, *Prosperity and Depression* (London: Alien & Unwin), 1964; Alvin H. Hansen, *Business Cycles and National Income* (New York: Norton), 1951.

14. John Sterman, "Modeling Managerial Behavior: Misperceptions of Feedback in a Dynamic Decisionmaking Experiment," *Management Science,* vol. 35, no. 3 (March 1989): 335.

15. When simulated by computer, the results for the "no strategy" strategy show that the retailer has the worst backlogs because he only starts receiving full

shipments once the supplier's backlogs are eliminated. This means that retailers would be especially vulnerable under this strategy—which is precisely why most retailers place larger orders in the real world.

16. In the simulation game, total costs are computed by assessing $1.00 cost for each backlog unit (each week) and $0.50 for each inventory unit (each week), and by summing the resulting costs of each position to calculate a total team cost. An average cost for a four-stage game of thirty-five weeks is $2,028 (Sterman, "Modeling Managerial Behavior"), 331-39, corresponding to a cost of about $1,270 for thirty weeks in a three-stage game. The total team cost for the "do nothing" strategy is about $825.

17. Potentially, the players could learn from their experience in the game, in ways that players in real production-distribution systems cannot learn—if they were able to play the game repeatedly and to understand, collaboratively, how their decisions interact in the larger system. The beer game would then be a "microworld."

18. Because the game is usually not played with the different positions in regular contact, there is little opportunity to observe how the players fare in face-to-face interactions. Nonetheless, as the teams currently operate, most team members become consumed in blaming one another for their problems. Other decision-making simulations are designed to deal more directly with the dynamics of team learning.

19. A common example of seeing patterns of behavior in business is "trend analysis," so that a firm can best *respond* to shifting demographic trends or changing customer preferences.

20. William Manchester, *The Glory and the Dream* (Boston: Little, Brown), 1974, 80-81.

21. It is also possible to redesign the physical structure of the game, although this was not an option for the players when the game was first played. For example, you could redesign the information system so that wholesalers and breweries, as well as retailers, had current information on retail sales. Or, you could eliminate the middlemen entirely and have breweries supply retailers directly. Redesigning the physical system (physical flows of goods, people, and materials; information; rewards and other factors outside the individual decision makers' immediate control) is an important leadership function in real life. But success depends on leaders' systemic understanding, just as changing individual ways of placing orders depends on systemic understanding. Thus, achieving systemic understanding is the primary task, from which redesigning physical systems, as well as operating policies, can follow.

CHAPTER 4
THE LAWS OF THE FIFTH DISCIPLINE

1. These laws are distilled from the works of many writers in the systems field: Garrett Hardin, *Nature and Man's Fate* (New York: New American Library),

1961; Jay Forrester, *Urban Dynamics,* Chapter 6 (Cambridge, Mass.: MIT Press), 1969; Jay Forrester, "The Counterintuitive Behavior of Social Systems," *Technology Review* (January 1971, pp. 52-68; Donella H. Meadows "Whole Earth Models and Systems," *Co-Evolution Quarterly* (Summer 1982): 98-108; Draper Kauffman, Jr., *Systems I: An Introduction to Systems Thinking,* (Minneapolis: Future Systems Inc.), 1980 (available through Innovation Associates, P.O. Box 2008, Framingham, MA 01701.

2. This and many other Sufi tales can be found in the books of Idries Shah, eg., *Tales of the Dervishes* (New York: Dutton), 1970, and *World Tales* (New York: Harcourt Brace Jovanovich), 1979.

3. George Orwell, *Animal Farm* (New York: Harcourt Brace), 1954.

4. D. H. Meadows, "Whole Earth Models and Systems."

5. Lewis Thomas, *The Medusa and the Snail* (New York: Bantam Books), 1980.

6. Charles Hampden Turner, *Charting The Corporate Mind: Graphic Solutions to Business Conflicts* (New York: Free Press), 1990.

CHAPTER 5
A SHIFT OF MIND

1. A comprehensive summary of the "cybernetic" and "servo-mechanism" schools of thought in the social sciences can be found in George Richardson, *Feedback Thought in Social Science and Systems Theory* (Philadelphia: University of Pennsylvania Press), 1990.

2. The use of this term reflects a viewpoint, as many supporters of the "terrorist" cause claim that they are fighting for freedom. I use the term only because it reflects a widespread view across a broad political spectrum, including much of the Middle East, that organized attacks on civilians warrant this label.

3. There are probably more self-described "systems analysts" in the U.S. Department of Defense, National Security Agency, and CIA than in all other branches of government. For their part, the Soviets have pioneered in systems theory; for the past forty years, probably more theoretical contributions have come from Soviet mathematicians than from those of any other country. In part, the Soviet government sponsored systems research because of the great dream to use sophisticated computer tools for state control of the national economy.

4. See Nancy Roberts, "Teaching Dynamic Feedback Systems Thinking: An Elementary View," *Management Science* (April 1978), 836-843; and Nancy Roberts, "Testing the World with Simulations," *Classroom Computer News,* January/February 1983, 28.

5. The principles and tools of systems thinking have emerged from diverse roots in physics, engineering, biology, and mathematics. The particular tools presented in this chapter come from the "system dynamics" approach pioneered by Jay Forrester at MIT. See, for example, *Industrial Dynamics* (Cambridge, Mass.: MIT Press), 1961; *Urban Dynamics* (Cambridge, Mass.: MIT Press),

1969; and "The Counterintuitive Behavior of Social Systems," *Technology Review* (January 1971), 52-68. This particular section owes a special debt to Donella Meadows, whose earlier article "Whole Earth Models and Systems," *Co-Evolution Quarterly* (Summer 1982), 98-108 provided the model and the inspiration for its development.

6. By contrast, many "Eastern" languages such as Chinese and Japanese do not build up from subject-verb-object linear sequences. David Crystal, *The Cambridge Encyclopedia of Language* (New York: Cambridge University Press), 1987.

7. The *Bhagavad-Gita,* or "The Lord's Song," translated by Annie Besant, reprinted in Robert O. Ballou, *The Bible of the World* (New York: Viking), 1939.

8. Robert K. Merton, "The Self-Fulfilling Prophecy," in Robert K. Merton, editor, *Social Theory and Social Structure* (New York: Free Press), 1968.

9. R. Rosenthal, "Teacher Expectation and Pupil Learning"; and R. D. Strom, editor, *Teachers and the Learning Process* (Englewood Cliffs, N.J.: Prentice-Hall); R. Rosenthal, "The Pygmalion Effect Lives," *Psychology Today,* September 1973.

10. This does not suggest that free-market forces are sufficient for all forms of balance and control needed in modern societies—delays, inadequate information, unrealistic expectations, and distortions such as monopoly power also reduce efficiency of "free markets."

11. More information on lean manufacturing can be found on the Lean Enterprise Web site at www.lean.org.

CHAPTER 6
NATURE'S TEMPLATES: IDENTIFYING THE PATTERNS THAT CONTROL EVENTS

1. Two are presented in detail below, and eight altogether are used in this book. This is roughly half the archetypes that professional systems thinkers "carry in their heads."

2. Initial curricula building on generic structures have been developed. See Mark Paich, "Generic Structures," in *System Dynamics Review,* vol. 1, no. 1 (Summer 1985): 126-32; Alan Graham, "Generic Models as a Basis for Computer-Based Case Studies" (Cambridge, Mass.: System Dynamics Group Working Paper D-3947), 1988; Barry Richmond *et al., An Academic User's Guide to STELLA,* Chapters 8, 9 (Lyme, N.H.: High Performance Systems), 1987. David Kreutzer, "Introduction to Systems Thinking and Computer Simulation," *Lesley College Graduate Course Comp 6100,* 1987.

3. In this case, the balancing feedback process goes around the outside of the figure: from R&D budget, to increasing management complexity, longer product development times, reduced rate of new product introductions, and, eventually, back to smaller R&D budgets.

4. To my knowledge, Barry Richmond was the first to analyze this structure, which we have since found to be virtually endemic in management consulting firms, not to mention academic departments that grow rapidly, then become top heavy with tenured faculty.

5. Peter Senge, Art Kleiner, Charlotte Roberts, George Roth, Rick Ross, Bryan Smith, *The Dance of Change: The Challenges to Sustaining Momentum in Learning Organizations* (New York: Doubleday/Currency), 1999.

6. *Facts on File 1990* (New York: Facts on File).

7. This and the other "systems archetype" templates are reproduced with the permission of Innovation Associates, where they are used in the *Leadership and Mastery* and *Business Thinking: A Systems Approach* workshops.

8. Information on Alcoholics Anonymous can be found in the following books: *Alcoholics Anonymous,* 1976; *Living Sober,* 1975; *Twelve Steps and Twelve Traditions,* 1953; all published by Alcoholics Anonymous World Services, Inc., P.O. Box 459, Grand Central Station, New York, NY 10163.

CHAPTER 7
SELF-LIMITING OR SELF-SUSTAINING GROWTH

1. The model developed below derives from Jay Forrester's original studies of corporate growth: (Jay W. Forrester, "Modeling the Dynamic Processes of Corporate Growth," IBM Scientific Computing Symposium on Simulation Models and Gaming (December 1964), and J. W. Forrester, "Market Growth as Influenced by Capital Investment," *Industrial Management Review,* 1968, 83-105.

2. David Birch, *Job Creation in America* (New York: The Free Press), 1987, 18.

3. This figure is produced by computer simulation of the interrelationships of the WonderTech structure with a fixed delivery time standard. The simulation incorporates a simplifying assumption of an unlimited potential market, which was essentially true in WonderTech's early years. Even with realistic limits on the potential market, however, there is a dramatic improvement in behavior when the delivery time standard is held fixed. The simulation is done with STELLA, a systems thinking model building and simulation program available from High Performance Systems. The actual simulation model used is presented in Jay Forrester, 1968, and in P. Senge, "Systems Principles for Leadership," in *Transforming Leadership,* J. Adams, editor (Alexandria, Va.: Miles River Press), 1984.

CHAPTER 8
PERSONAL MASTERY

1. K. Inamori, "The Perfect Company: Goal for Productivity." Speech given at Case Western Reserve University, June 5, 1985.

2. A study by McKinsey & Co. from 1978–1993 entitled "The Journey" identified Hanover as one of only two companies to join the top quartile of the property and liability industry throughout the period. O'Brien retired as a consequence of a hostile takeover engineered by State Mutual, which had a majority share of the firm's ownership throughout this time period.

3. Henry Ford, *Detroit News,* February 7, 1926.

4. Robert Fritz, *The Path of Least Resistance* (New York: Fawcett-Columbine), 1989.

5. William O'Brien, *Character and the Corporation* (Cambridge, MA: SoL), 2006.

6. Ibid.

7. M. dePree, *Leadership is an Art* (New York: Doubleday), 1989.

8. George Bernard Shaw, *Man and Superman,* Preface (Penguin, 1950).

9. Pierre Wack, "Scenarios: Uncharted Ahead," *Harvard Business Review* (September/October 1985): 73–89.

10. This principle comes from the work of Robert Fritz, who calls it "structural tension." We shifted the terminology to avoid confusion with the word "structure" as used in systems thinking.

11. Bill Russell and Taylor Branch, *Second Wind: The Memoirs of an Opinionated Man* (New York: Random House), 1979.

12. Fritz's *Path of Least Resistance* delves into the reasons behind this habit.

13. Ibid.

14. Ibid.

15. David Kantor and William Lehr, *Inside the Family: Toward a Theory of Family Process* (San Francisco: Jossey-Bass), 1975.

16. The term "subconscious" has been used by many others, such as Freud and Jung, to represent phenomena somewhat different from those discussed here.

17. The following brief discussion borrows from many spiritual traditions, from developmental Christianity to Zen, but owes a special debt to the work of Robert Fritz (see note 3). Useful readings from these different traditions include, *Finding Grace at the Center,* editor Thomas Keating et al. (Still River, Mass.: St. Bede Publications), 1978; and Shunryu Suzuki Roshi, *Zen Mind, Beginner's Mind.* (New York and Tokyo: Weatherhill), 1975.

18. Quoted in Fritz, *The Path of Least Resistance.*

19. Weston Agor, *Intuitive Management: Integrating Left and Right Brain Management Skills* (Englewood Cliffs, N.J.: Prentice-Hall), 1984; Henry Mintzberg, "Planning on the Left Side and Managing on the Right," *Harvard Business Review* (July/August 1976): 49-58; Daniel Isenberg, "How Top Managers Think" *Harvard Business Review* (July/ August 1976): 49.

20. Karen Cook, "Scenario for a New Age; Can American Industry Find Renewal in Management Theories Born of Counterculture?" *New York Times Magazine,* September 25, 1988; Robert Lindsey, "Gurus Hired to Motivate Workers are Raising Fears of Mind Control," *New York Times,* April 17, 1987.

CHAPTER 9
MENTAL MODELS

1. H. Gardner, *The Mind's New Science* (New York: Basic Books), 1984, 1985.
2. C. Argyris, *Reasoning, Learning and Action: Individual and Organizational* (San Francisco: Jossey-Bass), 1982.
3. Thomas S. Kuhn, *The Structure of Scientific Revolutions* (Chicago: University of Chicago Press), 1962, 1970.
4. Ian Mitroff, *Break-Away Thinking* (New York: John Wiley), 1988.
5. The Detroit example also suggests that entire industries can develop mental models chronically out of touch with reality. In some ways, industries are especially vulnerable because all the individual members of the industry look to each other for standards of best practice. It may take someone from "outside the system," such as foreign competitors, with different mental models, to finally break the spell.
6. Pierre Wack, "Scenarios: Uncharted Waters Ahead," *Harvard Business Review* (September/October 1985), 72; and "Scenarios: Shooting the Rapids," *Harvard Business Review* (November/December 1985), 139.
7. "After the Middle East and the North African nations asserted themselves and took control of the oil in their lands, Shell's position was enhanced. It enjoyed an edge that has enabled it to come close to [its founder] Deterding's goal: eclipse Exxon as the world's largest oil company."—Milton Moskowitz in *The Global Marketplace* (New York: Macmillan), 1987.
8. The core values at Hanover, in addition to openness and merit, include "localness" (no decision should ever be made higher up than is absolutely necessary), and leanness (continually increasing the capacity to produce more, higher quality results with less resources).
9. C. Argyris and D. Schon, *Organizational Learning: A Theory of Action Perspective* (Reading, Mass.: Addison-Wesley), 1978; C. Argyris, R. Putnam, and D. Smith, *Action Science* (San Francisco: Jossey-Bass), 1985; C. Argyris, *Strategy, Change, and Defensive Routines* (Boston: Pitman), 1985.
10. Donald Schon, *The Reflective Practitioner: How Professionals Think in Action* (New York: Basic Books), 1983.
11. G. A. Miller, "The magical number seven plus or minus two: Some limits on our capacity for processing information," *Psychological Review,* vol. 63, 1956, 81-97.
12. I am indebted to Diana Smith for allowing me to reproduce these guidelines.
13. John Sterman, "Misperceptions of Feedback in Dynamic Decisionmaking," Cambridge, Mass.: MIT Sloan School of Management Working Paper WP-1933-87, 1987.

CHAPTER 10
SHARED VISION

1. Some facts about the man Spartacus come from Arthur Koestler's postscript to his novel *The Gladiator,* translated by Edith Simon (New York: Macmillan), 1939.
2. These cases of corporate vision have been analyzed by G. Hamel and C. K. Prahalad in "Strategic Intent," *Harvard Business Review,* May-June, 1989.
3. Kazuo Inamori, "The Perfect Company: Goal for Productivity," speech given at Case Western Reserve University, Cleveland, Ohio, June 5, 1985.
4. Max de Pree, *Leadership is an Art* (New York: Doubleday/Currency), 1989.
5. A. Maslow, *Eupsychian Management* (Homewood, Ill.: Richard Invin and Dorsey Press), 1965.
6. William Manchester, *The Glory and the Dream* (Boston: Little, Brown and Company), 1974.
7. G. Hamel and C. K. Prahalad, "Strategic Intent."
8. Ibid.
9. The ideas expressed in this section come from many hours of discussion with my colleagues at Innovation Associates, notably Charles Kiefer, Alain Gauthier, Charlotte Roberts, Rick Ross, and Bryan Smith.
10. M. Moskowitz, *The Global Marketplace* (New York: Macmillan Publishing Company), 1987.
11. "IBM's $5,000,000,000 Gamble," *Fortune,* September 1966, and "The Rocky Road to the Marketplace," *Fortune,* October 1966 (two-part article).

CHAPTER 11
TEAM LEARNING

1. W. Russell and T. Branch, *Second Wind: Memoirs of an Opinionated Man* (New York: Random House), 1979.
2. This diagram appeared originally in C. Kiefer and P. Stroh, "A New Paradigm for Developing Organizations," in J. Adams, editor, *Transforming Work* (Alexandria Va.: Miles Riler Press), 1984.
3. This section benefited especially from conversations with Bill Isaacs and with David Bohm, who was also very kind letting me reproduce many of his observations. See also William Isaacs, *Dialogue and the Art of Thinking Together* (New York: Currency), 1999.
4. David Bohm, *The Special Theory of Relativity* (New York: W. A. Benjamin), 1965.
5. Many of David Bohm's statements contained here come from a series of "dialogues" in which David participated in Cambridge and elsewhere for many years. I am deeply grateful for his permission to include them here, as well as excerpts from his book, with coauthor Mark Edwards, provisionally entitled *Thought, the Hidden Challenge to Humanity* (San Francisco: Harper & Row).

Other related books include *Wholeness and the Implicate Order* (New York: Ark Paperbacks), 1983; with F. D. Peat, *Science, Order, and Creativity* (New York: Bantam), 1987.

6. See, for example, E. Schein, *Process Consultation,* vol. 2 (Reading, Mass.: Addison Wesley), 1987.
7. C. Argyris, *Strategy, Change, and Defensive Routines* (Boston: Pitman), 1985.
8. Ibid.
9. Ibid.
10. See, for example, D. C. Wise and G. C. Lewis, "A Fire Sale in Personal Computers," Business Week, March 25, 1985, 289, and "Rocky Times for Micros," *Marketing Media Decisions,* July 1985.
11. Argyris, *Strategy, Change, and Defensive Routines.*
12. Interestingly, reduced threat in talking about sensitive issues is exactly what happens in "dialogue sessions," where the ground rules are such that concern for "right" or "wrong" insights quickly disappears. As dialogue sessions become a regular part of how teams work together, such threats perceived by team members may well decline generally.
13. In order to move beyond defenses, it helps to create a learning environment— what we call a microworld—in which people can openly explore their hesitancies about moving toward more openness. When people surface their hesitancies in such a setting, it's possible to design mini-experiments that help them to incrementally try out new ways of acting in the face of their concerns.
14. Donald Schon, *The Reflective Practitioner: How Professionals Think in Action* (New York: Basic Books), 1983.
15. The names and other specifics of this story are fictitious but the dialogue itself, and the background organizational issues it addressed, are real. The dialogue is reproduced from transcripts of the actual meeting (which is a common feature of our research on team learning), which are only shortened, not edited, in an attempt to preserve the feeling of the dialogue itself. I am indebted to Bill Isaacs for his help in organizing this material.
16. Michael Porter, *Competitive Advantage: Creating and Sustaining Superior Performance* (New York: Free Press), 1985, and Michael Porter, *Competitive Strategy: Techniques for Analyzing Industries and Competitors* (New York: Free Press), 1980.

CHAPTER 12
FOUNDATIONS

1. Chris Argyris, "Good Communication That Blocks Learning," *Harvard Business Review*, July-August, 1994, 77-85.
2. Jay Bragdon, *Living Asset Management* (Cambridge, Mass.: SoL), 2006 (forthcoming); Jim Collins, *Built to Last* (New York: HarperCollins), 1997.
3. Unilever recruited other businesses, governmental, and nongovernmental organizations to establish a global certification process for sustainable fisheries,

the Marine Stewardship Council. The company has also started related initiatives focused on sustainable agriculture and water conservation. See the Web site www.unilever.com

4. Sayra Pinto, Jasson Guevera, and Molly Baldwin, "Living the Change You Seek: Roca's Core Curriculum for Human Development," *Reflections, the SoL Journal*, vol. 5, no. 4. For more on Roca, see the Web site www.roca.org.

5. As we are using the terms here, you can be a "user of a tool" but you are a "practitioner of organizational learning."

6. Arie de Geus, *The Living Company* (Boston: Harvard Business School Press), 2002.

7. Dee Hock, *One From Many; Visa and the Rise of Chaordic Organizations* (San Francisco: Berrett-Koehler), 2005.

8. Gregory Bateson, *Steps To and Ecology of Mind* (New York: Ballantine), 1972

9. Anne Murray Allen and Dennis Sandow, "The Nature of Social Collaboration," *Reflections, the SoL Journal*, vol. 6, no. 2.

10. Murray Allen and Sandow, op cit., 1.

CHAPTER 13
IMPETUS

1. For example, the IFC formulated its first explicit goals around sustainability in 2002, built on the belief that improving projects' impact beyond the financial bottom line—to include corporate governance, and environment and social sustainability measures—makes good business sense.

2. Robert Axelrod and Michael Cohen, *Harnessing Complexity: Organizational Implications of a Scientific Frontier* (New York: Basic Books), 2000.

3. The following comments are based on Khoo Boon Hui's speech at the Knowledge Management Asia conference, November 2, 2004, along with further conversations.

CHAPTER 14
STRATEGIES

1. This diagram has gone through many versions since it was first introduced in *The Fifth Discipline Fieldbook*, although the basic distinctions have remained the same.

2. The symbolism of the triangle and the circle suggest what is apparent and what is less obvious, what is "above the surface" and what is "below the surface." Skillful organizational leaders, like skillful teachers, know that they cannot cause the deep learning cycle to change anymore than teachers can cause students to learn. What they can do is create an environment within which learning is more likely to occur. This is the meaning of strategic architecture.

3. Taken-for-granted assumptions are regarded by Edgar Schein as the deepest

level of culture. The other two levels in Schein's framework are artifacts (dress, speech, style of meetings, etc.) and expressed values (such as official mission statements) are both easier to change than underlying assumptions. See Edgar Schein, *The Corporate Culture Survival Guide* (San Francisco: Jossey-Bass), 1999.

4. The basic connections shown around the deep learning cycle simplify the many feedback interactions that exist among these elements. For example, practices shape skills and capabilities because they provide recurring opportunities to learn particular skills, but the reverse is also true in the sense that our current skills determine our practices, what we are good at doing,

5. A check-in gives every member of a group an opportunity to reflect and share their thoughts prior to beginning a meeting. See Peter Senge, et al., *The Dance of Change*, 192.

6. Adapted from Marilyn Darling, David Meador, and Shawn Patterson, "Cultivating a Learning Economy," *Reflections, the SoL Journal*, vol. 5, no. 2.

7. Ann Graham, "The Learning Organization: Managing Knowledge for Business Success," Economist Intelligence Unit, New York, 1996.

8. Ibid.

9. George Roth and Art Kleiner, *Car Launch: The Human Side of Managing Change* (New York: Oxford University Press), 1999.

10. Art Kleiner, *The Age of Heretics* (New York: Currency), 1996.

11. Peter Senge, et al, *The Dance of Change: The Challenges to Sustaining Momentum in Learning Organizations* (New York: Doubleday/Currency), 1999.

12. William McDonough and Michael Braungart, *Cradle to Cradle: Remaking the Way We Make Things* (New York: North Point Press), 2002. For more specific information on the toxicological assessment, see www.greenblue.org, and the authors' Web site at www.mbdc.com.

13. PVC polyvinyl chloride is generally considered to be inert and nonharmful in a product like a shoe sole, but can release toxic gas in some manufacturing processes and when incinerated.

14. Margaret Wheatley's Web site is www.margaretwheatley.com. Her most recent book is *Finding Our Way* (San Francisco: Berrett-Koehler), 2005. See also *Leadership and the New Science* (San Francisco: Berrett-Koehler), 1999.

15. J. Clay, "Exploring the Links Between International Business and Poverty Reduction," Oxfam GB, Novib, Unilever, and Unilever Indonesia joint research project report, 2005. To download a copy of the report, see http://www.oxfam.org.uk.

16. This term was not used during the first decade of work on how systems thinking, personal and shared vision, and mental models could become integrated in practical work settings. Charles Kiefer and Peter Senge, "Metanoic Organizations, in J. Adams, *Transforming Work* (Alexandria, Va: Miles River Press), 1984.

CHAPTER 15
THE LEADER'S NEW WORK

1. The related paper, "The Leader's New Work," became one of MIT *Sloan Management Review*'s bestselling articles. Reprint 3211; Fall 1990, vol. 32, no. 1, 7–23.

2. See also, Peter Senge, "Leading Learning Organizations: The Bold, the Powerful, and the Invisible," in Frances Hesselbein, Marshall Goldsmith, and Richard Beckhard, *The Leader of The Future: New Visions, Strategies, and Practices for the Next Era* (San Francisco, CA: Jossey-Bass, Publishers), 1996 and Peter Senge and Katrin Kaeufer, "Communities of Leaders or No Leadership at All," in Ed. Subir Chuwdhury, *Management in the 21st Century* (London: Financial Times Publishing), 2000.

3. Juanita Brown and David Isaacs, *The World Café* (San Francisco: Berrett-Koehler), 2005.

4. Wanda Orlikowski, "Learning from Notes," *The Information Society,* 9, 1993, 237-250.

5. The four principles are: Inspire her to be healthy and active; Honor all stages of her life; Connect with her; Live and Work in Favor of the Future.

6. Robert Greenleaf, *Servant Leadership: a Journey into the Nature of Legitimate Power and Greatness* (New York: Paulist Press), 1977, 13.

7. H. Thomas Johnson is a world-famous accounting theorist, co-inventor of activity-based accounting, and coauthor of *Profit Beyond Measure* (2002), which documents radical innovations in performance management in companies like Toyota where the traditional centralized cost management system in manufacturing businesses has been replaced by local accountability for cost performance and innovation.

8. Sayra Pinto, Jaason Guevera, Molly Baldwin, "Living the Change You Seek: Roca's Core Curriculum for Human Development," ibid.

9. Robert Greenleaf, *op cit*, 13. See also Peter Block, *Stewardship* (San Francisco: Berrett-Koehler), 1996.

10. Eric Hoffer, *The True Believer* (New York: Harper Perennial), 2002.

11. Thomas Malone, *The Future of Work: How the New Order of Business will Shape Your Organization, Your Management Style, and Your Life* (Boston: Harvard Business School Press), 2004, 4. Malone argues that realizing the potential of IT also depends on managers with an orientation toward "cultivating" people.

12. As a regional director, Stocking was accountable for seventy-five trusts, each of which included hospitals and community services, approximately 180,000 medical and administrative staff.

13. Kahlil Gibran, *The Prophet* (New York: Knopf), 1923, 15.

14. Martin Luther King, "Letter from a Birmingham Jail," *American Visions,* January/February, 1986, 52-59.

CHAPTER 16
SYSTEMS CITIZENS

1. See Web site www.usccb.org/cchd/povertyusa/povfacts.shtml.
2. Adapted from George Roth, Art Kleiner, *Car Launch* (New York: Oxford University Press), 1999.
3. This diagram is based on a variety of relatively simple system dynamics models and simulation learning tools developed to study and improve non-experts' understanding of the basics of climate change. See John Sterman, Linda Booth Sweeney, "Cloudy Skies: Assessing Public Understanding of Global Warming," *System Dynamics Review,* Wiley and Sons, (18), 207-240, and http://web.mit.edu/jsterman/www/cloudy_skies.html.
4. CO_2 in the atmosphere also increases because all living systems—including human beings—produce the gas through respiration. As the total biomass of the planet increases, so does the amount of CO_2.
5. John Browne, "Rethinking Corporate Responsibility," *Reflections, the SoL Journal*, vol. 1, no. 4, 48-53. Recently Browne has been one of the first corporate advocates for "carbon stabilization," a target that requires dramatic reductions in CO_2 emissions, as shown below.
6. 2001 U.N. Intergovernmental Commission on Climate Change: "Climate Change 2001: The Scientific Basis. A Summary for Policymakers." Report of working group 1 of the Intergovernmental Panel on Climate Change, IPCC Third Assessment Report, available at www.ipcc.ch.
7. The concentration and temperature data are actually for measures in the lower levels of the atmosphere and upper levels of the oceans.
8. This data was also in the U.N. report from which the chart was taken, yet it was not displayed with the data on CO_2 emissions. Apparently, no one thought it sufficiently important to include with the data.
9. Many scientists claim that stabilizing CO_2 concentrations will take a 70 percent or more reduction in emission because the carbon sinks that sequester carbon are highly saturated due to the unusually high levels in the atmosphere. See chart in *Scientific American* (September, 2005, 47), showing high and low projections for emissions.
10. At the end of the session in Europe, a woman told me that her 8-year-old son would ask her "How big is the bathtub?" I relayed this question to my colleague John Sterman, who has been researching people's perceptions of climate change for several years. He suggested that the best answers could be found in the NASA ice core studies of long-term fluctuations in atmospheric gases. There I found that in 1850, CO_2 was already near its cyclic peak, a level reached approximately every 50,000 years. Today it is 30 percent higher than at any time in the past 450,000 years, suggesting that we are now well beyond the historic "size of the bathtub."
11. Unilever, one of the largest consumer goods product companies in the world, has identified sustainable agriculture, sustainable fishing, and water as strate-

gic initiatives, and undertaken diverse projects internally and in collaboration with others, in all three areas. See Web site www.unilever.com

12. Partly because of this inefficiency, hydrogen in sufficient quantities for operating fuel cells will come largely from the hydrocarbons in fossil fuels (primarily natural gas) by a process that also releases CO_2 although in smaller amounts than is released by burning coal or natural gas. To realize their long term potential, more efficient fuel cells could utilize hydrogen created from splitting water molecules, using energy from a nonfossil fuel source (such as wind, geothermal, solar, or nuclear). In such a system, hydrogen is a "carrier" rather than a source of energy, allowing potential energy generated from solar to be stored until is was needed.

13. In Saillant's first five years as CEO, the unit cost of Plug Power's core product fell 82 percent. A 2005 study of its overall industry segment showed that Plug's share of total economic value had grown from 4 percent to 24 percent from 2000 to 2005, and the company moved from fifth to first in its sector, based on public market data.

14. Plug Power's primary product is a PEM (proton exchange membrane) fuel cell. This is the largest selling of three basic fuel cell designs currently in the marketplace. By sharing their methods widely, they aim to demonstrate that zero-to-landfill design principles can benefit the entire industry. They have, in fact, influenced the U.S. Fuel Cell Council, the industry trade group, to adopt sustainability principles.

15. Roger Saillant, speech given at Bowdoin College on October 5, 2004.

16. "Mugged: Poverty in Your Coffee Cup," Oxfam International, September 2002, available from www.maketradefair.org.

17. Even for those who benefit from cheap, abundant food, future production is at risk. Since 1945, soil degradation has affected 1.2 billion hectares of agricultural land globally, an area the size of China and India combined. Loss of the world's arable land continues at about ten million hectares per year. Irrigation for the production of food accounts for 70 percent of the water withdrawn from freshwater systems for human use. Of that, only 30-60 percent is returned for downstream use, making irrigation the largest net user of fresh water globally. See Jason Clay, "World Agriculture and the Environment: a commodity-by-commodity guide to impacts and practices," Washington, D.C.: Island Press, 2004; Stanley Wood, Kate Sebastian, and Sara J. Scherr, "Pilot Analysis of Global Ecosystems: Agroecosystems (Washington, DC: World Resources Institute), 2000.

18. Chris Pomfret, speech at IPA Sustainability Conference, May 2002.

19. Initial corporate participants included General Mills; Nutreco, the worlds largest fish farming company; Sadia, one of Brazil's few multinational food companies; Sysco, the largest distributor of food products in the world, and fifteen others. The NGOs included World Wildlife Fund, The Nature Conservancy, Oxfam, and a half dozen local NGOs. The Kellogg Foundation, a major funder of local sustainable agriculture projects, was not only an initial funder but a participant. See "The Sustainable Food Laboratory: a multi-

stakeholder, multi-continent project to create sustainable food supply chains" at www.glifood.org and www.sustainer.org.

20. Developed by The Sustainability Institute, and based on forty years of systems research on global agricultural commodities, this theory is developed in depth in "Commodity System Challenges: Moving Sustainability into the Mainstream of Natural Resource Economics," Sustainability Institute Report, April, 2003, available from www.sustainer.org.

21. Some would argue that the real winners are consumers who get cheap goods and investors who make money in the unsustainable expansion and then liquidate their investments before profits deteriorate completely. But all people may suffer from unsustainable food supply chains and the consequent social and environmental damage may also affect rich and poor alike.

22. The initial protytping initiatives included "framing" (developing new ways in which mainstream citizens can connect their values to sustainable agriculture); "small fisheries" (improving market access for responsible small fishermen developing sustainable aquaculture); "responsible commodities and investment" (improving investor and buyer screens to drive international adoption of better social and environmental practices), "small farmer access" (improving livelihoods of family producers in Latin America through inovative market structures and infrastructure investments); regional food supply to schools and hospitals" (building regional networks to improve quality of food in particular institutions); "supply chain projects" (developing transparency in production practices and financial flows for specific supply chins); and a "business coalition" (a group of businesses driving more sustinable practices in a manner that brings economic stability).

23. Adam Kahane, *Solving Tough Problems* (San Francisco: Berrett-Koehler), 2005.

24. The systems thinking movement in education now encompasses thousands of educators in hundreds of schools. For an extensive resource list, see www.solonline.org; also The Creative Learning Exchange Web site at www.clex.org; and the Waters Foundation at www.watersfoundation.org.

CHAPTER 17
FRONTIERS

1. H. Thomas Johnson, *Relevance Lost: The Rise and Fall of Management Accounting* (Boston: Harvard Business School Press), 1991.

2. H. Thomas Johnson and Anders Broms, *Profit Beyond Measure* (New York: Free Press), 2000.

3. Toyota's market capitalization has come close to equalling and occasionally has exceeded the sum of the "Big Three" (GM, Ford, and Daimler-Chrysler) during the past two decades (Johnson, 2000).

4. Peter Senge and Goren Carstedt, "Innovating Our Way to the Next Industrial Revolution," *Sloan Management Review*, Winter, 2001. The terms "technolog-

ical" and "biological nutrients" that flow in continual cycles of use and reuse come from Mcdounough and Braungart, *Cradle to Cradle*. A list of resources with descriptions of the use of this idea in China's industrial planning can be found at www.solonline.org.

5. Joyce Fletcher, *Disappearing Acts: Gender, Power, and Relational Practice at Work* (Cambridge, Mass.: MIT Press), 1999.

6. See www.solonline.org for more information on the "Women Leading Sustainability" project and the SoL Sustainability Consortium.

7. For more on the SEED project see www.seed.slb.com. For more on the educational ideas behind the project, see Seymour Papert, *Mindstorm* (New York: Basic Books) 1980; also Michael Resnick, "Lifelong Kindergarten" in Ed. David Aspin, *International Handbook of Lifelong Learning* (New York: Springer), 2001.

8. See Web site www.urdt.net.

9. See Web site. www.kufunda.org.

10. Peter Senge, C. Otto Scharmer, Joseph Jaworski, Betty Sue Flowers, *Presence: An Exploration of Profound Change in People, Organizations, and Society* (New York: Doubleday/Currency), 2005. See also C. Otto Scharmer, *Theory U* (Cambridge, Mass.: SoL), 2006 (forthcoming).

11. An article based on Knuth's experiences is "Stories from An African Learning Village," *Reflections, the SoL Journal*, vol 6. no. 8-10. See Web site www.solonline.org; also see www.kufunda.org.

CHAPTER 18
THE INDIVISIBLE WHOLE

1. The following is reprinted with permission from "Whose Earth," by Russell Schweickart, in *The Next Whole Earth Catalog*, Stewart brand, editor (New York: Point Foundation/Random House), 1980.

2. One recent product was the beautiful book *The Home Planet*, edited by Kevin Kelley, with photographs and reflections from many astronauts and cosmonauts. The book was released at Christmas, 1988, the first book ever published simultaneously in the United States (Reading, Mass.: Addison-Wesley) and the U.S.S.R.

3. This hypothesis has been advanced by several scientists. For a good introduction to the idea and the supporting data, see Jay Lovelock, *Gaia: A New View of Life on Earth* (New York: Oxford University Press), 1979.

APPENDIX 2
SYSTEMS ARCHETYPES

1. Many people in the system dynamics field have contributed to identifying and coding these archetypes, or (as they are often called), "generic structures." I

would particularly like to thank Jennifer Kemeny, Michael Goodman, Ernst Diehl, Christian Kampmann, Daniel Kim, Jack Nevison, and John Sterman for their contributions.

APPENDIX 3
THE U PROCESS

1. Senge, et al, *Presence: An Exploration of Profound Change in People, Organizations, and Society* (New York: Doubleday/Currency), 2005; Adam Kahane, *Solving Tough Problems* (San Francisco: Berrett-Koehler), 2005; and C. Otto Scharmer, *Theory U* (Cambridge, Mass.: SoL), 2006 (forthcoming).

ACKNOWLEDGMENTS

In writing this book, I have often felt more like a reporter than an author. The work of so many people is treated, and the work of so many more lies behind the scenes, that my biggest fear is that I will forget someone who should be on these pages.

So I will proceed chronologically, in hope that this will be the most foolproof strategy. My introduction to systems thinking as a management and leadership discipline came from Jay W. Forrester, and he has been my mentor for some twenty years now. My debt to Jay is vast—obviously for his wisdom, less obviously for his enduring standards of excellence, most subtly for his commitment to always focus on the most important problems rather than the most tractable.

Harriet Rubin and Arie de Geus were instrumental in getting this project launched. Many thanks to Harriet for her belief (still to be proven out) in a first-time author. Her genuine enthusiasm for this project and uncanny intuitions were a continual delight. I learned to always listen to her comments, especially when my "academic mind" tried to intervene. Arie introduced me to the idea of learning organizations many years ago, then suggested that a book on the subject was in order over two years ago. Unfortunately, his duties at Shell precluded having as much of a role in producing the book as I would have liked. But his thinking and passion for the idea are evident nonetheless.

Many colleagues at MIT, Harvard, and Innovation Associates contributed significantly to particular aspects of the book: John Ster-man, Jennifer Kemeny, and Daniel Kim contributed to the systems thinking chapters; Bill Isaacs and Diana Smith helped enormously with the material on mental models and team learning; Charlie Kiefer, Charlotte Roberts, and Bryan Smith lent their considerable expertise in the areas of personal mastery and building shared vision. Alain Gauthier read the entire manuscript and offered many helpful suggestions. A special thanks to David Bohm and Chris Argyris for helping me to draw so extensively on their seminal works.

The practical experience and much of the inspiration lying behind this effort come from opportunities over the years to work with leaders who endeavor to live what is herein described—alas there are more of you than I could ever list. Especially helpful for this project have been my good friends Bill O'Brien of Hanover Insurance, Ed Simon of Herman Miller, and Ray Stata of Analog Devices. Each gave patiently of his time and generously of his spirit. Thank you also to Bart Bolton of Digital; and Geri Prusko, Bob Bergin, and Paul Stimson of Hanover for helping with specific applications discussions.

Don Ryan's artwork was critical to my concept of a book that would be more than a series of "linear" statements strung together. Thanks also to Janet Coleman of Doubleday for one thousand forms of assistance in "getting it done." Meanwhile, Janet Gould and Nan Lux kept our research center afloat while I disappeared; and Angela Lipinski, in addition to helping me, as always, with whatever needed to get done, simply handled the rest of my outside professional obligations throughout my hibernation. Robert Fritz's moral support meant a great deal because he too had learned to "book-write," becoming a remarkably good author remarkably quickly (as behooves someone whose expertise is creating). Michael Goodman's and Donella Meadows's support meant a great deal, just because it always does.

Three colleagues warrant special thanks. Bill Isaacs and Daniel

Kim helped with virtually all facets of the project, bringing to bear critical areas of expertise and helping to mold the overall product. Daniel even took on the onerous task of completing all the notes and references (with assistance from researcher Judith Bruk). Without Art Kleiner, who served as writing coach, critic, editor, and for certain key sections (like the story of "Lover's Beer"), coauthor, this book would simply not be the same book. Last summer he asked me to describe my thesis for the book in a sentence—that was the beginning of a thorough refocusing and reorganizing (and eventual rewriting) of a manuscript I had been "puttering with" for over a year. I will never forget his patience, tireless (or near tireless) effort and unflagging spirit. But, I bet he and Faith will not miss my 3 a.m. calls.

Lastly, thank you to my son Nathan for being my daily teacher about the joys and sorrows of living life as a learner, and thanks beyond thanks to Diane. Just about the time I started to move into "high gear" to reshape the book, our newest son, Ian, arrived. Caring for both "projects" simultaneously was enough work for four parents. Thanks, Diane, for your patience and your perseverance. Most of all, thank you for sharing the vision. I always knew that you wouldn't let me settle for less than was possible.

ACKNOWLEDGMENTS
FOR REVISED
EDITION

Obviously, the material for this new edition would never have been written without the inspiration and assistance from the many gifted masters of "the art and practice" of building learning organizations we interviewed, and from whose efforts we drew the examples and insights included in this book:

Vivienne Cox of BP; Marv Adams and Jeremy Seligman of Ford; Anne Murray Allen (retired) and Greg Merten (retired) of Hewlett-Packard; Les Omatoni of the Hewlett-Woodmere School District; Ilean Galloway and David Marsing (retired) of Intel; Dorothy Berry of the International Finance Corporation; Marianne Knuth of Kufunda Village; Darcy Winslow of Nike; Barbara Stocking of Oxfam; Roger Saillant of Plug Power; Molly Baldwin, Omar Ortez, Tun Krouch, Marina Rodriguez, Seroem Phong, Anisha Chablani, and Susan Ulrich of Roca; Salim al-Ayadh of Saudi Aramco; Hal Hamilton of the Sustainability Institute; Andre van Heemstra and Brigitte Tantawy-Monsou of Unilever; and Mieko Nishimizu (retired) of the World Bank.

For active managers especially, being cited in a book like this is a double-edged sword. On the one hand, all are justifiably proud of what they and their colleagues have accomplished, and, I hope, having their words and stories included here constitutes a small and appreciated acknowledgment. But no one person or organization needs to be hoisted up onto a pedestal and treated as a paragon of successful innovation. Whenever writers ask me for examples of "learning organizations," I always say, "There are no models, only learners." Everyone struggles. No one has "arrived." For every few steps forward there are always steps backwards, or at least sideways. So, for their willingness to have their stories shared in the spirit of helping others rather than being exemplars of all that is right, I am especially grateful.

I would also like to add a special thanks to a group of friends and colleagues who have helped develop the global SoL network, the "innovation in learning infrastructure" that is the overarching strategic focus for many of us. The basic aim of SoL, a self-governing network that grew out of the MIT Organizational Learning Research Center, is to foster partnerships among practitioners (e.g. managers), consultants, and researchers to build and share practical knowledge. All of the interviewees are active in the SoL network. In addition, I drew extensively on the work of many others who were not formally interviewed, some of whom are named above but many who are not. The latter include: Goran Carstedt (formerly of Volvo and IKEA); Robert Hanig; Sherry Immediato, SoL's Managing Director; Katrin Kaeufer, Otto Scharmer and Wanda Orlikowski of MIT; Joe Laur and Sara Schley of the SoL Sustainability Consortium; John Leggate of BP; Dennis Sandow; Don Seville of the Sustainability Institute; Rich Teerlink (formerly of Harley-Davidson); Nick Zenuick (formerly of Ford); C. Will Zhang, Mette Husemoen, Kai Sung and Stephen Meng of SoL China; and of course Arie de Geus. It has been a joy to work with each, in many cases for over twenty years and in settings around the world.

Lastly, without the help and partnership of Nina Kruschwitz, who served as managing editor and overall coordinator for the project, I would never have undertaken this revision in the first place. Nina and I have worked together for some fifteen years, through the series of *Fifth Discipline* fieldbooks and more recently, *Presence*. Her steadfast good humor and gentle presence made the daily deadlines into a continuing process of reflection ("What really needs to be said here?") and discovery ("Oh, that . . ."). Thank you.

INDEX

Visit www.solonline.org
for other Fifth Discipline resources.